A Dictionary of

BIBLICAL
ALLUSIONS
IN
ENGLISH
LITERATURE

A Dictionary of

BIBLICAL ALLUSIONS IN ENGLISH LITERATURE

Walter B. Fulghum, Jr.
CENTRAL CONNECTICUT STATE COLLEGE

HOLT, RINEHART and WINSTON, Inc.
New York · Chicago · San Francisco · Toronto · London

Copyright © 1965 by Holt, Rinehart and Winston, Inc.
All Rights Reserved
Library of Congress Catalog Card Number 65–19349
22958–0115
Printed in the United States of America

For Helen and David

preface

The book that everybody knows about, few read. There was a time, perhaps, when authors could take it for granted that most of their readers had a wide knowledge of the Bible, as of the Greek and Roman classics. But this assumption, as any teacher of literature knows, would be a doubtful one today. Many stories and characters of the Bible are familiar in a general way to readers of literature, but few of us know the Bible in sufficient detail to recognize, let alone understand, many of the Biblical allusions common in our language and literature. The purpose of this book is to help the intelligent reader in two ways: first, to locate an allusion in the Bible itself; and, second, to understand the allusion's meaning and use in literature.

Allusion here is interpreted broadly; it includes Biblical words, phrases, people, and places most frequently mentioned in literature. For each allusion the reader will find pronunciation when necessary, the location in the Bible, relevant passages from the Bible, and examples of uses of the allusion in English and American authors. It is true that Biblical words and phrases are sometimes used by writers and speakers who are not conscious of the origin of the words and who do not intend a specific allusion. Some references of this kind are included here if they are ultimately of Biblical origin. Cross references within the text itself are indicated by the use of small caps. Separate, complete entries will be found in the alphabetical listing for these words in small caps.

The King James translation is used, not only because it is the supreme literary version of the Bible, but also because most English and American authors since 1611 have used it. Where other translations were the source, such as probably the Wyclif Bible and the Vulgate for Chaucer, the Bishops' and Genevan Bibles for Shakespeare, or the Douay Version for Catholic writers, note has been made if the differences are significant.

There are so many Biblical allusions in English literature that a book of this kind can make only a selection of the most frequent ones. Therefore this text does not reduce the need for a good Biblical dictionary, encyclopedia, or concordance. Nor should it replace the reading of the Bible itself. It is hoped that this work will stimulate a wider and more careful reading of the Bible, because a thorough knowledge of it is essential to an understanding of both our literary and religious heritages.[1]

---

[1]Because of the many Biblical subjects in painting, sculpture, and music, this book should also be of value to students of the fine arts.

With the increasing use of modern translations—which are generally more accurate than the King James Bible—many of the older, more beautiful words and phrases are being lost today. It is hoped that this book, in addition to its practical function, will help to preserve something of our Biblical linguistic inheritance.

W. B. F., Jr.

New Britain, Connecticut
September 1965

A Dictionary of

BIBLICAL
ALLUSIONS
IN
ENGLISH
LITERATURE

AARON
(âr'ŭn)

Exod. 4:14–17,
27–31; 7:8–12;
32:1–6; Num.
17:1–11;
20:12–29

Aaron was the son of Amram the Levite, brother of Moses and Miriam, and head of the priesthood called Levites (Num. 18:1–7). He was Moses' spokesman and helper during the TEN PLAGUES; his rod turned into a serpent before Pharoah, and swallowed the Egyptians' rods also turned serpents (Exod. 7:8–12). He made the GOLDEN CALF from the earrings of the people while Moses was away on Mount Sinai (Exod. 32:1–6). To quiet the murmurings of the people the Lord caused Aaron's rod to bud and bring forth blossoms and almonds (Num. 17:1–11). The Lord refused to permit both Moses and Aaron to enter the promised land because they had rebelled against His word at the water of Meribah; and on His order Moses stripped Aaron of his garments and put them upon Eleazar his son. Aaron died, was buried on Mount Hor, and was mourned for thirty days by all Israel (Num. 20:12–29).

In "Absalom and Achitophel," Dryden calls the rebel Levites "Aaron's race."

Pope, in *An Essay on Man*, writes of the danger of uncontrolled passion:

> And hence one MASTER PASSION in the breast,
> Like Aaron's serpent, swallows up the rest.

In *Democratic Vistas*, Walt Whitman, attacking the corruption of our great cities, says that the "sole object" of business is, "by any means, pecuniary gain. The magician's serpent in the fable ate up all the other serpents; and money-making is our magician's serpent, remaining sole master of the field." The sculptor Kenyon, in Hawthorne's *The Marble Faun*, describes the making of his statue of Cleopatra: "I kindled a great fire within my mind, and threw in the material,—as Aaron threw the gold of the Israelites into the furnace,—and in the midmost heat uprose Cleopatra, as you see her." In "The Relic," Whittier tells of a cane cut from wood remaining after the burning of Pennsylvania Hall:

> Pure thoughts and sweet like flowers unfold.
>   And precious memories round it cling,
> Even as the Prophet's rod of old
>   In beauty blossoming:
> And buds of feeling, pure and good,
> Spring from its cold unconscious wood.

Cotton Mather, in "The Life of John Eliot," says that Eliot welcomed Nehemiah Walter as his successor as Pastor of Roxbury "with the tender Affections of a Father. The good Old Man like Old *Aaron*, as it were disrobed himself, with an

unspeakable Satisfaction, when he beheld his Garments put
upon a Son so dear unto him."

ABADDON
(*à·băd'ŭn*)

Rev. 9:11

"And they had a king over them, which is the angel of the
bottomless pit, whose name in the Hebrew tongue is Abaddon,
but in the Greek tongue hath his name Apollyon" [*à·pol'yŭn*].
Abaddon, in Hebrew "destruction," or "abyss," means (1) hell
or the bottomless pit (Rev. 9:1, 2, 11), and (2) the angel of
hell, sometimes the Devil himself. Abaddon was the king over
the locusts of torment who had stings in their tails like scor-
pions. Milton calls the bottomless pit Abaddon, but Bunyan,
in *Pilgrim's Progress,* calls the field overcome by Christian,
Apollyon. In "Childe Roland" Browning's knight meets "A
great black bird, Apollyon's bosom friend." The first of Dylan
Thomas's "Two Sonnets" begins:

> Altarwise by owl-light in the halfway-house
> The gentleman lay graveward with his furies;
> Abaddon in the hang-nail cracked from Adam,°

ABEDNEGO   *see FIERY FURNACE*

ABEL

Gen. 4:1–15;
Matt. 23:35

Abel was the younger brother of Cain, sons of Adam and Eve.
Cain slew him because the Lord had respect for Abel's offering
of "the firstlings of his flock" but not for Cain's "fruit of the
ground," a deed reflecting perhaps the historic conflict between
pastoral and agricultural peoples. Jesus spoke of "the blood of
righteous Abel." In *The Shepheardes Calendar,* Spenser praises
the righteous Abel, humble and devout; he was

> the first shepherd
> and lived with little gayne:
> As meeke he was, as meeke mought be,
> simple, as simple sheepe.
> Humble, and like in eche degree
> the flocke, which he did keepe.
> Often he used of hys keepe
> a sacrifice to bring.
> Nowe with a Kidde, now with a sheepe
> the Altars hallowing.
> So lowted he unto hys Lord,
> such favour couth he fynd,
> That sithens never was abhord,
> the simple shepheards kynd.

° From *The Collected Poems of Dylan Thomas.* Copyright 1953 by Dylan
Thomas. © 1957 by New Directions. Reprinted by permission of the publishers, New Directions, J. M. Dent & Sons, and the Literary Executors of
the Dylan Thomas Estate.

Dryden, in "To My Honoured Kinsman, John Driden," tells of his kinsman's love of hunting:

> And often have you brought the wily fox
> To suffer for the firstlings of the flocks.

In Joyce's *Ulysses* Napoleon says, "Madam, I'm Adam. And Able was I ere I saw Elba."

ABIGAIL
(ăb′·ĭ·gāl)

I Sam. 25:2–42

Abigail, wife of the rich but "churlish and evil" Nabal [nā′băl], was "a woman of good understanding, and of a beautiful countenance," a resourceful and loyal "handmaid." She saved Nabal from David, who sought revenge because Nabal, despite David's protection of his shepherds, refused David's request for supplies. After a night of heavy drinking, Nabal died, shocked by the news of what Abigail had done, and Abigail later married David. "Behold," she said to him, "let thine handmaid be a servant to wash the feet of the servants of my lord." In literature Abigail has been a name given to the loyal lady's maid. In Chaucer's "Tale of Melibee," Prudence, wife of Melibee, defends the wisdom and integrity of women against his doubts. Though some have been bad, she argues, "yet han men founde ful many a good womman, and ful discret and wis in conseillyng . . . . Abygail delivered Nabal hir housebonde fro David the kyng, that wolde have slayn hym, and apaysed the ire of the kyng by hir wit and by hir good conseillyng." In *An Apology for Smectymnuus,* Milton, defending the acrimonious character of the controversial rhetoric of his time, cites the story: in "going against Nabal, in the very same breath when he had just before named the name of God," David vowed not "to leave any alive of Nabal's house that pisseth against the wall" (v. 22). And then he repeated the expression to Abigail to explain the effect of her blessed intervention.

ABISHAG
(ăb′ĭ·shăg)

I Kings 1:1–4;
2:13–25

When "king David was old and stricken in years," Abishag a Shunamite was brought to him that he might "get heat . . . . The damsel was very fair, and cherished the king, and ministered to him: but the king knew her not." After David's death Adonijah his son sought her for his wife, but Solomon refused, keeping her perhaps for his own. Some writers have speculated that Abishag may have been the "black but comely" Shulamite (from the village of Shulem or Shunem) beloved by Solomon in The Song of Solomon (1:5; 6:13). In *Don Juan* Byron describes, with some inaccuracy, Don Juan's near suffocation hiding in Julia's bed while her husband searched the room:

> Of his position I can give no notion:
> 'Tis written in the Hebrew Chronicle,
> How the physicians, leaving pill and potion,
>   Prescribed, by way of blister, a young belle,
> When old King David's blood grew dull in motion,
>   And that the medicine answer'd very well;
> Perhaps 't was in a different way applied,
> For David lived, but Juan nearly died.

More accurately Aldous Huxley's aging Earl of Hauberk, in *After Many a Summer*, records in his diary: "I have tried King David's remedy against old age and found it wanting. Warmth cannot be imparted, but only evoked; and where no lingering spark persists, even tinder will not raise a flame." In "Provide, Provide," Robert Frost writes that

> The witch that came (the withered hag)
> To wash the steps with pail and rag
> Was once the beauty Abishag.*

ABOMINATION OF DESOLATION

Dan. 9:27; 11:31; 12:11; I Macc. 1:54; 6:7; Matt. 24:15; Mark 13:14

The expression, meaning something extremely hateful or disgusting, probably refers to the image of Zeus which Antiochus Epiphanes forced the Jews to set up on the altar of the Temple. The exact meaning that Jesus gave it is uncertain (Mark 13:14). In Blake's *Jerusalem*, the "destroyers of Jerusalem" are those

> Who pretend to Poetry that they may destroy imagination
> By imitation of Nature's Images drawn from Remembrance.
> These are the Sexual Garments, the Abomination of Desolation,
> Hiding the Human Lineaments . . . .

ABRAHAM

Gen. 11:26—25:10

He was the first patriarch, the founder of the Hebrew people. His earlier name Abram meant "exalted father," and when the Lord changed his name to Abraham He called him "the father of many nations" (Gen. 17:5). With his wife Sarai, later Sarah, and Lot "his brother's son" he migrated from his birthplace, Ur of the Chaldees, over the Fertile Crescent by way of Haran to Canaan, the PROMISED LAND. In "The Castle of Indolence," James Thomson paints an idyllic picture of Abraham's wandering:

> What time Dan Abraham left the Chaldee land,
> And pastured on from verdant stage to stage.

Where fields and fountains fresh could best engage.
Toil was not then. Of nothing took they heed,
But with wild beasts the silvan war to wage,
And o'er vast plains their herds and flocks to feed.
Blest sons of nature they! true golden age indeed!

His son ISHMAEL, with his mother Hagar, Sarah's handmaiden, was cast out to become a wanderer and a wild man. At the age of ninety-one Sarah laughed when she discovered that she was to bear a son, for it had "ceased to be with Sarah after the manner of women." Abraham was one hundred. The child was named Isaac, meaning "he shall laugh."

In the story "I and My Chimney," by Herman Melville, the narrator says that his elderly wife "seems to think that she is to teem on and be inexhaustible forever. She doesn't believe in old age. At that strange promise in the plain of Mamre, my old wife, unlike old Abraham's, would not have jeeringly laughed within herself." John Selden, in *Table Talk*, tells about a university preacher, being forbidden to "meddle with anything but what was in the text," one day preached upon the words "Abraham begot Isaac." Sticking to the text for "a good way, at last he observed that Abraham was resident; for if he had been nonresident he could never have begot Isaac . . . ." For the story of Abraham's sacrifice see ISAAC. Abraham and Sarah were buried in the Cave of Machpela [măk·pē′là], which Abraham had purchased for Sarah.

ABRAHAM'S BOSOM

Luke 16:22–23

When Lazarus the beggar died, he "was carried by the angels into Abraham's bosom." When the rich man, at whose gate Lazarus had been laid, died, he went to hell and looked up "being in torment, and [saw] Abraham afar off, and Lazarus in his bosom." It means paradise, heavenly rest and peace. King Richard, in Shakespeare's *Richard III*, consoles himself on his murder of the young princes in the Tower: "The sons of Edward sleep in Abraham's bosom." And in *Henry V*, when Pistol announces Falstaff's death, and Bardolph wishes he were with Falstaff "wheresome'er he is, either in heaven or hell," the good Hostess exclaims: "Nay, sure, he's not in hell; he's in Arthur's bosom, if ever man went to Arthur's bosom." Wordsworth, in the sonnet "It Is a Beauteous Evening, Calm and Free," addresses his daughter Caroline:

If thou appear untouched by solemn thought,
Thy nature is not therefore less divine:
Thou liest in Abraham's bosom all the year;

ABSALOM

II Sam. 3:3;
13–18

Absalom was the popular but rebellious son of David, famous "for his beauty; from the sole of his foot even to the crown of his head there was no blemish in him." His hair, which he polled "at every year's end," was heavy and luxuriant. Counseled by Hushai and the treacherous ACHITOPHEL, Absalom rebelled against his father. Before the final battle David gave orders saying, "Deal gently for my sake with the young man, even with Absalom." Defeated, Absalom rode away on a mule but was caught up in the "thick boughs of a great oak" by his hair, "and the mule that was under him went away." Joab, David's captain, thrust three darts through the heart of Absalom. When David was informed he lamented: "O my son Absalom, my son, my son Absalom! would God I had died for thee, O Absalom, my son, my son!" Absalom's fame during the Middle Ages for physical beauty is reflected in the Prologue of Chaucer's *The Legend of Good Women.* The "Balade," sung in praise of Alceste, queen of the God of Love, begins: "Hyd, Absalom, thy gilte tresses clere." Dryden, in "Absalom and Achitophel," depicts Charles II as prolific King David.

> Of all [his] numerous progeny was none
> So beautiful, so brave, as Absalom:
> Whether, inspired by some diviner lust,
> His father got him with a greater gust
> Or that his conscious destiny made way,
> By manly beauty, to imperial sway.

The king, in Tennyson's *Becket,* sends his herald to say to those who threaten Becket, "The King commands you, upon pain of death,/ That none should wrong or injure your Archbishop." And Folot adds, "Deal gently with the young man Absalom." Whittier's poem "To the Thirty-Ninth Congress" calls for forgiveness and mercy in settling the reconstruction.

> Alas! no victor's pride is ours;
> We bend above our triumphs won
> Like David o'er his rebel son.

ACCURSED THING

Joshua 6:18; 7:1,
11, 13, 15

Joshua warned his people before the fall of Jericho to "keep yourselves from the accursed thing, lest ye make yourselves accursed, when ye take of the accursed thing . . ." But ACHAN "took of the accursed thing, and the anger of the Lord was kindled against the children of Israel." So Achan, with all his family, his cattle and spoils, was stoned with stones and burned with fire. The accursed thing may have been a pagan idol;

perhaps it was simply heathen spoils. In "Christ's Hospital Five and Thirty Years Ago," Charles Lamb tells how at the school after meals "L" was seen carrying away from the table "disreputable morsels" of meat which later, it was reported, he carried "out of bounds [in] a large blue check handkerchief . . . . This then must be the accursed thing."

ACELDAMA
(à·sĕl'dà·mà)

Acts 1:19; Matt.
27:7, 8

Peter said that Judas "purchased a field with the reward of iniquity; and falling headlong, he burst asunder in the midst, and all his bowels gushed out. And it was known unto all the dwellers at Jerusalem; insomuch as that field is called in their proper tongue, Aceldama, that is to say, The field of blood." Matthew's account said that the chief priests took Judas's thirty pieces of silver, blood money, "and bought with them the potter's field, to bury strangers in. Wherefore that field was called, The field of blood, unto this day." Today the word commonly means a battlefield, a place of bloodshed. Francis Thompson's poem "Whereto Art Thou Come" draws an analogy between Judas and the man who betrays truth. He betrays

> but himself:
> And with his kiss's rated traitor-craft
> The Haceldama of a plot of days
> He buys, to consummate his Judasry
> Therein with Judas' guerdon of despair.

Thomas De Quincey, in *The English Mail-Coach,* tells a mother about her son's heroism in battle, but not that his regiment was already "lying stretched, by a large majority, upon one bloody aceldama." Thomas Jefferson wrote a letter to Benjamin Waterhouse, in June 1822, expressing fear that the Unitarians might "fall into the fatal error of fabricating formulas of creed and confessions of faith, the engines of which so soon . . . made of Christendom a mere Aceldama."

ACHAN
(ā'kăn)

Joshua 7:16–25

Greedy Achan stole sacred spoils and took "the accursed thing" during the siege of Jericho. For this by the Lord's command, he and all his family were stoned to death in the Valley of Achor. In *The Anatomy of Melancholy,* Robert Burton attacks the evils of literary patronage. Covetousness, he says, is "the root of all these mischiefs, which Achan-like compel them to commit sacrilege . . . that kindles God's wrath, brings . . . vengeance, and an heavy visitation upon themselves and others." After Jane, in Charlotte Brontë's novel, *Jane Eyre,* has learned about her lover's mad wife locked in an attic room, Rochester explains, saying, "[I do not] mean to torment you with the hideous associations and recollections of Thornfield Hall—this accursed place—this tent of Achan."

ACHITOPHEL *see AHITHOPHEL*

ADAM

*Gen. 1:26–27;
2:7,15—4:26*

Adam was the first man, formed by God from the dust of the ground. The name Adam, which first appears in the King James version at Genesis 2:19, is from the Hebrew word *adam* meaning simply "man"; it is a play upon the Hebrew word *adamah* which means "cultivated ground." Innocent before "the fall," Adam sinned by eating the fruit—not an apple—from the TREE OF KNOWLEDGE; was cursed by God to eat his bread "in the sweat of thy face . . . till thou return unto the ground: for out of it wast thou taken"; then expelled with Eve from "the garden of Eden, to till the ground from which he was taken."

Adam as the innocent man, living in idyllic peace and purity, before the fall is a common theme in literature. In *Paradise Lost,* Milton pictures Adam and Eve living in naked simplicity.

> Nor those mysterious parts were then conceal'd,
> Then was not guiltie shame, dishonest shame
> Of natures works, honor dishonorable,
> Sin-bred, how have ye troubl'd all mankind
> With shews instead, mere shews of seeming pure,
> And banisht from man's life his happiest life,
> Simplicity and spotless innocence.

Adam was "the goodliest man of men since borne." So Falstaff, in Shakespeare's *Henry IV, Part I,* makes merry with Prince Hal, saying, "I am now of all humours that have showed themselves humours since the old days of Goodman Adam." Melville's innocent Billy Budd "in many respects was little more than a sort of upright barbarian, much such perhaps as Adam presumably might have been ere the urbane Serpent wriggled himself into his company."

Adam is known in literature more commonly as the first sinner, the source with Eve of "original sin"; he is "old Adam" who fell through sexual sin. In Chaucer's "The Monk's Tale," he is one of the men fallen from high degree: although he was "not bigeten of mannes sperme unclene . . .

> for misgovernaunce
> Was dryven out of hys hye prosperitee
> To labour, and to helle, and to meschaunce,

Chaucer's Wife of Bath said about her fifth husband Jankyn reading to her about wicked wives, that if women had written stories, "By God! . . .

> They wolde han writen of men moore wikkednesse
> Than al the mark of Adam may redresse.

Shakespeare's Archbishop of Canterbury, in *Henry V*, says of Prince Hal, after his father's death, that

> his wildness, mortified in him,
> Seem'd to die too. Yea, at that very moment
> Consideration like an angel came
> And whipp'd th'offending Adam out of him,
> Leaving his body as a paradise
> T'envelop and contain celestial spirits.

And in *Love's Labour's Lost*, Biron says that the lady-killer Boyet

> pins wenches on his sleeve;
> Had he been Adam, he had tempted Eve.

Professor Teufelsdröckh, in Carlyle's *Sartor Resartus*, says all men are tried by temptation. "Not so easily can the old Adam, lodged in us by birth, be dispossessed."

"Adam's profession" was that of a gardener. The grave-diggers in *Hamlet* discuss their ancient profession.

FIRST CLOWN. . . . Come, my spade. There is no ancient gentlemen but gardeners, ditchers, and grave-makers: they hold up Adam's profession.

SECOND CLOWN. Was he a gentleman?

FIRST CLOWN. A' was the first that ever bore arms.

SECOND CLOWN. Why, he had none.

FIRST CLOWN. What, art a heathen? How dost thou understand the Scripture? The Scripture says "Adam digged:" could he dig without arms?

Well known, of course, in Shakespeare's time was the old rhyme:

> When Adam delved and Eve span,
> Where was then the gentleman?

Hand labor, hard work, says Kipling in "The Glory of the Garden," makes English gardens beautiful.

> Oh, Adam was a gardener, and God who made him sees
> That half a proper gardner's work is done upon his knees.

"Adam's apple" is a term based upon the ancient belief that, in spite of the fact that apples are nowhere mentioned in Genesis—it was possibly a pomegranate—a piece lodged in Adam's throat. The "second Adam" or the "new Adam" refers to Jesus Christ.

ADULLAM
(*à·dŭl'ăm*)

I Sam. 22:1–2

The cave to which David fled to escape Saul's wrath. There "every one that was in distress, and every one that was in debt, and every one that was discontented, gathered themselves unto him." Thomas Hardy, in *The Mayor of Casterbridge,* says that Mixen Lane in the lowest section of the town was "the Adullam of all the surrounding villages. It was the hiding-place of those who were in distress, and in debt, and trouble of every kind . . . ."

AGAG
(*ā'gāg*)

I Sam. 15:8–33

Agag was king of the Amalekites; the prophet Samuel ordered King Saul to destroy him and all his people and possessions. But Saul spared Agag, and Samuel himself, after severely condemning Saul, "hewed Agag in pieces before the Lord in Gilgal." In Dryden's poem "Absalom and Achitophel," Agag probably represents one of the Catholic peers executed in 1680, in part upon the false testimony of Titus Oates, called Corah by Dryden. Corah's zeal made him despise his prince,

> And Corah might for Agag's murder call,
> In terms as coarse as Samuel used to Saul.

In "The King's Missive," Whittier depicts Governor Endicott, stern Puritan, angered at the Quakers in his path.

> Shall I spare? Shall I pity them? God forbid!
> I will do as the prophet to Agag did:
> They come to poison the wells of the Word.
> I will hew them in pieces before the Lord.

AHAB

*I Kings
16:29—22:40*

Ahab, king of Israel, married JEZEBEL, daughter of a king of Sidon, adopted her pagan worship of Baal, and was rebuked by Elijah, who was then forced to flee. Killed in battle, Ahab was brought to Samaria where "one washed the chariot in the pool of Samaria; and the dogs licked up his blood." In "Elegy IV," Milton compares his tutor Thomas Young, abroad as chaplain to English merchants in Hamburg, to Elijah in "the trackless wilds and desert wastes of Arabia fled from the hands of King Ahab, and from thy hands too, ruthless woman of Sidon." Melville's Captain Ahab, in *Moby Dick,* says Peleg to Ishmael, "ain't Captain Bildad; no, he ain't Captain Peleg;

he's Ahab, boy; and Ahab of old, thou knowest, was a crowned king!" To which Ishmael prophetically replies, "And a very vile one. When that wicked king was slain, the dogs, did they not lick his blood?"

AHASUERUS   *see ESTHER*

AHITHOPHEL
(ȧ·hĭth'·ō·phŭl)

II Sam.
15:12—17:23

Ahithophel, whose name means "foolish brother," was a trusted counselor of King David who deserted to join Absalom's revolt. He advised Absalom to go "in unto his father's concubines in the sight of all Israel," then to permit him to pursue David with twelve thousand men and to kill him. When Absalom rejected this counsel in favor of Hushai's, Ahithophel "got him home to his house, and put his household in order, and hanged himself, and died. . . ." Ahithophel's unsavory reputation is reflected in Shakespeare's *Henry IV, Part II*, when Falstaff curses a merchant who refuses him credit, calling him "a whoreson Achitophel!" And Dryden's Achitophel in "Absalom and Achitophel" represents the Earl of Shaftesbury, counselor of Absalom—Duke of Monmouth against David—Charles II. Of the rebels high in power

> . . . the false Achitophel was first;
> A name to all succeeding ages cursed:
> For close designs, and crooked counsels fit;

AHOLAH AND AHOLIBAH
(ȧ·hōl'lȧ,
ȧ·hŏl'ĭ·bȧ)

Ezek. 23:1–44

Aholah, meaning "her own tent," and Aholibah, meaning "my tent [is] in her," were two sisters who "committed whoredoms in Egypt . . . in their youth: there were their breasts pressed, and there they bruised the teats of their virginity." Symbols of the unfaithfulness of Samaria and Jerusalem in turning to foreign gods, they were severely punished by God. In *An Apology for Smectymnuus*, Milton opposes the "Romish liturgy" as a garnishing of the gospel: "What was that which made the Jews, figured under the names of Aholah and Aholibah, go a whoring after all the heathen's inventions, but they saw a religion gorgeously attired and desirable to the eye?" Hardy's Tess of the D'Urbervilles came to accept her rape passively, believing that "if she should have to burn for what she had done, burn she must . . . . Like all village girls, she was well grounded in the Holy Scriptures, and had dutifully studied the histories of Aholah and Aholibah and knew the inferences to be drawn therefrom."

AJALON   *see JOSHUA, SUN AND MOON STAND STILL*

ALL FLESH IS GRASS   *see FLESH IS GRASS*

ALL IS VANITY

Eccles. 1:2

Ecclesiastes begins: "The words of the Preacher, the son of David, king in Jerusalem. Vanity of vanities, saith the Preacher, vanity of vanities; all is vanity." The Preacher—the K. J. translation of the Hebrew "koheleth," also known as Koheleth [kō·hĕl'·ĕth]—was traditionally thought to be Solomon. The words of Desdemona in *Othello*, after Othello has accused her of being a whore, probably allude to this passage:

> I cannot say "whore,"
> It doth abhor me now I speak the word.
> To do the act, that might the addition earn
> Not the world's mass of vanity could make me.

Browning's sensual bishop, in "The Bishop Orders His Tomb at Saint Praxed's Church," begins his deathbed plea for a luxurious tomb with, "Vanity, saith the preacher, vanity!" And in *Moby Dick*, Melville, reflecting upon man's tragedy writes: "the truest of all book's is Solomon's, and Ecclesiastes is the fine hammered steel of woe. 'All is vanity.' ALL. This wilful world hath not got hold of unchristian Solomon's wisdom yet." James Thompson's description of Dürer's "Melancholia" in the conclusion of "The City of Dreadful Night" is a profound expression of Victorian pessimism; in the picture is the sense

> That none can pierce the vast black veil uncertain
> Because there is no light beyond the curtain;
> That all is vanity and nothingness.

ALL THINGS IN COMMON

Acts 2:44–45;
4:32–35

The first Christians lived a communal life, sharing the wealth according to need. "And all that believed were together, and had all things common; and sold their possessions and goods, and parted them to all men as every man had need." As the queen lies dying in Tennyson's *Queen Mary*, she hears voices in the night crying out against kingship, priesthood and privilege, crying to God that he would "send again, according to His promise, the one King, the Christ, and all things in common, as in the day of the first church, when Christ Jesus was King." In "The Two Races of Men," Charles Lamb says that the borrower has great contempt for money. "What near approaches doeth he make to the primitive community,—to the extent of one half of the principle at least!" And in William D. Howells's *A Traveler from Altruria,* the Altrurian says that his "civilization is strictly Christian, and dates back to . . . the first Christian commune after Christ. It is a matter of history with us that one of these communists, when they were dispersed, brought the gospel to our continent; he was cast away on our eastern coast on his way to Britain."

AMAZIAH
(ăm·à·zī'à)

Amos 7:10–14

Amaziah was the priest of Bethel who complained to King Jeroboam about Amos's radical prophesying, saying, "Amos hath conspired against thee in the midst of the house of Israel: the land is not able to bear all his words." And he advised Amos to go back to Judah where he came from; "But prophesy not again any more at Bethel: for it is the king's chapel, and it is the king's court." Milton, in *Eikonoklastes,* tells how Charles I in prison longed for his own obsequious chaplains instead of the ministers sent by Parliament who always preached repentance to him. They were "as dear and pleasing as Amaziah, the priest of Bethel, was to Jeroboam. These had learned well the lesson that would please: 'Prophesy not against Bethel, for it is the king's chapel, the king's court;' and had taught the king to say of those ministers, which the parliament had sent, 'Amos hath conspired against me, the land is not able to bear all his words.' "

AMOS

Book of Amos

Amos was a herdsman of the southern village of Tekoa in Judah who went up to Bethel in Samaria to preach a religion of social justice and righteousness. He attacked economic exploitation and privilege, and priests who stressed ritual above righteousness. He incurred the wrath of Amaziah, priest of Bethel, who appealed to King Jeroboam to have Amos expelled for sedition. His prophecy of punishment for Israel "because they sold the righteous for silver, and the poor for a pair of shoes" is reflected in Whittier's "Cassandra Southwick" about the Quaker girl in Salem who was put up for sale into slavery for failure to pay a fine for nonattendance at church. One sea captain objected vigorously.

"Well answered, worthy captain, shame on their cruel laws!"
Ran through the crowd in murmurs loud the people's just applause.
"Like the herdsman of Tekoah, in Israel of old,
Shall we see the poor and righteous again for silver sold?"

Izaak Walton, in *The Compleat Angler*, sees Amos as a fisherman because like Job he mentioned fishhooks. This was in his attack upon the rich women of Samaria: "ye kine of Bashan, which oppress the poor, which crush the needy . . . . The Lord God will take you away with hooks, and your posterity with fishhooks." Walton says that fishing is appropriate to devout and humble men like Amos, who it is easy to believe was "not only a shepherd, but a good-natured plain fisherman." When Amaziah attacked him, Amos said, "I was no prophet, neither was I a prophet's son; but I was an herdman, and a gatherer of sycomore fruit." John Bunyan said of himself, "I am no poet, nor poet's son, but a mechanic."

ANAK, ANAKIM

(ā'năk,
ăn'*à*·kĭm)

*Num. 13:22,
28–33; Deut.
1:28*

Joshua's spies sent ahead to "search the land of Canaan" returned to report that "there we saw the giants, the sons of Anak, which come of the giants: and we were in our own sight as grasshoppers . . . ." Joshua ultimately drove them from the land. Dreaming of a meeting with his dead friend Hallam, Tennyson, in *In Memoriam*, as he watched the maidens sailing his shallop "gain strength and grace / And presence lordlier than before," said, I

> wax'd in every limb;
> I felt the thews of Anakim,
> The pulses of a Titan's heart.

In "Hawthorne and His Mosses," Melville says that if we read Shakespeare's contemporaries thoroughly, we will "be amazed at the wondrous ability of those Anaks of men . . . ."

ANANIAS

(ăn·*à*·nī'ăs)

Acts 5:1–10

In the early Christian days when "they had all things common," Ananias and his wife Sapphira [să·fī'rà] "sold a possession, and kept back part of the price . . . and brought a certain part, and laid it at the apostles' feet." When Peter accused Ananias of having lied unto God, he "fell down and gave up the ghost." About three hours later Sapphira also lied about the deception and was struck dead. Ananias is known as a deceiver or liar. In Ben Jonson's *The Alchemist*, when Subtle the alchemist learns the name of the Puritan deacon, Ananias, sent to make a deal, he exclaims,

> Out, the varlet
> That cozen'd the apostles! Hence, away!
> Flee, mischief! had your holy consistory
> No name to send me, of another sound,
> Than wicked Ananias?

In *Sesame and Lilies,* Ruskin says that most of us think not of "what we are to do, but of what we are to get; and the best of us are sunk into the sin of Ananias . . . we want to keep back part of the price . . . ." When Billy Budd, in Melville's *Billy Budd,* kills the deceitful Claggart, Captain Vere says, "It is the divine judgment of Ananias! . . . Struck dead by an angel of God. Yet the angel must hang."

ANATHEMA MARANATHA
(à·năth'·ê·mà măr·à·năth'à)

I Cor. 16:22

Paul wrote, "If any man love not the Lord Jesus Christ, let him be Anathema Maranatha." The word "anathema" (Gr. *anathema*) originally meaning anything devoted, to a god, for example, but coming later to mean devoted to evil, hence cursed—the two words together were thought to mean accursed. But *maranatha,* an Aramaic word, is now known to mean "our Lord has come" or "will come"; hence should be taken separately. In literature the traditional "double curse" is the usual sense, as in Macaulay's comment, in his essay on Milton, that after the death of Cromwell, "the principles of liberty were the scoff of every grinning courtier, and the Anathema Maranatha of every fawning dean." And in "The Jewish Cemetery at Newport," Longfellow pictures persecution of the Jews:

> Anathema maranatha! was the cry
> That rang from every town, from street to street;
> At every gate the accursed Mordecai
> Was mocked and jeered, and spurned by Christian feet.

ANGEL OF LIGHT

II Cor. 11:14

Paul, speaking of false apostles who transform themselves into the apostles of Christ, said, "And no marvel; for Satan himself is transformed into an angel of light." In Shakespeare's *The Comedy of Errors,* when the courtesan asks the wrong Antipholus for the chain he promised her, and he tells his servant Dromio that she is the devil himself, Dromio says, "Nay, she is worse, she is the devil's dam; and here she comes in the habit of a light wench: and therefore comes that the wenches say 'God damn me;' that's as much to say 'God make me a light wench.' It is written, they appear to men like angels of light: light is an effect of fire, and fire will burn; ergo, light wenches will burn. Come not near her." In Samuel Butler's *The Way of All Flesh,* Ernest's marriage to Ellen fails to save him from sin: "It seemed to him that in his attempt to be moral

he had been following a devil which had disguised itself as an
angle of light."

ANOINTED OF THE LORD   *see THE LORD'S ANOINTED*

ANTICHRIST   John wrote, "Little children . . . as ye have heard that anti-
                   christ shall come, even now are there many antichrists." And,
I John 2:18, 22;   "He is antichrist, that denieth the Father and the Son." The
4:3   antichrist would be finally conquered by the Second Coming
                   of Christ. He is referred to as "the man of sin" in II Thes-
                   salonians 2:1–12, and as the beast in Revelation 13; Babylon is
                   his city in Revelation 17—19. The term has been applied vari-
                   ously to the Roman Empire, to Nero and Caligula, to Mahomet,
                   to the Pope and the Roman Catholic Church by the Puritans,
                   and to Napoleon, Stalin, and Hitler. In Ben Jonson's *The
                   Alchemist,* the deacon Ananias tries to be rid of the crude
                   country boy, Kastril, saying, "Avoid, Sathan! / Thou look'st
                   like antichrist, in that lewd hat." Newman, in *Apologia pro
                   Vita Sua,* said that his early reading of the Protestant Bishop
                   Newman firmly convinced him "that the Pope was the Anti-
                   christ predicted by Daniel, St. Paul, and St. John." And in
                   Shaw's *Saint Joan,* Monseigneur says that Joan's writing letters
                   to the English king "giving him God's command" was "the
                   practice of the accursed Mahomet, the anti-Christ."

APOCALYPSE
(ă·pŏk′á·lĭps)

The word, from Greek *apokalypsis* meaning "disclosure," does
not appear in the Bible; it refers to the book of Revelation,
called also the Apocalypse of John. Apocalyptic writings deal
with hidden or secret meanings, prophecies of danger, and a
millenial future. In *The House of Fame,* Chaucer describes the
goddess of Fame seated on her throne; it was a great wonder
that she had as many eyes as

> weren on the bestes foure
> That Goddis trone gunne honoure,
> As John writ in th' Apocalips.

In *Paradise Lost,* as Satan approaches the Garden of Eden
intent upon corrupting Adam and Eve, Milton writes,

> O for that warning voice, which he who saw
> Th' Apocalyps, heard cry in heaven aloud,
> Then when the Dragon, put to second rout,
> Came furious down to be reveng'd on men.

APOLLYON   *see ABADDON*

APPLE   *see FORBIDDEN FRUIT*

APPLE OF HIS EYE

Deut. 32:10; Ps. 17:8; Prov. 7:2
When the Lord found Jacob "in the waste howling wilderness . . . he kept him as the apple of his eye." The phrase, referring at first to the pupil of the eye thought to be a round ball, means something very precious. At the Christmas dinner, in Joyce's *A Portrait of the Artist as a Young Man,* the Irish, who have been called by Mr. Dedalus "a priestridden Godforsaken race," are stoutly defended by Dante: "If we are a priestridden race we ought to be proud of it! They are the apple of God's eye. *Touch them not,* says Christ, *for they are the apple of My eye.*" And Henry Adams in *Mont-Saint-Michel and Chartres* says that Saint Bernard "was regarded as the apple of the Virgin's eye."

APPLE OF KNOWLEDGE   *see FORBIDDEN FRUIT*

APPLES OF SODOM

Deut. 32:32
In "Moses' Song of God's Faithfulness," the enemy's "vine is of the vine of Sodom, and of the fields of Gomorrah: their grapes are grapes of gall, their clusters are bitter." Later writers told of apple trees of the Dead Sea area whose fruit was full of ashes, so that the phrase, as "Dead Sea Fruit" or "Dead Sea Apple" means something bitter or disappointing. When Satan, in Milton's *Paradise Lost,* tells the devils in hell of his success in corrupting Adam and Eve, the forbidden tree suddenly appears before them. Then

> greedily they pluck'd
> The Fruitage fair to sight, like that which grew
> Neer that bituminous Lake where Sodom flam'd;
> This more delusive, not the touch, but taste
> Deceav'd; they fondly thinking to allay
> Thir appetite with gust, instead of Fruit
> Chewd bitter ashes, which th'offended taste
> With spattering noise rejected.

In *Childe Harold's Pilgrimage,* Byron says,

> Life will suit
> Itself to Sorrow's most detested fruit,
> Like to the apples on the Dead Sea's shore,
> All ashes to the taste.

And Trollope, in *Framley Parsonage*, writes, "I will not say that the happiness of marriage is like the Dead Sea fruit—an apple which, when eaten, turns bitter ashes in the mouth."

ARK, NOAH'S   *see NOAH'S ARK*

ARK OF BULRUSHES   *see MOSES AND ARK OF BULRUSHES*

ARK OF THE COVENANT

Exod. 25:10–22;
Deut. 31:9; Josh.
3:17; 6:4–11;
I Sam. 4, 5, 6, 7;
I Chron. 13:3–14;
15:1–29

The Ark of the Covenant, called also the Ark of God or the Ark of the Testimony, was the cabinet containing Moses' two tables of the Law, and was housed in the Holy of Holies, a chamber within the Tabernacle. Made of shittim (acacia) wood, overlaid with pure gold, fitted with four rings and staves for carrying, it supported the mercy seat flanked by two cherubims with sheltering wings. Here God said to Moses, "I will meet with thee, and I will commune with thee from above the mercy seat . . . ." It was carried by the Levites through the wilderness, across the Jordan and around the walls at the fall of JERICHO; it was captured by the Philistines, returned joyously by David to Jerusalem, and finally installed in Solomon's temple. It was later lost, perhaps destroyed by Nebuchadnezzar.

In Milton's *Paradise Lost*, Raphael tells Adam of the construction of the Ark of the Covenant:

> By his prescript a Sanctuary is fram'd
> Of cedar, overlaid with Gold, therein
> An Ark, and in the Ark his Testimony,
> The Records of his Cov'nant, over these
> A Mercie-seat of Gold between the wings
> Of two bright Cherubim . . . .

Bertha, the maiden fair, in Keats's "The Eve of St. Mark," is "perplexed with a thousand" Biblical things such as "the Covenantal Ark / With its many mysteries, / Cherubim and golden mice." When the Philistines, "smitten for keeping the ark," wanted to send it back, they were told they must return with it as "a trespass offering . . . five golden emerods and five golden mice." Hardy, in *Tess of the D'Urbervilles*, describes the family dresser standing importantly up in front of the moving van "like some Ark of the Covenant that they were bound to carry reverently."

ARMAGEDDON
(är·mȧ·gĕd′ŭn)

Rev. 16:16

From the Hebrew *har*, "mountain," and *megiddon*, the Plain of Megiddo, in the Plain of Esdraelon where great battles had taken place; Armageddon is the field where the forces of good and evil will clash before Judgment Day, or commonly today any final, decisive battle. In "Rantoul," Whittier pictures an antislavery congressman:

> We seemed to see our flag unfurled,
> Our champion waiting in his place
> For the last battle of the world,
> The Armageddon of the race.

H. L. Mencken, in "Puritanism as a Literary Force," comments on the "supernaturalization of politics" in America. "There has not been a presidential contest since Jackson's day without its Armageddons, its marching of Christian soldiers . . . ."

ASHES   see DUST AND ASHES

ASHES AND SACKCLOTH   see SACKCLOTH AND ASHES

ASHTORETH; ASHTAROTH, pl.
(ăsh′·tĕr·ĕth)

Judg. 2:13; 10:6;
I Sam. 7:3–4; I
Kings 11:5, 33

Ashtoreth, also called Asherah [ȧ·shē′rȧ], in Greek form Astarte, was the Canaanite and Phoenician goddess of love and fertility. Sometimes called "the queen of heaven" in reference to Jeremiah (7:18; 44:17–19), she was the counterpart of the Greek Aphrodite or Venus, and the Babylonian Ishtar. Her worship was associated with the male god Baal and the phallic pole or sacred tree called the "GROVE"; in her temples sacred prostitution lured the backsliding Hebrews—Solomon for one. She is one of the fallen devils in Milton's *Paradise Lost*:

> With these in troop
> Came Astoreth, whom the Phoenicians call'd
> Astarte, Queen of Heav'n, with crescent Horns;
> To whose bright Image nightly by the Moon
> Sidonian Virgins paid their Vows and Songs,
> In Sion also not unsung, where stood
> Her Temple on th'offensive Mountain, built
> By that Uxorious King, whose heart though large,
> Beguil'd by fair Idolatresses, fell
> To Idols foul.

Swinburne, in "Dolores" a poem to "Our Lady of Pain," asks of lovers long ago, "Where are they, Cottytto or Venus, / Astarte or Ashtaroth, where?" And Poe, in "Ligeia," may have coined the name of the "wan and the misty-winged Ashtophet," who presided over his marriage to Ligeia, from Ashtaroth and TOPHET. The spelling of Ashtoreth (Ashtaroth) is inconsistent in literature.

ASMODEUS He was the demon in the Book of Tobit, of the Apocrypha,
(ăz·mô·dē'ŭs) who killed the seven husbands of Sara, who then married Tobias, son of Tobit. He was driven from Media into Egypt fast bound by Tobias using a charm made from a fish burnt over perfumed coals. In Milton's *Paradise Lost*, as Satan approached the garden of Eden, he was entertained by its perfumed air,

> better pleas'd
> Then Asmodeus with the fishie fume,
> That drove him, though enamourd, from the Spouse
> Of Tobits Son, and with a vengeance sent
> From Media post to Egypt, there fast bound.

AT EASE IN ZION

Amos 6:1 The prophet Amos attacked the complacent, luxury-loving rich, saying, "Woe to them that are at ease in Zion, and trust in the mountain of Samaria." In *Culture and Anarchy*, Matthew Arnold contrasts Hellenism with Hebraism: "Socrates is terribly at ease in Zion. Hebraism . . . has always been severely preoccupied with an awful sense of the impossibility of being at ease in Zion; of the difficulties which oppose themselves to man's pursuit or attainment of that perfection of which Socrates talks so hopefully." Charles Lamb, in "Christ's Hospital Five and Thirty Years Ago," contrasts two teachers: one demanding, the other easygoing. While the other students were "battering their brains over Xenophon and Plato . . . we were enjoying ourselves at our ease in our little Goshen."

AT THE FEET OF   see SIT AT THE FEET OF

AVENGER OF BLOOD   see CITY OF REFUGE

AZAZEL   see SCAPEGOAT

BAAL; BAALIM, pl.

(bā′ăl,
bā′ăl·ĭm)

*Judg. 2:11–14;
3:7*

Baal was the Canaanite and Phoenician male god of fertility, consort of Ashtoreth or Astarte, worshiped with licentious ceremonies on the high places among the groves or phallic poles. Queen Jezebel brought Baal worship into Israel, Elijah contested his prophets on Mount Carmel, and Jeremiah and King Josiah denounced their Hebrew followers. The Baalim and Ashtoreth were among the fallen devils on the Plain of Hell in Milton's *Paradise Lost.* And in *Paradise Regained,* Christ rejects Satan's temptation of worldly kingdoms, citing the Israelites who "wrought their own captivity" through worship of "the deities of Egypt, Baal next, and Ashtaroth, / And all the idolatries of heathen round . . . ." In *Sartor Resartus,* Carlyle's Professor Teufelsdröckh writes "that there are 'true priests,' as well as Baal-priests, in our own day . . . ."

BABEL
(bā′běl)

Gen. 11:1–9

Babel, meaning "the gate of God," is the Hebrew name for Babylon, city on the Plain of Shinar [shī′nēr]. When "the whole earth was of one language," the people tried to build a tower whose top would reach unto heaven. For their presumption "the Lord did there confound the language of all the earth: and from thence did the Lord scatter them abroad upon the face of all the earth." Babel thus means an impracticable scheme, or great confusion. The original Tower of Babel was a platformed, seven-storied tower called a ziggurat, built for the worship of the Babylonian god Marduk. In *A Defense of Poetry,* Shelley attacks the "vanity of translation" as a confusion of tongues: "to seek to transfuse from one language into another the creations of a poet . . . is the burthen of the curse of Babel." Byron, in his "Dedication" to *Don Juan,* says of Wordsworth's lengthy *Excursion,* "he who understands it would be able / To add a story to the Tower of Babel." In "The Bell Tower," Melville says of the fallen bell tower, "Like Babel's, its base was laid in a high hour of renovated earth, following the second deluge . . . . No wonder that, after so long and deep submersion, the jubilant expectation of the race should, as with Noah's sons, soar into Shinar aspiration."

BABES AND SUCKLINGS *see OUT OF THE MOUTH OF BABES AND
SUCKLINGS*

BABYLON   Capital of Babylonia and later Chaldea on the Euphrates River,
(băb'ĭ·lŏn)   mentioned many times in the Bible from Genesis 10:10 to
                     Revelations, and the scene of the Exile, it was known for its
                     wealth, grandeur, and wickedness. Isaiah's prophecy of Baby-
                     lon's fall into hell (14:4; 21:9) as well as its grandeur are
                     reflected in Poe's "The City in the Sea." The city is seen not
                     by "rays from the holy heaven come down,"

> But light from out the lurid sea
> Streams up the turrets silently—
> Gleams up the pinnacles far and free—
> Up domes—up spires—up kingly halls—
> Up fanes—up Babylon-like walls—

And in conclusion,

> Down, down that town shall settle hence,
> Hell, rising from a thousand thrones,
> Shall do it reverence.

And Francis Thompson, in *The Night of Forbearing*, says that
the greatness of the human heart lies in its creative genius:
"Our towns are copied fragments from our breast; / And all
man's Babylons strive but to impart / The grandeurs of his
Babylonian heart."

BABYLON AS SCARLET WOMAN, WHORE

Rev. 17:1–7; 18   An angel showed St. John the Divine a vision of "the great
                     whore that sitteth upon many waters . . . . I saw a woman sit
                     upon a scarlet coloured beast . . . having seven heads and ten
                     horns. And the woman was arrayed in purple and scarlet
                     colour, and decked with gold and precious stones and pearls,
                     having a golden cup in her hand full of abominations and
                     filthiness of her fornication: And upon her forehead, was a
                     name written, MYSTERY, BABYLON THE GREAT, THE
                     MOTHER OF HARLOTS AND ABOMINATIONS OF THE
                     EARTH." Radical Protestants of the past have interpreted the
                     scarlet woman as being the Roman Catholic Church seated in
                     Rome; the K.J. title of Revelations 17 is "The Woman on the
                     Seven Hills." In *Eikonoklastes,* Milton argues that God's saints
                     have the right to overthrow those European kings whose power
                     comes not from God, "but from the beast; and are counted no
                     better than his ten horns. 'These shall hate the great whore,'
                     and yet 'shall give their kingdoms to the beast that carries
                     her; they shall commit fornication with her,' and yet 'shall
                     burn her with fire,' and yet 'shall lament the fall of Babylon,'

where they fornicated with her." Charles Lamb wrote Mrs.
Wordsworth a letter saying that the abstract notion of the
East India Company is "pretty, rather poetical, but as she
makes herself manifest by the persons of such beasts, I loathe
and detest her as the scarlet what-do-you-call-her of Babylon."
Carlyle, in "Characteristics," describes the "frightful Puffing"
of advertising as "a perfect 'Babylon, the mother of Abomina-
tions,' in very deed making the world 'drunk' with the wine of
her iniquity . . . ." And the relation of Hawthorne's *The
Scarlet Letter* to this passage is clear when Governor Bellingham
says of Pearl, "We might have judged that such a child's
mother must needs be a scarlet woman, and a worthy type of
her of Babylon."

BACA, VALE OF
(bā'·ca)

Ps. 84:5, 6

"Blessed is the man whose strength is in thee . . . . Who
passing through the valley of Baca make it a well; the rain
also filleth the pools." Although the word "Baca" means
"weeping," leading some to believe that the expression "vale
of tears" is based on this passage, Baca trees are balsams which
exude "tears" of gum, and the Valley of Baca was a dry valley
through which pilgrims passed on route to Jerusalem. In
"Hazel Blossoms," Whittier thinks of the hazel as a divining
rod:

> O Love! the hazel-wand may fail,
>   But thou canst lend the surer spell,
> That, passing over Baca's vale,
>   Repeats the old-time miracle,
>   And makes the desert-land a well.

BALAAM
(bā'lăm)

Num. 22–24

Balaam was a heathen soothsayer living east of the Jordan at
Pethor, who would not utter curses against the Hebrews; he
pronounced blessings only. Later, however, he induced the
Hebrews to sin (Num. 31) and was subsequently remembered
disparagingly. In literature he is chiefly known by the animal
story of "Balaam's Ass." (Num. 22:1–35) At the request of
Balak, king of Moab, "Balaam rose up in the morning, and
saddled his ass, and went with the princes of Moab" to curse
the Israelites. But "the ass saw the angel of the Lord standing
in the way, and his sword drawn in his hand: and the ass
turned aside out of the way . . . and Balaam smote the ass, to
turn her into the way." Three times Balaam smote her; then
"the Lord opened the mouth of the ass, and she said unto
Balaam, "What have I done unto thee, that thou has smitten

me three times?" The Lord then opened Balaam's eyes, and
he repented and would not curse the Israelites. Robert Herrick's
poem "Upon Julia's Fall" tells how Julia fell from her horse.

> The wanton Ambler chanc'd to see
> Part of her leggs sincereitee:
> And ravish'd thus, It came to passe,
> The Nagge (like to the Prophets Asse)
> Began to speak, and would have been
> A telling what rare sights h'ad seen:
> And had told all; but did refraine,
> Because his Tongue was ty'd againe.

In *Culture and Anarchy,* Matthew Arnold says that the Protestant attitude toward the Bible differs little from the Catholic's
attitude toward his church: "The mental habit of him who
imagines that Balaam's ass spoke, in no respect differs from
the mental habit of him who imagines that a Madonna of
wood or stone winked." D. H. Lawrence wrote Mabel Luhan
excusing himself for going to Ceylon rather than accepting her
invitation to visit Taos: "It is vile of us to put off Taos for the
moment. But I have a Balaam's Ass in my belly which won't
budge, when I turn my face west. I can't help it. It just suddenly swerves away in me. I will come. But I detour."

BALAK, BALAC   *see BALAAM*

BALM IN GILEAD

Jer. 8:22   The Lord asks why his people are not healed of their sins:
"For the hurt of the daughter of my people am I hurt . . . .
Is there no balm in Gilead; is there no physician there? why
then is not the health of the daughter of my people recovered?"
The Israelites carried on trade in the aromatic and medicinal
herbs from Gilead (Gen. 37:25). In Poe's "The Raven," the
lover asks,

> "On this home by Horror haunted—tell me truly, I implore—
> Is there—*is* there balm in Gilead?—tell me—tell me, I implore!"
> Quoth the raven, "Nevermore."

Tom Sawyer, in Mark Twain's novel, said of Aunt Polly who
was obsessed with patent medicines and "all manner of reme-
dies" that "she never suspected that she was not an angel of
healing and the balm of Gilead in disguise, to the suffering
neighbors." Edwin Arlington Robinson's "Old King Cole" lives

with outward calm, but inwardly he suffers: "For grief like mine there is no balm / In Gilead, or in Tilbury Town."°

BARABBAS
(ba·răb′ăs)

Matt. 27:16–26;
Mark 15:7–15;
John 18:40

Barabbas was the thief at the trial of Jesus who was released instead of Jesus. He was called also a seditionist and murderer by Luke (23:19) and Mark (15:7). In Tennyson's *Becket,* Becket exiled from England blames Rome: "Why should this Rome, this Rome / still choose Barabbas rather than the Christ, / Absolve the left-hand thief and damn the right?" Attacking unjust profits, Ruskin in *Time and Tide,* argues that theft is the cardinal sin in the New Testament: "Although Barabbas was a leader of sedition, and a murderer besides . . . —yet St. John in curt and conclusive account of him, fastens again on the theft."

BASHAN
(bā′shăn)

Num. 21:33;
32:33; Deut.
3:1–14; Ps. 22:12

Bashan, meaning "the fruitful," was a high, fertile land east of the Sea of Galilee, famed for its grain, cattle, sheep, and strong men. Psalm 22:12 mentions "strong bulls of Bashan," and Amos addresses luxury-loving wives as "ye kine of Bashan." King Og, its most famous ruler, "remained of the remnant of giants; behold, his bedstead was a bedstead of iron . . . nine cubits was the length thereof, and four cubits the breadth of it . . ." (about 13 by 6 feet). He was slain with all his people by Moses. Mark Antony, in Shakespeare's *Antony and Cleopatra,* scolding Cleopatra for entertaining Thyreus' wooing for Caesar, declares, "O, that I were / Upon the hill of Basan, to outroar / The horned herd! for I have savage cause . . . ." In *The Autocrat of the Breakfast Table,* O. W. Holmes tells of the British love of puns: "Lord Bacon playfully declared himself a descendant of Og, the King of Bashan." In *Absalom and Achitophel,* Dryden attacked corpulent Thomas Shadwell as King Og:

> Og, from a treason-tavern rolling home.
> Round as a globe, and liquor'd ev'ry chink,
> Goodly and great he sails behind his link.
> With all this bulk there's nothing lost in Og,
> For ev'ry inch that is not fool is rogue:
> A monstrous mass of foul corrupted matter,
> As all the devils had spew'd to make the batter.

BASILISK   *see COCKATRICE*

°Reprinted with permission of The Macmillan Company from *Collected Poems* by E. A. Robinson. Copyright 1916 by E. A. Robinson. Renewed 1944 by Ruth Nivison.

BATHSHEBA   *see DAVID AND BATHSHEBA*

BEAM IN THINE OWN EYE   *see MOTE IN THY BROTHER'S EYE*

BEARS OF ELISHA   *see ELISHA*

BEAST WITH TEN HORNS   *see BABYLON AS SCARLET WOMAN, WHORE*

BEATITUDES

Matt. 5:3–12;
Luke 6:20–23

The beatitudes are Jesus' statements regarding those who are blessed—from the Latin *beatus*, "made happy"; they are a preface to the incomparable Sermon on the Mount. They begin: "Blessed are the poor in spirit; for theirs is the kingdom of heaven." In Shakespeare's *Henry IV, Part I*, Falstaff, when he heard that his old buddy, Prince Hal, had become king, said to Pistol, "I am Fortune's steward . . . . Blessed are they that have been my friends; and woe to my Lord Chief Justice." When Billy Budd, in Melville's novel *Billy Budd*, was impressed into the navy, the master of Billy's ship said to the naval lieutenant, ". . . you are going to take away my peacemaker." " 'Well,' answered the Lieutenant . . . 'blessed are the peace-makers, especially the fighting peacemakers.' " Thoreau wrote to Parker Pillsbury about "the present condition of things in this country": "Blessed were the days before you read a President's message. Blessed are the young, for they do not read the President's message. Blessed are they who never read a newspaper, for they shall see Nature, and, through her, God."

BEDLAM   *see BETHLEHEM*

BEELZEBUB
(bē·ĕl′zē·bŭb)

Matt. 10:25;
12:24–27; Mark
3:22; Luke
11:15–19

Derived from the O.T. *Baal-zebub* [bā′ȧl-zē′bŭb] (II Kings 1:2, 3, 6, 16) meaning "Lord of the heavenly habitation," a god of the Philistines, Beelzebub, meaning "Lord of the flies," became in the N.T. "the prince of the devils." In Shakespeare's *Macbeth*, the porter responds to the knocking at the gate with, "Knock, knock, knock! Who's there, i' the name of Beelzebub?" In Milton's *Paradise Lost*, he is Satan's chief who advances Satan's own secret plan before the council of the devils to make an attack on man. Ishmael, in *Moby Dick*, says that such queer castaway characters become whale men "that Beelzebub himself might climb up the side . . . to chat with the captain, and not create any unsubduable excitement in the forecastle."

BE FRUITFUL AND MULTIPLY

Gen. 1:22, 28;
9:1, 7

At the creation God said to both animals and man, and later to Noah and his sons, "Be fruitful and multiply." Chaucer's Wife of Bath in the Prologue to her tale speaks of her five former husbands—and her readiness for a sixth: there is no definition of the number of husbands a woman may have:

> Men may devyne and glosen, up and doun,
> But wel I wot, express, withoute lye,
> God bad us for to wexe and multiplye;
> That gentil text kan I wel understonde.

And Adam, in Milton's *Paradise Lost,* laments his fall:

> All that I eate or drink, or shall beget,
> Is propagated curse. O voice once heard
> Delightfully, Encrease and multiply,
> Now death to heare! For what can I encrease
> Or multiply, but curses on my head?

BEGINNING OF WISDOM   *see FEAR OF THE LORD IS THE BEGINNING OF WISDOM*

BEHEMOTH
(bē·hē′mŏth)

Job 40:15–24

The behemoth, the word meaning "great beast," was some enormous water animal, possibly the hippopotamus; it was cited by the voice of the Lord out of the whirlwind as evidence of the Lord's supreme creative power. In *Paradise Lost,* Raphael pictures him probably as the elephant in describing the creation to Adam: "scarce from his mould / Behemoth biggest born of Earth upheav'd / His vastness:" William Vaughan Moody, in "Menagerie," speaks of voices of his "ancient kindred / . . . Grotesque and monstrous voices, heard afar / Down ocean caves when behemoth awoke." ° And O. W. Holmes, in *The Autocrat of the Breakfast Table,* tells of being caught in tight places "until our bones . . . cracked as if we had been in the jaws of Behemoth."

BEL AND THE DRAGON

"The History of
the Destruction
of Bel and the
Dragon," Apoc.

Bel, the same as Baal, was the Babylonian-Assyrian sun-god of earth and air. By scattering ashes on the temple floor, Daniel exposed the false priests of Bel, who secretly ate the sacrificial food at night. The Dragon, also worshiped by the Babylonians, was killed when Daniel fed it pitch, fat, and

°Reprinted by permission of Houghton Mifflin Company.

hair. In Ben Jonson's *The Alchemist*, the Puritan pastor Tribulation Wholesome describes the deceitful alchemist and his confederates as "profane as Bel and the Dragon." Carlyle, in *Shooting Niagara: And After?*, says England can be rebuilt permanently if men would behave "like the sons of Adam, and not like the scandalous . . . sons of Bel and the Dragon."

BELIAL
(bē'lĭ · ăl)

Deut. 13:13;
Judg. 19:22; I
Sam. 1:16; 2:12;
II Cor. 6:15

Belial, meaning "wicked," "lawless," is a personification of evil in the O.T. usually used with "man," "son," "daughter," "children"; in the N.T. it means Satan. In *Paradise Lost*, Milton made Belial one of the most lewd and subtle but dignified devils in hell: "a fairer person lost not Heav'n." In *Paradise Regained*, Belial was "the disolutest spirit that fell, / The sensuallest, and after Asmodai / The fleshliest incubus," who advised Satan to tempt Christ with sexual pleasure. Satan rejected his advice, saying he judged all others by himself: "Thou thyself doat'st on womankind, admiring / Thir shape, thir colour, and attractive grace, / None are, thou thinks't, but taken with such toys." In Dryden's *Absalom and Achitophel*, the Sons of Belial were the Whig conspirators against Charles II. The spiteful monk in Browning's "Soliloquy of the Spanish Cloister" will slip his "scroflus French novel" into Brother Lawrence's sieve; "Simply glance at it, you grovel / Hand and foot in Belial's gripe:"

BELLS AND POMEGRANATES

Exod. 28:33–35;
39:24–26

The Lord directed that there should be "a golden bell and a pomegranate upon the hem" of Aaron's robe so that "his sound shall be heard when he goeth in unto the holy place before the Lord, and when he cometh out, that he die not." Poems by Robert Browning were published in a series entitled "Bells and Pomegranates." Walter Pater, in *Miscellaneous Studies*, told of the vivid impression made on him as a child when he read of "the bells and pomegranates attached to the hem of Aaron's vestment, sounding sweetly as he glided over the turf of the holy place."

BELSHAZZAR
(běl · shăz'ĕr)

Dan. 5:1–30

Belshazzar, meaning "Bel protect the king," and called inaccurately the son of Nebuchadnezzar (he was the son of Nabonidus), was the last Chaldean king of Babylon. He gave "a great feast to a thousand of his lords" using "the golden and silver vessels, which his father Nebuchadnezzar had taken

out of the temple . . . in Jerusalem." When he saw the HAND-
WRITING ON THE WALL "his thoughts troubled him, so that the
joints of his loins were loosed, and his knees smote one against
another." In "Hawthorne and His Mosses," Melville praised
the story "A Select Party," saying Hawthorne had "builded
[an] august dome of sunset clouds, and served them on a
richer plate than Belshazzar's when he banqueted his lords in
Babylon." In *Eikonoklastes*, Milton ridiculed Charles II's claims
of fevered shaking, calling it "Belshazzar's palsy," and saying
that it was his own people's petitions which had "shaken all
his joints with such a terrible ague."

BE NOT YE CALLED RABBI

Matt. 23:7-8

Jesus said of the Scribes and Pharisees, who loved "greetings in
the markets, and to be called of men, Rabbi, Rabbi . . . . But
be not ye called Rabbi: for one is your Master, even Christ;
and all ye are brethren." The word Rabbi means "master" or
"teacher." In Chaucer's "Summoner's Tale," the friar, having
been hoaxed by Thomas, rushes to his friend, a lord, who
greets him as master.

> "No maister, sire," quod he, "but servitour,
> Though I have in scole swich honour.
> God liketh not that 'Raby' men us calle,
> Neither in market ne in youre large halle."

And in *Culture and Anarchy*, Matthew Arnold opposes to
Jacobism, which loves a Rabbi—an authoritarian or dictator—
culture: "However much it may find to admire in personages
[such as Compte, Buckle, or Mill], it nevertheless remembers
the text: 'Be not ye called Rabbi!' and it soon passes on from
any Rabbi."

BETHANY   *see LAZARUS, RAISING OF*

BETHEL   *see HOUSE OF GOD*

BETHESDA, POOL OF
(bĕ·thĕz′dả)

John 5:1-9

A pool in Jerusalem having five porches, where when "an
angel went down at a certain season into the pool, and troubled the water: whosoever then first after the troubling of the
water stepped in was made whole of whatsoever disease he
had." There Jesus saw a cripple who had waited thirty-eight
years because, he explained, "I have no man . . . to put me
into the pool: while I am coming, another steppeth down before

me." Jesus said unto him, "Rise, take up thy bed, and walk,"
and "immediately the man was made whole." Robert Burton,
in *The Anatomy of Melancholy*, writes that patrons neglect
university men and favor their own clerks: "Whilst we lie
waiting here as those sick men did at the Pool of Bethesda
till the angel stirred the water, expecting a good hour, they
step between and beguile us of our preferment." In "Bethesda,"
by Arthur Hugh Clough, a divine stranger approached the
invalid, "and breathing hope into the sick man's face, / Bade
him take up his bed, and rise and go." When Henchard, in
Hardy's *The Mayor of Casterbridge*, opened his door for his
daughter Elizabeth-Jane, Joshua Jopp, seeking employment,
"stepped forward like the quicker cripple at Bethesda, and
entered in her stead." Timid Theobald Pontifex, in Butler's
The Way of All Flesh, meeting "one of the prettier and more
agreeable girls" at a university party was usually "cut out by
someone less bashful than himself, and he sneaked off, feeling,
as far as the fair sex was concerned, like the impotent man
at the pool of Bethesda."

BETHLEHEM

Matt. 2:1

Bethlehem was the town in Judea where Jesus was born. The
word "bedlam" comes from the hospital of St. Mary of Bethlehem in London for the insane. In "The Medal," Dryden
attacks religious dissenters as "A conventicle of gloomy sullen
saints; / A heaven like Bedlam, slovenly and sad, / Fore-
doom'd for souls with false religion mad." Tennyson, in "Sir
John Oldcastle," writes of the little town of Lutterworth where
Wycliff, translator of the Bible into English, lived:

> Not least art thou, thou little Bethlehem
> In Judah, for in thee the Lord was born;
> Nor thou in Britain, little Lutterworth
> Least, for in thee the word was born again.

BETHULIA   *see JUDITH*

BETTER TO MARRY THAN TO BURN

I Cor. 7:7–9

The apostle Paul, a bachelor, giving advice on marriage, said,
"For I would that all men were even as I myself. But every
man has his proper gift of God . . . I say therefore to the
unmarried and widows, It is good for them if they abide even
as I. But if they cannot contain, let them marry: for it is better
to marry than to burn." Chaucer's Wife of Bath, in the Prologue to her tale, said,

I woot wel that th' apostle was a mayde;
But nathelees, though that he wroot and sayde
He wolde that every wight were swich as he,
Al nys but conseil to virginitee.

She said Paul would not oppose her marrying a sixth husband:

th' apostle seith that I am free
To wedde, a Goddes half, where it liketh me.
He seith that to be wedded is no synne;
Bet is to be wedded than to brynne.

And in Hardy's *Tess of the D'Urberville's,* Alec jests about forsaking his preaching to woo Tess again: "I believe that if the bachelor-apostle, whose deputy I thought I was, had been tempted by such a pretty face, he would have let go the plough for her sake as I do!"

BEULAH
(bū'là)

Isa. 62:4

Beulah, meaning "married," was the name given to Israel after the Exile: thy land shall be called "Beulah: for the Lord delighteth in thee, and thy land shall be married." In Bunyan's *Pilgrim's Progress,* it is the paradisiacal land where the pilgrims pause before crossing the River of Death. In his essay "John Bunyan," Macaulay wrote that Bunyan passed through fierce religious conflicts, a "Valley of the Shadow of Death . . . to that bright and fruitful land of Beulah." And Robert Louis Stevenson, in "Walt Whitman," said, "The Enchanted Ground of dead-alive respectability is next, upon the map, to the Beulah of considerate virtue."

BIRTHRIGHT   *see SOLD HIS BIRTHRIGHT FOR A MESS OF POTTAGE*

BLESSED ARE THEY   *see BEATITUDES*

BLIND LEAD THE BLIND

Matt. 15:14;
Luke 6:39

When his disciples told Jesus that he had offended the Pharisees, he replied, "Let them alone: they be blind leaders of the blind. And if the blind lead the blind, both shall fall into the ditch." Professor Teufelsdröckh, in Carlyle's *Sartor Resartus,* commented on the ineffectiveness of university education, "It is written, When the blind lead the blind, both shall fall into the ditch." Whittier, in "The Problem," wrote about labor relations:

The home-pressed question of the age can find
No answer in the catch-words of the blind

> Leaders of the blind. Solution there is none
> Save in the Golden Rule of Christ alone.

And Van Wyck Brooks, in *The Ordeal of Mark Twain*, said that Mark Twain's marriage was "a case of the blind leading the blind. Mark Twain had thrown himself into the hands of his wife; she, in turn, was merely the echo of her environment."

BLOOD CRIETH FROM THE GROUND

Gen. 4:10

When Cain killed Abel, the Lord said, "What hast thou done? the voice of thy brother's blood crieth unto me from the ground." In Shakespeare's *Richard II*, Bolingbroke accused Mowbray of plotting the Duke of Gloucester's death: he

> like a traitor coward
> Sluiced out his innocent soul through streams of blood:
> Which blood, like sacrificing Abel's, cries,
> Even from the tongueless caverns of the earth,
> To me for justice and rough chastisement;

Benjamin Franklin, in the *Narrative of the Late Massacres*, wrote that the guilt for the massacre of the Indians "will lie on the whole land till Justice is done . . . . The Blood of the Innocent, will cry to Heaven for Vengeance." And in Whittier's "Toussaint L'Ouverture" there "Burst on the startled ears of men / That voice which rises unto God, / Solemn and stern,—the cry of blood."

BLOOD OF THE LAMB, WASHED IN THE

Rev. 7:14

A great multitude clothed with white robes gathered before the throne and the Lamb were "they which came out of great tribulation, and have washed their robes, and made them white in the blood of the Lamb." In *A Defense of Poetry*, Shelly said that the errors of great poets are minor, "they have been washed in the blood of the mediator and redeemer, Time." The refrain of Vachel Lindsay's "General William Booth Enters into Heaven" is "Are you washed in the blood of the Lamb?"* The hippopotamus in T. S. Eliot's "The Hippopotamus" rises toward heaven: "Blood of the Lamb shall wash him clean / And him shall heavenly arms enfold. . . ."†

---

*Reprinted with permission of The Macmillan Company from *Collected Poems* by Vachel Lindsay. Copyright 1913 by The Macmillan Company.

†From "The Hippopotamus" in *Collected Poems 1909–1962* by T. S. Eliot. Reprinted by permission of Harcourt, Brace & World, Inc., and Faber and Faber, Ltd.

BOANERGES
(bō·a·nûr′jēz)

Mark 3:17

Jesus surnamed James and John "Boanerges, which is, The sons of thunder," because, said Jerome, of their fiery eloquence. Others say because of their violent tendencies: Jesus rebuked them because they would "command fire to come down from heaven, and consume" the Samaritans (Luke 9:51–56). The word means "sons of rage, soon angry." Cotton Mather, in *Magnalia Christi Americana*, said that John Eliot in his preaching against "Carnality" and "Indulgence in sensual Delights" was a "right *Boanerges* . . . he spoke as many *Thunderbolts* as *Words*." In "Sea Dreams" Tennyson writes of a ranting, anti-Catholic preacher, "Our Boanerges with his threats of doom / And loud-lunged Antibabylonianisms." Emily Dickinson's locomotive, in "I like to see it lap the miles," neighs like Boanerges.

BOAZ   *see RUTH*

BONE OF MY BONE

Gen. 2:23

When the Lord God made Eve "and brought her unto the man, Adam said, This is now bone of my bones, and flesh of my flesh." This is the Hebrew "genitive superlative" repeated in other phrases such as "servant of servants," "holy of holies," "King of Kings," and "Song of Songs." Hamlet says to Horatio, of flattery and good judgment,

> Give me that man
> That is not passion's slave, and I will wear him
> In my heart's core, ay, in my heart of heart,
> As I do thee.

In Tennyson's "Rizpah" a mother gathers the fallen bones of her son, who had been hung in chains on the gallows, to bury them secretly in the churchyard.

> Flesh of my flesh was gone, but bone of my bone was left—
> I stole them all from the lawyers—and you, will you call it a theft?—
> My baby, the bones that had suck'd me, the bones that had laughed and had cried—
> Theirs? O no! they are mine—not theirs—they had moved in my side.

And Jane, in Charlotte Brontë's *Jane Eyre*, says of her marriage to Rochester after ten years, "No woman was ever nearer to her mate than I am: ever more absolutely bone of his bone, flesh of his flesh."

BONES, DRY   *see VALLEY OF DRY BONES*

BOOK OF LIFE

Rev. 3:5;
20:12–15; 21:27

"And I saw the dead, small and great, stand before God; and
. . . the book was opened, which is the book of life: and the
dead were judged out of those things which were written in
the books, according to their works . . . . And whosoever was
not found written in the book of life was cast into the lake of
fire." Several references are made in the Bible to the book
kept by God listing those destined for the joys of eternal life
(Ps. 69:28; Dan. 12:1 ff.; Luke 10:20; Philippians 4:3). In Shakespeare's *Richard II*, Mowbray, after their banishment by Richard, said to Bolingbroke, who questioned his loyalty, "If ever
I were traitor, / My name be blotted from the book of life, /
And I from Heaven banished as from hence!" In Thomas
De Quincey's *Suspiria de Profundis*, Our Lady of Sighs visits
the Pariah, the Jew, and the English criminal banished to
Norfolk Island—those "blotted out from the books of remem-
brance in sweet far-off England." And in *Confessions of an
English Opium Eater*, De Quincey, saying that opium recalls
forgotten memories of past years, is convinced "that the dread
book of account which the Scriptures speak of is, in fact, the
mind of each individual."

THE BOOKS WERE OPENED

Dan. 7:10

In Daniel's vision of the final judgment "ten thousand stood
before" the "Ancient of days," and "the judgment was set,
and the books were opened." In Tennyson's "Sea Dreams" a
young man meets an older man who has defrauded him, and
asks to see his books:

> "The books, the books!" but he, he could not wait,
> Bound on a matter of life and death;
> When the great Books—see Daniel seven and ten—
> Were open'd, I should find he meant me well;

Ruskin, in *Sesame and Lilies*, writes that some do not believe
in immortality; others believe that "within these five, or ten
or twenty years, for every one of us the judgment will be set,
and the books opened."

BOTTOMLESS PIT   *see ABADDON*

BOW THE KNEE TO RIMMON   *see RIMMON*

BRAND OF CAIN   *see MARK OF CAIN*

BREAD CAST UPON WATERS   *see CAST THY BREAD UPON THE WATERS*

BREAK BREAD   *see LAST SUPPER*

BRICKS WITHOUT STRAW

Exod. 5:6–19

When Moses and Aaron asked permission for three days' release for a religious feast in the wilderness, Pharoah accused them of letting the people off from their burdens, and "commanded the same day the taskmasters of the people . . . saying, Ye shall no more give the people straw to make brick, as heretofore: let them go and gather straw for themselves." Because straw was essential as the binding material for the Nile mud, the frequent interpretation of bricks made without straw is incorrect: the hardships were doubled when the Hebrews were forced to gather their own straw which had previously been supplied to them. Arguing against seeking for religious authorities beyond the Bible itself, Milton, in *Of Prelatical Episcopacy*, says that he is doing his "utmost endeavour to recall the people of God from this vain foraging after straw . . . ." In *The Anatomy of Melancholy*, Robert Burton, criticizing literary patrons, many of whom are ignorant and corrupt, says that "[hard taskmasters they prove] they take away their straw and compel them to make their number of brick." Professor Teufelsdröckh, in Carlyle's *Sartor Resartus*, says that for many years "had the poor Hebrew, in this Egypt of an Auscultatorship, painfully toiled, baking bricks without stubble . . . ."

BROAD IS THE WAY   *see STRAIT IS THE GATE, NARROW IS THE WAY*

BROKEN AND CONTRITE HEART

Ps. 51:17

The Lord delights not in burnt offerings. "The sacrifices of God are a broken spirit: a broken and a contrite heart, O God, thou wilt not despise." Rebecca expresses her devotion to God, in Scott's *Ivanhoe*, in this hymn:

> But Thou hast said, The blood of goat,
> The flesh of rams I will not prize;
> A contrite heart, a humble thought,
> Are mine accepted sacrifice.

In "Recessional" Kipling writes:

> The tumult and the shouting dies;
> The Captains and the Kings depart:
> Still stands Thine ancient sacrifice,
> An humble and a contrite heart.

BROOK CHERITH   *see ELIJAH FED BY RAVENS*

BROTHER'S KEEPER   *see MY BROTHER'S KEEPER*

BRUISED (BROKEN) REED

II Kings 18:21;
Isa. 36:6

King Hezekiah is warned not to trust Egypt: "Now, behold, thou trustest upon the staff of this bruised reed, even upon Egypt, on which if a man lean, it will go into his hand, and pierce it . . ." (Isa. 42:3; Matt. 12:20). Of the Lord's elect Isaiah also wrote, "A bruised reed shall he not break, and the smoking flax shall he not quench . . . ." In *Night Thoughts*, Young wrote, "Lean not on Earth, 'twill pierce thee to the heart; / a broken reed at best, but oft, a spear." In his sonnet to Keats, Longfellow reads Keats's epitaph, that his name "was writ in water"; then says,

> Rather let me write:
> "The smoking flax before it burst to flame
> Was quenched by death, and broken the bruised reed."

In "The Eternal Goodness," Whittier writes that if his "heart and flesh are weak / To bear an untried pain, / The bruised reed He will not break, / But strengthen and sustain."

BULL(S) OF BASHAN   *see BASHAN*

BULRUSHES   *see MOSES AND ARK OF BULRUSHES*

BURNING BUSH

Exod. 3:1–4

When Moses was keeping the flock of Jethro, his father-in-law, in Midian, "the angel of the Lord appeared unto him in a flame of fire out of the midst of a bush: and he looked, and, behold, the bush burned with fire, and the bush was not consumed." During the Middle Ages the burning bush was a usual symbol of the Virgin, as in Chaucer's Prologue to the "Prioress's Tale," where the Prioress invokes the Virgin's aid:

> O mooder Mayde! o mayde Mooder free!
> O bussh unbrent, brennynge in Moyses sighte,

> That ravyshedest doun fro the Deitee . . .
> Help me to telle it in thy reverence!

In "Good-Bye" Emerson wrote,

> I laugh at the lore and the pride of man,
> At the sophist schools and the learned clan;
> For what are they all, in their high conceit,
> When man in the bush with God may meet.

BURY THE DEAD   *see LET THE DEAD BURY THEIR DEAD*

BY BREAD ALONE

Deut. 8:3; Matt. 4:4; Luke 4:4
The Devil tempted Jesus, after fasting forty days and forty nights in the wilderness, saying, "If thou be the Son of God, command that these stones be made bread." Jesus replied, "It is written, Man shall not live by bread alone, but by every word that proceedeth out of the mouth of God." In Milton's *Paradise Regained,* when Satan tempts Jesus in the same way,

> the Son of God reply'd.
> Think'st thou such force in Bread? is it not written . . .
> Man lives not by Bread only, but each Word
> Proceeding from the mouth of God;

And Milton wrote his Athenian friend Leonard Philares about his failing eyesight: "But if, as is written, 'Man shall not live by bread alone, but by every word that proceedeth out of the mouth of God,' what should prevent one from resting likewise in the belief that his eyesight lies not in his eyes alone, but enough for all purposes in God's leading and providence?"

BY THE RIVERS OF BABYLON

Ps. 137:1
The psalm sung in memory of the Exile in Babylonia begins, "By the rivers of Babylon, there we sat down, yea, we wept, when we remembered Zion." The captors "required of us mirth, saying, Sing us one of the songs of Zion." The Prayer Book version begins "By the waters of Babylon . . . ." Izaak Walton tells, in his *Life of Dr. John Donne,* how Donne grieved at his wife's death: "as the Israelites sate mourning by the rivers of Babylon when they remembered Sion, so he gave some ease to his oppressed heart by thus venting his sorrow." Swinburne's poem celebrating Italy's resistance to Austrian tyranny, titled "Super Flumina Babylonis," begins "By the waters of Babylon we sat down and wept, / Remembering thee, / That for ages

of agony hast endured, and slept, / And wouldst not see." In
The Waste Land, T. S. Eliot writes,

> The nymphs are departed.
> And their friends, the loitering heirs of City directors;
> Departed, have left no addresses.
> By the waters of Leman I sat down and wept . . . .°

CAIAPHAS
(kā′yȧ·făs)

Matt. 26:3, 57;
John 11:49–54;
18:14, 24, 28

Caiaphas, the high priest, after Jesus had raised Lazarus from
the dead, said to the Pharisees and chief priests, ". . . it is
expedient for us, that one man should die for the people, and
that the whole nation perish not. And this spake he not of
himself: but being high priest that year, he prophesied that
Jesus should die for that nation." In *An Apology for Smectymnuus,* Milton refers to his opponent as "as perfect a
hypocrite as Caiaphas"; and, in the *Tetrachordon,* Milton says
that "modern interpreters . . . will make [St. Paul] a prophet
like Caiaphas, to speak the word not thinking, nay, denying to
think." In Tennyson's *Queen Mary,* when Archbishop Cranmer,
condemned to burning, is brought before the people weeping,
to confess his conversion, Father Cole says, "Behold him,
brethren . . . . Weep with him if ye will, / . . . Yet it is expedient for one man to die, / Yea for the people, lest the
people die."

CAIN

Gen. 4:1–17

Cain, Adam and Eve's first son, was "a tiller of the ground";
when the Lord favored the offering of his brother Abel, a
shepherd, but not Cain's offering, Cain "was very wroth," and
he "rose up against Abel his brother, and slew him." The
Lord then cursed Cain, saying, "When thou tillest the ground,
it shall not henceforth yield unto thee her strength; a fugitive
and a vagabond shalt thou be in the earth." In his essay "Of
Envy," Bacon wrote, "Cain's envy was the more vile and
malignant towards his brother, Abel, because when his sacrifice
was better accepted there was nobody to look on." King
Claudius, after the play in *Hamlet,* said, "O, my offense is rank,
it smells to heaven; / It has the primal eldest curse upon't, / A
brother's murder." Ancient tradition held that Cain used the
jawbone of an ass, as in Hamlet's remark at the gravedigger's
scene, "How the knave jowls it [a skull] to the ground, as if
it were Cain's jaw-bone, that did the first murder!" In the
old tapestries Cain was distinguished by a yellow, sandy-colored
beard.

°From *Collected Poems 1909–1962* by T. S. Eliot. Reprinted by permission of Harcourt, Brace & World, Inc., and Faber and Faber, Ltd.

CAIN'S CITY

Gen. 4:17

After he was cursed by the Lord to be a wanderer in the earth, Cain "builded a city, and called the name of the city, after the name of his son, Enoch." In *The History of the World,* Sir Walter Raleigh wrote that "the first city of the world was built by Cain, which he called Enoch, of whom were the Henochii before remembered." The Henochii, said Raleigh, dwelt after the flood "towards the east side of Eden where Cain dwelt." Cain's city, as are Cain's children, is associated with evil and corruption in literature. In *Billy Budd,* Melville writes that natural virtues seem to be "exceptionally transmitted from a period prior to Cain's City and citified man."

CALF OF GOLD   *see GOLDEN CALF*

CALVARY

Luke 23:33

Calvary, or Golgotha, is the place where Christ was crucified. The word "Calvary," from the Latin *calvaria,* meaning "skull," is the translators' word for the Aramaic *gūlgūlthā* (Matt. 27:33; Mark 15:22; John 19:17). The N.T. Greek *kranion* also meant "skull." At the abdication scene in Shakespeare's *Richard II,* the Bishop of Carlisle warns that if Bolingbroke is crowned, "The blood of English shall manure the ground / . . . and this land be called / The field of Golgotha and dead men's skulls." In Carlyle's *Sartor Resartus,* Professor Teufelsdröckh experienced religious doubt, when life was about to "grind me limb from limb. O, the vast, gloomy solitary Golgotha, and Mill of Death!"; and a battlefield is described by Carlyle as a place of desolation: "the kind seedfield lies a desolate, hideous Place of Skulls." Emily Dickinson frequently used the word "Calvary" to express her own sorrow, as in: "Title divine is mine / The Wife without / The Sign, / Acute degree / Conferred on me— / Empress of Calvary." °

CAMEL GO THROUGH AN EYE OF A NEEDLE

Matt. 19:24

After the rich young man "went away sorrowful: for he had great possessions," Jesus said, "It is easier for a camel to go through the eye of a needle, than for a rich man to enter into the kingdom of God." Imprisoned, Richard, in Shakespeare's *Richard II,* reflects upon the difficulty of finding words to express his feelings: "the word itself is set against the word: / As thus, 'Come, little ones,' and then again, / 'It is as hard to come as for a camel / To thread the postern of a small needle's

° From *Poems by Emily Dickinson* by Emily Dickinson (Boston, Little, Brown and Co.).

eye.' " Mark Twain wrote, in his *Notebook*, "It is easier for a cannibal to enter the Kingdom of Heaven through the eye of a rich man's needle than it is for any other foreigner to read the terrible German script." And Caitlin Thomas, in *Leftover Life to Kill*, reflecting on her poverty in Italy after Dylan's death, wrote, "It is as hard for a poor man to pass through the eye of a corrugated bodkin as to enter the house of a rich man."

CANA
(kā′nä)

John 2:1–11

Jesus, invited to a marriage in Cana of Galilee, turned water into wine. The ruler of the feast observed that whereas most men hold the worse wine for the end, "thou hast kept the good wine until now." In Chaucer's Prologue to "The Wife of Bath's Tale," the Wife says that she was told that she should wed only once because "Christ ne wente never but onis / To weddyng in the Cane of Galilee." Robert Herrick, in "To the Water Nymphs, Drinking at the Fountain," wrote:

> Or else sweet Nimphs do you but this;
> To th' Glasse your lips encline;
> And I shall see by that one kisse,
> The Water turn'd to Wine.

In "The Holy Grail," by Tennyson, King Arthur called on Lancelot last of all the knights to report on their quests: "Perhaps, like him of Cana in Holy Writ. / Our Arthur kept his best until the last."

CANAAN, LAND OF   see PROMISED LAND

CANAAN, SON OF HAM

Gen. 9:18–27

Ham, the father of Canaan, looked on Noah, his father, lying drunk and uncovered in his tent. When "Noah awoke from his wine, and knew what [Ham] had done unto him . . . he said, Cursed be Canaan; a servant of servants shall he be unto his brethren." Because the word "servant" meant "slave" and because tradition held that the Africans descended from Ham, this passage has been used by some to justify Negro slavery and segregation. Sir Walter Raleigh, in *The History of the World,* said that the Egyptians knew about the first age of man partly "from Mizraim, the son of Cham, who had learnt the same of Cham, and Cham of his father, Noah." In his *History of New York,* Washington Irving said that America was discovered late because Noah had only three sons among whom to divide the earth: Asia went to Shem, Europe to Japhet, and

Africa to Ham. In "Letter from a Missionary of the Methodist Episcopal South," Whittier tells of the forming of a vigilance committee to send all Yankees back up north: "[the rough river boatman] cursed the niggers— / Fulfilling the word of prophecy, 'Cursed be Canaan.' " The slaver in Stephen Vincent Benét's *John Brown's Body* justifies his slave trafficking, saying, "I get my sailing-orders from the Lord. / . . . It's down there [in the Bible], Mister, / Down there in black and white—the sons of Ham— / Bond-servants—sweat of their brows." ° In the beginning of *Troilus and Criseyde*, Chaucer writes, "For I, that God of Loves servantz serve, / Ne dar to Love, for myn unliklynesse." And Charles Lamb, in "The Two Races of Men," says that lenders "are born degraded. 'He shall serve his brethren.' "

CANDLE UNDER A BUSHEL   *see LIGHT (CANDLE) UNDER A BUSHEL*

CAST PEARLS BEFORE SWINE

Matt. 7:6

Jesus, in the Sermon on the Mount, said, "Give not that which is holy unto the dogs, neither cast ye your pearls before swine, lest they trample them under their feet, and turn again and rend you." In Sonnet XII, Milton, writing about the hostile reactions to his liberal views on divorce, said that he was beset by a barbarous noise "Of Owles and Cuckoes, Asses, Apes and Doggs . . . / But this is got by casting Pearl to Hoggs . . . ." A Wyclifite defends translation of the Bible into English in Whittier's "Sir John Oldcastle": "The Gospel, the priest's pearl, flung down to swine— / The swine, lay-men, lay-women, who will come, / God willing, to outlearn the filthy friar." Miss Dobbin, in Sarah Orne Jewett's "The Dulham Ladies," said sadly that she had always tried, "to elevate people's thoughts and direct them into higher channels. But as for that Woolden woman, there is no use in casting pearls before swine!"

CAST THE FIRST STONE   *see WOMAN TAKEN IN ADULTERY*

CAST THY BREAD UPON THE WATERS

Eccles. 11:1

One of the proverbs in Ecclesiastes says, "Cast thy bread upon the waters: for thou shalt find it after many days," expressing the idea of doing good without assurance of reward. In *The*

°From *John Brown's Body* by Stephen Vincent Benét, published by Holt, Rinehart and Winston, Inc. Reprinted by permission of Brandt & Brandt.

Man That Corrupted Hadleyburg, by Mark Twain, Mrs. Richards said after learning of the reward left for whoever had been kind to the stranger, "What a fortune for that kind man who set his bread afloat upon the waters!" Frank Harris, in his biography *Bernard Shaw,* said that Shaw never risked a penny "in any form of public entertainment, theatrical or other. When it came to putting in work, he could cast his bread upon the waters recklessly . . . ." Writing of the success of Louisa May Alcott and her father's books, Van Wyck Brooks, in *New England: Indian Summer,* said, "Louisa had entranced her public as a chronicler of the Alcott household, which had cast its bread upon the waters and found it after many days."

CATTLE UPON A THOUSAND HILLS

Ps. 50:10

God says he will not reprove his people for their sacrifices, nor take their bullocks and goats, "For every beast of the forest is mine, and the cattle upon a thousand hills." In "Boswell's Life of Johnson," Carlyle said that the world has misunderstood Boswell, "figuring him . . . simply of the bestial species, like the cattle on a thousand hills." And Thoreau said, in *Walden,* as he listened to a cattle train, "And hark! here comes the cattle-train bearing the cattle of a thousand hills, sheepcots, stables, and cow-yards in the air . . . ."

CHALICE   *see GRAIL*

CHAM (HAM)   *see CANAAN, SON OF HAM*

CHARIOT OF FIRE

II Kings 2:11;
Mal. 4:5, 6

As ELIJAH THE TISHBITE and ELISHA were talking about what Elijah could do for Elisha before Elijah was taken away, "It came to pass, as they still went on, and talked, that, behold, there appeared a chariot of fire, and horses of fire, and parted them both asunder; and Elijah went up by a whirlwind into heaven." It was long expected that Elijah would return again. In Milton's *Paradise Regained,* the disciples, disturbed by Christ's long absence in the wilderness, thought that he might be "for a time caught up to God, as once / . . . the great Thisbite who on fiery wheels / Rode up to Heaven, yet once again to come." Robert Southey, in *The Life of Nelson,* writes of "the most splendid" death of Nelson that "if the chariot and horses of fire had been vouchsafed for Nelson's translation, he could scarcely have departed in a brighter blaze of glory." Emily

Dickinson wrote: "Elijah's wagon knew no thill, / Was innocent of wheel, / Elijah's horses as unique / As was his vehicle." °

CHEBAR, RIVER OF   see EZEKIEL

CHILDREN OF LIGHT

Luke 16:8; John 12:35–36

A. To the people gathered for the feast of the Passover Jesus said, "Yet a little while is the light with you. Walk while ye have the light, lest darkness come upon you . . . While ye have light, believe in the light, that ye may be the children of light." In *Culture and Anarchy,* Matthew Arnold said that the Philistine is "the enemy of the children of light or servants of the idea." Edwin Arlington Robinson, in "The Children of the Night," a poem dealing with religious doubt, concluded: "Let us, the Children of the Night, / Put off the cloak that hides the scar! / Let us be Children of the Light / And tell the ages what we are." † B. Jesus told his disciples about "a certain rich man which had a steward" who gave inaccurate accounting; Jesus said, "The lord commended the unjust steward, because he had done wisely: for the children of this world are in their generation wiser than the children of light." G. K. Chesterton, in *Charles Dickens,* said that in his early life Dickens might be called worldly: "the children of this world are in their generation infinitely more sensitive than the children of light." Frances Trollope, in *Domestic Manners of the Americans,* said, "The State legislators may truly be said to be 'wiser in their generation than the children of light,' and they ensure their safety by forbidding light to enter among" the slaves. The climax to James Joyce's story "Grace," in *Dubliners,* is a sermon on this text delivered to a congregation of businessmen by Father Purdom "with resonant assurance. It was one of the most difficult texts in all the Scriptures, he said, to interpret properly."

CHILDREN OF THIS WORLD   see CHILDREN OF LIGHT

CHILDREN'S TEETH ARE SET ON EDGE   see FATHERS HAVE EATEN A SOUR GRAPE

CHRIST   see JESUS

° From *Poems by Emily Dickinson* by Emily Dickinson, by permission of Little, Brown and Co. Copyright 1914, 1942 by Martha Dickinson Bianchi.
† From *The Children of the Night* by E. A. Robinson. Reprinted by permission of Charles Scribner's Sons.

CHRIST CRUCIFIED   *see JESUS, CRUCIFIXION*

CHRIST WALKING ON THE WATER   *see JESUS, WALKING ON THE WATER*

CITY OF DAVID   *see ZION*

CITY OF GOD   *see NEW JERUSALEM*

CITY OF REFUGE

Deut. 4:41–43;
Josh. 20:1–9

Moses and Joshua appointed six cities of refuge "that the slayer that killeth any person unawares and unwittingly may flee thither: and they shall be your refuge from the avenger of blood" (Josh. 20:5; Exod. 21:13). Refuge was granted "until he stand before the congregation in judgment" (Num. 35:12). De Quincey, in *The Spanish Military Nun,* said that "oftentimes the Hebrew fugitive to a city of refuge, flying for his life before the avenger of blood" would sink into sleep as he knelt before the city gate. In "Swendenborg," Emerson said, "If we tire of the saints, Shakespeare is our city of refuge." Dr. Jekyll, in Stevenson's *Dr. Jekyll and Mr. Hyde,* said, "Jekyll was now my city of refuge; let but Hyde peep out an instant," and men would slay him.

CLAY   *see DUST, CLAY*

CLEAN AND UNCLEAN ANIMALS   *see NOAH'S ARK*

CLEAR AS A CRYSTAL   *see RIVER OF WATER OF LIFE*

CLOUD LIKE A MAN'S HAND

I Kings 18:44–45

ELIJAH on Mount Carmel, prophesying rain for King Ahab, sent his servant to look toward the sea seven times. The seventh time the servant reported, "Behold, there ariseth a little cloud out of the sea, like a man's hand . . . . And it came to pass . . . that the heaven was black with clouds and wind, and there was a great rain." The expression, often "a cloud no bigger than a man's hand," means a small hint of a greater thing to come. Describing a rising storm, Whittier, in "Storm on Lake Asquam," wrote: "A cloud, like that the old-time Hebrew saw / On Carmel prophesying rain, began / To lift itself o'er wooded Cardigan, / Growing and blackening." D. H. Lawrence, in *Letters,* said he felt like "a ship becalmed . . .

waiting for some wind to blow me back to town . . . . I look like Elijah, or Elisha, whichever it was, for a cloud as big as a man's hand." And H. S. Canby said that in *John Brown's Body* Benét "knows how to raise the cloud no bigger than a man's hand with his opening scene on a [slave ship]."

CLOVEN HOOF

Lev. 11:3, 7, 26; Deut. 14:7

The law for clean animals fit for food and sacrifice given by Moses said, "Whatsoever parteth the hoof, and is clovenfooted, and cheweth the cud . . . that shall ye eat." Because Satan was later pictured as being cloven-footed, or cloven-hoofed, the term came to mean devilish. In *The Compleat Angler,* Izaak Walton's hunter says he could mention many more than the usual animals hunted, "especially those creatures which Moses in the Law permitted to the Jews, which have cloven hoofs and chew the cud . . . ."

CLOVEN TONGUES OF FIRE *see PENTECOST*

COAT OF MANY COLORS

Gen. 37:3, 23, 32

"Now Israel [Jacob] loved Joseph more than all his children, because he was the son of his old age: and he made him a coat of many colours." Joseph's envious brothers, after selling Joseph into slavery, dipped the coat in goat's blood and brought it to Jacob, who then said, "It is my son's coat; an evil beast hath devoured him." The more accurate modern translations, "a long robe with sleeves" or "a tunic with long sleeves," reflect the fact that such a garment, distinguishing the chief and his heir, would be a cause of the brothers' envy. In *Cape Cod,* Thoreau described a beachcomber: he had on "a coat of many pieces and colors, though it was mainly the color of the beach, as if it had been sanded." In *Billy Budd,* Melville described the look on Claggart's face when Captain Vere suggested that Claggart might be lying about Billy: it was "a look such as might have been that of the spokesman of the envious children of Jacob deceptively imposing upon the troubled patriarch the blood-dyed coat of young Joseph."

COCKATRICE

Isa. 11:8; 14:29; 59:5; Jer. 8:17

"Out of the serpent's root shall come forth a cockatrice, and his fruit shall be a fiery flying serpent." The Hebrew word *tsepha* is variously translated "cockatrice," "adder," "viper," "asp"; and it is later called a "basilisk." It was believed to be a deadly serpent hatched from a cock's egg, which could kill even with its breath or its glance. In Shakespeare's *Twelfth Night*, Sir Toby Belch plans to set Sir Andrew and Viola, disguised as the page boy Cesario, against each other: "This will so fright them both that they will kill one another by the look, like cockatrices."

COCK CROW

Matt. 26:34, 74, 75

Before the crucifixion Jesus said to Peter, "Verily, I say unto thee, That this night, before the cock crow, thou shalt deny me thrice." Peter did so; at the third time "immediately the cock crew. And Peter remembered the word of Jesus, which was said unto him, Before the cock crow, thou shalt deny me thrice. And he went out and wept bitterly." In Tennyson's *Harold*, when King Edward tells Harold that he is going to send Edith to the "cloister'd, solitary life," Harold says, "No, no, no!" Edward replies, "Treble denial of the tongue of flesh, / Like Peter's when he fell, and thou wilt have / To wail for it like Peter." Longfellow, in *Evangeline*, described the farmyard at Grand Pré "where crowed the cock, with the selfsame / Voice that in ages of old had startled the penitent Peter." A man is questioned about knowing a criminal, in Thomas Hardy's "In the Servant's Quarters." He denies everything: "—His face convulses as the morning cock that moment crows, / And he droops, and turns, and goes."

COMFORTERS OF JOB   *see JOB'S COMFORTERS*

COMMUNION   *see LAST SUPPER*

CONSIDER THE LILIES   *see LILIES OF THE FIELD*

CONTRITE HEART   *see BROKEN AND CONTRITE HEART*

CORAH   *see KORAH, CORAH*

CORRUPTIBLE AND INCORRUPTIBLE; CORRUPTION AND INCORRUPTION

I Cor. 15:42–44, 52–54

Paul, writing about the resurrection of the dead, said, "It is sown in corruption; it is raised in incorruption: It is sown in dishonor; it is raised in glory." At the last trump of judgment, "the dead shall be raised incorruptible . . . . For this corruptible must put on incorruption, and this mortal must put on immortality." In "Boswell's Life of Johnson," Carlyle, writing of Boswell's character, said, "James Boswell belonged, in his corruptible part, to the lowest classes of mankind; a foolish, inflated creature . . . but in his corruptible there dwelt an incorruptible, all the more impressive and indubitable for the strange lodging it had taken." Emerson, in "The American Scholar," said that "the new deed . . . detaches itself from the life like a ripe fruit, to become a thought of the mind. Instantly it is raised, transfigured; the corruptible has put on incorruption." In *Moby Dick*, Melville tells how the fragrant ambergris comes from "the inglorious bowels of a sick whale . . . . Now that the incorruption of this most fragrant ambergris should be found in the heart of such decay; is this nothing? Bethink thee of that saying of St. Paul in Corinthians, about corruption and incorruption; how we are sown in dishonor, but raised in glory."

COUNSEL OF PERFECTION   see RICH YOUNG RULER

CRIPPLE OF BETHESDA   see BETHESDA, POOL OF

CROSSING OF THE RED SEA   see RED SEA

CROWN OF THORNS

Matt. 27:29;
Mark 15:17; John
19:2–5

Condemned to crucifixion, Jesus was taken by Pilate's soldiers into the common hall; "and when they had platted a crown of thorns, they put it upon his head . . . and they bowed the knee before him, and mocked him, saying, Hail, King of the Jews!" In *Eikonoklastes*, Milton, replying to King Charles's defender, who had said that Charles "had rather wear a crown of thorns with our Saviour," wrote, "They who govern ill those kingdoms which they had a right to, have to our Saviour's crown of thorns no right at all. Thorns they may find enow of their own gathering, and their own twisting . . . but to wear them as our Saviour wore them, is not given to them that suffer by their own demerits." In *In Memoriam*, Tennyson dreams of his suffering:

> I wander'd from the noisy town,
>   I found a wood with thorny boughs;
>   I took the thorns to bind my brows,
> I wore them like a civic crown;
>
> I met with scoffs, I met with scorns
>   From youth and babe and hoary hairs:
>   They call'd me in the public squares
> The fool that wears a crown of thorns.

CRUMBS WHICH FELL FROM THE RICH MAN'S TABLE   *see*
          LAZARUS AND DIVES

CRYING IN THE WILDERNESS   *see VOICE THAT CRIETH IN THE*
          WILDERNESS

CRY OF BLOOD   *see BLOOD CRIETH FROM THE GROUND*

CUP   *see GRAIL*

CURSED BE CANAAN   *see CANAAN, SON OF HAM*

CURSE GOD AND DIE   *see JOB'S WIFE*

CURSE OF CAIN   *see MARK OF CAIN*

CURSE THE DAY I WAS BORN

Job 3:1–11   When Satan "smote Job with sore boils," Job "opened his mouth, and cursed his day," saying, "Let the day perish wherein I was born, and the night in which it was said, There is a man child conceived . . . . Why died I not from the womb? why did I not give up the ghost when I came out of the belly?" In Chaucer's "The Clerk's Tale," Griselda's father, upon hearing that Griselda had been sent home by her husband, "Curseth the day and tyme that nature / Shoop hym to been a lyves creature." In Butler's *The Way of All Flesh*, when Ernest, in Miss Snow's room for the purpose of religious conversion, was interrupted by the worldly Townley intent upon a different purpose, he blushed more scarlet than ever, slunk off, "and cursed the hour that he was born." And in Hardy's *Jude the Obscure*, as Jude lay dying alone outside the walls of Christminster College where he had never been able to go, he heard cheers from the games and whispered to himself, "Let the day perish wherein I was born, and the night in which it was said, 'There is a man child conceived.' . . . Why died I not from the womb? Why did I not give up the ghost when I came out of the belly?" ("Hurrah!")

DAGON   Dagon, meaning fish, was a Philistine agricultural god, with an
(dā'gŏn) upper half man and a lower half fish. Samson pulled down the
          pillars in the temple of Dagon in Gaza. And when the Philis-
Judg. 16:23,24; tines set the ark of God on the threshold of Dagon's house,
I Sam. 5:1–5   they found the next morning that "Dagon was fallen upon his face to the ground before the ark of the Lord; and the head

of Dagon and both the palms of his hands were cut off upon
the threshold; only the stump of Dagon was left to him." In
Milton's *Paradise Lost*, Dagon was one of the fallen angels:

> Next came one
> Who mourn'd in earnest, when the Captive Ark
> Maim'd his brute Image, head and hands lopt off
> In his own Temple, on the grunsel edge,
> Where he fell flat, and sham'd his Worshipers:
> Dagon his name, Sea Monster, upward Man
> And downward fish . . . .

In *Moby Dick*, Melville says that the story that St. George
killed a dragon, not a whale, "will fare like that fish, flesh,
and fowl idol of the Philistines, Dagon by name; who being
planted before the ark of Israel, his horse's head and both the
palms of his hands fell off from him, and only the stump or
fishy part of him remained." Charles Lamb, in "Grace before
Meat," said that "a man should be sure . . . that while he is
pretending his devotions otherwise, he is not secretly kissing
his hand to some great fish—his Dagon—with a spiritual con-
secration of no ark but the fat tureen before him." And William
Bradford said, in *Of Plymouth Plantation*, that John Endicott
changed the name of Thomas Morton's Merry-Mount to Mount
Dagon.

DAILY BREAD *see OUR DAILY BREAD*

DANIEL

*The Book of
Daniel; The
History of
Susanna*

A. Daniel was a faithful young Jew in Babylon, during the
reigns of Nebuchadnezzar, Belshazzar, and Darius, who interpreted dreams and predicted the future in apocalyptic terms,
inspiring the Jews to religious devotion and hope for the
future. In literature Daniel is most commonly associated with
the stories of the FIERY FURNACE, NEBUCHADNEZZAR, the HAND-
WRITING ON THE WALL at Belshazzar's feast, and the LAW OF
THE MEDES AND THE PERSIANS. B. In the apocryphal book,
The History of Susanna, Daniel is the clever lawyer who saves
Susanna from the unjust accusations of two elders. Daniel's
fame as an interpreter of dreams is reflected in Hawthorne's
The Scarlet Letter, when Chillingsworth asks a stranger, "Who
is the father of the babe held in Mistress Prynne's arms on the
scaffold?" The townsman answers, "Of a truth, friend, that
matter remaineth a riddle; and the Daniel who shall expound
it is yet a-wanting." Daniel as the clever young lawyer is the
allusion in Shakespeare's *The Merchant of Venice*, when Portia,
acting as a lawyer at the trial, tells Bassanio that "there is no

power in Venice / Can alter a decree established—" the con-
tract is binding. Shylock exclaims, "A Daniel come to judgement! yea, a Daniel! / O wise young judge, how I do honor
thee!" Portia then turns the tables on Shylock, as did Daniel
on the elders in the story of Susanna.

DARKNESS WHICH MAY BE FELT   *see PLAGUE OF DARKNESS*

DAUGHTERS OF MEN

Gen. 6:1–4

"When men began to multiply on the face of the earth . . .
the sons of God saw the daughters of men that they were fair;
and they took them wives of all which they chose . . . and
they bare children to them, the same became mighty men
which were of old, men of renown." Satan, in *Milton's Paradise
Regained,* rejected Belial's advice to tempt Christ with beautiful women, saying in effect don't judge others by yourself:

> Before the Flood thou with thy lusty Crew,
> False titl'd Sons of God, roaming the Earth
> Cast Wanton eyes on the daughters of men,
> And coupl'd with them, and begot a race.

The thought that "love could bind" the villagers of Aylmer
closer made the "hoar head of the baronet," in Tennyson's
"Aylmer's Field," "bristle up / With horror, worse than had
he heard his priest / Preach an inverted scripture, sons of
men, / Daughters of God . . . ." Fedallah, in Melville's *Moby
Dick,* is like one of "earth's primal generations . . . when
though, according to Genesis, the angels indeed consorted with
the daughters of men, the devils also . . . indulged in mundane
amours."

DAVID

*I Sam. 16—
I Kings 2; Ruth
4:18–22*

David, meaning "beloved" or "chieftain," was described by a
servant of Saul as the "son of Jesse the Bethlehemite, that is
cunning in playing, and a mighty valiant man, and a man of
war, and prudent in matters, and a comely person, and the
Lord is with him." Successor to Saul as king of Israel, David
is known in literature as the husband of many wives, including
Bathsheba and childless Michal, as "slayer of Goliath," as
"harpist and singer," as friend of Jonathan, as the father of
rebel ABSALOM, and as the ancestor of Jesus (Luke 1:32).
Dryden, in "Absalom and Achitophel," pictures Charles II as
David, a man after the Lord's own heart (I Sam. 13:14), and a
polygamist:

> Then Israel's monarch after Heaven's own heart,
> His vigorous warmth did variously impart

To wives and slaves; and, wide as his command,
Scattered his Maker's image through the land,.

But, wrote Dryden, Saul's daughter "Michal, of royal blood,
the crown did wear, / A soil ungrateful to the tiller's care:"
When David captured the ark from the Philistines and brought
it to Jerusalem, he "danced before the Lord with all his might."
Michal "saw king David leaping and dancing before the Lord,
and she despised him in her heart" (II Sam. 6:14–16). In Shaw's
Candida, when Candida is forced to choose between her
husband Morrell and the poet Marchbanks, Morrell tells Candida
that Marchbanks said that "you despised me in your heart."
Marchbanks replies, "No, no: I—I—it was David's wife. And it
wasn't at home: it was when she saw him dancing before all
the people." In Milton's *Paradise Regained*, Satan urges Jesus
to seize David's throne:

thy Kingdom though foretold
By Prophet or by Angel, unless thou
Endeavour, as thy Father David did,
Thou never shalt obtain.

DAVID AND BATHSHEBA

II Sam. 11 One evening King David, walking on the roof of his house,
"saw a woman washing herself; and the woman was very
beautiful to look upon." She was Bathsheba, the wife of Uriah
the Hittite. David sent for her, and later when she conceived,
he wrote Joab his captain, saying, "Set ye Uriah in the fore-
front of the hottest battle, and retire ye from him, that he
may be smitten, and die." Bathsheba mourned, and then became David's wife and the mother of Solomon. The Reverend
Dimmesdale, adulterer in Hawthorne's *The Scarlet Letter*, hung
the walls of his room with Gobelin tapestries depicting the
story of David and Bathsheba. When Tess, in Hardy's *Tess of
the D'Urbervilles*, told Angel Clare on their wedding night of
her past relations with another man, he deserted her. Later he
reconsidered: "he thought of the wife of Uriah being made a
queen; and he asked himself why he had not judged Tess . . .
by the will rather than by the deed."

DAVID AND GOLIATH

I Sam. 17 Goliath of Gath, the giant champion of the Philistines, covered
with armor, "had greaves of brass upon his legs . . . and the
staff of his spear was like a weaver's beam." Young David,
unarmed, "chose him five smooth stones out of the brook,"
and with his sling "smote the Philistine in his forehead, that

the stone sunk into his forehead; and he fell upon his face to
the earth." David then ran up to "the Philistine, and took his
sword, and drew it out of the sheath thereof, and slew him,
and cut off his head therewith." In Shakespeare's *Merry Wives
of Windsor*, Falstaff admits his weakness when "he was in the
shape of a woman," but "in the shape of a man, Master Brook,
I fear not Goliath with a weaver's beam." Thomas Hardy
describes the young furze cutter Humphrey as "being sheathed
in bulging leggings as stiff as the Philistine's greaves of brass."
Emily Dickinson wrote:

> I took my power in my hand
> And went against the world;
> 'Twas not so much as David had,
> But I was twice as bold.
>
> I aimed my pebble, but myself
> Was all the one that fell.
> Was it Goliath was too large,
> Or only I too small? °

DAVID AND NATHAN

II Sam. 12

When King David sinned with Bathsheba, ordering her husband
killed in order to marry Bathsheba, the Lord sent Nathan the
prophet to reprove David. Nathan told him the story of a rich
man who took a poor man's "one little ewe lamb, which he
had brought up and nourished . . . and was unto him as a
daughter." Angered, David said to Nathan, "As the Lord liveth,
the man that hath done this thing shall surely die . . . because
he had no pity!" Then said Nathan sternly to King David,
"Thou art the man." And the Lord "struck the child that
Uriah's wife bare unto David" dead. In Hardy's *The Return of
the Native*, poor Diggory Venn, who had lost Thomasin to the
gay Wildeve, pursued his trade in Thomasin's heath; to be
"near her, yet unseen, was the one ewe-lamb of pleasure left
to him." In *Modern Painters*, Ruskin demonstrates David's
gentlemanliness by recalling the Nathan story: when David's
"own story is told him under a disguise, though only a lamb is
now concerned, his passion about it leaves him no time for
thought. 'The man shall die'—note the reason—'because he had
no pity.' A vulgar man would assuredly have been cautious,
and asked, 'Who it was?' " In Emily Brontë's *Wuthering
Heights*, Mr. Lockwood dreamed that he spoke out against the

° From *Poems by Emily Dickinson* by Emily Dickinson (Boston, Little,
Brown and Co.).

famous Reverend Jabes Branderham for preaching an inter-
minable sermon on sin; then cried Jabes, "after a solemn
pause, leaning over his cushion, '*Thou art the man!*' " When
Elizabeth-Jane, in Hardy's *The Mayor of Casterbridge*, discovered that the wealthy Lucetta had stolen her lover, Elizabeth-Jane cried "in Nathan tones, 'You—have—married Mr.
Farfrae!' "

DAVID DANCED   *see DAVID*

DAVID, HARPIST, MUSICIAN

I Sam. 16:14–23

When "the Spirit of the Lord departed from Saul, and an evil
spirit from the Lord troubled him," his servants brought him
David, who was "a cunning player on a harp." When "the
evil spirit from God was upon Saul, David took an harp, and
played with his hand: so Saul was refreshed, and was well, and
the evil spirit departed from him." When in Shakespeare's
Richard II, King Richard, a prisoner in Pomfret Castle, hears
music outside, he says,

> This music mads me, let it sound no more;
> For though it have holp madmen to their wits,
> In me it seems it will make wise men mad.

In Charlotte Brontë's *Jane Eyre*, when Jane returns to the
blinded Rochester, he tells her, "If Saul could have had you
for his David, the evil spirit would have been exorcised without the aid of a harp." At the town hall meeting, in Longfellow's "The Birds of Killingsworth," the Preceptor tries to
save the birds from slaughter, calling them "The street musi-
cians of the heavenly city, / . . . who made sweet music for
us all / In our dark hours, as David did for Saul."

DAY OF DOOM   *see JUDGMENT DAY*

DAY OF JUDGMENT   *see JUDGMENT DAY*

DAYS OF OUR YEARS   *see THREESCORE YEARS AND TEN*

DAYS SWIFTER THAN A WEAVER'S SHUTTLE   *see WEAVER'S SHUTTLE*

DEAD BURY THEIR DEAD   *see LET THE DEAD BURY THEIR DEAD*

DEAD LION   *see LIVING DOG BETTER THAN A DEAD LION*

DEAD SEA APPLES, FRUIT   *see APPLES OF SODOM*

O DEATH, WHERE IS THY STING?

I Cor. 15:55   Paul wrote that at the Last Judgment, when "this mortal shall have put on immortality, then shall be brought to pass the saying that is written, Death is swallowed up in victory. O death, where is thy sting? O grave, where is thy victory?" Thomas Campbell, in "The Last Man," reflecting on immortality, wrote that his soul would live again,

> By him recall'd to breath,
> Who captive led captivity,
> Who robb'd the grave of Victory,
> And took the sting from Death.

In *Walden*, Thoreau wrote that there is no stronger proof of immortality than the beauty of the light of an early morning in spring. "All things must live in such a light. O Death, where was thy sting? O Grave, where was thy victory, then?" Joyce, in *A Portrait of the Artist as a Young Man*, told of the preacher quoting Addison that only "the pious and believing Christian" can meet his end, saying in his heart:

> *O grave, where is thy victory?*
> *O death, where is thy sting?*

DEBORAH   Deborah, meaning "a bee," was "a prophetess, the wife of Lapidoth." She "dwelt under a palm tree" and "judged Israel
Judg. 4, 5   at that time." When the Canaanites oppressed Israel, she called Barak to lead an army against Sisera, captain of the Canaanite army. The great war ode known as "The Song of Deborah" (Judg. 5) celebrates the great victory by the River Kishon and the death of Sisera in the tent of JAEL. In Shakespeare's *Henry VI, Part I*, when Joan la Pucelle fought and overcame Charles of France, he cried, "Stay, stay thy hands! Thou art an Amazon / And fightest with the sword of Deborah." In Tennyson's *Enoch Arden*, Annie one sleepless night, longing for Enoch away at sea, seized her Bible, and "Suddenly put her finger on the text, / 'Under the palm tree.'" Closing the Book she dreamed of "her Enoch sitting on a height, / Under a palm-tree . . . happy and singing." In *The Princess* by Tennyson, Princess Ida sang a song of victory for her champions in a tournament. "But high upon the palace Ida stood / . . . Like that great dame of Lapidoth she sang: / 'Our enemies

have fallen, have fallen . . . .' " Whittier celebrated the victory
of Deborah and Barak in "Palestine":

> Hark, a sound in the valley! where, swollen and strong,
> Thy river, O Kishon, is sweeping along;
> Where the Canaanite strove with Jehovah in vain,
> And thy torrent grew dark with the blood of the slain.
>
> There sleep the still rocks and the caverns which rang
> To the song which the beautiful prophetess sang,
> When the princes of Issacher stood by her side
> And the shout of a host in its triumph replied.

DECALOGUE   see TEN COMMANDMENTS

DEEP CALLETH UNTO DEEP

Ps. 42:7

The Psalmist sings of his soul's thirst for God: "Deep calleth
unto deep at the noise of thy waterspouts: all thy waves and
thy billows are gone over me." In *Nature*, Emerson writes, "In
the uttermost meaning of the words, thought is devout, and
devotion is thought. Deep calls unto deep. But in actual life,
the marriage is not celebrated." Whittier speaks of Massachusetts' voice of freedom, in "Massachusetts to Virginia": "The
voice of Massachusetts! Of her free sons and daughters, / Deep
calling unto deep aloud, the sound of many waters!" Gerard M.
Hopkins, in "Nondum," writes of man's longing to know God:
"And still th' abysses infinite / Surround the peak from which
we gaze. / Deep calls to deep and blackest night / Giddies
the soul with blinding daze . . . ."

DEFERRED HOPE   see HOPE DEFERRED

DELIGHTETH TO HONOUR

*Esther 6:6, 7, 9,
11*

When Haman came to speak to King Ahasuerus about hanging
the despised Mordecai on the gallows, Ahasuerus said, "What
shall be done unto the man whom the king delighteth to
honour?" Haman thought in his heart, "To whom would the
king delight to do honour more than to myself?" and told the
king how to do him honor. But the king ordered Haman to so
honor Mordecai; which done Haman proclaimed, "Thus shall
it be done unto the man whom the king delighteth to honour,"
and then hastened home in shame. Charles Lamb, in "The Two
Races of Men," says that a borrower is like "the sea which
taketh handsomely at each man's hand. In vain the victim,
whom he delighteth to honour, struggles with destiny . . . ."

In *Moby Dick*, Melville's Ishmael says that "the world declines honoring us whalemen" because it considers us butchers. "Butchers we are, that is true. But butchers . . . of the bloodiest badge have been all Martial Commanders whom the world invariably delights to honor."

DELILAH   *see SAMSON AND DELILAH*

DELIVER US FROM EVIL   *see LEAD US NOT INTO TEMPTATION*

DEN OF THIEVES

Matt. 21:12–13;
Mark 11:15–17;
Luke 19:45–46

Jesus "went into the temple of God, and cast out all of them that sold and bought in the temple, and overthrew the tables of the moneychangers, and the seats of them that sold doves. And said unto them, It is written, My house shall be called the house of prayer; but ye have made it a den of thieves." In Ben Jonson's *The Alchemist*, Ananias, the deacon, and Tribulation Wholesome, the pastor, now disillusioned with the alchemist, come to cart away the widows' and orphans' metals which they had previously brought to be transmuted into gold. Ananias explains to Lovewit, the owner of the house: we come "to bear away the portion of the righteous / Out of this den of thieves." Carlyle, in *Sartor Resartus*, said he had walked through Monmouth Street "with little feeling of 'Devotion': probably in part because the contemplative process is so fatally broken in upon by the brood of moneychangers who nestle in that church, and importune the worshipper with merely secular proposals." Ruskin, in *The Stones of Venice*, said that "the meanest trades of the city push their counters" up into the porches of St. Marks; "Nay, the foundations of its pillars are themselves the seats—not 'of them that sell doves' for sacrifice, but of the vendors of toys and caricatures." James Joyce, in *A Portrait of the Artist as a Young Man*, standing on the library steps watches the flight of birds and considers his decision to give up priesthood for writing: "But was it for this folly that he was about to leave for ever the house of prayer and prudence into which he had been born . . . ?"

DEPART IN PEACE   *see SIMEON THE JUST*

DEVIL   *see SATAN*

DEVIL (SATAN) CHAINED

Rev. 20:1–2

St. John the Divine "saw an angel come down from heaven, having the key of the bottomless pit and a great chain in his hand. And he laid hold on the dragon, that old serpent which is the Devil, and Satan, and bound him a thousand years . . . ." In "Lenvoy de Chaucer A Bukton," Chaucer writes of the sorrow and woe of marriage:

> I wol not seyn how that yt is the cheyne
> Of Sathanas, on which he gnaweth evere;
> But I dar seyn, were he out of his peyne,
> As by his wille he wolde be bounde nevere.

In "The Man of Law's Tale," Chaucer describes the Sultan's mother as a "serpent under femynynytee, / Like to the serpent depe in helle ybounde!" From the day of Christ's birth, in Milton's "On the Morning of Christ's Nativity":

> Th' old Dragon under ground
> In straiter limits bound,
>   Not half so far casts his usurped sway,
> And wrath to see his Kingdom fail,
> Swindges the scaly Horrour of his foulded tail.

DEVILS BELIEVE, AND TREMBLE

Jas. 2:19

James wrote, "Thou believest that there is one God; thou doest well: the devils also believe, and tremble." Carlyle, in "Boswell's Life of Johnson," said that "the life of every good man . . . preaches to the eye and heart and whole man, so that Devils even must believe and tremble." Melville, in *Billy Budd,* said that even the evil Claggart had a conscience, "for though consciences are unlike as foreheads, every intelligence, not including the Scriptural devils who 'believe and tremble,' has one."

DIANA OF THE EPHESIANS

Acts 19:23–28, 34–35

Diana of the Ephesians was the fertility goddess of many breasts, worshiped in the temple of Ephesus. Demetrius and other craftsmen made silver shrines for Diana. When Paul preached against gods made with hands, the people "were full of wrath, and cried out, saying, Great is Diana of the Ephesians." Henry Adams, in *The Dynamo and the Virgin,* discussing the Puritan notion that sex was sin, said that in other ages sex was strength. "Everyone, even among Puritans, knew that . . . Diana of Ephesus . . . was goddess because of her force; she was the animated dynamo; she was reproduction—the greatest and most mysterious of all energies; all she needed was to be fecund." Matthew Arnold, in *Discourses in America*, discussing "the unsound majority," compared the Ephesians worshiping Diana to the Frenchman who is "a worshipper of the great goddess Lubricity." Thomas Paine, in *The Age of Reason*, argued that "the Christian church sprung out of the tail of heathen mythology . . . . The statue of Mary succeeded the statue of Diana of Ephesus."

DIE DAILY

I Cor. 15:31

Paul wrote to the Corinthians, "And why stand we in jeopardy every hour? I protest by your rejoicing which I have in Christ Jesus our Lord, I die daily." In Shakespeare's *Macbeth*, Macduff, offering his services to Malcolm, said,

> Thy royal father
> Was a most sainted king: the queen that bore thee,
> Oftener upon her knees than on her feet,
> Died every day she lived.

In his *Life of Dr. John Donne*, Izaak Walton said that in Donne's final illness he "fell into a fever, which . . . hastened him into so visible a consumption that his beholders might say, as St. Paul of himself, 'He dies daily.'" In "Hebraism and Hellenism," Matthew Arnold said of the Greek notion of felicity, " 'C'est le bonheur des hommes,'—when? . . . when they exercise themselves in the law of the Lord day and night?—no; when they die daily?—no."

DIVES   *see LAZARUS AND DIVES*

DIVIDE SHEEP FROM GOATS   *see SEPARATE SHEEP FROM GOATS*

DIVIDED AGAINST ITSELF   *see HOUSE DIVIDED AGAINST ITSELF*

A DOG RETURNETH TO HIS VOMIT

Prov. 26:11; II Pet. 2:22

One of the proverbs on fools: "As a dog returneth to his vomit, so a fool returneth to his folly." In Shakespeare's *Henry IV, Part II*, the Archbishop of York addresses the commonwealth as a "beastly feeder" so full of the king

> That thou provokest thyself to cast him up.
> So, so, thou common dog, didst thou disgorge
> Thy glutton bosom of the royal Richard;

And now thou wouldst eat thy dead vomit up,
And howl'st to find it.

In Bunyan's *Pilgrim's Progress,* Hope explains why Temporary refused to accompany Christian: "when the power of guilt weareth away, that which provoked them to be religious ceaseth. Wherefore they naturally turn to their own course again, even as we see the Dog that is sick of what he has eaten: he vomits and casts up all; . . . but now when his sickness is over . . . he turns him about and licks up all; and so it is true which is written, The Dog is turned to his own vomit again." And Jonathan Edwards, in *Personal Narrative,* tells how as a boy he "entirely lost those affections and delights" of religion, "and returned like a dog to his vomit, and went on in the ways of sin."

DOGS LICKED HIS SORES   *see LAZARUS AND DIVES*

DOOMSDAY   *see JUDGMENT DAY*

DOORKEEPER IN THE HOUSE OF MY GOD

Ps. 84:10

The psalm offering consolation in exile: "I had rather be a doorkeeper in the house of my God, than to dwell in the tents of wickedness." Izaak Walton, in his *Life of Dr. John Donne,* said that when Donne was converted and entered the clergy, "he was now gladder to be a doorkeeper in the house of God than he could be to enjoy the noblest of all temporal enjoyments." In Whittier's "Letter from a Missionary . . . to a Distinguished Politician," a missionary from the Methodist Episcopal Church South, who has been busy fighting Yankee abolitionists, writes hoping for "a quiet berth in Washington": "Better to be / Door-keeper in the White House, than to dwell / Amidst these Yankee tents . . . ."

DOUBTING THOMAS

John 20:24–29

Thomas, one of the twelve disciples of Jesus, said after the Crucifixion, "Except I shall see in his hands the print of the nails, and put my finger into the print of the nails, and thrust my hand into his side, I will not believe." After eight days, when Thomas did these things and was convinced, Jesus said unto him, "Thomas, because thou hast seen me, thou hast believed: blessed are they that have not seen, and yet have believed." Thomas Paine, in *The Age of Reason,* said, "But it

appears that Thomas did not believe the resurrection; and, as
they say, would not believe without having ocular and manual
demonstration himself. *So neither will I.;* and the reason is
equally as good for me, and for every other person, as for
Thomas." In *The Undying Fire,* H. G. Wells's Dr. Barrack
said, "My mind is a sceptical mind . . . . I want things I can
feel and handle. I am an Agnostic by nature and habit and
profession. A Doubting Thomas born and bred." Arthur H.
Clough, in "In Stratis Viarum," reflects upon true believers in
a great city:

> Blessed are those who have not seen,
>   And who have yet believed
> The witness, here that has not been,
>   From heaven they have received.

DO UNTO OTHERS   *see GOLDEN RULE*

DOVE OF NOAH

Gen. 8:8–12   When the ark rested upon the mountains of Ararat, Noah
"sent forth a dove from him, to see if the waters were abated
. . . . But the dove found no rest for the sole of her foot . . . ."
After seven days he sent the dove forth again, and this time
the dove came in "and, lo, in her mouth was an olive leaf
pluckt off: so Noah knew that the waters were abated from off
the earth." Because the olive branch is a symbol of peace,
Noah's dove has become the dove of peace, as well as a
messenger. The falconer, in Izaak Walton's *The Compleat
Angler,* argues that birds have a "political use": ". . . tis not to
be doubted that the dove was sent by Noah, to give him
notice of land when to him all appeared to be sea, and the
dove proved a faithful and comfortable messenger." In Byron's
The Bride of Abydos, Selim the seafarer calls Zuleika his lover
to be his guide: "Thou, my Zuleika, share and bless my bark; /
The dove of peace and promise to mine ark!" In Byron's *Don
Juan,* Donna Inez sent her son Don Juan away on a ship from
Cadiz: "As if a Spanish ship were Noah's ark, / To wean him
from the wickedness of earth, / And send him like a dove of
promise forth." And in the same book, a beautiful white bird
"not unlike a dove" flew over a boat of shipwrecked seamen:
"And had it been the dove from Noah's ark, / Returning there
from her successful search, / Which in their way that moment
chanced to fall, / They would have eat her, olive branch and
all."

DOVE OF PEACE   see *DOVE OF NOAH*

DRAGON   see *SERPENT AS THE DEVIL*

DREAM DREAMS, OLD MEN

Joel 2:28; Acts 2:17

Joel wrote that God will pour out his spirit upon all flesh; "and your sons and your daughters shall prophesy, your old men shall dream dreams, your young men shall see visions:" In Dryden's "Absalom and Achitophel," Achitophel urges Absalom to rebel against David: "[You are] the people's prayer, the glad diviner's theme, / The young men's vision, and the old men's dream!" Washington Irving, in "The Legend of Sleepy Hollow," says that everyone who resides for a time in the valley unconsciously imbibes "the visionary propensity" of its inhabitants: "However wide awake they may have been before they entered that sleepy region . . . they begin to grow imaginative—to dream dreams, and see apparitions." S. M. Crothers, in "Every Man's Natural Desire to Be Somebody Else," arguing that business often narrows a man, said (not accurately), "The old prophet declared that the young men dream dreams and the old men see visions, but he did not say anything about the middle-aged men. *They* have to look after the business end."

DRY BONES   see *VALLEY OF DRY BONES*

DURA, PLAIN OF   see *NEBUCHADNEZZAR*

DUST AND ASHES

Gen. 18:27; Job 30:19; 42:6

As Abraham pleaded with the Lord to spare Sodom because of the righteous therein, he said, "Behold now, I have taken upon me to speak unto the Lord, which am but dust and ashes." And Job, bewailing his suffering, said, "He hath cast me into the mire, and I am become like dust and ashes." And when Job finally answered the Lord out of the whirlwind, he said, "Wherefore I abhor myself, and repent in dust and ashes." Hence the phrase expresses humility, worthlessness, and repentance. In Shakespeare's *King John*, young Arthur pleads with Hubert sent by King John to burn out Arthur's eyes: "There is no malice in this burning coal; / The breath of heaven has blown his spirit out / And strew'd repentant ashes on his head." In *Tess of the D'Urbervilles*, Hardy said of Tess after Alec had raped her, "Hate him she did not quite; but he was dust and ashes to her . . . ." In the same book, after her husband Angel Clare had left her, Tess felt that in her "was the record of a pulsing life which had learnt too well, for its years, the dust and ashes of things . . . ."

DUST, CLAY

Gen. 2:7; 3:19;
Job 10:9; 33:6;
Isaiah 64:8

"And the Lord God formed man of the dust of the ground . . . ." "In the sweat of thy face shalt thou eat bread, till thou return unto the ground; for out of it wast thou taken: for dust thou art, and unto dust shalt thou return." Job complained bitterly of God's cruelty to him, saying, "Remember, I beseech thee, that thou hast made me as the clay; and wilt thou bring me into dust again?" In Hebrew *adamah*, translated "dust of the ground," is a pun on *adam*, translated "man" in Genesis 2:7, and as "man" or "Adam" elsewhere. In Shakespeare's *Hamlet*, when Rosencrantz and Guildenstern asked what he had done with Polonius's body, Hamlet replied, "Compounded it with dust, whereto 't is kin." In "Uses of Great Men," Emerson said, "Man, made of the dust of this world, does not forget his origin . . . ." Longfellow, in "A Psalm of Life," said,

> Life is real! Life is earnest!
> And the grave is not its goal;
> Dust thou art, to dust returnest,
> Was not spoken of the soul.

Melville's narrator, in "I and My Chimney," communes with his pipe about the future of their friend the chimney: "But, indeed, we sons of clay, that is my pipe and I, are no whit better than the rest." When Theodore, in Mark Twain's *The Mysterious Stranger*, told Satan of the burning of eleven young girls as witches, Satan replied that "what the human race did was of no consequence. And he said he had seen it made; and it was not made of clay; it was made of mud—part of it was, anyway."

EARTH OPENETH HER MOUTH, AND SWALLOWETH THEM   *see KORAH, CORAH*

EASE IN ZION   *see AT EASE IN ZION*

EAST OF EDEN   *see LAND OF NOD*

EDEN, GARDEN OF

Gen. 2:8–14

"And the Lord God planted a garden eastward in Eden; and there he put the man whom he had formed. And out of the ground made the Lord God to grow every tree that is pleasant to the sight, and good for food; the tree of life also in the midst of the garden, and the TREE OF KNOWLEDGE of good and evil. And a river went out of Eden to water the garden; and from thence it was parted, and became into four heads." The word "Eden" in Hebrew means "delight." The word "Paradise," meaning in Greek "park" or "garden," comes from St. Jerome's Vulgate translation, and is used for both Eden and heaven, or a state of bliss. In Shakespeare's *Richard II*, the Duke of Gaunt, in his noble speech on England, calls it "This other Eden, demi-paradise . . . ." In Milton's *Paradise Lost*, Satan, in the shape of a cormorant, sits in the Tree of Life viewing Eden. It was

> A Heaven on Earth: for blissful Paradise
> Of God the Garden was, by him in the East
> Of Eden planted . . . .
> Out of the fertil ground he caus'd to grow
> All Trees of noblest kind for sight, smell, taste;
> And all amid them stood the Tree of Life,
> High eminent, blooming Ambrosial Fruit
> Of vegetable Gold; and next to Life
> Our Death the Tree of Knowledge grew fast by,
> Knowledge of Good bought dear by knowing ill.

In *De Profundis*, Oscar Wilde recalled his Oxford days: "I wanted to eat of the fruit of all the trees in the garden of the world . . . . My only mistake was that I confined myself so exclusively to the trees of what seemed to me the sun-lit side of the garden, and shunned the other side for its shadow and its gloom." D. H. Lawrence, in *Studies in Classic American Literature*, said that Melville "found in Typee the paradise he was looking for . . . . But Paradise. He insists on it. Paradise. He could even go stark naked, like before the Apple episode." Edwin Arlington Robinson, in "Ben Jonson Entertains a Man from Stratford,"[*] pictures Shakespeare in a gloomy mood:

> Today the clouds are with him, but anon
> He'll out of 'em enough to shake the tree
> Of life itself and bring down fruit unheard of,
> And, throwing in the bruised and whole together,
> Prepare a wine to make us drunk with wonder.

EGYPTIAN DARKNESS   *see PLAGUE OF DARKNESS*

EGYPT'S FIRSTBORN   *see FIRSTBORN OF EGYPT*

[*] Reprinted with permission of The Macmillan Company from *Collected Poems* by E. A. Robinson. Copyright 1916 by E. A. Robinson. Renewed 1944 by Ruth Nivison.

ELIAS   *see ELIJAH, THE TISHBITE*

ELIJAH CONTESTS WITH PROPHETS OF BAAL

I Kings 18:17–40   Because King Ahab sinned in following Baalim, Elijah on Mount Carmel challenged the prophets of Baal to a test of the true God. Baal's prophets built an altar of wood and called "on the name of Baal from morning even until noon" to send fire, but there was no answer. Then "Elijah mocked them, and said, Cry aloud: for he is a god: either he is talking, or he is pursuing, or he is in a journey, or peradventure he sleepeth, and must be awaked." And the Baal prophets "cried aloud, and cut themselves after their manner with knives and lancets, till the blood gushed out upon them." Then Elijah built an altar of wood surrounded by a trench, and he poured water over it until the trench was filled. He prayed to the Lord God, and fire came down which burned all "and licked up the water that was in the trench." In *An Apology for Smectymnuus,* Milton justified argument by laughter: "I would ask, to what end Elijah mocked the false prophets? Was it to show his wit, or to fulfil his humor? Doubtless we cannot imagine that great servant of God had any other end . . . but to teach and instruct the poor mislead people." Swinburne, in "Hymn to Man," mocks Christians as did Elijah the prophets of Baal:

> Cry aloud till his godhead awaken; what doth he to sleep and to dream?
> Cry, cut yourselves, gash you with knives and with scourges, heap on to you dust;
> Is his life but as other gods' lives? is not this the Lord God of your trust?

In *Tess of the D'Urbervilles,* Hardy asks, after Tess's rape, "Where was Tess's guardian angel? . . . Perhaps, like that other god of whom the ironical Tishbite [spoke], he was talking, or he was pursuing, or he was in a journey, or he was sleeping and not to be awaked." In Mark Twain's "The Stolen White Elephant," Captain "Hurricane" Jones tells the story of "Isaac" and the prophets of Baal: Isaac "graveled the prophets of Baal every way he could think of. Says he, 'You don't speak up loud enough; your god's asleep, like enough, or maybe he's taking a walk; you want to holler you know—or words to that effect; I don't recollect the exact language.' " Then Isaac struck a match "and pff! up the whole thing blazes like a house afire! Twelve barrels of *water?* Petroleum, sir, PETROLEUM! That's what it was."

ELIJAH FED BY RAVENS

I Kings 17:2–7

Elijah cursed the sinful King Ahab with drought, and the Lord told him to hide by the Brook Cherith [chē'rĭth], where he would be fed by the ravens. "And the ravens brought him bread and flesh in the morning, and bread and flesh in the evening; and he drank of the brook." In *Paradise Regained,* Milton described Christ hungering in the wilderness and dreaming of meats and drinks:

> Him thought, he by the Brook Cherith stood
> And saw the Ravens with their horny beaks
> Food to Elijah bringing Even and Morn,
> Though ravenous, taught to abstain from what they brought.

Izaak Walton's falconer, in *The Compleat Angler,* said birds have "political use": "And when God would feed the Prophet Elijah after a kind of miraculous manner, he did it by ravens, who brought him meat morning and evening." Butler, in *The Way of All Flesh,* told of a Salvator Rosa painting, hanging in the dining room, of "Elijah or Elisha (whichever it was) being fed by the ravens in the desert. There were the ravens in the upper right-hand corner with bread and meat in their beaks and claws, and there was the prophet in question in the lower left-hand corner looking longingly up towards them." When Ernest was very small he was disturbed that the food never actually reached the prophet; so one day "with a piece of bread and butter traced a greasy line right across it from the ravens to Elisha's mouth, after which he had felt more comfortable."

ELIJA'S FIERY CHARIOT   *see CHARIOT OF FIRE*

ELIJAH'S MANTLE

I Kings 19:19; II Kings 2:8–14

Elijah found Elisha "plowing with twelve yoke of oxen before him . . . and Elijah passed by him and cast his mantle upon him" (I Kings 19:19). Just before Elijah went into heaven in "a chariot of fire," Elisha asked, ". . . let a double portion of thy spirit be upon me." Then as Elijah "went up by a whirl-wind into heaven," Elisha "took up the mantle of Elijah that fell from him and went back and stood by the bank of Jordan" (II Kings 2:9, 13). At the conclusion of Dryden's "Mac Flecknoe," Flecknoe, the poet of dullness, sinking down, lets fall his mantle on his son Mac Flecknoe, or Thomas Shadwell:

> Sinking he left his drugget robe behind,
> Borne upwards by a subterranean wind.

The mantle fell to the young prophet's part,
With double portion of his father's art.

In the Dedication to the second edition of his poems, Robert
Burns said, "The poetic genius of my country found me, as the
prophetic bard Elijah did Elisha—at the plow; and threw her
inspiring mantle over me." Melville, in *Billy Budd*, describes
the daybreak of Billy's hanging: "Like the prophet in the chariot disappearing in heaven and dropping his mantle to Elisha,
the withdrawing night transferred its pale robe to the peeping
day."

ELIJAH, THE TISHBITE

*I Kings 17–19; II
II Kings 1–2*

Elijah, meaning "Yahweh is my God," was a Tishbite—where
the Tishbites lived is uncertain. A great prophet of the ninth
century B.C., he was known by New Testament writers as
Elias, the Greek form of his name. Elijah as the founder of the
Carmelites is suggested in Chaucer's "The Summoner's Tale"
by the begging friar:

"For who kan teche and werchen as we konne?
And that is nat of litel tyme," quod he.
"But syn Elye was, or Elise,
Han freres been, that fynde I of record,
In charitee, ythanked be oure Lord!"

The belief is based upon Elijah's contest on Mt. Carmel with
the prophets of BAAL. Elijah denounced AHAB and JEZEBEL for
their sins, and he stayed with the widow of Zarephath
[zăr′ê·făth], who fed him a little cake before she gathered
two sticks. Ernest as a young minister, in Butler's *The Way of
All Flesh*, made a "horrid faux pas" when he preached one
morning when the Bishop was present "upon the question what
kind of little cake it was that the widow of Zarephath had
intended making when Elijah found her gathering a few sticks.
He demonstrated that it was a seed cake. . . . The Bishop was
very angry." Elijah rose into heaven in a CHARIOT OF FIRE,
and his mantle fell to ELISHA.

ELISHA

*I Kings: 16–21;
II Kings 2, 4–9,
13*

Elijah found Elisha, a prosperous farmer's son, plowing and
appointed him to be his successor. Elisha also became a great
prophet of the ninth century B.C., performing many miracles
and acting as counselor to several kings. When Elisha saw
Elijah ascend in a chariot of fire into heaven, he cried,
"My father, my father, the chariot of Israel, and the horsemen thereof." In *Magnalia Christi Americana*, Cotton Mather

said that when John Eliot died, "all-devouring *Death* . . . slighted all those Lamentations of ours, *My Father, My Father, the Chariots of Israel, and the Horsemen thereof!*" At Bethel Elisha was mocked by little children calling him "bald head"; angered, he cursed them "and there came forth two she bears out of the wood, and tare forty and two children of them." In "The Old Benchers of the Inner Temple," Charles Lamb said that Thomas Coventry "made a solitude of children wherever he came, for they fled his presence, as they would have shunned an Elisha bear. His growl was as thunder in their ears . . . ." When the son of the woman of Shunem died, Elisha "went up, and lay upon the child, and put his mouth upon his mouth, and his eyes upon his eyes, and his hands upon his hands: and he stretched himself upon the child; and the flesh of the child waxed warm." Tennyson, in *In Memoriam,* expressed his grief upon the return of Arthur Hallam's body to England:

> Ah yet, ev'n yet, if this might be,
> I, falling on his faithful heart,
> Would breathing thro' his lips impart
> The life that almost dies in me.

Elisha cured Naaman [nā′á·măn], the captain of the king of Syria, of leprosy. Forced to return with his Syrian master, Naaman carried "two mules' burden of earth" back with him with which to build an altar unto the Lord. In Butler's *The Way of All Flesh,* the narrator, attending Theobald's old church, "felt as Naaman must have felt on certain occasions when he had to accompany his master on his return after having been cured of his leprosy." Elisha saw a carpenter's axhead fall into the water, and the man said, "Alas, Master! for it was borrowed." Elisha "cut down a stick, and cast it in thither; and the iron did swim." In *Animadversions,* Milton attacked his opponent's false metaphor: you will have to ground your argument "better than from this metaphor, which you may now deplore as the axehead that fell into the water and say, 'Alas, master, for it was borrowed,' unless you have as good a faculty to make iron swim, as you had to make light froth sink."

EMMAUS
(ĕ·mā′ŭs)

Luke 24:13–35

Three days after Jesus' resurrection, two of his followers walked from Jerusalem to the village of Emmaus, talking of all the things which had happened. Jesus joined them, "but their eyes were holden that they should not know him." Thinking him a stranger, they told him of the crucifixion, burial, and resurrection. Then Jesus said to them, "O fools, and slow of heart to believe all that the prophets have spoken . . . ." and he "expounded unto them in all the scriptures the things concerning himself." And he ate supper with them; then "their eyes were opened, and they knew him . . . and he vanished out of their sight." Arthur Hugh Clough, in "Easter Day," asked

> What if at Emmaus' inn, and by Capernaum's Lake,
> Came One, the bread that brake—
> Came One that spake as never mortal spake,
> And with them ate, and drank, and stood, and walked about?
> Ah! "some" did well to "doubt"!

In Butler's *The Way of All Flesh*, Althea, "as nearly a freethinker as anyone could be," once called the narrator's attention "to a note in her prayer-book which gave an account of the walk to Emmaus with the two disciples, and how Christ had said to them, 'O fools and slow of heart to believe ALL that the prophets have spoken'—the 'all' being printed in small capitals." In Hardy's *The Mayor of Casterbridge*, Henchard and Farfrae—his rival in business and love—"sat stiffly side by side at the darkening [tea] table, like some Tuscan painting of the two disciples supping at Emmaus. Lucetta, forming the third and haloed figure was opposite them . . . ."

ENDOR   *see WITCH OF ENDOR*

ENOCH
(ē′nŭk)

Gen. 4:17–18;
5:18–23

At Genesis 4:17–18, Enoch was a son of Cain, who named the first city after him; at Genesis 5:18–23 he was the son of Jared and the father of Methuselah, a man who "walked with God" (cf. Heb. 11:5). Carlyle, in *Heroes and Hero Worship*, said that Napoleon was inferior to Cromwell: "no such sincerity as in Cromwell . . . no silent walking, through long years, with the Awful Unnamable of this Universe; 'walking with God,' as he called it." In Hawthorne's *The Scarlet Letter*, when the Reverend Dimmesdale consults Chillingworth about his illness and says if it were God's will he would be willing to die, Chillingworth says that often young "saintly men, who walk with God, would fain" die. And later, when he longs to confess, Dimmesdale would say from his pulpit, "I, in whose daily life you discern the sanctity of Enoch,—I, whose footsteps, as you suppose, leave a gleam along my earthly track . . . I, your pastor . . . am utterly a pollution and a lie!"

ENTER INTO THY CLOSET

Matt. 6:6

In the Sermon on the Mount Jesus gave instructions about prayer. Do not as the hypocrites "pray standing in the synagogues and in the corners of the streets, that [you] may be seen of men . . . . But . . . when thou prayest, enter into thy closet, and when thou hast shut thy door, pray to thy Father which is in secret; and thy Father which seeth in secret shall reward thee openly." In *The Crown of Wild Olive*, Ruskin said that one may worship anywhere, anytime. Pray not, he said, "as thy hypocrites . . . standing in the *churches* [we should translate it] that they may be seen of men. But . . . enter into thy closet, and when thou hast shut thy door, pray to thy Father,—which is not in chancel nor in aisle, but 'in secret.'" In "The Over-Soul," Emerson said that man should learn "that the Highest dwells with him . . . . But if he would know what the great God speaketh, he must 'go into his closet and shut the door' as Jesus said."

ENTER YE IN AT THE STRAIT GATE   *see STRAIT IS THE GATE AND NARROW IS THE WAY*

ESAU

Gen. 25:21–34; 27; 33

Esau, meaning "hairy," was the eldest son of Isaac and Rebekah, and the twin brother of Jacob. When Rebekah conceived, "the children struggled together within her . . . twins in her womb." "And the first came out red, all over like an hairy garment; and they called his name Esau . . . . And after that came his brother out, and his hand took hold on Esau's heel; and his name was called Jacob . . . ." In *Eikonoklastes,* Milton said that Charles I meant "no good to either independent or presbyterian . . . . Those twins, that strove enclosed in the womb of Rebecca, were the seed of Abraham . . . ." Melville, in *Moby Dick,* said that whales produce "but one at a time; though in some few known instances giving birth to an Esau and Jacob." Esau became "a cunning hunter, a man of the field . . . ." In a letter to John Hamilton Reynolds, Keats asked why modern poets should be as limited as Wordsworth and Hunt, "when we can wander with Esau?" After he SOLD HIS BIRTHRIGHT FOR A MESS OF POTTAGE to Jacob, and lost his father's blessing to his brother, he hated Jacob and "said in his heart, The days of mourning for my father are at hand; then will I slay my brother Jacob." In *The Way of All Flesh*, Samuel Butler wrote that Ernest's marriage to Ellen, his mother's maid, was worse than his wedding to the church: "He had learned nothing by experience: he was an Esau—one of those wretches whose hearts the Lord had hardened."

ESHCOL, GRAPES OF

Num. 13:17–27

Eshcol [ĕsh′cŏl], meaning "cluster of grapes," was the valley or brook near Hebron from which spies sent out by Moses, as the Israelites approached Canaan, brought back "one cluster of grapes, and they bare it between two upon a staff . . . ." The spies reported, "We came unto the land whither thou sentest us, and surely it floweth with milk and honey; and this is the fruit of it." William Bradford, in *Of Plymouth Plantation,* tells of the expedition bringing back the Indian corn to the Pilgrims on Cape Cod. "And so, like the men from Eshcol, carried with them of the fruits of the land and showed their brethren; of which, and their return, they were marvelously glad and their hearts encouraged." In "To E. Fitzgerald," Tennyson tells of his attempt at a vegetarian diet. Failing, he "tasted flesh again," then dreamed of "climbing icy capes / And glaciers, over which there roll'd / To meet me long-arm'd vines with grapes / Of Eshcol hugeness." In "The Fruit-Gift," Whittier writes of receiving a gift of a basket of fruit:

> Thrilled with a glad surprise, methought I knew
> The pleasure of the homeward turning Jew,
> When Eshcol clusters on his shoulders lay,
> Dropping their sweetness on his desert way.

ESTHER

Book of Esther

Esther was the beautiful and courageous heroine, the queen of the Persian King Ahasuerus (Xerxes) in Shushan (Susa), who with the aid of her guardian and cousin Mordecai saved her people from destruction by the wicked Haman. The name "Esther," which may mean "star," probably derives from Ishtar, the Babylonian goddess of love. Her Jewish name Hadassah means "myrtle." At the climax of a seven-day feast, King Ahasuerus [à·hăz′û·e′rŭs] ordered Queen Vashti to appear before his drunken guests. Refusing, she was deposed. Esther was selected to replace her from among the fairest young virgins of the kingdom—a sort of Miss Persia contest in which every maid went through twelve months of "purifications, to wit, six months with oil of myrrh, and six months with sweet odours, and with other things for the purifying of the women." Her cousin Mordecai "sat in the king's gate" and aroused the ire of Haman, the king's chief counselor, because he refused

to bow down before him. Haman plotted to kill all the captive
Jews and hang Mordecai on a high gallows, but Esther persuaded the king to reverse things. Haman and his ten sons
were hanged on the gallows built for Mordecai and the Jews
slew all their enemies. The "day of feasting and gladness" in
celebration became the Feast of Purim held on "Mordecai's
day."

Tennyson's Princess Ida, in *The Princess*, is proud of the
independence of the girls in her women's college:

> We move, my friend,
> At no man's beck, but know ourself and thee,
> O Vashti, noble Vashti! Summon'd out
> She kept her state, and left the drunken king
> To brawl at Shushan underneath the palms.

In *The Reason of Church Government*, Milton draws a parallel
between Christ and Ahasuerus. "If Christ be the church's
husband, expecting her to be presented before him a pure
unspotted virgin; in what could he show his tender love to her
more than in prescribing his own ways, which he best knew
would be to the improvement of her health and beauty, with
much greater care doubtless than the Persian king could appoint
for his queen Esther those maiden dietings and set prescriptions of baths and odors, which may render her at last the
more amiable to his eye?" Mordecai's suffering is reflected in
Charles Lamb's description of a "poor relation" as "a Mordecai in your gate," and in Longfellow's poem "The Jewish
Cemetery at Newport," which tells of the persecutions of the
Jews: "At every gate the accursed Mordecai / Was mocked
and jeered and spurned by Christian feet." The bell maker, in
Melville's story "The Bell Tower," talks to the magistrates
about hanging his fine clock-bell: ". . . when Haman there is
fixed on this, his lofty tree, then, gentlemen, will I be most
happy . . . ."

ETHIOPIAN CHANGE HIS SKIN   *see LEOPARD CHANGE HIS SPOTS*

EUCHARIST   *see LAST SUPPER*

EUROCLYDON   *see PAUL SHIPWRECKED*

EVE   Eve was the first woman, Adam's wife, made by God as "an
               help meet for him" from Adam's rib. Deceived by the serpent,
Gen. 1:26–28;   she ate the forbidden fruit of the tree of knowledge, gave it
2:18—4:26   "also unto her husband," was cursed by God "in sorrow [to]

bring forth children," and with Adam was expelled from the
Garden of Eden. The name "Eve" is from the Hebrew *hawwah*,
meaning "life." The "mother of all living," Eve bore first Cain,
then Abel and Seth.

In Milton's *Paradise Lost*, Adam tells the angel Raphael of
the creation of Eve. Though sleeping, he saw God

> Who stooping op'nd my left side, and took
> From thence a Rib, with cordial spirits warme,
> And Life-blood streaming fresh; wide was the wound,
> But suddenly with flesh fill'd up & heal'd:
> The Rib he formd and fashond with his hands;
> Under his forming hands a Creature grew,
> Manlike, but different sex, so lovely faire,
> That what seemd fair in all the World, seemd now
> Mean, or in her summd up, in her containd,
> And in her looks, which from that time infus'd
> Sweetness into my heart, unfelt before,
> And into all things from her Aire inspir'd
> The spirit of love and amorous delight.

With Adam she was all innocence and purity before the fall,
naked and unashamed. Satan watched them unobserved in
Milton's account:

> Two of far nobler shape erect and tall,
> Godlike erect, with native Honour clad
> In naked Majestie seemd Lords of all . . .
> She as a vail down to the slender waste
> Her unadorned golden tresses wore
> Dissheveld, but in wanton ringlets wav'd
> As the Vine curles her tendrils, which impli'd
> Subjection, but requir'd with gentle sway,
> And by her yeilded, by him best receivd,
> Yeilded with coy submission, modest pride,
> And sweet reluctant amorous delay.

Emily Dickinson pictures Eve's innocence in a short poem:

> Not when we know
> The Power accosts,
> The garment of Surprise
> Was all our timid Mother wore
> At Home, in Paradise.*

Byron's picture, in *Don Juan*, of the innocent pair is more
cynical. Don Juan's mother was as pure and perfect as Eve.

*From *Poems by Emily Dickinson* by Emily Dickinson, by permission
of Little, Brown and Co. Copyright 1914, 1942 by Martha Dickinson Bianchi.

> Perfect she was, but as perfection is
>   Insipid in this naughty world of ours,
> Where our first parents never learn'd to kiss
>   Till they were exiled from their earlier bowers,
> Where all was peace, and innocence, and bliss
>   (I wonder how they got through the twelve hours)

However, Eve is also in literature the sinner, the weaker vessel, the temptress and cause of Adam's fall. Chaucer's Wife of Bath was lectured by her fifth husband, Jankyn, on woman's wickedness.

> Upon a nyght Jankyn, that was our sire,
> Redde on his book, as he sat by the fire,
> Of Eva first: that for hir wikkednesse
> Was al mankind brought to wreccednesse . . . .

In "The Nun's Priest's Tale," Chaucer's Chauntecleer bewails taking his wife's advice:

> Wommenes conseils been ful ofte cold;
> Wommenes conseils brought us first to wo,
> And made Adam fro Pardys to go,
> There-as he was ful myrie and well at ese . . . .

Don Adriano de Armado, in Shakespeare's *Love's Labour's Lost*, wrote the King that he had arrested Jaquenetta because she had "sorted and consorted" unlawfully with one Costard. She was the "weaker vessel . . . a child of our grandmother Eve, a female; or for thy more sweet understanding, a woman." When Milton's Eve uses her female charm to lure Adam to the "compleating of the mortal Sin Original," their love turns to lust.

> As with new Wine intoxicated both
> They swim in mirth, and fansie that they feel
> Divinitie within them breeding wings
> Wherewith to scorn the Earth: but that false Fruit
> Farr other operation first displaid,
> Carnal desire enflaming, hee on Eve
> Began to cast lascivious Eyes, she him
> As wantonly repaid; in Lust they burne:
> Till Adam 'gan Eve to dalliance move.

EWE LAMB   *see DAVID AND NATHAN*

EXPULSION   *see FLAMING SWORD*

EYE FOR AN EYE

Exod. 21:23–25;
Lev. 24:20; Deut.
19:21

For various offenses against one's fellow man, the law of Moses prescribed the "lex talionis," or the law of retaliation: "thou shalt give life for life, eye for eye, tooth for tooth, hand for hand, foot for foot, burning for burning, wound for wound, stripe for stripe." In Tennyson's *Becket*, King Henry criticizes the bishops for their "laxity": you bishops hailed into your courts a cleric who had "violated / The daughter of his host, and murdered him / . . . But since your canon will not let you take / Life for a life, ye but degraded him / Where I had hang'd him." In Emily Brontë's *Wuthering Heights*, Mrs. Heathcliff tells Ellen Dean that "on only one condition" could she hope to forgive Heathcliff. "It is, if I may take an eye for an eye, a tooth for a tooth; for every wrench of agony return a wrench: reduce him to my level." And in "Compensation," Emerson wrote that "all things are double, one against the other.—Tit for tat; an eye for an eye; a tooth for a tooth; blood for blood; measure for measure; love for love."

EYE HATH NOT SEEN

I Cor. 2:9

In his first epistle to the Corinthians, Paul wrote of the hidden wisdom of God: "But as it is written, Eye hath not seen, nor ear heard, neither have entered into the heart of man, the things which God hath prepared for them that love him." In Shakespeare's *A Midsummer Night's Dream*, Bottom awakens and calls his friends, saying, "I have had a most rare vision . . . . The eye of man hath not heard, the ear of man hath not seen, man's hand is not able to taste, his tongue to conceive, nor his heart to report, what my dream was." Thomas De Quincy, in *Autobiographical Sketches*, wrote that when he went to see his sister the day after she died, he saw through the window a brilliant summer day: ". . . it was not possible for the eye to behold, or for the heart to conceive, any symbols more pathetic of life and the glory of life."

EYE OF A NEEDLE   *see CAMEL GO THROUGH AN EYE OF A NEEDLE*

EZEKIEL
(ē·zēk′yĕl)

Book of Ezekiel

Ezekiel, meaning "God strengthens," was a prophet-priest of the sixth century B.C. who was "watchman" over a group of the Israelites during exile in Babylon by the river of Chebar. He used visions based in large part upon images from Babylonian

art, e.g., the vision of WHEELS WITHIN WHEELS. He used allegory, as in the story of AHOLAH AND AHOLIBAH, and in the
VALLEY OF DRY BONES. The Lord said unto Ezekiel, "Son of
man, I have made thee a watchman unto the house of Israel . . . ." John Woolman relates in his *Journal* how he was
impelled to speak out once concerning "drinking and vain
sports" in a public house, while "reading what the Almighty
said to Ezekiel, respecting his duty as a watchman . . . ."

FAITH, HOPE, AND CHARITY

I Cor. 13:13   In his first epistle to the Corinthians, Paul wrote, "And now
abideth faith, hope, charity, these three; but the greatest of
these is charity." In Ben Jonson's *The Alchemist,* Sir Epicure
Mammon speaks to Subtle the alchemist, who is cheating him,
about Surly, who is skeptical about the whole business: "This
great gent'man you must bear withal: / I told you he had
not faith." Surly replies, "And little hope, sir; / But much
less charity, should I gull myself." In *Vanity Fair,* Thackeray
says that he is going to "occasionally step down and talk about"
his characters. There will be silly and wicked ones; "Such
people there are living and flourishing in the world—Faithless,
Hopeless, Charityless; let us have at them, dear friends, with
might and main." In "The Mystery of Life and Its Arts,"
Ruskin said that we have to turn youths' courage from war to
mercy, "their intellect from dispute of words to discernment of
things . . . . And then, indeed, shall abide, for them, and for us,
an incorruptible felicity, and an infallible religion; shall abide
for us Faith, no more to be assailed by temptation . . . shall
abide with us Hope, no more to be quenched by the years that
overwhelm . . . —shall abide for us, and with us, the greatest
of these; the abiding will, the abiding name of our Father. For
the greatest of these is Charity."

FAITH WITHOUT WORKS

Jas. 2:14–26   James wrote, "Yea, a man may say, Thou hast faith, and I
have works: shew me thy faith without thy works, and I will
shew thee my faith by my works . . . . But wilt thou know, O
vain man, that faith without works is dead? Was not Abraham
our father justified by works, when he had offered Isaac his
son upon the altar? Seest thou how faith wrought with his
works, and by works was faith made perfect?" In the Prologue

to Chaucer's "The Second Nun's Tale," is an Invocation to Mary:

> And, for that feith is deed withouten werkis,
> So for to werken yif me wit and space,
> That I be quit fro thennes that moost derk is!

In *The American Crisis*, Thomas Paine, rallying America to resist, said, ". . . throw not the burden of the day upon Providence, but 'show your faith by your works,' that God may bless you." And in *Cape Cod*, Thoreau told how the Reverend Samuel Osborne "introduced improvements in agriculture" such as peat culture in the colonies, but was condemned and dismissed by the ecclesiastical council for his unorthodox ideas. "But he was fully justified, methinks, by his works in the peat meadow; one proof of which is, that he lived to be between ninety and one hundred years old."

THE FALL

Gen. 3

Because of their sin of disobedience in eating of the FORBIDDEN FRUIT of the TREE OF KNOWLEDGE, Adam and Eve, tempted by the serpent, were expelled from the Garden of Eden. God condemned Eve saying, ". . . in sorrow thou shalt bring forth children"; and Adam, saying, "In the sweat of thy face shalt thou eat bread, till thou return unto the ground . . . ." In Shakespeare's *Richard II*, the Queen, upon hearing her gardener's tale of King Richard's overthrow, said,

> Thou, old Adam's likeness, set to dress the garden,
> How dares thy harsh rude tongue sound this unpleasing news?
> What Eve, what serpent hath suggested thee
> To make a second fall of cursed man?

Milton begins *Paradise Lost* with the statement of his theme:

> Of Mans First Disobedience, and the Fruit
> Of that Forbidden Tree, whose mortal taste
> Brought Death into the World, and all our woe,
> With loss of Eden, till one greater Man
> Restore us, and regain the blissful Seat . . . .

In *Don Juan*, Byron writes of the Russian Queen Catherine's frequent infidelities:

> how man *fell* I
> Know not, since knowledge saw her branches stript
> Of her first fruit; but how he falls and rises,
> *Since, thou* hast settled beyond all surmises.

FALL OF JERICHO   *see JERICHO*

FALL OF SPARROW   *see SPARROW'S FALL*

FAMILIAR SPIRIT   *see WITCH OF ENDOR*

FATHER, FORGIVE THEM

Luke 23:34

When Jesus was crucified on Calvary, he said, "Father, forgive them; for they know not what they do." In Chaucer's *Troilus and Criseyde*, Pandarus came to see Criseyde after Troilus had left her; he reached under the sheet and kissed her. Chaucer said,

> I passe al that which chargeth noughte to seye.
> What! God foryaf his deth, and she also
> Foryaf, and with here uncle gan to pleye,
> For other cause was ther noon than so.

As Jane was recovering from her fainting spell at Mrs. Reed's, in Charlotte Brontë's *Jane Eyre*, she thought, "Yes, Mrs. Reed, to you I owe some fearful pangs of mental suffering. But I ought to forgive you, for you knew not what you did . . . ." And in Longfellow's *Evangeline*, Father Felician stills the strife of his congregation caused by the seizure of their lands and the orders to leave:

> Lo! where the crucified Christ from his Cross is gazing upon you!
> See! in those sorrowful eyes what meekness and holy compassion!
> Hark! how those lips still repeat the prayer, "O Father, forgive them!"
> Let us repeat it now, and say, "O Father, forgive them."

FAT OF THE LAND

Gen. 45:18

When Pharaoh heard of the visit of Joseph's brethren, he was pleased, and told Joseph to send his brethren back to Canaan, "And take your father and your households, and come unto me: and I will give you the good of the land of Egypt, and ye shall eat the fat of the land." Thomas Hood said of the workingman, in "The Lay of the Laborer," that he was

> Still one Adam's heirs,
> Though doom'd by chance of birth
> To dress so mean, and to eat the lean
> Instead of the fat of the earth . . . .

William Dean Howells, in "My Mark Twain," said that Mark Twain "had a magnificent scheme for touring the country with Aldrich and Mr. G. W. Cable and myself, in a private car, with a cook of our own, and every facility for living on the fat of the land." And Carl Sandburg, in *Abraham Lincoln: The Prairie*

Years, said that when Lincoln was seven, "There were times when they lived on the fat of the land and said God was good; other times when they just scraped along and said they hoped the next world would be better than this one."

FATHERS HAVE EATEN A SOUR GRAPE

Jer. 31:29–30;
Ezek. 18:2–3

Jeremiah and Ezekiel taught individual responsibility as against inherited, or group, guilt: "In those days they shall say no more, The fathers have eaten a sour grape, and the children's teeth are set on edge. But every one shall die for his own iniquity: every man that eateth the sour grape, his teeth shall be set on edge." In Butler's *The Way of All Flesh,* when Mr. George Pontifex ate or drank to excess, "young people knew that they had better look out. It is not as a general rule the eating of sour grapes that causes the children's teeth to be set on edge. Well-to-do parents seldom eat many sour grapes; the danger to the children lies in the parents eating too many sweet ones." In *Walden,* Thoreau comments on the burden of holding "superfluous property" and the superiority of savage life: "What mean ye by saying . . . that the fathers have eaten sour grapes, and the children's teeth are set on edge?" Ezekiel said, "As I live, saith the Lord God, ye shall not have occasion any more to use this proverb in Israel . . . ." And in "The Pit and the Pendulum," Poe says, "I forced myself to ponder upon the sound of the crescent as it should pass across the garment— upon the peculiar thrilling sensation which the friction of cloth produces on the nerves. I pondered over all this frivolity until my teeth were on edge."

FATTED CALF

Luke 15:23, 27,
30

When the PRODIGAL SON returned home, his father received him joyfully, saying, "And bring hither the fatted calf, and kill it; and let us eat, and be merry." In Shakespeare's *The Comedy of Errors,* when Dromio of Syracuse asks his master about a picture of old Adam, and Antipholus asks, "What Adam?" Dromio replies, ". . . that Adam that keeps the prison: he that goes in the calf's skin that was killed for the Prodigal." In "Mackery End, in Hertfordshire," Charles Lamb says that he and his sister Bridget were welcomed hospitably by their country cousins: "The fatted calf was made ready, or rather was already so, as if in anticipation of our coming." Oliver Wendell Holmes, in "Jonathan Edwards," said that Edwards's

God was "a piece of iron machinery which would have held back the father's arms stretching out to embrace his son, and shed the blood of the prodigal, instead of that of the fatted calf."

FEAR OF THE LORD IS THE BEGINNING OF WISDOM

Ps. 111:10; Prov. 9:10

This psalm, in praise of the Lord, concludes: "The fear of the Lord is the beginning of wisdom: a good understanding have all they that do his commandments: his praise endureth forever." In Bunyan's *Pilgrim's Progress*, Christian discusses "the good use of fear" with Hope, who says, "I do believe, as you say, that fear tends much to men's good, and to make them right at their beginning to go on Pilgrimage." Christian replies, "Without doubt it doth, if it be right; for so says the Word, The fear of the Lord is the beginning of Wisdom." Matthew Arnold, in *God and the Bible*, argued that the new liberalism could not replace religion: ". . . however poorly men may have got on when their governing idea was: *The fear of the Lord is the beginning of wisdom,* they can get on even less by the governing idea that *all men are born naturally free and equal.*"

FEET OF CLAY

Dan. 2:31–33

Daniel told King NEBUCHADNEZZAR the dream which Nebuchadnezzar had forgotten and which none of his magicians or astrologers could reveal. "Thou, O king, sawest . . . a great image, whose brightness was excellent . . . . His legs [were] of iron, his feet part of iron and part of clay. Thou sawest till that a stone . . . smote the image upon his feet that were of iron and clay, and brake them to pieces." In Tennyson's "Merlin and Vivien" in *Idylls of the King*, Merlin condemns Vivien for slandering King Arthur's knights: "She is like the harlots who . . . / Inflate themselves with some insane delight, / And judge all nature from her feet of clay." In *Studies in Classic American Literature*, D. H. Lawrence said that when Melville came home from his South Sea travels, he married: "No more Typees. No more paradises . . . . A home: a torture box. A wife: a thing with clay feet." And in Albee's *The American Dream*, Grandma tells Mrs. Barker about Mommy and Daddy's son: ". . . it didn't have a head on its shoulders, it had no guts, it was spineless, its feet were made of clay . . . just dreadful things."

FELL AMONG THIEVES

Luke 10:30   Jesus' parable of the GOOD SAMARITAN was about "a certain
man who went down from Jerusalem to Jericho, and fell among
thieves, which stripped him of his raiment, and wounded him,
and departed, leaving him half dead." In *Sartor Resartus*,
Carlyle said that Professor Teufelsdröckh is a "Traveller from
a far Country; more or less footsore and travel-soiled; has
parted with road-companions; fallen among thieves, been
blistered with bug-bites, [and] poisoned by bad cookery." In
Treasure Island, Stevenson said that Dick "had been well
brought up before he came to sea and fell among bad companions." Butler, in *The Way of All Flesh*, said about Ernest,
now a pastor, after meeting his old college friend Townley,
"Then came an even worse reflection; how if he had fallen
among material thieves as well as spiritual ones?"

FIAT LUX   *see LET THERE BE LIGHT*

FIELD OF BLOOD   *see ACELDAMA*

FIERY FURNACE

Dan. 3   King NEBUCHADNEZZAR set up "an image of gold . . . in the
plain of Dura, in the province of Babylon," and all peoples
fell down and worshiped it except Shadrach, Meshach, and
Abednego [shā′drăk, mē′shăk, à·bĕd′nê·gō]. Nebuchadnezzar,
full of fury, had these men "bound in their coats, their hosen,
and their hats . . . and cast into the midst of the burning fiery
furnace." The furnace was so "exceeding hot, the flame . . .
slew those men that took up Shadrach, Meshach, and Abednego." But the Lord spared them—not a hair of their heads
was singed—and "the king promoted Shadrach, Meshach, and
Abednego in the province of Babylon." In Shakespeare's
Henry VIII, Northumberland tries to moderate Buckingham's
hatred for Cardinal Wolsey: "Be advis'd; / Heat not a furnace
for your foe so hot / That it do singe yourself." In Milton's
Eikonoklastes, Charles I prophesied that those who had " 'cast
black scandals on him' " would be " 'blasted by the same
furnace of popular obloquy, wherein they sought to cast his
name and honor.' I believe that not a Romish gilded portrai-
ture gives a better oracle than a Babylonish golden image
could do, to tell us truly who heated that furnace of obloquy,
or who deserves to be thrown in, Nebuchadnezzar, or the

three kingdoms." In *Moby Dick*, Melville, describing the extraction of whale oil, says that after execution, the whale "is condemned to the pots, and, like Shadrach, Meshach, and Abednego, his spermaceti, oil, and bone, pass unscathed through the fire."

FIG LEAVES

Gen. 3:7

When Eve and Adam—"the woman" and "her husband"—did eat of the fruit of the tree of knowledge, "the eyes of them both were opened, and they knew that they were naked; and they sewed fig leaves together, and made themselves aprons." In *Don Juan*, Byron wrote of love in high English places:

> Adam exchanged his Paradise for ploughing,
>   Eve made up millinery with fig leaves—
> The earliest knowledge from the tree so knowing,
>   As far as I know, that the church receives:
> And since that time it need not cost much showing,
>   That many of the ills o'er which man grieves,
> And still more woman, spring from not employing
> Some hours to make the remnant worth enjoying.

Henry Adams, in *The Education of Henry Adams*, asked why "the Woman" was unknown in America. "For evidently America was ashamed of her, and she was ashamed of herself, otherwise they would not have strewn fig-leaves so profusely all over her. When she was a true force, she was ignorant of fig-leaves, but the monthly-magazine-made American female had not a feature that would have been recognized by Adam."

FILTHY LUCRE

I Tim. 3:3, 8

Timothy wrote on the qualifications of bishops and deacons: they must be, among other things, "not greedy of filthy lucre." The setting of Chaucer's "The Prioress's Tale" was within a great city in Asia—

> a Jewerye,
> Sustened by a lord of that contree
> For foule usure and lucre of vileynye,
> Hateful to Christ and to his compaignye;

Robert Burton, in *The Anatomy of Melancholy*, attacked the evils of literary patronage, saying that greed is the chief fault: "Some out of that insatiable desire of filthy lucre, to be enriched, care not how they come by it *per fas et negas*, hook or crook, so they have it."

FIRE AND BRIMSTONE

Gen. 19:24; Luke 17:29; Rev. 20:10; 21:8

As LOT fled, "the Lord rained upon Sodom and upon Gomorrah brimstone and fire from the Lord out of heaven . . ." and destroyed them. In Revelation, fire and brimstone refer to hell: "And the devil that deceived them was cast into the lake of fire and brimstone" to be "tormented day and night for ever and ever." There "the fearful, and unbelieving, and the abominable, and murderers, and whoremongers, and sorcerers, and idolaters, and all liars, shall have their part in the lake which burneth with fire and brimstone: which is the second death." In Bunyan's *Pilgrim's Progress*, Christian tells Obstinate and Pliable, who try to dissuade him from his journey, ". . . you dwell in the City of Destruction, the place also where I was born . . . and dying there, sooner or later, you will sink lower than the grave, into a place that burns with Fire and Brimstone . . . ." In Stephen Crane's *The Red Badge of Courage*, veterans told tales of "tattered and eternally hungry men . . . they'll charge through hell's fire an' brimstone t'git a holt on a haversack, an' sech stomachs ain't a-lastin' long." Mark Twain, in *The Mysterious Stranger*, said that old Ursula, Father Peter's cook and housekeeper, "could tell everyday lies fast enough and without taking any precautions against fire and brimstone on their account . . . ."

FIRE THAT IS NOT QUENCHED   *see WORM THAT DIETH NOT*

FIREBRANDED FOXES   *see SAMSON'S FIREBRANDED FOXES*

FIRSTBORN OF EGYPT

Exod. 11:4–6; 12:29–30

The tenth plague that the Lord brought upon Pharaoh and the Egyptians: "And it came to pass, that at midnight the Lord smote all the firstborn in the land of Egypt, from the firstborn of Pharaoh that sat on his throne unto the firstborn of the captive that was in the dungeon; and all the firstborn of the cattle." In Shakespeare's *As You Like It*, Jacques ends his song bemoaning the hardship of exile in the forest, and says, "I'll go to sleep, if I can; if I cannot, I'll rail against all the first-born of Egypt." When Jane Eyre, in Charlotte Brontë's *Jane Eyre*, about to marry Rochester, learns that he has a mad wife, she says, "My hopes were all dead—struck with a subtle doom, such as, in one night, fell on all the first-born in the land of Egypt." In Butler's *The Way of All Flesh*, Theobald reflected upon his son Ernest's shortcomings at Dr. Skinner's school. "Then his thoughts turned to Egypt and the tenth plague. It seemed to him that if the little Egyptians had been anything like Ernest, the plague must have been something very like a blessing in disguise. If the Israelites were to come to England now he should be greatly tempted not to let them go." And Butler wrote that after Ernest had left home, "It had been a bitter pill to Theobald to lose his power of plaguing his first-born."

FIRST SHALL BE LAST AND THE LAST SHALL BE FIRST

Matt. 19:30;
20:16

When Peter asked what those shall have who "have forsaken all, and followed thee?" Jesus replied, they "shall receive an hundredfold, and shall inherit everlasting life. But many that are first shall be last; and the last shall be first." In Bunyan's *Pilgrim's Progress,* when Christian saw Faithful ahead of him and called for him to wait until he caught up, Faithful refused. "At this Christian was somewhat moved, and putting to all his strength, he quickly got up with Faithful, and did also overrun him, so the last was first." In Tennyson's *Mizpah*, a mother who picked up the bones of her boy hanged on the gallows and secretly buried them thought of the forgiveness of the Lord: "He'll never put on the black cap except for the worst of the worst, / And the first may be last—I have heard it in church—and the last may be first."

FISHERS OF MEN

Matt. 4:18–20;
Mark 1:16–17

As Jesus was walking by the sea of Galilee, he saw Simon Peter and Andrew his brother "casting a net into the sea: for they were fishers. And he said unto them, Follow me, and I will make you fishers of men." In Chaucer's "The Summoner's Tale," the hypocritical friar boasts of his devotion:

> I walke, and fisshe Christen mennes soules,
> To yelden Jhesu Crist his propre rente;
> To sprede his word is set al myn entente.

In Tennyson's *Harold,* Harold, shipwrecked on the shore, accused Rolf, a fisherman approaching with lights, of having betrayed them. "Fishermen? devils! / Who, while ye fish for men with your false fires, / Let the great devil fish for your own souls." Rolf replied, "Nay then, we be liker the blessed apostles; *they* were fishers of men, Father Jean says." In *Cape Cod,* Thoreau told how in Provincetown a clerk refused to list a town Representative as "Fisherman," substituting "Master Mariner." "So much for American democracy," said Thoreau.

"I reminded him that Fisherman had been a title of honor with
a large party ever since the Christian era at least."

FIVE THOUSAND, FEEDING   *see LOAVES AND FISHES*

FLAMING SWORD

Gen. 3:24   Because Adam and Eve sinned by eating of the FORBIDDEN
FRUIT of the TREE OF KNOWLEDGE, God expelled them from
the Garden of Eden. "So he drove out the man; and he
placed at east of the garden of Eden Cherubims, and a flaming
sword which turned every way, to keep the way of the tree
of life." It is believed that it was the angel Michael who held
the flaming sword at the gate of Eden. The preacher, in Joyce's
A Portrait of the Artist as a Young Man, tells the young men of
the expulsion: "And then the voice of God was heard in that
garden, calling his creature man to account: and Michael,
prince of the heavenly host, with a sword of flame in his hand,
appeared before the guilty pair and drove them forth . . . ."
In Shaw's *Candida*, the poet Marchbanks tells Candida's husband of the evening he has just spent with Candida. He "approached the gate of Heaven . . . . Then she became an angel;
and there was a flaming sword that turned every way, so that
I couldn't go in; for I saw that that gate was really the gate
of Hell."

FLESH IS GRASS

Isa. 40:6–7; I Pet.   The voice that cried in the wilderness said, "Cry. And he
1:24   said, What shall I cry? All flesh is grass, and all the goodliness
thereof is as the flower of the field: The grass withereth, the
flower fadeth . . . surely the people is grass." In *Don Juan*,
Byron speaks of fame. Not a pinch of dust remains of King
Cheops's mummy:

> But I, being fond of true philosophy,
>   Say very often to myself, "Alas!
> All things that have been born were born to die,
>   And flesh (which Death mows down to hay) is grass."

In Shaw's *Back to Methuselah*, Zoo reproves The Elderly
Gentleman, who seems proud of his age: "Yes, Daddy, but it
is not the number of years we have behind us, but the number
we have before us that makes us careful . . . to find out the
truth about everything. What does it matter to you whether
anything is true or not? your flesh is grass: you come up like
a flower, and wither in your second childhood."

FLESH IS WEAK

Matt. 26:41;
Mark 14:38

In GETHSEMANE Jesus, finding Peter asleep, said, "What, could ye not watch with me one hour? Watch and pray, that ye enter not into temptation: the spirit indeed is willing, but the flesh is weak." The Biblical idea of the frailty of the flesh became proverbial by the Middle Ages. In Shakespeare's *Henry IV, Part I,* Prince Hal chastizes Falstaff for cozening Mistress Quickly. Falstaff replies, "Dost thou hear, Hal? Thou knowest in the state of innocency Adam fell, and what should poor Jack Falstaff do in the days of villainy? Thou seest I have more flesh than another man, and therefore more frailty." In Shakespeare's *Richard II,* Bolingbroke, banished by King Richard, says, "Banished this frail sepulcher of our flesh." In *Don Juan,* Byron wrote of the trials of virtue in hot countries:

> That howsoever people fast and pray,
> The flesh is frail, and so the soul undone;
> What men call gallantry, the gods adultery,
> Is much more common where the climate's sultry.

FLESH OF MY FLESH   *see BONE OF MY BONE*

FLESH POTS OF EGYPT

Exod. 16:3

The children of Israel "murmured against Moses and Aaron in the wilderness," saying unto them, "Would to God we had died by the hand of the Lord in the land of Egypt, when we sat by the flesh pots, and when we did eat bread to the full; for ye have brought us forth into this wilderness, to kill this whole assembly with hunger." In literature the expression now frequently means longing for material things, for luxuries of a sinful kind. In his *Autobiography,* Benjamin Franklin said that his friend Keimer "suffer'd grievously" from their vegetarian project; he "long'd for the flesh pots of Egypt, and order'd a roast pig." In *Nature,* Emerson said that "Some theosophists have arrived at a certain hostility . . . towards matter, as the Manichean and Plotinus. They distrusted in themselves any looking back to these flesh-pots of Egypt. Plotinus was ashamed of his body."

FLOOD

Gen. 6–8

Because "the wickedness of man was great in the earth," the Lord sent a flood to destroy "both man, and beast, and the creeping thing, and the fowls of the air; for it repenteth me that I have made them." Noah, by God's instructions, made an ark (See NOAH'S ARK) into which he took his sons, his wife, his sons' wives; and seven of every clean beast, male and female, and two of "beasts that are not clean," male and female (Genesis 6:20 and 7:15 say two of all kinds). It rained "forty days and forty nights," and when the rains ended, Noah's ark rested "upon the mountains of Ararat." Noah, his family, and the animals then went forth to repopulate the earth. In Chaucer's "The Miller's Tale," "hende Nicholas" persuaded carpenter John to get up in a tub on the ceiling because that night "shall fall a reyn, and that so wilde and wood, / That half so greet was nevere Noees flood." While John slept, Nicholas made merry with young Alison, John's wife. Later, hearing an anguished cry, "Help! water! water! help, for Goddes herte!" John, thinking "Allas, now comth Nowelis flood!" cut the cord in two and crashed in a swoon. Nicholas and Alison "tolden every man that he was wood, / He was agast so of Nowelis flood . . . ." And in Shakespeare's *The Comedy of Errors*, Dromio of Syracuse tells his master of his lady, a kitchen wench who sweats so that "a man may go over shoes in the grime of it." Says his master, "That's a fault that water will mend." "No, sir," says Dromio, "'tis in grain; Noah's flood could not do it."

FLY IN THE OINTMENT

Eccles. 10:1

One of the proverbs in Ecclesiastes: "Dead flies cause the ointment of the apothecary to send forth a stinking savour: so doth a little folly him that is in reputation for wisdom and honour." Charles Lamb, in "Poor Relations," defines a poor relation as, among other things, "a fly in your ointment." In *Studies in Classical American Literature*, D. H. Lawrence said that Melville loved Typee, but had to escape. "The very freedom was a torture to him. Its ease was slowly horrible to him. This time *he* was the fly in the odorous tropical ointment." And Aldous Huxley said, in *The Olive Tree*, "There is only one fly in the ointment offered by commercial propagandists; they want your money."

FOOLISH VIRGINS   *see PARABLE OF THE WISE AND FOOLISH VIRGINS*

FORBIDDEN FRUIT

Gen. 3:1–6

God forbade Adam and Eve to eat or touch the fruit of the tree of knowledge lest they die. Although the phrase "forbidden fruit" appears nowhere in the Bible, and "apple" is not mentioned in Genesis, they commonly refer to this passage. Shakespeare's ninety-third sonnet concludes: "How like Eve's apple doth thy beauty grow, / If thy sweet virtue answer not thy show!" In *Areopagitica*, Milton argues that good and evil in this world "grow up together almost inseparably . . . . It was from out the rind of one apple tasted, that the knowledge of good and evil . . . leaped forth into the world." In Joyce's *A Portrait of the Artist as a Young Man*, the preacher tells the boys how the serpent promised Eve "that if she and Adam ate of the forbidden fruit they would become as Gods . . . ." D. H. Lawrence, in *Studies in Classic American Literature*, said that Melville's Fayaway in *Typee* was "a laughing little Eve, naked with him, and hankering after no apple of knowledge, so long as he would just love her when he felt like it."

FORTY DAYS AND FORTY NIGHTS *see FLOOD*

FOUGHT A GOOD FIGHT

II Tim. 4:7

Paul, anticipating his own death, wrote to Timothy, "I have fought a good fight, I have finished my course, I have kept the faith: Henceforth there is laid up for me a crown of righteousness, which the Lord, the righteous judge, shall give me at that day . . . ." In Chaucer's "The Second Nun's Tale," St. Cecilia tells Maximus and others whom she has converted, in anticipation of their coming deaths:

> Ye han for soothe ydoon a greet bataille,
> Your cours is doon, your feith han ye conserved.
> Gooth to the corone of lif that may nat faille;
> The rightful Juge, which that ye han served,
> Shal yeve it yow, as ye han it deserved.

Charles Lamb, in "Mrs. Battle's Opinions on Whist," said that Mrs. Battle had no use for "insufferable triflers" at cards. She played for keeps. "She fought a good fight; cut and thrust."

FOUND WANTING *see WEIGHED IN THE BALANCES AND FOUND WANTING*

FOUR RIVERS OF EDEN

Gen. 2:10–14

"And a river went out of Eden to water the garden; and from thence it was parted, and became into four heads." The first, Pison [pī'son] which "compasseth the whole land of Havilah" [hăv'ĭ·lä], may be the Arabian and Persian gulfs or the upper western branch of the Nile. The second, Gihon [gī'hon] which "compasseth the whole land of Ethiopia," may be upper eastern branch of the Nile. The third, Hiddekel [hĭd'ê·kĕl], which "goeth toward the east of Assyria," is the Tigris; and the "fourth river is the Euphrates." In *Paradise Lost,* Milton says that Satan entered Eden from an underground part of the Tigris River. There was a place

> Where Tigris at the foot of Paradise
> Into a Gulf shot underground, till part
> Rose up a Fountain by the Tree of Life;
> In with the River sunk, and with it rose
> Satan involv'd in rising Mist . . .

In *Cape Cod,* Thoreau quotes Humboldt telling how Columbus "approaching the New World" and perceiving its beauty supposed "that he was approaching the garden of Eden, the sacred abode of our first parents. The Orinoco seemed to him one of the four rivers which . . . flowed from Paradise, to water and divide the surface of the earth, newly adorned with plants."

FRAILTY OF FLESH   *see FLESH IS WEAK*

FROGS   *see PLAGUE OF FROGS*

GABRIEL

Dan. 8:16; 9:21;
Luke 1:19, 26

Gabriel, meaning "God is mighty," was a messenger of God. He interpreted a vision to Daniel, announced the birth of John the Baptist to Zacharias and Elizabeth, and the birth of Jesus to Mary. In Milton's *Paradise Lost,* Gabriel is "the winged Warriour," "chief of the Angelic Guards" of the Gate of Paradise. Uriel warns him of the approach of Satan, and Gabriel promises, ". . . in at this Gate none pass / The vigilance here plac't, but such as come / Well known from Heav'n." Emily Dickinson, in "Forever Cherished Be the Tree," remembering that Gabriel did not reveal himself to Zacharias until asked, and not to Mary at all, writes of two robins coming to her apple tree "from the sky / Two Gabriels . . . ."

> They registered in Nature's book
> As Robin—Sire and Son,
> But angels have that modest way
> To screen them from renown.°

And in *A Portrait of the Artist as a Young Man,* by Joyce, Stephen awoke one morning, a poem in his heart. "O! in the

° From *Poems by Emily Dickinson* by Emily Dickinson, by permission of Little, Brown and Co. Copyright 1914, 1942 by Martha Dickinson Bianchi.

virgin womb of the imagination the word was made flesh. Gabriel the seraph had come to the virgin's chamber."

GADARENE SWINE

Matt. 8:28–32;
Mark 5:1–13;
Luke 8:26–33

In the country of the Gadarenes [găd·a·rēn'] Jesus met a man possessed with devils, who said, "My name is Legion: for we are many." "And all the devils besought him, saying, Send us into the swine, that we may enter into them. And forthwith Jesus gave them leave. And the unclean spirits went out, and entered into the swine: and the herd ran violently down a steep place into the sea, (they were about two thousand;) and were choked in the sea." In Shakespeare's *The Merchant of Venice,* when Bassanio invites Shylock to dine with him, Shylock replies, "Yes, to smell pork; to eat of the habitation which your prophet the Nazarite [the Nazarene] conjured the devil into." Shaw, in his Preface to *Saint Joan,* speaking of "Modern Education Which Joan Escaped," said that "To Joan and her contemporaries we should appear as a drove of Gadarene swine, possessed by all the unclean spirits cast out by the faith and civilization of the Middle Ages, running violently down a steep place into a hell of high explosives."

GAIN THE WHOLE WORLD   *see WHAT IS A MAN PROFITED, IF HE SHALL GAIN THE WHOLE WORLD?*

GAMALIEL, PAUL'S TEACHER   *see SIT AT THE FEET OF*

GARDEN OF EDEN   *see EDEN, GARDEN OF*

GATE OF HEAVEN

Gen. 28:16–17

When "Jacob awaked out of his sleep," during which he had his vision of a ladder (see JACOB'S LADDER), he said, "Surely the Lord is in this place; and I knew it not. And he was afraid, and said, How dreadful is this place! this is none other but the House of God, and this is the gate of heaven." Shakespeare, in the sonnet beginning, "When, in disgrace with fortune and men's eyes," said, after feelings of despair:

> Haply I think on thee—and then my state,
> Like to the lark at break of day arising
> From sullen earth, sings hymns at heaven's gate;

In "Absalom and Achitophel," Dryden said of Elkanah Settle, a poet who had satirized him, that he was a dog, but not treasonable. " 'T were a pity treason at his door to lay, /

Who makes heaven's gate a lock to its own key." And in *Uncle Tom's Cabin,* Harriet Beecher Stowe said that Augustine St. Clare's religion varied: "up to Heaven's gate in theory, down in earth's dust in practice."

GATES OF PEARL   *see STREETS OF GOLD*

GAZA
(gā'·zà)

Judg. 16:1–3, 21

Gaza, meaning "the strong place," was one of the chief cities of the Philistines. Samson visited a harlot there, and when the Gazites "compassed him in, and laid wait" to kill him in the morning, Samson "arose at midnight, and took the doors of the gate of the city, and the two posts, and went away with them, bar and all, and put them upon his shoulders, and carried them up to the top of an hill that is before Hebron" [hē'brŭn]. When the Philistines finally captured Samson, they "put out his eyes, and brought him down to Gaza, and bound him with fetters of brass; and he did grind in the prison house." Chaucer relates the gates of Gaza story in "The Monk's Tale."

> By verray force at Gazan, on a nyght,
> Maugree Philistiens of that citee,
> The gates of the toun he hath up plyght,
> And on his bak ycaryed hem hath hee
> Hye on an hill whereas men myghte hem see.

In Shakespeare's *Love's Labour's Lost,* Moth tells his master, Don Armado, of Samson, a man "of good repute and carriage." He was "a man of good carriage, great carriage, for he carried the town gates on his back like a porter . . . ." Don Armado replies, "O well-knit Samson! strong-jointed Samson! I do excell thee in my rapier as much as thou didst me in carrying gates." In Milton's *Samson Agonistes,* Samson speaks of his imprisonment in Gaza:

> Promise was that I
> Should Israel from Philistian yoke deliver;
> Ask for this great Deliverer now, and find him
> Eyeless in Gaza at the Mill with slaves,
> Himself in bonds under Philistian yoke.

GEHENNA   *see TOPHET(H)*

GENERATION OF VIPERS

Matt. 3:7; 12:34;
23:33

Jesus denounced the scribes, Pharisees and Sadducees as the "generation of vipers," meaning the offspring of vipers. "How can ye," he said, "escape the damnation of hell?" In Shakespeare's *Richard II,* when King Richard lands in Wales and learns that some of his followers have gone over to Bolingbroke, he says, "Oh, villains, vipers, damned without redemption!" In Shakespeare's *Troilus and Cressida,* Paris ribs Pandarus for thinking only of doves and love. "Hot blood begets hot thoughts, and hot thoughts beget hot deeds, and hot deeds is love." Pandarus replies, "Is this the generation of love,—hot blood, hot thoughts, and hot deeds? Why they are vipers. Is love a generation of vipers?" Aldous Huxley, in *After Many a Summer Dies the Swan,* said, "Who are the Scribes and Pharisees? Simply the best citizens; the pillars of society; all right thinking men. In spite of which, or rather because of which, Jesus calls them a generation of vipers."

GETHSEMANE
(gĕth · sĕm′à · nè)

Matt. 26:36;
Mark 14:32

Gethsemane, meaning wine or oil press, was the garden on the Mount of Olives where Jesus went after the LAST SUPPER with his disciples to pray. "Then saith he unto them, My soul is exceeding sorrowful, even unto death: tarry ye here, and watch with me." At midnight he was arrested. Swinburne, in "Super Flumina Babylonis," wrote of the suffering of Italy under Austrian tyranny: "And the north was Gethsemane, without leaf or bloom, / A garden sealed." Emily Dickinson, in "All Overgrown by Cunning Moss," on the death of Charlotte Brontë, spoke of Charlotte's travels and return to the confinement of Haworth:

> Gathered from any wanderings,
> Gethsemane can tell
> Through what transporting anguish
> She reached the asphodel! °

In *Studies in Classic American Literature,* D. H. Lawrence wrote of Captain Ahab's weariness and suffering before his final fight with Moby Dick: "It is the Gethsemane of Ahab, before the last fight: the Gesthemane of the human soul seeking the last self-conquest, the last attainment of extended consciousness—"

GET THEE BEHIND ME (HENCE), SATAN

Matt. 4:10; Luke
4:1–8

The devil tempted Jesus in the wilderness, "taking him up into an high mountain, shewed unto him all the kingdoms of the world in a moment of time. And the devil said unto him, All

---

° From *Poems by Emily Dickinson* by Emily Dickinson (Boston, Little, Brown and Co.).

this power will I give thee . . . . If thou therefore wilt worship
me . . . ." "And Jesus answered and said unto him, Get thee
behind me, Satan: for it is written, Thou shalt worship the Lord
thy God, and him only shalt thou serve." In Milton's *Paradise
Regained*, Satan brought Christ to a high mountain and tempted
him with "great and glorious Rome" and the "Kingdoms of
the world" if "thou wilt fall down, / And worship me as thy
superior Lord . . . ." Jesus replied:

> Wert thou so void of fear or shame,
> As offer them to me the Son of God,
> To me my own, on such abhorred pact,
> That I fall down and worship thee as God?
> Get thee behind me; plain thou now appear'st
> That Evil one, Satan for ever damn'd.

Shaw, in the Preface to *Back to Methuselah*, arguing against
conventional "allopathic education," said, "Homeopathic education has not yet been officially tried . . . . A body of schoolmasters inciting their pupils to infinitesimal peccadilloes with
the idea of provoking them to exclaim, 'Get thee behind me,
Satan' . . . would certainly do less harm than our present
educational allopaths do . . . ."

GIANTS IN THE EARTH

Gen. 6:4

"There were giants in the earth in those days; and also after
that, when the sons of God came in unto the daughters of men,
and they bare children to them, the same became mighty men
which were of old, men of renown." The "wickedness of man
was [so] great in the earth" that the Lord sent the Flood to
punish them. In *Beowulf*, Beowulf presents to King Hrothgar
the ancient sword of the giants brought from Grendel's cave.
On its hilt was written an account of "a battle long ago, when
a flood, a rushing sea, slew the race of giants; they had lived
boldly; that race was estranged from the eternal Lord. The
Ruler gave them final requital for that in the surge of the
water." * John Dryden, in "To My Dear Friend Mr. Con-
greve," wrote of the Elizabethans: "Strong were our sires, and
as they fought they writ. / Conqu'ring with force of arms,
and dint of wit; / Theirs was the giant race, before the flood
. . . ." In *Life on the Mississippi*, Mark Twain, after recounting
the many historical events from the discovery of the river by
La Salle to the time of modern commerce, said, "Truly, there

*From the Everyman edition of *Anglo Saxon Poetry*. Translation by
R. K. Gordon.

were snails in those days." And in *Innocents at Home*, he said that every rich strike in the mining days created one or two very rich men: "There were nabobs in those days."

GIBEON   *see JOSHUA, SUN AND MOON STAND STILL*

GIBEONITES   *see HEWERS OF WOOD AND DRAWERS OF WATER*

GIDEON

Judg. 6–8

Gideon was a man of religious zeal, a clever military leader of the Israelites against the Midianites and the Amalekites. He asked God to show his will "If thou wilt save Israel by my hand . . . ." He asked that if I "put a fleece of wool in the floor; and if the dew be on the fleece only, and it be dry upon all the earth beside, then shall I know that thou wilt save Israel by my hand . . . ." And so it was; next morning he "wringed the dew out of the fleece, a bowl full of water." A second time the opposite occurred: the fleece was dry, the dew was on the ground. With three hundred men he defeated a multitude of Midianites and Amalekites. He gave his men trumpets, pitchers, and lamps; they surrounded the enemy, and "blew the trumpets, and brake the pitchers, and held the lamps in their left hands . . . and cried, The sword of the Lord, and of Gideon . . . and all the host ran, and cried, and fled." In *Past and Present*, Carlyle says that if one has courage, patience, and faith, work will be rewarded. "Like Gideon thou shalt spread out thy fleece at the door of thy tent; see whether under the wide arch of Heaven there be any bounteous moisture or none. Thy heart and life-purpose shall be as a miraculous Gideon's fleece, spread out in silent appeal to Heaven; and from the kind Immensities [will come] blessed dew—moisture." In "Christ's Hospital Five and Thirty Years Ago," Lamb compared two teachers: one easygoing, the other severe. Severe Boyer's "thunders rolled innocuous for us; his storms came near, but never touched us; contrary to Gideon's miracle, while all around were drenched, our fleece was dry." In Bunyan's *Pilgrim's Progress*, when Christian reached The House Beautiful, they took him into the Armory and "shewed him some of the Engines with which some [the Lord's] Servants had done wonderful things. They shewed him . . . the Pitchers, Trumpets and Lamps too, with which Gideon put to flight the Armies of Midian."

GIFT OF TONGUES   *see PENTECOST*

GIRD UP HIS LOINS

I Kings 18:46; II Kings 4:29; 9:1

A common figurative but practical expression in the Bible, meaning "Tighten your belt and get ready to go": "And the hand of the Lord was on Elijah; and he girded up his loins, and ran before Ahab to the entrance of Jezreel." In Bunyan's *Pilgrim's Progress*, when Christian had fallen to "musing in the midst of my dumps" at the Strait Gait, Good-will comforted him. "Then *Christian* began to gird up his loins, and to address himself to his Journey." In Butler's *The Way of All Flesh*, Mr. Hawke preached to the Cambridge students: "Oh! my young friends, turn, turn, turn, now while it is called today . . . stay not even to gird up your loins; look not behind you for a second, but fly into the bosom of Christ . . . ." In *Civil Disobedience*, Thoreau said that those who behold the truth of "the Bible and the Constitution . . . where it comes trickling into this lake or that pool, gird up their loins once more, and continue their pilgrimage toward its fountainhead."

GIVE US THIS DAY OUR DAILY BREAD   *see OUR DAILY BREAD*

GLORY IS DEPARTED   *see ICHABOD*

GLORY TO GOD IN THE HIGHEST   *see PEACE, GOOD WILL TOWARD MEN*

GNASHING OF TEETH   *see WEEPING AND GNASHING OF TEETH*

GO, AND DO THOU LIKEWISE   *see GOOD SAMARITAN*

GO, AND HE GOETH; COME, AND HE COMETH

Matt. 8:9

A centurion asked Jesus to heal his servant, saying, "For I am a man under authority, having soldiers under me: and I say to this man, Go, and he goeth; and to another, Come, and he cometh . . . ." Convinced of the centurion's faith, Jesus healed the servant. In *The Stones of Venice*, Ruskin said that it is no slavery for a workman to work for another man if he can work with free expression. "It is often the best kind of liberty,— liberty from care. The man who says to one, Go, and he goeth, and to another, Come, and he cometh, has, in most cases, more sense of restraint and difficulty than the man who obeys him." Thomas De Quincey, in *Confessions of an English Opium Eater,* said of his dreams, some of which he could summon up as a child could, and some not, that "a child said to me when

I questioned him on this matter, 'I can tell them to go, and they go; but sometimes they come when I don't tell them to come.' Whereupon I told him that he had almost as un-limited command over apparitions as a Roman centurion over his soldiers."

GO AND SIN NO MORE   *see WOMAN TAKEN IN ADULTERY*

GOD AND MAMMON   *see MAMMON*

GO DOWN TO THE SEA IN SHIPS

Ps. 107:23

"Oh that men would praise the Lord . . . for his wonderful works . . . !" "They that go down to the sea in ships, that do business in great waters; These see the works of the Lord, and his wonders in the deep." In *Moby Dick*, Melville contrasts merchant ships, which "are but extension bridges," with the Nantucketer who draws his "living from the bottomless deep itself . . . he alone resides and riots on the sea; he alone in Bible language, goes down to it in ships . . . . There is his home; there lies his business . . . ." John Masefield may have had this passage in mind in "Sea Fever," which begins, "I must go down to the seas again, to the lonely sea and the sky, / And all I ask is a tall ship, and a star to steer her by . . . ." °

GOD SAVE THE KING

I Sam. 10:24; II Sam. 16:16; II Kings 11:12; II Chron. 23:11

Samuel gathered all the people together and sent for Saul. "And they ran and fetched him thence: and when he stood among the people, he was higher than any of the people from his shoulders and upward. And Samuel said to all the people, See ye him whom the Lord hath chosen, that there is none like him among all the people? And all the people shouted, and said, God save the king." The expression, which in the original Hebrew means "(long) live the King," appears several times in the Bible. In *The Vision of Judgement*, Byron said of the death of George the Third:

> "God save the king!" It is a large economy
> In God to save the like; but if he will
> Be saving, all the better; for not one am I
> Of those who think damnation better still:

°Reprinted with permission of The Macmillan Company from *Collected Poems* by John Masefield. Copyright 1912 by The Macmillan Company. Renewed 1940 by John Masefield. Permission also granted by The Society of Authors and Dr. John Masefield, O. M.

In "A Chapter on Ears," Charles Lamb says he has no ear for
music. He is sentimentally disposed to harmony, but organically
incapable of a tune. "I have been practising 'God save the
King' all my life . . . and am not arrived, they tell me, within
many quavers of it. Yet hath the loyalty of Elia never been
impeached."

GOG AND MAGOG

(gŏg, mā'gŏg)

Rev. 20:8

Although Gog is mentioned as prince of the country of Magog
in Ezekiel 38:2–3, most allusions refer to the passage in Revelation. At the end of the MILLENIUM, "when the thousand years
are expired, Satan shall be loosed out of his prison, And shall
go out to deceive the nations which are in the four quarters of
the earth, Gog and Magog, to gather them together to battle:
the number of whom is as the sand of the sea." Thus they
represent two nations who will war against the people of God.
Their giant statues are at the Guildhall of London: porters of
the royal palace, descendants of an ancient race of giants and
demons. In "A Chapter on Ears," Charles Lamb says that at
a concert of his Catholic friend, "I am converted, and yet a
Protestant;—at once *malleus hereticorum* . . . . three heresies
center in my person:—I am Marcion, Ebion, and Cerinthus—
Gog and Magog—what not?" Lord Macaulay, in "Lord Clive,"
said that "The Hungarian, in whom the trembling monks
fancied that they recognized the Gog or Magog of prophecy,
carried back the plunder of the cities of Lombardy to the
depths of the Pannovian forests." Bernard Berenson, in "My
Utopia," in 1952, said, "Having reached the shady side of my
seventy-ninth year, I regret at times that I cannot hope to see
the outcome of this gogmagogery of a war."

GOLDEN BOWL BE BROKEN

Eccles. 12:6

The poem on old age, a reminder to youth, pictures the last
days before death: "Or ever the silver cord be loosed, or the
golden bowl be broken, or the pitcher be broken at the
fountain . . . ." In "The Iron Gate," read on his seventieth
birthday, Oliver Wendell Holmes wrote of his sense of old age:

> And sad "Ecclesiastes, or the Preacher,"—
> Has he not stamped the image on my soul,
> In that last chapter, where the worn-out Teacher
> Sighs o'er the loosened cord, the broken bowl?

Poe's "Lenore" begins: "Ah, broken is the golden bowl!—the
spirit flown forever!" In "The Pride of the Village," Washington Irving told how the maiden deserted by her lover "felt a

conviction that she was hastening to the tomb . . . . The silver cord that had bound her to existence was loosed . . . ." And Melville, in "I and My Chimney," tells how his wife opposed both his pipe and his enormous chimney. "But my spouse, who likes the smoke of my tobacco as little as she does that of the soot, carries on war against both. I live in continual dread lest, like the golden bowl, the pipes of me and my chimney shall yet be broken."

GOLDEN CALF

Exod. 32:1–14; 33:3, 5, 9

When "Moses delayed to come down out of the mount," the people asked Aaron to make them gods: "for as for this Moses, the man that brought us out of the land of Egypt, we wot not what is become of him." So Aaron, Moses' brother and chief priest, gathered the golden earrings from the ears of the wives and sons and daughters, and with a graving tool made "a molton calf." The Lord's wrath waxed hot against his "stiff-necked people," but Moses persuaded him to repent "of the evil which he thought to do unto his people." In Ben Jonson's *The Alchemist,* Sir Epicure Mammon promises to make Surly rich; no more, he says, shall "the sons of Sword and Hazard fall before / The golden calf, and on their knees, whole nights, / Commit idolatry with wine and trumpets . . . ." Arthur Hugh Clough, in "The New Sinai," warns against worshiping the golden calf of atheism:

> "The Man that went the cloud within
>   Is gone and vanished quite;
> He cometh not," the people cried,
>   "Nor bringeth God to sight:
> Lo these thy gods, that safety give,
>   Adore and keep the feast!"
> Deluding and deluded cries
>   The Prophet's brother—Priest:
> And Israel all bows down to fall
>   Before the gilded beast.

And Matthew Arnold, in *Culture and Anarchy,* says that the term "[Philistine] gives the notion of something particularly stiff-necked and perverse in the resistance to light and its children."

GOLDEN RULE

Matt. 7:12; Luke 6:31

Jesus' teaching to his disciples, "Therefore all things whatsoever ye would that men should do to you, do ye even so to them," is known as the Golden Rule. The phrase does not, however, appear in the Bible; and the wording commonly begins "Do unto others . . ." perhaps influenced by the form of the catechism. In *Walden,* discussing philanthropy, Thoreau said that the Indians were sometimes superior to the missionaries who offered them consolation as they burned them at the stake; "and the law to do as you would be done by fell with less persuasiveness on the ears of those who, for their part, did not care how they were done by . . . ." In Melville's *Moby Dick,* Ishmael reasons that since the will of God is "to do to my fellow man what I would have my fellow man to do to me," and since the heathen Queequeg is his fellow man and he would wish Queequeg to join him in his Presbyterian worship, therefore "I must then unite with him in his; ergo I must turn idolater."

GOLGOTHA   *see CALVARY*

GOLIATH   *see DAVID AND GOLIATH*

GOMORRAH   *see SODOM AND GOMORRAH*

GOOD AND FAITHFUL SERVANT   *see PARABLE OF THE TALENTS*

GOOD FIGHT   *see FOUGHT A GOOD FIGHT*

GOOD FOR NOTHING   *see SALT OF THE EARTH*

GOOD SAMARITAN

Luke 10:30–37   When "a certain lawyer stood up, and tempted" Jesus, asking "who is my neighbour?" Jesus answered with the parable of the good Samaritan. He stopped to help the man who "fell among thieves," binding up his wounds and "pouring in oil and wine." He took him to an inn and gave the host two pence to take care of him, promising to pay more if necessary. A Levite and a certain priest had passed him by. The lawyer decided that the one who showed mercy was the neighbor; "Then said Jesus unto him, Go, and do thou likewise." The Samaritans were a people disliked by the Jews (John 4:9). The phrase "good Samaritan" is not in the Bible. Butler, in *The Way of All Flesh,* said that Ernest, after a disillusioning meeting with his old college friend Townley, "began to feel as though, if he was to be saved, a good Samaritan must hurry up from somewhere—he knew not whence." In Byron's *Don*

Juan, Gulbeyaz, the favorite of the harem into which Don Juan has been smuggled, sheds a tear in sympathy with his sorrow over his lost Haidée. Byron wrote:

> female hearts are such a genial soil
> For kinder feelings, whatsoe'er their nation,
> They naturally pour the "wine and oil,"
> Samaritans in every situation . . . .

Carlyle, in "Boswell's Life of Johnson," said that after Johnson resigned a secure position as usher at Market Bosworth, he learned to be content with humble human things: ". . . is there not already an actual realized human Existence, all stirring and living on every hand of him? Go thou and do likewise!"

GOOD THING COME OUT OF NAZARETH

John 1:46

Philip asked Nathanael to become a disciple of Jesus, saying, "We have found him, of whom Moses in the law, and the prophets, did write, Jesus of Nazareth, the son of Joseph. And Nathanael said unto him, Can there any good thing come out of Nazareth? Philip said unto him, Come and see." In Washington Irving's "The Legend of Sleepy Hollow," after Ichabod Crane disappeared, Hans Van Ripper consigned Ichabod's "magic books and poetic scrawl" to the flames and determined from then on "to send his children no more to school; observing, that he never knew any good come of this same reading and writing." In Hardy's *Tess of the D'Urbervilles,* Mrs. Clare had not met her daughter-in-law, Tess, who had been a dairymaid; but her son's "enthusiasm for Tess had infected her through her maternal sympathies, till she had almost fancied that a good thing could come out of Nazareth—a charming woman out of Talbothay's Dairy." In *The Gilded Age,* Mark Twain said that the district called the Knobs of East Tennessee "had a reputation like Nazareth, as far as turning out any good thing was concerned."

GOOD TIDINGS OF GREAT JOY

Luke 2:10

At Jesus' birth, "there were shepherds in the same country abiding in the field, keeping watch over their flock by night. And, lo, the angel of the Lord came upon them . . . and they were sore afraid. And the angel said unto them, Fear not: for, behold, I bring you good tidings of great joy, which shall be to all people." In *The English Mail-Coach,* Thomas De Quincey tells of his vision of a child that "rode in a carriage as frail as flowers . . . as if danger there were none. 'O, baby!' I exclaimed, 'shalt thou be the ransom for Waterloo? Must we, that carry tidings of great joy to every people, be messengers of ruin to thee?' " In "The City of Dreadful Night," James Thomson gives an ironic sermon to his "Melancholy Brothers . . . battling black floods without an ark."

> And now at last authentic word I bring,
> Witnessed by every dead and living thing;
>   Good tidings of great joy for you, for all:
> There is no God; no Fiend with names divine
> Made us and tortures us; if we must pine,
>   It is to satiate no Being's gall.

GO TO THE ANT, THOU SLUGGARD

Prov. 6:6–9

One of the warnings against idleness: "Go to the ant, thou sluggard; consider her ways, and be wise: Which having no guide, overseer, or ruler, Provideth her meat in the summer, and gathereth her food in the harvest. How long wilt thou sleep, O sluggard? When wilt thou arise out of thy sleep?" In Bunyan's *Pilgrim's Progress*, Christian fell asleep in "a pleasant Arbour" on "the Hill called Difficulty." "Now as he was sleeping, there came one to him and awaked him, saying, Go to the Ant, thou sluggard; consider her ways and be wise." In *A Free Commonwealth*, Milton argued that to commit government to a king is laziness. Were we "aught else but sluggards or babies, we need depend on none but God and our own counsels, our own . . . industry! 'Go to the ant, thou sluggard,' saith Solomon; 'consider her ways, and be wise; which having no prince, ruler, or lord, provides her meat in summer, and gathers her food in the harvest': which evidently shows us, that they who think the nation undone without a king . . . love not so much true spirit and understanding in them as a pismire."

GOURD OF JONAH   *see JONAH'S GOURD*

GRAIL

*Matt. 26:26–28;
Luke 22:20; I
Cor. 11:25–28*

The Grail is also called the Holy Grail, Sangreal (Sangraal), the cup or chalice. At the Last Supper Jesus "took of the cup, and gave thanks, and gave it to [his disciples], saying, Drink ye all of it; for this is my blood of the new testament, which is shed for the many for the remission of sins." Medieval legend held that Joseph of Arimathea preserved the cup, caught some of Jesus' blood in it at the Crucifixion, and then brought it to Glastonbury in England, where it later disappeared. The quest for the Holy Grail was a central theme of the Arthurian romances as in Malory's *Morte d'Arthur*. It was also held to be the dish at the Last Supper from which Jesus ate the Paschal lamb with his disciples. More recently it has been interpreted as a primitive female sexual symbol associated with the bleeding spear, as in T. S. Eliot's *The Waste Land.* In *Of Reformation in England,* Milton said, of the luxury found in the church after Constantine, that "former times had wooden chalices and golden priests, but they, golden chalices and wooden priests." Tennyson's "The Holy Grail" tells the story of "The cup, the cup itself, from which our Lord / Drank at the last sad supper with his own." And in "Directive," Robert Frost tells of a stolen drinking cup hidden in an old cedar tree: "A broken drinking goblet like the Grail / Under a spell so the wrong ones can't find it . . . ."*

GRAIN OF MUSTARD SEED

Matt. 13:31–32

A parable of Jesus. "The kingdom of heaven is like to a grain of mustard seed, which a man took, and sowed in his field: Which indeed is the least of all seeds: but when it is grown, it is the greatest among herbs, and becometh a tree, so that the birds of the air come and lodge in the branches thereof." Carlyle, in "Boswell's Life of Johnson," said of the variety and power of Johnson's writing, "Admire also the greatness of Literature; how a grain of mustard-seed cast into its Nile-waters, shall settle in the teeming mould, and be found, one day, as a Tree, in whose branches all the fowls of heaven may lodge." Alexander Henderson, in *Aldous Huxley,* said that Huxley "has only to note an idea, and it proliferates rapidly into a vast foliage, like the Biblical seed of mustard sprouting into a lodging for the fowls of the air."

GRAVEN IMAGE

Exod. 20:4–5

The second of the Ten Commandments is "Thou shalt not make unto thee any graven image, or any likeness of any thing that is in heaven above, or that is in earth beneath, or that is in the water under the earth." Verse 5 prohibits the worship of these images, or idols: "Thou shalt not bow down thyself to them, nor serve them." In "A Plea for Captain John Brown," Thoreau argued that many Christians are hypocritical about slavery: "The curse is the worship of idols . . . and the New Englander is just as much an idolator as the Hindoo. John Brown was an

*From *Complete Poems of Robert Frost.* Copyright 1923, 1945 by Holt, Rinehart and Winston, Inc. Copyright 1936, 1951 by Robert Frost. Copyright © 1964 by Lesley Frost Ballantine. Reprinted by permission of Holt, Rinehart and Winston, Inc. and Jonathan Cape, Ltd.

exception, for he did not set up even a political graven image
between him and his God."

GRAVE, WHERE IS THY VICTORY?   *see O DEATH, WHERE IS THY STING?*

GRAVES WERE OPENED

Ezek. 37:12-13;
Matt. 27:52-53

When Jesus "yielded up the ghost" on the Cross, "the graves
were opened; and many bodies of the saints which slept arose,
and came out of the graves after his resurrection, and went into
the holy city, and appeared unto many." Shakespeare, in *Hamlet,* some believe, may have had this passage in mind, when
Horatio, on the platform at Elsinore, said, "A little ere the
mightiest Julius fell, / The graves stood tenantless and the
sheeted dead / Did squeak and gibber in the Roman streets
. . . ." More probable are Prospero's words, in *The Tempest,*
when he addresses the elves, the demipuppets, by whose aids
he has exercised his magical powers: "graves at my command
/ Have waked their sleepers, oped, and let 'em forth / By my
so potent art." In "The Crucifixion," Whittier wrote:

> The dead are waking underneath!
> Their prison door is rent away!
> And, ghastly with the seal of death
> They wander in the light of day!

GREATER THAN I CAN BEAR   *see MY PUNISHMENT IS GREATER THAN I CAN BEAR*

GREATEST OF THESE IS CHARITY   *see FAITH, HOPE, AND CHARITY*

GREAT GRASSHOPPERS

Nah. 3:17

Nahum denounced Nineveh for its wickedness. "Woe to the
bloody city! it is all full of lies and robbery . . . thy captains
[are] as the great grasshoppers, which camp in the hedges in
the cold day, but when the sun ariseth they flee away, and their
place is not known where they are." In his comments on his
"Ode on the Departing Year," Coleridge denounced England
for the wickedness of its wars. "Thy crowned are as the locusts;
and thy captains as the great grasshoppers which camp in the
hedges in the cool day; but when the sun ariseth they flee away,
and their place is not known where they are." Edwin Arlington
Robinson, in "The Man against the Sky," says of those men
who faced death guided by "a blind attendance on a brief ambi-

tion," "Nahum's great grasshoppers were such as these, / Sun scattered and soon lost."°

GREEN PASTURES

Ps. 23:2

The Twenty-Third Psalm begins: "The Lord is my shepherd; I shall not want. He maketh me to lie down in green pastures: he leadeth me beside the still waters." In Coleridge's *The Wanderings of Cain*, the shade of Abel cries out to Cain in bitterness: "Thou eldest born of Adam . . . cease to torment me. I was feeding my flocks in green pastures by the side of quiet rivers, and thou killedst me; and now I am in misery." In *In Chancery*, Galsworthy said, ". . . from those green pastures where Forsytes flourish—Mayfair and Kensington, St. James and Belgravia . . . the people swarmed down on to the roads where death would presently pass . . . . " And in *A Mencken Chrestomathy*, H. L. Mencken said a college diploma lifts one "over a definite fence, and maketh him to lie down in greener pastures."

GROVE(S)

Judg. 3:7; I Kings 16:33; II Kings 17:10; 21:3, 7; 23:4-7, 14-15

"And the children of Israel did evil in the sight of the Lord . . . and served Baalim and the groves." Ahab "made a grove; and Ahab did more to provoke the Lord God of Israel to anger than all the kings of Israel that were before him." Groves were phallic poles set up in "high places" associated with the Canaanite worship of the fertility goddess Asherah [á·shē′rá] or ASHTORETH, and BAAL the male god. Both King Ahab, with Jezebel, and King Ahaz sinned in worshiping the grove. In Hardy's *Tess of the D'Urbervilles*, when Alec d'Urberville gave up preaching to return to Tess, he said to her, "But you may well despise me now! I thought I worshipped on the mountains, but I find I still serve in the groves! Ha! ha!" Robert Frost, in "New Hampshire," speaking of the Freudian "new school of the pseudo-phallic," wrote,

> Agreed in frowning on these improvised
> Altars the woods are full of nowadays,
> Again as in the days when Ahaz sinned
> By worship under green trees in the open . . . .
> Even to say the groves were God's first temples
> Comes too near to Ahaz' sin for safety.†

°Reprinted with permission of The Macmillan Company from *Collected Poems* by E. A. Robinson. Copyright 1916 by E. A. Robinson. Renewed 1944 by Ruth Nivison. .

†From *Complete Poems of Robert Frost*. Copyright 1923, 1945 by Holt, Rinehart and Winston, Inc. Copyright 1936, 1951 by Robert Frost. Copyright © 1964 by Lesley Frost Ballantine. Reprinted by permission of Holt, Rinehart and Winston, Inc., and Jonathan Cape, Ltd.

HAGAR   see ISHMAEL

HALT AND THE BLIND   see MAIMED, THE HALT, THE BLIND

HAM   see CANAAN, SON OF HAM

HAMAN   see ESTHER

HAND AGAINST EVERY MAN   see ISHMAEL

HANDWRITING ON THE WALL

Dan. 5:5–30   This phrase, which appears nowhere in the Bible and means today a prediction of misfortune, is derived from the story of Belshazzar's feast. As the thousand lords drank wine there "came forth fingers of a man's hand, and wrote over against the candlestick upon the plaister of the wall of the king's palace" the words MENE, MENE, TEKEL, UPHARSIN. "Then was king Belshazzar greatly troubled, and his countenance was changed in him, and his lords were astonished." In Carlyle's *Sartor Resartus*, Professor Teufelsdröckh said that he resisted all religious doubts in youth: "Had a . . . miraculous Handwriting on the wall, convincingly proclaimed to me *This thou shalt do* . . . I would have done it, had it been leaping into the infernal Fire." And Thomas Hardy, in *The Return of the Native*, describing the night festival fire at Eustacia Vye's house on Egdon Heath, tells of "a small human hand, in the act of lifting pieces of fuel into the fire; for all that could be seen the hand, like that which troubled Belshazzar, was there alone."

HANGED OUR HARPS UPON THE WILLOWS

Ps. 137:2   The Psalmist sang of the sorrows of exile. "By the rivers of Babylon, there we sat down, yea, we wept, when we remembered Zion. We hanged our harps upon the willows in the midst thereof." The Hebrews refused to sing songs demanded as entertainment by their Babylonian captors. The schoolmistress, in William Shenstone's "The Schoolmistress," sang Psalms sweetly in her garden.

> Sweet melody! to hear her then repeat
> How Israel's sons, beneath a foreign king,
> While taunting foeman did a song entreat,
> All, for the nonce, untuning every string,
> Unhung their useless lyres—small heart had they to sing.

In *The Compleat Angler*, Izaak Walton's Piscator cites this psalm to argue that sitting by a river fosters contemplation: ". . . the children of Israel, who having in a sad condition banished all mirth and music from their pensive hearts and having hung up their mute harps upon the willow trees growing by the rivers of Babylon, sat down upon those banks bemoaning the ruins of Sion and contemplating their own sad condition." And the modern ballad "There Is a Tavern in the Town" may also echo this Psalm.

> Adieu, adieu, kind friends adieu!
> I can no longer stay with you.
> I will hang my heart on a weeping willow tree,
> And may the world go well with thee!

HARDEN HIS HEART

Exod. 4:21; 7:13, 22; 8:15; 9:12; Matt. 19:8

When Moses, upon God's command, started his return to Egypt with his wife and sons, the Lord said unto him, "When thou goest to return into Egypt, see that thou do all those wonders before Pharaoh, which I have put in thy hand: but I will harden his heart, that he shall not let the people go." And Pharoah's heart was hardened during the ten plagues. In *Common Sense*, Thomas Paine said that he wished for reconciliation with King George, but from the moment of April 1775, "I rejected the hardened, sullen-tempered Pharaoh of England forever . . . ." In Samuel Butler's *The Way of All Flesh*, Ernest, finding that his marriage to Ellen was failing, saw that "he had learned nothing by experience: he was . . . one of those wretches whose hearts the Lord had hardened." In Shaw's *Saint Joan*, after Joan has defended the truth of her voices, the Archbishop says to her, "I see that I am speaking in vain to a hardened heart."

HARMLESS AS DOVES   *see WISE AS SERPENTS, AND HARMLESS AS DOVES*

HATE NOT HIS FATHER, AND MOTHER, AND WIFE, AND CHILDREN, AND BRETHREN, AND SISTERS

Luke 14:26

Jesus said to a great multitude with him, "If any man come to me, and hate not his father, and mother, and wife, and children, and brethren, and sisters, and his own life also, he cannot be my disciple." In Bunyan's *Pilgrim's Progress*, the Evangelist counsels Christian against Mr. Worldly Wiseman's attempt to "render the Cross odious . . . The King of glory hath told thee, that . . . He that comes after him, and hates not his father, and mother, and wife, and children, and brethren and sisters, yea and his own life also, he cannot be my disciple." In Butler's *The Way of All Flesh*, Ernest's friend, reflecting upon what Ernest had told him "about his prison meditations," said that "he was trying to give up father and mother for Christ's sake . . . he was giving them up because he thought they hindered him in the pursuit of his truest and most lasting happiness." In "Compensation," Emerson said that greatness of thought has dangers. "With every influx of light comes new danger . . . He . . . must bear witness to the light . . . . He must hate father and mother, wife and child."

HAUGHTY SPIRIT BEFORE A FALL　　*see PRIDE GOETH BEFORE . . . A FALL*

HE THAT HATH, TO HIM SHALL BE GIVEN　　*see WHOSOEVER HATH, TO HIM SHALL BE GIVEN*

HE THAT RUNS MAY READ

Hab. 2:2　　Habakkuk [hȧ·băk′ŭk], denouncing the Chaldeans, says he will stand on the watchtower and "watch to see what he will say unto me, and what I shall answer when I am reproved." The Lord says to him, "Write the vision, and make it plain upon tables, that he may run that readeth it." This means: so that one may read it swiftly, or on the run. The common form of the expression is that of Cowper, in "Tirocinium," and Tennyson, in "The Flower" which concludes: "Read my little fable; / He that runs may read." In *Sartor Resartus*, Carlyle said that there are "sham metaphors" in our language, "which may be called its false stuffings, superfluous show-cloaks and tawdry woolen rags: whereof he that runs and reads may gather whole hampers,—and burn them." Macaulay, in "Milton," said that the Puritans were most remarkable men. "The odious and ridiculous parts of their character lie on the surface. He that runs may read them . . . ."

HE THAT WATERETH

Prov. 11:25　　One of the proverbs on the just balance of things: "The liberal soul shall be made fat: and he that watereth shall be watered also himself." In "Compensation," Emerson said, "All things are double, one against another.—Tit for tat . . . . He that watereth shall be watered himself." Ruskin, in *Sesame and Lilies*, said, "We have seen that the duties of bishop and pastor

are to see and feed; and, of all who do so it is said, 'He that
watereth, shall be also watered himself.' But the reverse is truth
also. He that watereth not, shall be withered himself."

HEAP COALS OF FIRE UPON HIS HEAD

Prov. 25:22; Rom.
12:20

"If thine enemy be hungry, give him bread to eat; and if he be
thirsty, give him water to drink: For thou shalt heap coals of
fire upon his head, and the Lord shall reward thee." Or, as in
Romans, "Be not overcome of evil, but overcome evil with
good." In Tennyson's "Romney's Remorse," the painter Romney, who had forsaken his wife and children for his art and then
taken them back, to be nursed by his wife in his half-mad old
age, says he has made

> The wife of wives a widow-bride, and lost
> Salvation for a sketch.
>   I am wild again!
> The coals of fire you heap upon my head
> Have crazed me.

In "John Underhill," Whittier told how the sinner Captain
Underhill, banished by Boston, repented, and became a preacher
of the Word in foreign lands.

> And the heart of Boston was glad to hear
> How he harried the foe on the long frontier,
> And heaped coals on the land against him barred,
> The coals of his generous watch and ward.

HEAVENLY CITY   see NEW JERUSALEM

HEAVEN'S GATE   see GATE OF HEAVEN

HEM OF HIS GARMENT

Matt. 9:20–22;
14:34–36

When Jesus was in the land of Gennesaret [gĕn·ĕs'à·rĕt] the
people brought to him all that were diseased, "And besought
him that they might only touch the hem of his garment: and
as many as touched were made perfectly whole." Francis
Thompson's "The Kingdom of God" concludes,

> Yea, in the night, my Soul, my daughter,
> Cry,—clinging Heaven by the hems;
> And lo, Christ walking on the water
> Not of Gennesareth, but Thames!

Oliver Wendell Holmes, in *The Autocrat of the Breakfast
Table*, said that "all men are afraid of books, who have not

handled them. Do you suppose our dear *didascalos* [referring to James Russell Lowell] over there ever read *Poli Synopsis* or consulted *Castelli Lexicon*, while he was growing up to their stature? Not he; but virtue passed through the hem of their parchment and leather garments whenever he touched them." In "The Man That Corrupted Hadleyburg," by Mark Twain, the Richards family received a letter from the stranger who had exposed the hypocrisy of the other leading citizens of the town, saying, "Your honesty is beyond reach of temptation . . . . This town is not worthy to kiss the hem of your garment."

HEROD AGRIPPA I

Acts 12:20–23

Herod Agrippa I, the grandson of HEROD THE GREAT, was ruler of Israel from A.D. 41 to 44. He is known in literature chiefly for his spectacular death. He made an oration before the people of Tyre and Sidon, "And the people gave a shout, saying, It is the voice of a god, and not of a man. And immediately the angel of the Lord smote him, because he gave not God the glory: and he was eaten of worms, and gave up the ghost." In Tennyson's "The Palace of Art," the poet's soul in her palace of art prospered for three years: "on the fourth she fell / Like Herod, when the shout was in his ears, / Struck thro' with pangs of hell." Longfellow, in "The Birds of Killingworth," seems to have confused Herod Agrippa I with Herod the Great. After the birds were all killed, Killingworth was devastated by caterpillars and insects.

> Devoured by worms, like Herod, was the town,
>   Because, like Herod, it had ruthlessly
> Slaughtered the Innocents.

HEROD ANTIPAS
(ăn′tĭ·păs)

Matt. 14:1–12;
Mark 6:17–28

Herod Antipas, the son of HEROD THE GREAT, was tetrarch of Galilee from 4 B.C. to A.D. 39. When John the Baptist rebuked Herod for his unlawful marriage to Herodias [hē·rō′dĭ·ăs], his brother Philip's wife, Herod imprisoned him. Herodias' daughter, by later tradition Salome [sà·lō′mê]—she is not named in the story—danced before Herod at his birthday feast. Pleased, he promised "to give her whatsoever she would ask. And she, being before instructed of her mother, said Give me here John Baptist's head in a charger." Herod was sorry, but he gave the order, and John the Baptist's "head was brought in a charger, and given to the damsel: and she brought it to her mother." The Pardoner, in Chaucer's "The Pardoner's Tale," attributes Herod's act to drunkenness.

> Herodes, whoso wel the stories soghte,
> Whan he of wyn was repleet at his feeste,
> Right at his owene table he yaf his heeste
> To sleen the Baptist John, ful gilteless.

In Shakespeare's *Antony and Cleopatra,* when Alexas says to Cleopatra, "Herod of Jewry dare not look upon you / But when you are well pleased," Cleopatra replies, "That Herod's head / I'll have: but how, when Antony is gone / Through whom I might command it?" In Browning's "Fra Lippo Lippi," the Prior condemns Fra Lippo Lippi's realistic painting on the cloister wall, saying "Give us no more body than shows soul."

> "Oh, that white smallish female with the breasts,
> She's just my niece . . . Herodias, I would say,—
> Who went and danced and got men's heads cut off!
> Have it all out!"

HERODIAS   *see HEROD ANTIPAS*

HEROD THE GREAT

Matt. 2:1–16

King Herod, ruler of the Jews from 37 to 4 B.C., was the fierce tyrant who, when he first heard of the birth of Jesus in Bethlehem sent the wise men to "search diligently for the young child . . . that I may come and worship him also." When the wise men failed to return, Herod was "exceeding wroth, and sent forth, and slew all the children that were in Bethlehem, and in all the coasts thereof, from two years old and under . . . ." This act is known as the slaughter, or massacre, of the innocents. Herod was played in the medieval mystery plays as a roaring ranter; hence the expression to "out-herod Herod," as in Shakespeare's *Hamlet.* Hamlet advises the players to use restraint: "O, it offends me to the soul to hear a robustious periwig pated fellow tear a passion to tatters . . . to split the ears of the groundlings . . . it out-herods Herod . . . ." Herod's first impulse to worship the child is probably alluded to when Charmian, in Shakespeare's *Antony and Cleopatra,* asks the Soothsayer to tell her fortune. "Good now, some excellent fortune! . . . let me have a child at fifty, to whom Herod of Jewry may do homage." In Shakespeare's *Henry V,* Henry threatens the destruction of Harfleur: surrender or you will see

> Your naked infants spitted upon pikes,
> Whiles the mad mothers with their howls confused
> Do break the clouds, as did the wives of Jewry
> At Herod's bloody-hunting slaughtermen.

In Melville's *Moby Dick,* the sailors are transfixed passing some

rocky islands and hearing cries "so plaintively wild and un-
earthly—like half-articulated wailings of the ghosts of all
Herod's murdered Innocents." In Mark Twain's *Tom Sawyer,*
Tom got Ben Rogers to whitewash the fence for him. As Ben
"worked and sweated in the sun, the retired artist sat on a barrel
in the shade close by, dangled his legs, munched his apple, and
planned the slaughter of more innocents."

HEWERS OF WOOD AND DRAWERS OF WATER

Josh. 9:3–27 When Joshua was conquering Canaan, the crafty Gibeonites,
posing as people from a far country, made a league of peace
with Joshua. When the ruse was discovered, "that they were
neighbors, and that they dwelt among them," Joshua spoke
unto them, saying, "Now therefore ye are cursed, and there
shall none of you be freed from being bondmen, and hewers
of wood and drawers of water for the house of my God." In
"The Knight's Tale," Chaucer said of Arcite when he became
page with Emily's chamberlain, "Well konde he hewen wode,
and water bere, / For he was young and myghty for the
nones . . . ." In "The Hind and the Panther," Dryden tells a
fable of the "Swifts," "the giants of the swallow kind, / Large-
limb'd, stout-hearted, but of stupid mind, / For Swisses, or for
Gibeonites design'd." Carlyle, in "Boswell's Life of Johnson,"
said that Johnson was a giant worker: "With giant's force he
toils, since such is his appointment, were it but at hewing of
wood and drawing of water."

HIDE HIS (YOUR) LIGHT UNDER A BUSHEL   *see LIGHT(CANDLE) UNDER A BUSHEL*

HINNOM, VALLEY OF   *see TOPHET(H)*

HIP AND THIGH   *see SMITE THEM HIP AND THIGH*

HOLOFERNES   *see JUDITH*

HOLY GRAIL   *see GRAIL*

HOLY GROUND   *see PUT OFF THY SHOES*

HOLY OF HOLIES

Exod. 26:31–34 This was "the most holy place," the sacred inner chamber of
the tabernacle in which was kept the ark of the testimony, or
ARK OF THE COVENANT. It is *sanctum sanctorum* in the Vulgate

version. In Carlyle's *Sartor Resartus,* Professor Teufelsdröckh tells of the profound influence made on him by his religious mother: "such things . . . reach inwards to the very core of your being; mysteriously does a Holy of Holies build itself into visibility in the mysterious deeps . . . ." In "Life without Principle," Thoreau said that men admit much rubbish to their minds. "Think of admitting the details of a single case of the criminal court into our thoughts, to stalk profanely through their very *sanctum sanctorum* for an hour . . . ." In *Moby Dick,* when the harpooner Tashtego fell into the sperm whale's head, Melville said, "Now, had Tashtego perished in that head, it had been a very precious perishing; smothered in the very whitest and daintiest of fragrant spermaceti; coffined, hearsed, and tombed in the secret inner chamber and sanctum sanctorum of the whale."

HONEY OUT OF THE CARCASE OF THE LION   *see OUT OF THE EATER CAME FORTH MEAT*

HOPE AS AN ANCHOR

Heb. 6:19 Paul wrote to the Hebrews that in "hope we have as an anchor of the soul, both sure and steadfast . . . ." In *Hyperion,* Keats said of Asia, one of the fallen Titans at council:

> Even as Hope upon her anchor leans,
> So leant she, not so fair, upon a tusk
> Shed from the broadest of her elephants.

William Hazlitt, in "On Familiar Style," said that florid writers with their "gaudy style" used as their stock in trade "Personifications, capital letters, seas of sunbeams . . . Brittania with her shield, or Hope leaning on an anchor."

HOPE DEFERRED

Prov. 13:12 "Hope deferred maketh the heart sick: but when the desire cometh, it is a tree of life." Macaulay, in "Samuel Johnson," said that Johnson's "roughness and violence which he showed in society" were the result of many bitter calamities and deprivations which he had suffered, "by that deferred hope which makes the heart sick." In Butler's *The Way of All Flesh,* as Ernest's friend was on his way to tell Theobald and Christina of Ernest's imprisonment, he recalled "Christina's long years of hope deferred that maketh the heart sick, before she was married . . . ."

HOREB, MOUNT   *see SINAI*

HOREB, ROCK IN   *see SMITE THE ROCK*

HORNS OF THE ALTAR

Exod. 21:13–14;
27:2; I Kings
1:50–53; 2:28–29

The altar of the burnt offerings in the Tabernacle and the Temple had four projections like horns at the corners. A criminal or fugitive found sanctuary by clinging to the horns of the altar. In *The English Mail-Coach,* De Quincey sees a vision of a woman: "Clinging to the horns of the altar, voiceless she stood —sinking, rising, raving, despairing." In *Ivanhoe,* Scott said, "Vows are the knots which tie us to Heaven—they are the cords which bind the sacrifice to the horns of the altar . . . ." And in "Massachusetts to Virginia," Whittier asked if Massachusetts must help recapture Virginia's fugitive slaves.

> We hunt your bondmen, flying from Slavery's hateful hell;
> Our voices, at your bidding, take up the bloodhound's yell;
> We gather, at your summons, above our fathers' graves,
> From Freedom's holy altar-horns to tear your wretched slaves.

HORNS OF MOSES   *see MOSES' FACE SHONE*

HOSEA

Book of Hosea

Hosea married an unfaithful wife, Gomer, who followed after lovers. In Hardy's *Tess of the D'Urbervilles,* Alec D'Urberville, having wronged her, proposes to Tess a second time: "The words of the stern prophet Hosea . . . come back to me . . . 'And she shall follow after her lover, but she shall not overtake him; and she shall seek him, but shall not find him; then shall she say, I will go and return to my first husband; for then was it better with me than now' " (Hos. 2:7). Alec changed the plural masculine pronouns to singular. Hosea, representing God, is merciful and forgiving; he suffers for Gomer, or Israel, and receives her back to their home. Hosea wrote, "For I desired mercy, and not sacrifice; and the knowledge of God more than burnt offerings." In "The Human Sacrifice," Whittier, attacking capital punishment, asks that God may enlighten the blind eye responsible for cruel hangings:

> Soften his hard, cold heart, and show
> The power which in forbearance lies,
> And let him feel that mercy now
> Is better than old sacrifice!

In the conclusion of Marc Connelly's *The Green Pastures,* God confers with Hezdrel, who is facing death fighting Herod. Hezdrel says he "ain't skeered" because he believes in the God of Hosea. God asks if he isn't the same as the God of Moses. "No," replies Hezdrel contemptuously. "Dat ol' God of wrath and vengeance? We have de God dat Hosea preached to us . . . . De God of Mercy . . . he ain't a fearsome God no mo." God then asks Hezdrel how Hosea found that mercy. "De only way he could find it . . . Through sufferin'."

HOUSE DIVIDED AGAINST ITSELF

Matt. 12:22–25

When the Pharisees heard that Jesus healed "one possessed with a devil, blind, and dumb" they said, "This fellow doth not cast out devils, but by Beelzebub the prince of the devils. And Jesus knew their thoughts, and said unto them, Every kingdom divided against itself is brought to desolation; and every city or house divided against itself shall not stand." Good is not likely to come out of evil, nor evil out of good. In Shakespeare's *Richard II*, when the Bishop of Carlisle hears of Richard's abdication, he prophesies the division that will ultimately lead to the Wars of the Roses:

> Oh, if you raise this house against this house,
> It will the woefulest division prove
> That ever fell upon this cursed earth.

In "A Plea for Captain John Brown," Thoreau spoke of the division among the Northerners themselves over the slavery question: "Our foes are in our midst and all about us. There is hardly a house but is divided against itself, for our foe is all but the universal woodenness of both head and heart."

HOUSE IN BETHANY

Matt. 26:6–13; John 12:1–8

When Jesus was in the house of Simon the leper in Bethany, Mary took "a pound of ointment of spikenard, very costly, and anointed the feet of Jesus, and wiped his feet with her hair: and the house was filled with the odour of the ointment." In "The Ballad of Reading Gaol," Oscar Wilde wrote:

> And every human heart that breaks,
> In prison cell or yard,
> Is as that broken box that gave
> Its treasure to the Lord,
> And filled the unclean leper's house
> With the scent of costliest nard.

Walter Pater, in "The Child in the House" in *Miscellaneous Studies*, wrote of the deep religious impressions made upon him during childhood. "Sentiment, congruous . . . only with . . . the deep, effusive unction of the House of Bethany, was assumed as the due attitude for the reception of our every-day existence."

HOUSE NOT MADE WITH HANDS

II Cor. 5:1   Paul wrote to the Corinthians contrasting our earthly with our heavenly house. "For we know that if our earthly house of this tabernacle were dissolved, we have a building of God, an house not made with hands, eternal in the heavens." Coleridge, in "Youth and Age," thinks of his body now and in youth:

> *When* I was young?—Ah, woful When!
> Ah! for the change 'twixt Now and Then!
> This breathing house not built with hands . . . .

Browning, in "By the Fire-Side," wonders about the future of his happy marriage:

> When earth breaks up and heaven expands,
> How will the change strike me and you
> In the house not made with hands?

And, in "Milton," Macaulay said, in praise of the Puritans, "Their palaces were houses not made with hands."

HOUSE OF GOD

Gen. 28:17   When Jacob awoke from his dream of the ladder (see JACOB's LADDER), he was afraid and said, "How dreadful is this place! this is none other but the house of God, and this is the Gate of Heaven." He took the stones he had used for his pillow and set up a pillar, "And he called the name of that place Bethel." Bethel means "house of God," and the phrase became common in the Bible. In *Areopagitica*, Milton, defending sects and schisms, said, ". . . there must be many schisms and many dissections made in the quarry and in the timber ere the house of God can be built." Cotton Mather, in "The Life of John Eliot," said that "his family was a little *Bethel*, for the Worship of God constantly and exactly maintained in it." James R. Lowell, in "The Cathedral," said:

> Let us be thankful when, as I do here,
> We can read Bethel on a pile of stones,
> And, seeing where God *has* been, trust in Him.

HOUSE OF MANY MANSIONS   *see MANY MANSIONS*

HOUSE OF PRAYER   *see DEN OF THIEVES*

HOUSE OF RIMMON   *see RIMMON*

HOW ARE THE MIGHTY FALLEN

II Sam. 1:19, 25, 27

This is the refrain in David's lament for the deaths of Saul and Jonathan. "The beauty of Israel is slain upon thy high places: how are the mighty fallen!" When Tess's humble father, in Hardy's *Tess of the D'Urbervilles*, learning of his descent from an ancient family, asks the parson what he should do about it, the latter replies, "O—nothing, nothing; except chasten yourself with the thought of 'how are the mighty fallen.' " In Somerset Maugham's *Of Human Bondage*, Philip comments on Thorpe Athelny's unusual name. Mr. Athelny replies, "It's a very old Yorkshire name. Once it took the head of my family a day's hard riding to make the circuit of his estates, but the mighty are fallen. Fast women and slow horses."

HOWLING WILDERNESS

Deut. 32:10

Moses, praising the Lord, recalled the days of old when he found Jacob "in a desert land, and in the waste howling wilderness; he led him about, he instructed him, he kept him as the apple of his eye." In *Vanity Fair*, Thackeray defended Becky Sharp's "much talked-of parties," saying that "if every person is to be banished from society who runs into debt and cannot pay —if we are to be peering into everybody's private life . . . why, what a howling wilderness and intolerable dwelling Vanity Fair would be." In Carlyle's *Sartor Resartus*, Professor Teufelsdröckh told of educating himself in poverty outside the university; it was a wild desert, a "waste, and howling with savage monsters." And in *The Maine Woods*, Thoreau said, "Generally speaking, a howling wilderness does not howl; it is the imagination of the traveller that does the howling."

HOW LONG, O LORD?   *see LORD, HOW LONG?*

I AM THAT I AM

Exod. 3:14

When God spoke to Moses from the BURNING BUSH appointing him to deliver Israel from Egyptian bondage, Moses asked his name. "And God said unto Moses, I AM THAT I AM: and he said, Thus shalt thou say unto the children of Israel, I AM hath sent me unto you." The Hebrew name for God YHVH, from which "Jehovah" comes, is related to the verb "to be," *hayah*. Lowell, in "New England Two Centuries Ago," said that Puritanism lost its religious passion after the death of Cromwell, becoming more a matter of forms: "Become traditional, repeating the phrase without the spirit, reading the present backward as if it were written in Hebrew, translating Jehovah by 'I was' instead of 'I am,'—it was no more like its former self . . . ." In Byron's *Don Juan*, Donna Inez, Juan's mother, asserts that there is an analogy between the English and Hebrew languages: " 'Tis strange—the Hebrew noun which means 'I am,' / The English always use to govern d—n."

ICHABOD

I Sam. 4:21

When Phineas's wife, who "was with child, near to be delivered," heard that the Philistines had captured the ark of God, and that Phineas and her father-in-law were dead, she gave birth to a son. "And she named the child Ichabod, saying, The glory is departed from Israel: because the ark of God was taken . . . ." The name means "inglorious." Washington Irving said of his ungainly hero in "The Legend of Sleepy Hollow" that "the cognomen of Crane was not inapplicable to his person." So perhaps the given name "Ichabod." Whittier's poem "Ichabod," attacking Daniel Webster for his speech favoring the Fugitive Slave Law, begins: "So fallen! so lost! the light withdrawn / Which once he wore! / The glory from his grey hairs gone / Forevermore." Thomas Henry Huxley, in "A Liberal Education," said that some people "declare that ignorance makes bad workmen; that England will soon be unable to turn out cotton goods . . . cheaper than other people; and then, Ichabod! Ichabod! the glory will be departed from us."

IF ANY WOULD NOT WORK, NEITHER SHOULD HE EAT

II Thess. 3:10

Paul wrote to the Thessalonians, reminding them how, when he had visited them before, he had worked for his bread with them: "For even when we were with you, this we commanded you, that if any would not work, neither should he eat." In *Sesame and Lilies*, Ruskin said that our duty is in part to feed people. "It is quite true, infallibly true, that if any man will not work, neither should he eat—think of that, and every time you sit down to your dinner, ladies and gentlemen, say solemnly, before you ask a blessing, 'How much work have I done today for my dinner?' " In "Compensation," Emerson said, "All things are double, one against another.—Tit for tat . . . . Who doth not work shall not eat."

IF THY RIGHT HAND (EYE) OFFEND THEE

Matt. 5:29–30

In the Sermon on the Mount, Jesus said, "And if thy right eye offend thee, pluck it out, and cast it from thee . . . . And if thy right hand offend thee, cut it off, and cast it from thee; for it is profitable for thee that one of thy members should perish, and not that thy whole body should be cast into hell." In Shakespeare's *Richard II* the Duke of York opposes Bolingbroke, pardoning his treacherous son Aumerle:

> If thou do pardon, whosoever pray,
> More sins for this forgiveness prosper may.
> This fester'd joint cut off, the rest rest sound;
> This let alone will all the rest confound.

In the following complete poem of eight lines from "A Shropshire Lad," A. E. Housman writes on being stoical in meeting troubles.

> If it chance your eye offend you,
>   Pluck it out, lad, and be sound:
> 'Twill hurt, but here are salves to friend you,
>   And many a balsam grows on ground!
>
> And if your hand or foot offend you,
>   Cut it off, lad, and be whole;
> But play the man, stand up and end you,
>   When your sickness is your soul.°

IN ALL HIS GLORY   *see LILIES OF THE FIELD*

IN HIS OWN IMAGE

Gen. 1:26–27   The creation of man in the first chapter of Genesis: "And God said, Let us make man in our image, after our likeness . . . . So God created man in his own image, in the image of God created he him; male and female created he them." In Milton's *Paradise Lost*, the angel Raphael tells Adam of the creation: God said, "Let us make now Man in our image, Man / In our similitude . . . ." Gerard M. Hopkins, in "Nondum," writes of man's longing to see God:

> We guess; we clothe Thee, unseen King,
>   With attributes we deem are meet;
> Each in his own imagining
>   Sets up a shadow in Thy seat . . . .†

And Santayana, in "On My Friendly Critics," said, "My atheism, like that of Spinoza, is true piety towards the universe and

---

°From "A Shropshire Lad"—Authorized Edition—from *The Collected Poems of A. E. Housman*. Copyright 1940 by Holt, Rinehart and Winston, Inc. Reprinted by permission of Holt, Rinehart and Winston, Inc., The Society of Authors, and Jonathan Cape, Ltd.

†From *Poems of Gerard Manley Hopkins*, W. H. Gardner, ed. (New York, Oxford University Press, Inc.). Copyright 1948 by Oxford University Press, Inc.

denies only gods fashioned by men in their own image, to be servants of their human interests."

IN MY FATHER'S HOUSE   *see MANY MANSIONS*

IN OUR LAND   *see VOICE OF THE TURTLE*

IN PRINCIPIO   *see IN THE BEGINNING*

IN SPIRIT AND IN TRUTH   *see SAMARITAN WOMAN*

IN THE BEGINNING

Gen. 1:1; John 1:1 The Bible begins with the Hymn of Creation: "In the beginning God created the heaven and the earth." Saint John begins: "In the beginning was the Word, and the Word was with God, and the Word was God." In *Beowulf*, at King Hrothgar's court there were the sound of harp and the song of the minstrel: "He who could tell of men's beginning from olden time spoke of how the Almighty wrought the world . . . ." * In the Prologue to *The Canterbury Tales*, Chaucer said the Friar

> was the beste beggere in his hous;
> For though a widwe hadde noght a sho,
> So plesaunt was his *In principio*
> Yet wolde he have a ferthing er he wente. . .

This referred to the practice of medieval friars repeating *In principio erat verbum* as they visited from house to house. In Chaucer's "The Nun's Priest's Tale," Chauntecleer praises his wife Pertelote's beauty, declaring that everything he says is true:

> For al so siker as *In principio*,
> *Mulier est hominis confusio,*—
> Madame, the sentence of this Latyn is,
> "Womman is mannes joye and al his blis."

In *Sartor Resartus* Carlyle's Professor Teufelsdröckh says that all men, like Adam, are subject to temptation: "Life is warfare between necessity and freedom; in the beginning, especially, a hard-fought battle."

INNOCENT AS DOVES   *see WISE AS SERPENTS, AND HARMLESS AS DOVES*

---

*From the Everyman edition of *Anglo Saxon Poetry*. Translation by R. K. Gordon.

IRON DID SWIM   *see ELISHA*

ISAAC

Gen. 21:1–8;
22:1–14

When Isaac, meaning "he shall laugh," was born to Abraham and Sarah, she gave him the name because, being ninety-one, as she said, "God hath made me to laugh, so that all that hear will laugh with me." Abraham was one hundred. God tested Abraham by commanding him to sacrifice Isaac as a burnt offering, long a Canaanite practice. As "Abraham stretched forth his hand, and took the knife to slay his son," the voice of an angel from heaven commanded him to stop. Then Abraham "lifted up his eyes, and looked, and behold behind him a ram caught in a thicket by his horns: and Abraham took the ram, and offered him up for a burnt offering in the stead of his son." In Fielding's *Joseph Andrews*, Mr. Adams the parson tells Joseph that love should be subservient to duty. "Had Abraham so loved his son Isaac as to refuse the sacrifice required, is there any of us who would not condemn him?" Whittier concludes "The Human Sacrifice," a protest against capital punishment, with:

> My brother man, Beware!
> With that deep voice, which from the skies
> Forbade the Patriarch's sacrifice,
> God's angel cries, Forbear!

In *Billy Budd*, Melville said that when the stern Captain Vere told Billy of his death sentence for killing Claggart, he may "have caught Billy to his heart, even as Abraham may have caught young Isaac on the brink of resolutely offering him up in obedience to the exacting behest." And in Butler's *The Way of All Flesh*, when Ernest's friend told him of his inheritance, noting that Ernest could not tell his father and mother, who would suffer because they had not received it, Ernest replied, "No, no, no, it would be too cruel; it would be like Isaac offering up Abraham and no thicket with a ram in it near at hand."

ISCARIOT   *see JUDAS ISCARIOT*

ISHMAEL

Gen. 16,
17:23–26;
21:9–21

Convinced that she could bear no children, Sarai (Sarah) asked Abraham to go in unto Hagar, her maid, so that Sarai might obtain children. But Sarai later became jealous and persecuted Hagar; and when Isaac was born to Sarai, Abraham, at Sarai's request, drove Hagar away with her son Ishmael. An angel told Hagar that Ishmael "will be a wild man; his hand will be against every man, and every man's hand against him." And "God was with the lad; and he grew, and dwelt in the wilderness, and became an archer." In "The Two Races of Men," Charles Lamb told about Ralph Bigod, Esq., a prodigious borrower and lender, who knew how to lose his money in many ways: ". . . out away from him it must go peremptorily, as Hagar's offspring into the wilderness." Samuel Butler, in *The Way of All Flesh*, said of Dr. Skinner, the stern schoolmaster, that "his hand was very properly a heavy one. His hand was against them [his students], and theirs was against him." Hardy, in *The Return of the Native*, said of Egdon Heath, the "furzy, briary wilderness" home of Eustacia Vye, who felt herself to be cast out of civilization, that it was an "untameable Ishmaelitish thing . . . . Civilization was its enemy." Melville's narrator in *Moby Dick* is Ishmael, who escapes from civilization by going whaling. D. H. Lawrence, in *Studies in Classic American Literature*, calls him "Ishmael the hunted. But much more, Ishmael the hunter."

ISRAEL   see *JACOB WRESTLES WITH AN ANGEL*

IT WAS GOOD

Gen. 1:4, 12, 18, 21, 25, 31

When God created light on the first day, he "saw the light, that it was good." On the third day, God created the dry land, Earth, and the Seas, "And God saw that it was good." And so on through the six days of creation. On the sixth day, when God created man, "behold, it was very good." In "The Uses of Great Men," Emerson said that if we are sensitive to elemental things, "light and darkness, heat and cold . . . sweet and sour," they will "circle us round in a wreath of pleasures . . . . The eye repeats every day the finest eulogy on things—'He saw that they were good.'" And in "Self-Reliance," Emerson said that "prayer is the contemplation of the facts of life from the highest point of view . . . . It is the spirit of God pronouncing his works good." In "The Number of Two," Robert Herrick said,

> God hates the Duall number . . .
> And when He blest each sev'rall Day, whereon
> He did his curious operation;
> Tis never read there (as the Fathers say)
> God blest His work done on the second day:
> Wherefore two prayers ought not to be said,
> Or by our selves, or from the Pulpit read.

And in *The Stones of Venice*, Ruskin said that man must confess in his architecture to imperfection. Only God's work achieves perfection; ". . . ours may never have that sentence written upon it,—'And behold, it was very good.'"

I WAS A STRANGER   *see STRANGER, AND YE TOOK ME IN*

JABAL   *see TUBAL-CAIN*

JACOB AND LABAN

(lā'băn)

Gen. 30:25–43

When it was time for Jacob to return home with his two wives, Leah and Rachel, he agreed with Laban, his father-in-law, to take "all the speckled and spotted cattle" and goats as his share. Then "Jacob took him rods of green poplar . . . and pilled white strakes in them . . . ." And when the flocks came in to the watering troughs to drink, Jacob held the rods before the stronger cattle. "And the flocks conceived before the rods, and brought forth cattle ringstraked, speckled, and spotted." So "the feebler were Laban's, and the stronger Jacob's. And the man increased exceedingly, and had much cattle . . . ." In *The Merchant of Venice*, Shakespeare, probably using the Bishops' Bible, has Shylock tell the story to justify his lending principles.

> Mark what Jacob did.
> When Laban and himself were compromis'd
> That all the eanlings which were streak'd and pied
> Should fall as Jacob's hire, the ewes, being rank,
> In the end of autumn turned to the rams,
> And, when the work of generation was
> Between these wooly breeders in the act,
> The skilful shepherd pill'd certain wands
> And, in the doing of the deed of kind,
> He stuck them up before the fulsome ewes,
> Who then conceiving did in eaning time
> Fall parti-colour'd lambs, and those were Jacob's.
> This was a way to thrive, and he was blest;
> And thrift is blessing, if men steal it not.

In "Sleep and Poetry," Keats attacked the mechanical aspects of eighteenth-century poetry: "ye taught a school / Of dolts to smooth, inlay, and clip, and fit, / Till, like the certain wands of Jacob's wit, / Their verses tallied." In *Captain Stormfield's Visit to Heaven*, Mark Twain said the young saints "wear wings all the time—blazing red ones, and blue and green, and gold, and variegated, and rain-bowed, and ring-streaked-and-striped—and nobody finds fault."

JACOB, LEAH, AND RACHEL

Gen. 29:15–30

Jacob loved Rachel and agreed to serve Laban her father seven years to win her. Rachel's elder sister "Leah was tender eyed; but Rachel was beautiful and well favored." On the wedding night, according to custom, Laban brought the veiled bride to Jacob's tent. "And it came to pass, that in the morning, behold, it was Leah . . . ." Laban said it was not the custom in his country "to give the younger before the firstborn." So Jacob, loving "Rachel more than Leah . . . served with him yet seven other years." In Hardy's *Far from the Madding Crowd*, Boldwood, in love with Bathsheba, is told by her maid Liddy that Bathsheba might marry six years later; he thinks, "Jacob had served twice seven for Rachel: what were six for such a woman as this?" In *Tess of the D'Urbervilles*, Angel Clare, in love with Tess, carried her three dairymaid friends across a flooded road. Then finally taking Tess in his arms, he whispered in her ear, "Three Leahs to get one Rachel."

JACOB'S LADDER

Gen. 28:10–19

When Jacob was traveling to Padan-Aram [pā′dăn], to escape Esau's fury and to get a wife, he slept one night. "And he dreamed, and behold a ladder set up on earth, and the top of it reached to heaven: and behold the angels of God ascending and descending on it." Awaking, he cried, ". . . this is none other but the house of god, and this is the gate of heaven." The "city was called Luz at the first," but "he called the name of that place Bethel . . . ." In Milton's *Paradise Lost*, Satan arrives at the Gate of Heaven, approached by stairs.

> The stairs were such as whereon Jacob saw
> Angels ascending and descending, bands
> Of Guardians bright, when he from Esau fled
> To Padan-Aram in the field of Luz,
> Dreaming by night under the open Skie,
> And waking cri'd, This is the Gate of Heav'n.

Thomas de Quincey, in "Literature of Knowledge and Literature of Power," said that what you owe to Milton is not knowledge, but power, "that is, exercise and expansion to your own latent capacity of sympathy with the infinite, where every pulse and each separate influx is a step upwards, a step ascending as upon a Jacob's ladder from earth to mysterious altitudes above the earth."

JACOB'S RODS, WANDS   *see JACOB AND LABAN*

JACOB WRESTLES WITH AN ANGEL

Gen. 32:24–32

One night as Jacob was returning home after serving Laban, he "wrestled a man with him until the breaking of day." The man asked to be let go "for the day breaketh," but Jacob would not let him go until he blessed Jacob. So he did, and changed Jacob's name to Israel, meaning, probably, "May God strive, contend, or rule." It was an angel of God, and "Jacob called the name of the place Peniel [pê·nī′ĕl, meaning "face of God"]: for I have seen God face to face . . . ." Izaak Walton, in *The Life of Dr. John Donne,* said that Donne doubted his qualifications for the clergy. "But God who is able to prevail wrestled with him, as the angel did with Jacob, and marked him . . . for his own . . . with a blessing of obedience to the motions of his blessed Spirit." Emily Dickinson told the story in her own way:

> A Little over Jordan,
> As Genesis record,
> An Angel and a Wrestler
> Did wrestle long and hard.

> Till, morning touching mountain,
> And Jacob waxing strong,
> The Angel begged permission
> To breakfast and return.

> "Not so," quoth wily Jacob,
> And girt his loins anew,
> "Until thou bless me, stranger!"
> The which acceded to:

> Light swung the silver fleeces
> Peniel hills among,
> And the astonished Wrestler
> Found he had worsted God!°

JAEL
(jā′ĕl)

Judg. 4, 5

Jael, meaning "wild goat," was the wife of Heber the Kenite. Defeated in battle against Deborah and Barak, Sisera, captain of the Canaanite army, "fled away on his feet to the tent of Jael the wife of Heber the Kenite." She gave him milk and a cover to sleep. "Then Jael Heber's wife took a nail of the tent [a tent peg], and took an hammer in her hand, and went softly unto him, and smote the nail into his temples, and fastened it into the ground: for he was fast asleep and weary. So he died." In Chaucer's "The Wife of Bath's Prologue," Jankyn, the fifth husband of the Wife of Bath, lectured her about treacherous wives: "And somme han dryve nayles in hir brayne, / While that they slepte, and thus they han hem slayne." Caliban, in Shakespeare's *The Tempest,* urges Stephano to make himself lord of Prospero's island: "Yea, yea, my lord. I'll yield him thee asleep, / Where thou mayst knock a nail into his head."

°From *Poems by Emily Dickinson* by Emily Dickinson, by permission of Little, Brown and Co. Copyright 1914, 1942 by Martha Dickinson Bianchi.

And Delilah, in Milton's *Samson Agonistes*, spurned by the blinded Samson, says that some day she shall become famous.

> Not less renown'd then in Mount Ephraim,
> Jael, who with inhospitable guile
> Smote Sisera sleeping through the Temples nail'd.

JAWBONE OF AN ASS

Judg. 15:15–17 The men of Judah delivered Samson to the Philistines with his arms bound with cords. He burst the cords, "found a new jawbone of an ass, and put forth his hand, and took it, and slew a thousand men therewith. And Samson said, With the jawbone of an ass, heaps upon heaps, with the jawbone of an ass have I slain a thousand men." This poem is attributed to Benjamin Franklin:

> Jack, eating rotten cheese, did say,
> Like Samson, I my thousands slay;
> I vow, quoth Roger, so you do.
> And with the self-same weapon too.

In Christopher Fry's *The Lady's Not for Burning*, Thomas, wanting to be hanged but thwarted when Jennet faints, says, "Oh, the delicate mistiming of women! She has carefully / Snapped in half my jawbone of an ass."

JEALOUS GOD   *see SINS OF THE FATHERS*

JEHU As Jehu, a commander, approached the palace of King Jehoram
(jē′hu) (Joram) intent upon killing the king, the watchman said that a
messenger's "driving is like the driving of Jehu the son of
II Kings 9:20 Nimshi; for he driveth furiously." In *Eikonoklastes*, Milton said that Charles II "forced the parliament to drive like Jehu." Dryden, in "The Medal," attacks the Earl of Shaftesbury as a fomenter of rebellion against monarchy:

> But this new Jehu spurs the hot-mouth'd horse;
> Instructs the beast to know his native force,
> To take the bit between his teeth, and fly
> To the next headlong step of anarchy.

In Galsworthy's *Over the River*, young Croom, driving "his old but newly-acquired two-seater," tells Clare he can make the long trip ahead: "I shall drive like Jehu. It's a good anodyne."

JEPHTHA'S DAUGHTER

Judg. 11:29–40

Jephtha, having agreed to lead the Israelites against the invading Ammonites, vowed to the Lord that if he would give him victory, then "whatsoever cometh forth of the doors of my house to meet me, when I return in peace from the children of Ammon, shall surely be the Lord's, and I will offer it up for a burnt offering." Returning victorious, Jephtha came "unto his house, and, behold, his daughter came out to meet him with timbrels and dances: and she was his only child . . . ." Before she was sacrificed, Jephtha's daughter asked her father, ". . . let me alone two months, that I may go up and down upon the mountains, and bewail my virginity, I and my fellows." Done, she returned to her father, "who did with her according to his vow which he had vowed: and she knew no man." In Chaucer's "The Physician's Tale," Virginius's daughter, facing a similar situation, pleads with her father:

> "Thanne yif me leyser, fader myn," quod she,
> "My deeth for to compleyne a litel space;
> For, pardee, Jepte yaf his doghter grace
> For to compleyne, er he hir slow, allas!
> And, God it woot, no thyng was hir trespas,
> But for she ran hir fader first to see,
> To welcome hym with greet solempnitee."

She fell into a swoon, then recovered, saying,

> "Blissed be God, that I shal dye a mayde!
> Yif me my deeth, er that I have a shame;
> Dooth with youre child youre wyl, a Goddes name!"

In *Hamlet,* Hamlet, feigning madness, addresses Polonius:

HAM. O Jephtha, judge of Israel, what a treasure hadst thou!
POL. What a treasure had he, my lord?
HAM. Why,
  "One fair daughter, and no more,
    The which he loved passing well."
POL. [*Aside*] Still on my daughter.
HAM. Am I not i' the right, old Jephtha?

And in "Mackery End, in Hertfordshire," Lamb wrote of himself and his sister housing together, "old bachelor and maid, in a sort of double singleness; with such tolerable comfort . . . that I, for one, find in myself no sort of disposition to go out upon the mountains, with the rash king's offspring, to bewail my celibacy."

JERICHO

Joshua 6

Under Joshua's command the armed men and seven priests, blowing trumpets of rams' horns and carrying the ark of the covenant, circled Jericho for seven days. On the seventh day, according to Joshua's directions, "when the people heard the sound of the trumpet, and the people shouted with a great shout, that the wall fell down flat, so that the people went up into the city, every man straight before him, and they took the city." In "Christ's Hospital Five and Thirty Years Ago," Charles Lamb told about a boy who smuggled a girl into his dormitory "for better than a week." But he couldn't keep a secret: suddenly he shouted "his good fortune to the world below; and, laying out his simple throat, blew such a ram's-horn blast, as (toppling down the walls of his own Jericho) set concealment any longer at defiance." In "Science and Culture," Thomas H. Huxley said that those who proposed to introduce physical science into education were "excommunicated by the classical scholars in their capacity of Levites in charge of the ark of culture . . . . Certainly the time was that the Levites of culture would have sounded their trumpets against its walls as against an educational Jericho." In the Preface to *Saint Joan*, Shaw said that Joan "did not expect besieged cities to fall Jerichowise at the sound of her trumpet, but, like Wellington, adapted her methods of attack to the peculiarities of the defence."

JESUS, CRUCIFIXION

Matt. 27; Mark 15; Luke 23; John 19

"And when they were come to the place, which is called Calvary, there they crucified him, and the malefactors, one on the right hand, and the other on the left" (Luke 23:33). In Milton's *Paradise Lost*, the angel Michael tells Adam of Christ's future death. He will die to save mankind.

> For this he shall live hated, be blasphem'd,
> Seis'd on by force, jud'g, and to death condemnd
> A shameful and accurst, naild to the Cross
> By his own Nation, slain for bringing Life;

Thoreau, in "A Plea for Captain John Brown," asked, why hang the man "sent to be the redeemer of those in captivity . . . ? You who pretend to care for Christ crucified, consider what you are about to do to him who offered himself to be the saviour of four millions of men." A. E. Housman, in "Carpenter's Son," wrote of the carpenter's son about to be hanged. He might have stayed at home and followed his father's trade.

Fare you well, for ill fare I:
Live, lads, and I will die.

Here hang I, and right and left
Two poor fellows hang for theft:
All the same's the luck we prove,
Though the midmost hangs for love.°

JESUS, ENTRY INTO JERUSALEM

Matt. 21:1–10;
Mark 11:1–11;
John 12:12–15

Jesus, before His betrayal, made His "triumphal entry" into Jerusalem riding on an ass. When the people heard that He was coming, they "took branches of palm trees, and went forth to meet him, and cried, Hosanna: Blessed is the King of Israel that cometh in the name of the Lord." In Tennyson's *Enoch Arden,* Annie dreams of Enoch her lover, happy, sitting on a height and singing,

Hosanna in the highest; yonder shines
The Sun of Righteousness, and there be palms
Whereof the happy people strowing cried
"Hosanna in the highest!"

In *Nature,* Emerson said, "Nature is thoroughly mediate. It is made to serve. It receives the dominion of man as meekly as the ass on which the Savior rode."

JESUS, RESURRECTION

Matt. 28; Mark
16; Luke 24;
John 20

At "dawn toward the first day of the week, came Mary Magdalene [măg′·dà·lē′nê] and the other Mary to see the sepulchre. And, behold, there was a great earthquake: for the angel of the Lord descended from heaven, and came and rolled back the stone from the door and sat upon it . . . . And the angel . . . said unto the women, Fear not ye: For I know that ye seek Jesus, which was crucified. He is not here: for he is risen, as he said . . . . And as they went to tell his disciples, behold, Jesus met them, saying, All hail. And they came and held him by the feet, and worshipped him" (Matt. 28:1–9). In Chaucer's "Tale of Melibeus," Prudence, when her husband Melibeus lectures her about woman's wickedness, replies, "And, sire, that ther hath been many a good womman, may lightly be preved . . . for the grete bountee that is in women, oure Lord Jhesu Christ, whan he was risen fro deeth to lyve,

°From "A Shropshire Lad"—Authorized Edition—from *The Collected Poems of A. E. Housman.* Copyright 1940 by Holt, Rinehart and Winston, Inc. Reprinted by permission of Holt, Rinehart and Winston, Inc., The Society of Authors, and Jonathan Cape, Ltd.

appeered rather to a woman than to his Apostles." In "Locksley Hall Sixty Years After," Tennyson advises young men, "Follow Light, and do Right—for man can half-control his doom— / Till you find the deathless Angel seated in the vacant tomb." In Butler's *The Way of All Flesh*, Ernest, as a young minister, tries to enlighten his skeptical neighbor Mr. Shaw, a tinker. At the latter's request, Ernest tells him the story of the Resurrection as told in St. John's Gospel. "I am sorry to say that Ernest mixed up the four accounts in a deplorable manner; he even made the angel come down and roll away the stone and sit upon it. He was covered with confusion when the tinker first told him without the book of some of his many inaccuracies, and then verified his criticisms by referring to the New Testament itself." In "Don'ts," D. H. Lawrence advises, ". . . Don't be a good little, good little boy / being as good as you can . . ."*

> A little fresh air in the money sty,
> knocked a little hole in the holy prison,
> done your own little bit, made your own little try
> that the risen Christ should be risen.

JESUS, TEMPTATION

Matt. 4:1–11;
Mark 1:12–13;
Luke 4:1–13

Jesus, after fasting forty days and forty nights in the wilderness, was tempted by the devil in various ways. For one, the devil took "him up into an exceeding high mountain," and offered him "all the kingdoms of the world." But Jesus said, "Get thee hence, Satan: for it is written, Thou shalt worship the Lord thy God, and him only shalt thou serve. Then the devil leaveth him . . . ." Milton's *Paradise Regained* is the supreme poetic version of this story in English literature. In Carlyle's *Sartor Resartus*, "The Everlasting Yea" begins with Professor Teufelsdröckh exclaiming, "Temptations in the Wilderness! . . . Have we not all to be tried with such?" It continues, "Our wilderness is the wide World in an Atheistic Century; our Forty Days are long years of suffering and fasting: nevertheless, to these also comes an end." In Somerset Maugham's *Of Human Bondage*, Philip felt a "wild exhilaration" looking down from a hill above Heidelberg. "Philip, as he stood there . . . thought how the tempter had stood with Jesus on a high mountain and shown him the kingdoms of the earth. To Philip, intoxicated with the beauty of the scene, it seemed that it was the whole world which was spread before him, and he was eager to step down and enjoy it. He was free from degrading fears and free from prejudice . . . . He was his own master at last. From old habit, unconsciously he thanked God that he no longer believed in Him."

JESUS, WALKING ON THE WATER

Matt. 14:25;
Mark 6:48; John
6:19

The disciples on a ship in the Sea of Galilee, called also Gennesaret, were "tossed with waves: for the wind was contrary. And in the fourth watch of the night Jesus went unto them, walking on the sea." Peter also walked on the water at Jesus' bidding, but he was afraid, until Jesus "stretched forth his hand, and caught him . . . ." The wind ceased, and then they "worshipped him, saying, Of a truth thou art the Son of God." In "Lycidas," Milton writes of the union of Lycidas' soul with God. "So Lycidas sunk low, but mounted high, / Through the dear might of him that walked the waves / . . . ." Francis Thompson, in "The Kingdom of God," spoke of God's presence here and now.

> Yea, in the night, my Soul, my daughter,
> Cry,—clinging Heaven by the hems;
> And lo, Christ walking on the water
> Not of Gennesareth, but of Thames!

And in Whittier's "Abraham Davenport," after the great dark day of 1870, the moon suddenly appeared. Over the ocean gleamed

> a line of light,
> Such as of old with solemn awe,
> The fishers by Gennesaret saw,
> When dry-shod o'er it walked the Son of God,
> Tracking the waves with light wher'er his sandals trod.

JEWISH HERCULES   *see SAMSON*

JEZEBEL

I Kings 16:31;
18:4, 13, 19;
21:1–25; II Kings
9:7–37

Jezebel, daughter of the King of Tyre and wife of King AHAB, brought the worship of Baal and Astarte to Ahab and the Israelites. She was denounced by the Hebrew prophets and by ELIJAH, who defeated her prophets in the contest on Mount Carmel. When Naboth refused to part with his vineyard which Ahab wanted, Jezebel sent "two men, sons of Belial . . . to bear witness against him saying, Thou didst blaspheme God and the king." Naboth was then stoned to death, and Elijah denounced Jezebel, saying, "The dogs shall eat Jezebel by the

wall of Jezreel." When King JEHU found Jezebel flirting at
him from her window in Jezreel, he ordered her thrown down:
"and some of her blood was sprinkled on the wall, and on
the horses: and he trod her under foot." And when "they
went to bury her . . . they found no more of her than the
skull, and the feet, and the palms of her hands," for the dogs
did eat the flesh of Jezebel. In Shakespeare's *Twelfth Night,*
Sir Andrew Aguecheek says, somewhat faultily, of Malvolio,
"Fie on him Jezebel!" In *An Apology for Smectymnuus,* Milton
defends himself against personal attacks: ". . . this loose railer
. . . like a son of Belial, without the hire of Jezebel, charges
me 'of blaspheming God and the king . . . .' " And in *Eikonoklastes,* Milton attacked the illegal actions of the king "especially to get vast sums of money . . . the seizing not of one
Naboth's vineyard, but of whole inheritances . . . ." F. R.
Higgins wrote about Queen Jezebel in "Song for the Clatter-
Bones":

> King Jehu he drove to her,
> She tipped him a fancy beck;
> But he from his knacky side-car spoke,
> "Who'll break that dewlapped neck?"
> And so she was thrown from the window;
> Like Lucifer she fell
> Beneath the feet of the horses and they beat
> The light out of Jezebel.

JOB

Book of Job

"There was a man in the land of Uz, whose name was Job;
and that man was perfect and upright, and one that feared
God, and eschewed evil." In order to test his loyalty, God permitted Satan to afflict Job with much suffering. Job's patience
and steadfastness were rewarded finally with prosperity and
happiness. In Chaucer's "The Clerk's Tale" of patient Griselda
are parallels to Job. She was a flower of wifely patience.

> Men speke of Job, and moost for his humblesse,
> As clerkes, whan hem list, konne wel endite,
> Namely of men, but as in soothfastnesse
> Though clerkes preise wommen but a lite,
> Ther kan no man in humblesse him acquite
> As womman kan, ne kan been half so trewe
> As wommen been, but it be falle of newe.

The Wife of Bath, in her Prologue told how she always got
her way with an old husband. She would say, when he became
enraged,

> Com neer, my spouse, lat me ba thy cheke!
> Ye sholde been al pacient and meke,
> And han a sweete spiced conscience,
> Sith ye so preche of Jobes pacience.
> Suffereth alwey, syn ye so wel kan preche.

In Shakespeare's *Othello*, when Othello accuses Desdemona of falseness, he cries:

> Had it pleas'd Heaven
> To try me with affliction; had they rain'd
> All kind of sores and shames on my bare head,
> Steep'd me in poverty to the very lips . . .
> I should have found in some place of my soul
> A drop of patience.

In Shakespeare's *Henry IV, Part II,* when the Chief Justice threatens to become Falstaff's physician to cure him of "the disease of not listening," Falstaff replies, "I am as poor as Job, my lord, but not so patient. Your lordship may minister the potion of imprisonment to me in respect to poverty; but how I should be your patient to follow your prescriptions, the wise may make some dram of a scruple . . . ."

JOB'S COMFORTERS

Job 16:2

Job's friends, Eliphaz, Bildad, and Zophar, tried to explain Job's sufferings by saying, in effect, that his sins must have been the cause. Then the "perfect and upright Job" answered and said, "I have heard many such things: miserable comforters are ye all." In "Characteristics," Carlyle said that "Napoleon was but a Job's comforter, when he told his wounded Staff-officer, twice unhorsed by cannon-balls, and with half his limbs blown to pieces: 'Vous vous écoutez trop!' " In *Don Juan,* Byron wrote of friends "Consoling us with—'Would you had thought twice! / Ah! if you had but follow'd my advice!' "

> O Job! you had two friends: one's quite enough,
> Especially when we are ill at ease;
> They're but bad pilots when the weather's rough,
> Doctors less famous for their cures than fees.

JOB'S WIFE

Job 2:9, 10

When Satan "smote Job with sore boils from the sole of his foot unto his crown," his wife said unto him, "Dost thou still retain thine integrity? curse God, and die." When Falstaff is exposed for all his vices, at the end of Shakespeare's *The Merry Wives of Windsor,* Page declares that he is "as poor as Job," and Ford replies, "And as wicked as his wife." Robert

Burns, in "Address to the Deil," reminds the devil of the "spitefu joke" he played on Job: "While scabs and botches did him gall, / Wi bitter claw, / And lows'd his ill-tongu'd, wicked scaul, / Was warst ava." In "The Man Against the Sky," E. A. Robinson pictures the man who "seeing in death too small a thing to fear, / He may go forward like a stoic Roman / Where pangs and terrors in his pathway lie— / Or, seizing the swift logic of a woman, / Curse God and die." *

JOHN OF PATMOS

(păt′mŏs)

Rev. 1:9

John of Patmos, or Saint John the Divine, was the author of the book of Revelation, or the Apocalypse. It was written on the penal island of Patmos in the Aegean Sea, where John had been banished, perhaps during the reign of Domitian, about A.D. 95. The island scene provided much imagery for John's visions of the NEW JERUSALEM, the Lamb of God, the fall of BABYLON, and JUDGMENT DAY. In Chaucer's "The Prioress's Tale," the Prioress says of the slain Christian child (Rev. 14:1–5):

> O martir sowded to virginitee!
> Now maystow syngen, folwynge evere in oon,
> The white Lamb celestial—quod she—
> Of which the grete evaungelist, Seint John,
> In Pathmost wroot, which seith that they that goon
> Biform this Lamb and synge a song al newe,
> That nevere fleshly wommen they ne knewe.

In Burns's "The Cotter's Saturday Night," the priestlike father reads from the sacred page, "How he, who lone in Patmos banished, / Saw in the sun a mighty angel stand, / And heard great Bab'lon's doom pronounc'd by Heaven's command."

And in "The Curse of the Charter-Breakers," Whittier says that modern "Priests of God" should be as vigorous as those of old. They are "God's interpreter . . . . Heralding the better day":

> Catching gleams of temple spires,
> Hearing notes of angel choirs,
> Where, as yet unseen to them,
> Comes the New Jerusalem!
> Like the seer of Patmos gazing,
> On the glory downward blazing;
> Till upon Earth's grateful sod
> Rests the City of our God!

* Reprinted with permission of The Macmillan Company from *Collected Poems* by E. A. Robinson. Copyright 1916 by E. A. Robinson. Renewed 1944 by Ruth Nivison.

JOHN THE BAPTIST

Matt. 3, 11, 14;
Mark 1, 6; Luke
3, 7; John 1, 3

Born of the aged priest Zacharias and Elizabeth, John the Baptist preached in the wilderness of Judea repentance and the coming of Christ. Known as the Precursor, John was "the voice of one crying in the wilderness. Prepare ye the way of the Lord, make his paths straight" (see VOICE THAT CRIETH IN THE WILDERNESS). Perhaps a NAZARITE, "John had his raiment of camel's hair, and a leathern girdle about his loins; and his meat was locusts and wild honey." He was beheaded by HEROD ANTIPAS at the request of Herodias and her daughter Salome. In Dryden's "Mac Flecknoe," Mac Flecknoe announces his successor, Thomas Shadwell, to the throne of dullness. Referring to Heywood and Shirley, he says:

> Even I, a dunce of more renown than they,
> Was sent before but to prepare the way:
> And coarsely clad in Norwich Drugget came
> To teach the Nations in thy greater name.

In "My First Acquaintance with Poets," William Hazlitt told about hearing Coleridge preach. "The idea of St. John came into mind, 'of one crying in the wilderness, who had his loins girt about, and whose food was locusts and wild honey.' " And in Joyce's *A Portrait of the Artist as a Young Man*, Stephen reflects upon his despairing friend Cranly: "the child of exhausted loins . . . . The exhausted loins are those of Elizabeth and Zachary. Then, he is the precursor. Item: he eats chiefly belly bacon and dried figs. Read locusts and wild honey. Also, when thinking of him, saw always a stern severed head or death mask . . . . Puzzled for the moment by saint John at the Latin gate. What do I see? A decollated precursor trying to pick the lock."

JOHN THE BAPTIST'S HEAD   *see HEROD ANTIPAS*

JONADAB THE RECHABITE
(rē′kà·bĭt)

Jer. 35

Jonadab [jŏn′à·dăb] or Jehonadab [jē·hŏn′á·dăb], was the son of Rechab [rē′kăb]. The pastoral Rechabites dwelled in tents and led strict, ascetic lives, abstaining from wines. Jonadab assisted Jehu in destroying King Ahab's Baal worship (II Kings 10:15–23). In Dryden's "Absalom and Achitophel," SHIMEI shunned wine: "And, that his noble style he might refine, / No Rechabite more shunned the fumes of wine." Theobald, in Butler's *The Way of All Flesh*, a believer in strict obedience of children and sober living, was impressed, when his son Ernest was born, with the tale of an Eastern traveler who "had come upon a remarkably hardy, sober, industrious little Christian community—all of them in the best of health—who had turned out to be the actual living descendants of Jonadab, the son of Rechab . . . ." Later, when Theobald learned that Ernest's grandfather had left a small legacy to Ernest, he reflected that "if Jonadab, the son of Rechab's father—or perhaps it might be simpler under the circumstances to say Rechab at once—if Rechab, then, had left handsome legacies to his grandchildren—why Jonadab might not have found those children so easy to deal with . . . ."

JONAH

Book of Jonah

Disobeying God's command to go preach to the Ninevites, Jonah took ship toward Tarshish. God sent a mighty tempest, and the sailors, discovering that Jonah was the cause, cast him into the sea. "Now the Lord had prepared a great fish to swallow up Jonah. And Jonah was in the belly of the fish three days and three nights." No mention is made of a whale. Jonah prayed for forgiveness, "And the Lord spake unto the fish, and it vomited out Jonah upon the dry land." Obeying the Lord's second command, Jonah went and preached to the Ninevites. They repented, but Jonah was very angry that the Lord showed mercy to them. So the Lord sent a gourd (see JONAH'S GOURD) to shade Jonah, then a worm to wither it, to teach Jonah the lesson of God's compassion for all men, Jews and gentiles. In *Cape Cod*, Thoreau commented on the curious things "which fishes have swallowed . . . jugs, and jewels, and Jonah." In Melville's *Moby Dick*, Ishmael attempts to discuss the "interior structural features" of the whale. "But have a care how you seize the privilege of Jonah alone; the privilege of discoursing upon the joists and beams; the rafters, ridge-pole, sleepers and underpinnings, making up the frame-work of leviathan; and belike of the tallow-vats, dairy rooms, butteries, and cheeseries in his bowels." And in his sermon to the sailors, in *Moby Dick*, Father Mapple retells the story—except for the part of the gourd. He begins: "Shipmates, this book, containing only four chapters—four yarns—is one of the smallest strands in the mighty cable of the Scriptures. Yet what depths of the soul Jonah's deep sealine sounds! What a pregnant lesson to us in this prophet! What a noble thing is that canticle in the fish's belly! How billow-like and boisterously grand!"

JONAH, BRINGER OF BAD LUCK

Jonah 1:4–12

Jonah, discovered to be the cause of the "mighty tempest in the sea" by the casting of lots, admits it, saying to his shipmates, "Take me, and cast me forth into the sea; so shall the sea be calm unto you: for I know that for my sake this great tempest is upon you." Kipling, in *Captains Courageous*, said, "A Jonah's anything that spoils the luck." In Emily Brontë's *Wuthering Heights*, a storm struck furiously about midnight, knocking down a portion of the chimney stack. Nelly said, "I felt some sentiment that it must be a judgment on us also. The Jonah, in my mind, was Mr. Earnshaw . . . ." In Tennyson's "The Wreck," a wife who has deserted her child and run away with a lover is caught in a storm at sea: ". . . I began to weep, / 'I am the Jonah, the crew should cast me into the deep.' "

JONAH'S GOURD

Jonah 4:6–11

Jonah became angry when the Lord did not destroy the repentant Ninevites, saying, "O Lord, take, I beseech thee, my life from me; for it is better for me to die than to live." And he went and sat outside the city to see what would become of it. The Lord made a gourd to grow over him for shade, and Jonah was exceeding glad. Then the Lord prepared a worm next day that "smote the gourd that it withered," and Jonah, faint, again wished that he might die. "Then said the Lord, Thou hast pity on the gourd, for the which thou hast not laboured, neither madest it grow; which came up in a night, and perished in a night. And should I not spare Nineveh, that great city, wherein are more than sixscore thousand persons that cannot discern between their right hand and their left hand . . . ?" Coleridge, in his comment on his "Ode on the Departing Year," said of England's past wars, "We have been proud and confident in our alliances and our fleets—but God has prepared the cankerworm, and will smite the gourds of our pride." In Hardy's *Far from the Madding Crowd*, Boldwood said about his loss of Bathsheba, "Yes, He prepared a gourd to shade me, and like the prophet I thanked him and was glad. But the next day He prepared a worm to smite the gourd and wither it; and I feel it is better to die than to live." Whittier's "The Pumpkin" celebrates pumpkins and pumpkin pies.

> Oh, greenly and fair in the lands of the sun,
> The vines of the gourd and the rich melon run . . .

Like that which o'er Nineveh's prophet once grew,
While he waited to know that his warning was true,
And longed for the storm cloud, and listened in vain
For the rush of the whirlwind and the red fire-rain.

JOSEPH AND POTIPHAR'S WIFE

Gen. 39:7–20   Joseph became overseer in Potiphar's [pŏt'ĭ·fẽr] house, and he "was a goodly person and well favored." His "master's wife cast her eyes upon Joseph; and she said, Lie with me. But he refused . . . ." One day when there were no men in the house, "she caught him by his garment, saying, Lie with me: and he left his garment in her hand, and fled, and got him out." The lady lied to her husband, and Joseph was imprisoned. In Sheridan's *School for Scandal,* when Sir Peter Teazle finds Lady Teazle hiding behind Joseph Surface's screen, Joseph jests, saying, "Ha! ha! ha! . . . I'll tell you, Sir Peter, though I hold a man of intrigue to be a most despicable character, yet, you know, it does not follow that one is to be an absolute Joseph either!" In "Self-Reliance," Emerson said that man should yield to "the devout motions of the soul . . . . Leave your theory, as Joseph his coat in the hand of the harlot and flee." In *Don Juan,* Byron describes Juan, caught in Julia's closet, grappling with Julia's husband.

Juan contrived to give an awkward blow,
    And then his only garment quite gave way;
He fled, like Joseph, leaving it; but there,
    I doubt, all likeness ends between the pair.

JOSEPH, JACOB'S SON

Gen. 30:22–24;   Joseph, meaning "increaser," was Rachel's first son and the
37—50   favorite of Jacob, who gave him the "COAT OF MANY COLORS." Because of his father's favoritism and his imprudent treatment of his brothers, they sold him into slavery. He became overseer in Potiphar's home in Egypt, resisted the blandishments of Potiphar's wife (see JOSEPH AND POTIPHAR'S WIFE); and then, because of his fame as interpreter of the dreams of, first, Pharaoh's butler and baker, then of Pharaoh himself, Pharaoh made him governor of Egypt. During a famine in Canaan, he received his brothers, then his father, and settled them in Goshen to enjoy "THE FAT OF THE LAND." Joseph died at the age of one hundred and ten, was embalmed, and his body was later taken back to Canaan. In Chaucer's "The Nun's Priest's Tale," Chauntecleer tries to persuade his wife, fair Pertelote, of the prophetic truth of dreams:

> Reed eek of Joseph, and ther shul ye see
> Wher dremes be somtyme—I sey nat alle—
> Warnynge of thynges that shul after falle.
> Looke of Egipte the kyng, daun Pharao,
> His bakere and his butiller also,
> Where they ne felte noon effect in dremes.

Pharaoh dreamed of "seven well favoured kine and fatfleshed" that were eaten up by seven "ill favoured and leanfleshed kine," then of seven withered and thin ears that devoured seven good ears of corn. Joseph interpreted these dreams to mean seven years of plenty and seven years of famine. In Shakespeare's *Henry IV, Part I,* when Prince Hal calls Falstaff "a stuffed cloak-bag of guts," an "old fat man," Falstaff replies, "if to be fat be to be hated, then Pharaoh's lean kine are to be loved." In "Samuel Johnson," Macaulay said that when Johnson started writing there was little hope of patronage or profits. "The lean kine had eaten up the fat kine. The thin and withered ears had devoured the good ears. The season of rich harvest was over, and the period of famine had begun."

JOSEPH OF ARIMATHEA   *see GRAIL*

JOSHUA, SUN AND MOON STAND STILL

Josh. 10:12–14 When the Lord sent great hailstones down upon the Amorites to help the children of Israel, Joshua "said in the sight of Israel, Sun, stand thou still upon Gibeon; and thou, Moon, in the valley of Ajalon. And the sun stood still, and the moon stayed, until the people had avenged themselves upon their enemies." In *Paradise Lost,* the angel Michael describes future battles of the world to Adam:

> Or how the sun shall in mid Heav'n stand still
> A day entire, and nights due course adjourne,
> Man's voice commanding, Sun in Gibeon stand,
> And thou Moon in the vale of Aialon,
> Till Israel overcome.

In the conclusion of "To His Coy Mistress" Andrew Marvell urges action. Let us

> tear our pleasures with rough strife
> Through the iron gates of life:
> Thus, though we cannot make our sun
> Stand still, yet we will make him run.

And in "Locksley Hall," Tennyson rejects the Romantic idea of a retreat to primitive life: he

held it better men should perish one by one,
Than that earth should stand at gaze like
Joshua's moon in Ajalon.

JOT OR TITTLE   *see TITTLE*

JUBAL

Gen. 4:21

Jubal was the son of Lamech and Adah, the brother of TUBAL-
CAIN: "he was the father of all such as handle the harp and
organ." In literature he is the founder of music and song. In
Chaucer's *The Book of the Duchess,* the Black Knight says that
he composed songs to his lady to keep him from idleness. I

> made songes thus a gret del,
> Althogh I koude not make so wel
> Songes, ne knewe the art al,
> As koude Lamekes sone Tubal [*sic*]
> That found out first the art of songe;
> For as hys brothers hammers ronge
> Upon hys anvelt up and doun,
> Therof he took the firste soun,—

Dryden, in "A Song for St. Cecilia's Day," wrote:

> What passion cannot music raise and quell!
> When Jubal struck the chorded shell,
> His listening brethren stood around,
> And, wondering, on their faces fell
> To worship that celestial sound.

In "A Chapter on Ears," Lamb told of his deficiency in music
appreciation. "It is hard to stand alone—in an age like this—
(constituted to the quick and critical perception of all har-
monious combinations . . . beyond all preceding ages, since
Jubal stumbled upon the gamut)—"

JUBILEE

Lev. 25:8–13;
Luke 4:18–21

The Jubilee year was one year after "the space of the seven
sabbaths of years." "Ye shall make the trumpet sound throughout all your land . . . and proclaim liberty . . . unto all the
inhabitants . . . and return every man unto his possession." The
word means "ram"; hence "ram's horn," which was blown.
In the Middle Ages, after fifty years of service, friars were
permitted to go alone, which was to "make their jubilee," as
in Chaucer's "The Summoner's Tale." The friar says that his
sacristan and infirmary chief "han been trewe freres fifty yeer;
/ That may now—God be thanked of his loone! / Maken thir
jubilee and walke allone." In the "Ode: Intimations of Immortality," Wordsworth expresses the joy of youth in springtime.

Ye blessèd Creatures, I have heard the call
Ye to each other make; I see
The heavens laugh with you in your jubilee
My heart is at your festival
My head hath its coronal,
The fulness of your bliss, I feel—I feel it all.

JUDAS ISCARIOT

(ĭs·kăr′ĭ·ŏt)

*Matt. 26:14–50;
27:3–5; Mark
14:10–11, 43–45;
Luke 22:3–6,
47–48; John
12:4–6; 13:26–30;
18:2–5; Acts
1:16–18*

Judas is the Greek form of the Hebrew "Judah," a common late Jewish name. Iscariot means "man of Kerioth" a town in southeast Judea. In GETHSEMANE, for thirty pieces of silver, Judas betrayed Jesus to the priests and elders, to whom he had said, "Whomsoever I shall kiss, that same is he: hold him fast." Then "forthwith he came to Jesus, and said, Hail, master: and kissed him." Then Judas repented, "cast down the pieces of silver in the temple, and departed, and went and hanged himself"—by tradition on an elder tree. In Shakespeare's *Henry VI, Part III*, when King Edward asks his brother Gloucester to kiss young Ned, the Prince of Wales, Gloucester does so, saying,

And that I love the tree from whence thou sprang'st,
Witness the loving kiss I give the fruit.
[Aside] To say the truth, so Judas kiss'd his master,
And cried, "All hail!" when as he meant all harm.

Here Shakespeare nods. In no early version of the Bible did Judas say "All Hail!" Jesus said this to Mary and Mary Magdalene when he met them after the Resurrection (Matt. 28:9 in the Bishops' Bible). In Shakespeare's *Richard II*, when King Richard is brought before the usurper Bolingbroke, he says,

I well remember
The favors of these men. Were they not mine?
Did they not sometime cry "All hail!" to me?
So Judas did to Christ. But he in twelve
Found truth in all but one; I, in twelve thousand, none.

In *Othello*, after killing Desdemona, Othello cried, "I kiss'd thee ere I killed thee: no way but this, / Killing myself, to die upon a kiss." And in *Love's Labour's Lost*, Holofernes plays the part of Judas Maccabaeus, in the pageant of the nine Worthies. He is gulled by the courtiers.

HOLOFERNES. Judas I am,—
DUMAIN. The more shame for you, Judas.
HOLOFERNES. What mean you, sir?
BOYET. To make Judas hang himself.

HOLOFERNES. Begin, sir; you are my elder.
BIRON. Well followed: Judas was hanged on an elder.

.   .   .   .   .   .

BOYET. Therefore, as he is an ass, let him go.
     And so adieu, sweet Jude! Nay, why dost thou stay?
DUMAIN. For the latter end of his name.
BIRON. For the ass to the Jude; give it him:
     —Jud-as, away!

In the old tapestries and paintings Judas is represented with red hair, a sign of treachery. In *As You Like It*, Rosalind weeps because Orlando has failed his appointment. She says, "His very hair is of the dissembling color." Celia replies, "Something browner than Judas's. / Marry, his kisses are Judas's own children."

JUDAS MACCABAEUS   *see MACCABEES*

JUDGE NOT, THAT YE BE NOT JUDGED

Matt. 7:1; Luke 6:37

In the Sermon on the Mount, Jesus said, "Judge not, that ye be not judged." In *A Defence of Poetry*, Shelley said that the best poets are the best men; accusations against them have little basis. "Consider how little is as it appears—or appears as it is; look to your own motives, and judge not, lest ye be judged." Swinburne, in "Hymn to Man," writing on the suffering inflicted on man by Christianity, said, "Thou are judged, O judge, and the sentence is gone forth against thee, O God." In his Second Inaugural Address, Lincoln said that in the Civil War both sides "read the same Bible, and pray to the same God . . . . It may seem strange that any men should dare to ask a just God's assistance in wringing their bread from the sweat of other men's faces; but let us judge not, that we be not judged."

JUDGMENT DAY

Matt. 10:15; 25:31–46; Rom. 14:10; Rev. 20:11–15

The day, called also the Day of Judgment, the day of the Last Judgment, the day of doom or doomsday, is the day when the Lord, on the judgment seat, will judge men and angels, sending them to punishment in everlasting fire, or to eternal reward. The trumpet of the Last Judgment will sound, and thunder will be heard. In Shakespeare's *Hamlet*, Horatio compares the Ghost's appearance to ancient omens such as "the moist star / . . . sick almost to doomsday with eclipse." When Macbeth sees the witches' show of Eight Kings, he cries out, "What, will the line stretch out to the crack of doom?" Emerson, in "Spiritual Laws," wrote, "The world is full of judgment days, and into every assembly that a man enters, in every action he attempts, he is gauged and stamped." Theobald Pontifex, in Butler's *The Way of All Flesh*, tells Mrs. Thompson, dying and fearful, that the one thing certain about death is that "we shall all appear before the Judgment Seat of Christ, and that the wicked will be consumed in a lake of everlasting fire." In Melville's *Moby Dick*, the harpooner Daggoo, "thundering with the butts of three clubbed handspikes on the forecastle deck, roused the sleepers with such judgment claps that they seemed to exhale from the scuttle . . . ."

JUDGMENT OF SOLOMON   *see SOLOMON'S JUDGMENT OF THE CHILD*

JUDGMENT SEAT   *see JUDGMENT DAY*

JUDITH

"Judith" of the Apocrypha

Judith was a beautiful and wealthy widow who, when Holofernes besieged the Jews in Bethulia, volunteered to save her people. She went to the tent of Holofernes, professing to come to help him against the sinful Jews, was received hospitably and entertained. At one feast Holofernes drank wine till he fell senseless on his bed; Judith seized his scimitar, "took hold of the hair of his head . . . smote twice upon his neck with all her might, and she took away his head from him." Returning to Bethulia with the head "in her bag of meat," Judith was welcomed joyously, and she lived honored and happy to the age of "an hundred and five." Chaucer's monk, in "The Monk's Tale," tells the tragedy of "Oloferne, which Fortune ay kist / So likerously":

> for al his pomp and al his myght,
> Judith, a womman, as he lay upright
> Slepynge, his heed of smoot, and from his tente
> Ful pryvely she stal from every wight,
> And with his heed unto hir toun she wente.

Chaucer's fondness for the story is evidenced by his use of it also in "The Man of Law's Tale" and in "The Tale of Melibee." Ishmael, in Melville's *Moby Dick*, described the severed head of the sperm whale "hoisted against the ship's side . . . . There, that blood-dripping head hung to the Pequod's waist like the giant Holoferne's from the girdle of Judith." In "I and My Chimney," Melville's narrator and his wife quarrel about their chimney. Says she, " 'So Holofernes will have his way, never mind whose heart breaks for it.' Holofernes is with her a pet name for any fell domestic despot."

JUSTIFIED BY WORKS   *see FAITH WITHOUT WORKS*

KEYS OF THE KINGDOM

Matt. 16:18–19 When Simon Peter told Jesus that he knew he was Christ the Son of God, Jesus blessed him, saying, ". . . thou art Peter, and upon this rock I will build my church; and the gates of hell shall not prevail against it. And I will give unto thee the keys of the kingdom of heaven . . . ." In Shakespeare's *Othello*, Othello accuses Desdemona of infidelity:

> I took you for that cunning whore of Venice
> That married with Othello. You, mistress,
> That have the office opposite to Saint Peter,
> And keep the gate of Hell . . . .
> We have done our course, there's money for your pains.
> I pray you turn the key, and keep our counsel.

In Milton's "Lycidas," St. Peter appears as a mourner.

> Last came, and last did go,
> The Pilot of the Galilean lake,
> Two massy Keyes he bore of metals twain,
> (The Golden opes, the Iron shuts amain).

In "Suspiria de Profundis," Thomas De Quincey says of "Our Lady of Tears," one of the "Sisters of Sorrows": "This sister, the elder, it is that carries keys more than papal at her girdle, which open every cottage and every palace."

KICK AGAINST THE PRICKS

Acts 9:5; 26:14 As Saul, on the road to Damascus, was struck with a great light and "heard a voice saying unto him, Saul, Saul, why persecutest thou me?" he said, "Who art thou Lord? And the Lord said, I am Jesus whom thou persecutest: it is hard for thee to kick against the pricks." Jesus meant to kick against goads, spikes, or sharp weapons: i.e., to complain about one's hurts. In "Truth," Chaucer wrote about self-control: "Gret reste stant in litel besinesse; / Be war also to sporne ayeyns an al:" In a letter to John Hamilton Reynolds, Keats compared the narrowness of modern poets with the greatness of the older poets like Milton: "I will have no more of Wordsworth or Hunt in particular . . . . Why should we kick against the pricks, when we can walk on roses?" And in *Don Juan*, Byron said of Don Juan, fresh from the Continent, as he sped along the road from Canterbury to London:

> Juan admired these highways of free millions:
> A country in all senses the most dear
>   To foreigner or native, save some silly ones,
> Who "kick against the pricks," just at this juncture,
> And for their pains get only a fresh puncture.

KILL THE FATTED CALF   *see FATTED CALF*

KINGDOM NOT OF THIS WORLD

John 18:36

Pilate, when Jesus was brought before him, asked, "Art thou the King of the Jews?" Jesus answered, "My kingdom is not of this world: if my kingdom were of this world, then would my servants fight, that I should not be delivered to the Jews: but now is my kingdom not from hence." In Tennyson's *Becket,* when John of Salisbury tells Becket that his return to England has aroused the world against him, Becket replies, "Why, John, my kingdom is not of this world." Salisbury says, "If it were more of this world it might be / More of the next. A policy of wise pardon / Wins here as well as there." In *The Way of All Flesh,* Butler, at the time of Mr. Pontifex's death, says that some men find happiness in having a higher moral standard than others. "If they go in for this, however, they must be content with virtue . . . whose rewards belong to a kingdom that is not of this world."

KINGDOM OF GOD IS WITHIN YOU

Luke 17:21

When the Pharisees asked Jesus when the kingdom of God should come, he answered, "The kingdom of God cometh not with observation: Neither shall they say, Lo here! or, lo there! for, behold, the kingdom of God is within you." Francis Thompson's "The Kingdom of God" begins:

> O world invisible, we view thee,
> O world intangible, we touch thee,
> O world unknowable, we know thee,
> Inapprehensible, we clutch thee!

In *Essays in Criticism, First Series,* Matthew Arnold, comparing Christian morality with that of Marcus Aurelius, said that in order to match the latter, Christianity "has to correct its apparent offers of external reward, and to say: *The kingdom of God is within you.*" And, in *Culture and Anarchy,* Arnold said, "Religion says: *The kingdom of God is within you;* and culture, in like manner, places human perfection in an internal condition, in the growth and predominance of our humanity proper . . . ."

KING OF KINGS

Ezek. 26:7; I Tim. 6:15

Paul wrote of Jesus, calling him "the blessed and only Potentate, the Kings of kings, and Lord of lords." The "genitive superlative" was a common form in the Bible, as for example:

"bone of my bones, flesh of my flesh" (Gen. 2:23), "servant of servants" (Gen. 9:25), "God of Gods, and Lord of Lords" (Deut. 10:17), "Song of Songs," and "HOLY OF HOLIES." The phrase "King of Kings" was used by Shakespeare in several plays. For example, in the beginning of *Henry VI, Part I*, at the funeral of King Henry V, the Bishop of Winchester said, "He was a king bless'd of the King of Kings." In Shaw's *Back to Methuselah*, "The Male Figure" introduces "The Female Figure," saying, "This is Cleopatra—Semiramis, consort of the king of kings, and therefore queen of queens . . . the king of kings and queen of queens are . . . thought-out and hand-made to receive the sacred Life Force."

KISHON RIVER   *see DEBORAH*

KISS THE HEM OF HIS GARMENT   *see HEM OF HIS GARMENT*

KNOCK, AND IT SHALL BE OPENED UNTO YOU   *see SEEK, AND YE SHALL FIND*

KNOW NOT WHAT THEY DO

Luke 23:34   When Jesus was crucified, He said, "Father, forgive them; for they know not what they do." In Shakespeare's *Henry VI, Part II*, when King Henry hears news of Jack Cade's rebellion, he says, "O graceless men! they know not what they do." In Somerset Maugham's *Of Human Bondage*, Philip comes to feel "a holy compassion" for the weaknesses of mankind. One must "accept the good of men and be patient with their faults. The words of the dying God crossed his memory: *Forgive them, for they know not what they do.*"

KOHELETH, THE PREACHER   *see ALL IS VANITY*

KORAH, CORAH
(kō′·rah)

Num. 16:1–40   Korah, a Levite, with Dathan (dā·than) and Abiram (ā·bī′·ram) led a rebellion against Moses and Aaron, saying, "Ye take too much upon you . . . ye lift yourselves up above the congregation of the Lord." As punishment, "the earth opened her mouth, and swallowed them up, and their houses, and all the men that appertained unto Korah, and all their goods." And a fire consumed all that followed them. In Bunyan's *Pilgrim's Progress*, Hope tells Christian that LOT'S WIFE is a caution and example that "we should shun her sin . . . so Korah, Dathan, and Abiram, with the two hundred and fifty men that perished in their sin . . . ." Dryden, in "The Hind and the Panther," satirized the Presbyterians as "a class" descended from Cora's people.

> When Corah with his brethren did conspire
> From Moses' hand the sov'reign sway to wrest,
> And Aaron of his ephod to devest:
> Till opening earth made way for all to pass,
> And could not bear the burden of a class.

In *Moby Dick*, Melville compares the sea and the land. Is not a miracle upon one a miracle upon the other? "Preternatural terrors rested upon the Hebrews, when under the feet of Korah and his company the live ground opened and swallowed them up forever; yet not a modern sun ever sets, but in precisely the same manner, the live sea swallows up ships and crews."

LABAN   see JACOB AND LABAN

LAKE OF FIRE AND BRIMSTONE

Rev. 19:20;
20:10; 21:8

This was Saint John's name for hell. Here not only was the devil cast, "but the fearful, and unbelieving, and the abominable, and sorcerers, and idolaters, and all liars, shall have their part in the lake which burneth with fire and brimstone: which is the second death" (cf. Rev. 2:11). It is also known as the bottomless pit (see ABADDON), or the pit of the dragon (Rev. 20:1–3). Milton's *Paradise Lost* starts picturing Satan "with his horrid crew [who] lay vanquisht, rowling in the fiery Gulfe . . . ." And "So stretcht out huge in length the Arch-fiend lay / chain'd on the burning Lake . . . ." In Charlotte Brontë's *Jane Eyre*, the stern Mr. Brocklehurst accuses Jane of deceit, saying, ". . . all liars will have their portion in the lake burning with fire and brimstone." In *Culture* and *Anarchy*, Arnold cited, as an example of excess of the middle class, a Wesleyan minister speaking before "an irritated population of Catholics." He exclaimed, "I say, then, away with the Mass! It is from the bottomless pit; and in the bottomless pit shall all liars have their part, in the lake that burneth with fire and brimstone."

LAMB TO THE SLAUGHTER

Isa. 53:7; Jer.
11:19; Acts 8:32

Isaiah wrote that Jehovah's anointed "hath borne our griefs, and carried our sorrows . . . he is brought as a lamb to the slaughter . . . so he openeth not his mouth." In "Cassandra Southwick," Whittier wrote of the girl about to be sold into slavery; she sat all night unsleeping, knowing she was to be "Dragged to their place of market, and bargained for and sold, / Like a lamb before the shambles, like a heifer from the fold." And in Shaw's *Androcles and the Lion*, Androcles says to a fellow Christian about to be cast into the arena, "Brother, brother: let them rage and kill: let us be brave and suffer. You must go: as a lamb to the slaughter."

LAME, THE HALT, THE BLIND　　*see MAIMED, THE HALT, THE BLIND*

LAMECH
(lā′mek)

Gen. 4:19–24

Lamech was one of the early patriarchs, the father of Noah in one genealogy, and the husband of two wives: Adah [ā′da̍], mother of JABAL and JUBAL; and Zillah [zil′la̍], mother of TU-BAL-CAIN. The "Song of Lamech" (Gen. 4:23–24), perhaps the oldest in the Bible, is a primitive song of boasting and revenge. Chaucer considered Lamech a bigamist. In "Anelida and Arcite," King Arcite was false to Queen Anelida:

> gret wonder was it noon
> Thogh he were fals, for hit is kynde of man,
> Sith Lamek was, that is so longe agoon,
> To ben in love as fals as ever he can;
> He was the firste fader that began
> To loven two, and was in bigamye;

Chaucer's Wife of Bath defends her five husbands by citing several holy men with a plurality of wives: "What rekketh me, thogh folk seye vileynye / Of shrewd Lameth and his big-amye?" In Tennyson's *Maud*, the young man who killed Maud's brother in a duel flees to France. He is "sick of a nameless fear. / Looking, thinking of all I have lost; / An old song vexes my ear; / But that of Lamech is mine."

LAND OF BEULAH　　*see BEULAH*

LAND FLOWING WITH MILK AND HONEY

Exod. 3:8; 13:5

God spoke to Moses out of the burning bush saying, "I have surely seen the affliction of my people which are in Egypt . . . And I am come down to deliver them out of the hand of the Egyptians, and to bring them up out of that land unto a good land and a large, unto a land flowing with milk and honey." Called also the PROMISED LAND, it was the land of the Canaanites and their neighbors—Palestine. In Tennyson's "The Lover's Tale," the lovers, walking on the mountain, look to view "A land of promise, a land of memory, / A land of promise flowing with milk / And honey, of delicious memories." Ishmael, in Melville's *Moby Dick*, says of New Bedford, "It is a land of oil, true enough: but not like Canaan; a land, also, of corn and wine. The streets do not run with milk; nor in the spring-time do they pave them with fresh eggs." In *Don Juan*, Byron, describing a great English banquet, wrote, "That happiness for man—the hungry sinner! / . . . much depends on dinner."

> Witness the lands which "flow'd with milk and honey,"
> Held out unto the hungry Israelites:
> To this we have added since, the love of money,
> The only sort of pleasure which requites.

LAND OF NOD

Gen. 4:16

After Cain was condemned to be a fugitive and vagabond in the earth, he "went out from the presence of the Lord, and dwelt in the land of Nod, on the east of Eden." The word "nod" here means "wandering"—not "sleep," though it is, of course, frequently used in this sense. Dryden, in his essay "Virgil and the Aeneid," said, "Ulysses travelled; so did Aeneas; but neither of them were the first travellers; for Cain went into the land of Nod before they were born: and neither of the poets ever heard of such a man." In *Moby Dick*, Ishmael tells how in the Spouter Inn, "I slid off into a light doze, and had pretty nearly made a good offing towards the land of Nod, when I heard a heavy footfall in the passage . . . ." Sir Walter Raleigh, in *The History of the World*, wrote that the Henochii, inhabitants of Cain's city called Enoch, were found after the flood dwelling "towards the east side of Eden where Cain dwelt."

LAND OF PROMISE   *see PROMISED LAND*

LAODICEAN
(lā·ŏd′·ĭ·sē′ăn)

Rev. 3:14–16

Saint John said, "And unto the angel of the church of the Laodiceans write; . . . I know thy works, that thou art neither cold nor hot: I would thou wert cold or hot. So then because thou art lukewarm, and neither cold nor hot, I will spue thee out of my mouth." In Butler's *The Way of All Flesh*, Ernest wrote an essay saying that we should not "feel very strongly upon any subject . . . We should be . . . somewhat lukewarm churchmen . . . The Church herself should approach as nearly to that of Laodicea as was compatible with her continuing to be a Church at all, and each individual member should only be hot in striving to be as lukewarm as possible." In *Back to*

Methuselah, Shaw said, "Thus the world is kept sane less by the saints than by the vast mass of the indifferent . . . Butler's preaching of the gospel of Laodicea was a piece of common sense founded on the observation of this."

LAPIDOTH   *see DEBORAH*

LAST JUDGMENT   *see JUDGMENT DAY*

LAST SHALL BE FIRST   *see FIRST SHALL BE LAST*

LAST SUPPER

Matt. 26:26–29;
Mark 14:22–25;
Luke 22:14–20;
I Cor. 11:20–25

The Lord's Supper, the eucharist from the Latin *eucharistia,* meaning "giving of thanks," or the Communion, was the last supper Jesus shared with His disciples before the Crucifixion. After Judas (See JUDAS ISCARIOT) had betrayed Him, "Jesus took bread, and blessed it, and brake it, and gave it to the disciples, and said, Take, eat; this is my body. And he took the cup, and gave thanks, and gave it to them, saying, Drink ye all of it; For this is my blood of the new testament, which is shed for many for the remission of sins." Browning, in "An Epistle," speaks of Jesus as He who "was born and lived, / Taught, healed the sick, broke bread at his own house, / Then died . . . ." In Whittier's "Snow Bound" the tale is told of the skipper, a "rare sea-saint," who offered himself to feed his starving sailors, when a school of porpoises suddenly appeared: " 'Take, eat,' he said, 'and be content; / These fishes in my stead are sent . . . .' " And in *Studies in Classic American Literature,* D. H. Lawrence said that Melville was horrified by the Typees' cannibalism, but "he might have spared himself his shudder . . . . If the savages liked to partake of their sacrament . . . and to say, directly: 'This is thy body, which I take from thee and eat. This is thy blood, which I sip in annihilation of thee,' why surely their sacred ceremony was as awe-inspiring as the one Jesus substituted."

LAST TRUMPET   *see TRUMPET OF LAST JUDGMENT*

LATCHET OF WHOSE SHOES

Mark 1:7; Luke
3:16

John the Baptist preached, saying, "There comes one mightier than I after me, the latchet of whose shoes I am not worthy to stoop down and unloose." In Chaucer's "The Squire's Tale," the falcon says of her lover that no faithless lover of the past could "by twenty thousand part, / Countrefete the sophymes of his art, / ne were worthy unbokelen his galoche . . ./"

Carlyle, in "Boswell's Life of Johnson," said that Hume and Johnson were half-men, who combined would make a whole man. "Till such whole man arrive for us . . . might the Heavens but bless poor England with half-men worthy to tie the shoe-latchets of these . . ." In the Preface to *Back to Methuselah,* Shaw compared recent religious painters, such as the technical experts Hilton and Haydon, with Giotto, "the latchet of whose shoes they were nevertheless not worthy to unloose."

LAW OF THE MEDES AND PERSIANS

Dan. 6:8;
Esther 1:19

When "the presidents and princes" under King Darius [dà·rī′us] turned against Daniel, they asked the King to establish a firm decree that "whosoever shall ask a petition of any God or man for thirty days, save of thee, O king, he shall be cast into the den of lions." King Darius signed the decree that could not be changed, "according to the law of the Medes and Persians, which altereth not." In Charlotte Brontë's *Jane Eyre,* Mr. Rochester tells Miss Eyre that he is going to assert his authority: "I am laying down good intentions, which I believe durable as flint . . . and at this moment I pass a law, unalterable as that of the Medes and Persians." In *Letters from the Earth,* Mark Twain wrote on etiquette. For example, "Never pay a morning call (of ceremony) before breakfast. Figuratively speaking, this law, like the laws of the Medes and Persians, is written in blood."

LAW UNTO THEMSELVES

Rom. 2:14

Paul wrote to the Romans that all men will be rewarded according to their deeds. "For when the Gentiles, which have not the law, do by nature the things contained in the law, these, having not the law, are a law unto themselves." The modern use of the phrase, sometimes in the sense of being headstrong or rebellious, does not reflect Paul's meaning accurately. In *The Scarlet Letter,* Hawthorne said of little Pearl, "skipping, dancing, and frisking fantastically among the hillocks of the dead people . . . . It was as if she had been made afresh, out of new elements, and must perforce be permitted to live her own life, and be a law unto herself, without her eccentricities being reckoned to her for a crime." In "Self-Reliance," Emerson said that self-reliance "demands something godlike" in a man, "to trust himself for a taskmaster. High in his heart . . . clear in his sight, that he may in good earnest be doctrine, society, law to himself . . . ."

LAY NOT UP TREASURES UPON EARTH

Matt. 6:19–20

In the Sermon on the Mount, Jesus said, "Lay not up for yourselves treasures upon earth, where moth and rust doth corrupt, and where thieves break through and steal: But lay up for yourselves treasures in heaven, where neither moth nor rust doth corrupt, and where thieves do not break through nor steal . . . ." In *The Reason of Church Government,* Milton wrote of his determination to speak freely about his religious opinions. "For me, I have determined to lay up as the best treasure and solace of a good old age . . . the honest liberty of free speech from my youth . . . in so dear a concernment as the church's good." In *Walden,* Thoreau wrote of the burden of owning property. Those who devote their lives to acquiring wealth "are employed, as it says in an old book, laying up treasures which moth and rust will corrupt and thieves break through and steal." In Melville's *Moby Dick,* Captain Bildad offered Ishmael a very small share of the whaling profits, called a "lay." Mumbling from his Bible, Bildad said, *"Lay* not up for yourselves treasures upon earth, where moth . . . and rust do corrupt, but *lay—"* Ishmael thought to himself, *"Lay,* indeed . . . and such a lay! the seven hundred and seventy-seventh! Well, old Bildad, you are determined that I, for one, shall not *lay* up many *lays,* here below, where moth and rust do corrupt. It was an exceedingly *long lay* that, indeed . . . ."

LAZARUS AND DIVES

(lăz′à·rŭs,
dī′vēz)

Luke 16:19–31

A parable of Jesus. Dives, meaning in Latin "rich" (the word does not appear in the Bible), was a rich man "clothed in purple and fine linen [who] fared sumptuously every day." Lazarus, meaning "without help," was a poor beggar, "laid at his gate, full of sores, and desiring to be fed with the crumbs which fell from the rich man's table: moreover the dogs came and licked his sores." Lazarus died and was "carried by the angels into Abraham's bosom"; the rich man died and was tormented in hell. He cried in vain to Abraham for mercy. In Chaucer's "The Summoner's Tale," a greedy begging friar sermonizes on the virtue of poverty and abstinence, contrasting the rich with the poor: "Lazar and Dives lyveden diversly, / And divers gerdon hadden they therby." Falstaff, in Shakespeare's *Henry IV, Part I,* describes his tatterdemalion company of soldiers as "slaves as ragged as Lazarus in the painted cloth where the glutton's dog licked his sores . . . ." And in the same play, Falstaff says to Bardolph, "I never see thy face but I think upon Hell-fire and

Dives that lived in purple, for there he is in his robes, burning, burning . . . ." In "Poor Relations," Charles Lamb defines a poor relation as "a Lazarus at your door." And Poe, in "Hop-Frog," says that court jesters were "always ready with sharp witticisms, at a moment's notice, in consideration of the crumbs that fell from the royal table."

LAZARUS, RAISING OF

John 11:1–44

Lazarus of Bethany, the brother of Mary and Martha and a friend of Jesus, died while Jesus was away, east of the Jordan. He was laid in a cave for four days, and when Jesus returned, ". . . he cried with a loud voice, Lazarus, come forth. And he that was dead came forth, bound hand and foot with grave-clothes . . . ." In *In Memoriam*, Tennyson, grieving over the death of his friend Arthur Hallam, speculates about immortality.

> When Lazarus left his charnel-cave,
>   And home to Mary's house returned,
>   Was this demanded—if he yearn'd
> To hear her weeping by his grave?

> "Where wert thou, brother, those four days?"
>   There lives no record of reply,
>   Which telling what it is to die
> Had surely added praise to praise.

> Behold a man raised up by Christ!
>   The rest remaineth unreveal'd;
>   He told it not; or something seal'd
> The lips of that Evangelist.

In Melville's *Moby Dick*, Ishmael, rescued from the sea after his first encounter with a whale, made his will and felt easier. "Besides, all the days I should now live would be as good as the days that Lazarus lived after his resurrection; a supplementary clean gain of so many months or weeks as the case may be. I survived myself . . . ."

LEAD US NOT INTO TEMPTATION

Matt. 6:13

The Lord's Prayer: "And lead us not into temptation, but deliver us from evil . . . ." In Shakespeare's *Hamlet*, Claudius, reflecting on his guilt after the play, tries to pray, but cannot:

> And what's in prayer but this two-fold force,
> To be forestalled ere we come to fall,
> Or pardon'd being down? Then I'll look up,
> My fault is past.

By "pardon'd being down," Claudius refers to "Forgive us our trespasses." At the conclusion of *The Man That Corrupted Hadleyburg*, Mark Twain said of the town of Hadleyburg, its hypocrisy in the face of temptation fully revealed, that "by act of Legislature—upon prayer and petition," it was allowed to "leave one word out of the motto that for many generations had graced the town's official seal." The new motto was: "Lead us into temptation." In Emily Brontë's *Wuthering Heights*, when Mrs. Heathcliff threatened Joseph with her "Black Art," Joseph gasped, "Oh, wicked, wicked! may the Lord deliver us from evil!" In Robert Frost's *A Masque of Reason*, God explains to Job that he permitted the Devil to afflict Job, but that he defended Job against "that committee" of comforters. He then suggests that Job might revise the Book of Prayer to say, "Deliver us from committees."°

LEAH   *see JACOB, LEAH, AND RACHEL*

LEAN KINE AND FAT KINE   *see JOSEPH, JACOB'S SON*

LEFT HAND   *see LET NOT THY LEFT HAND*

LEGION

Mark 5:9; Luke 8:30

When Jesus met the man possessed with devils, in the country of the Gadarenes, he asked him his name. The maniac replied, "My name is Legion: for we are many," meaning possessed by many devils. Jesus permitted the devils to enter a herd of GADARENE SWINE, and the man was cured. In Shakespeare's *Twelfth Night*, when Malvolio performs his antics before the Countess, Sir Toby says he's mad: "Which way is he, in the name of sanctity? If all the devils of hell be drawn in little, and Legion himself possessed him, yet I'll speak to him." In *Sartor Resartus*, Carlyle asks how Professor Teufelsdröckh fared during his period of "Indifference." By "the Satanic School" Carlyle means the poets Byron, Shelley, Keats, and their imitators. "Does Legion still lurk in him, though repressed; or has he exorcised that Devil's Brood? . . . We should . . . say that Legion, or the Satanic School, was now pretty well extirpated and cast out, but next to nothing introduced in its room."

°From *Complete Poems of Robert Frost*. Copyright 1923, 1945 by Holt, Rinehart and Winston, Inc. Copyright 1936, 1951 by Robert Frost. Copyright © 1964 by Lesley Frost Ballantine. Reprinted by permission of Holt, Rinehart and Winston, Inc., and Jonathan Cape, Ltd.

LEOPARD CHANGE HIS SPOTS

Jer. 13:23

Jeremiah said, when the people questioned in their hearts his prophecies of punishment to come, "Can the Ethiopian change his skin, or the leopard his spots? then may ye also do good, that are accustomed to do evil." In Shakespeare's *Richard II,* when King Richard hears Bolingbroke accuse Mowbray of treachery and murder, he tries to calm them, saying, "Rage must be withstood. / Give me his gage. Lions make leopards tame." Mowbray replies, "Yea, but not change his spots. Take but my shame, / And I resign my gage. My dear dear Lord / The purest treasure mortal times afford / Is spotless reputation." Robert Southey, in "Ode on Negotiations with Buonaparte in January 1814," cautioned against negotiations with Napoleon: "For sooner shall the Ethiopian change his skin, / Or from the leopard shall her spots depart, / Than this man change his old flagitious heart." In Eugene O'Neill's *The Hairy Ape,* when Mildred's aunt accuses her of insincerity and says that she prefers to be artificial, Mildred replies, "Yes, I suppose I do . . . . When a leopard complains of its spots, it must sound rather grotesque. Purr, little leopard. Purr, scratch, tear, kill, gorge yourself and be happy—only stay in the jungle where your spots are camouflage. In a cage they make you conspicuous."

LET NOT THY LEFT HAND KNOW

Matt. 6:3

In the Sermon on the Mount, Jesus said not to make a display of giving alms, "as the hypocrites do in the synagogues and in the streets . . . . But when thou doest alms, let not thy left hand know what thy right hand doeth." In *Sartor Resartus,* Carlyle spoke of the virtue of silence and secrecy. "Thought will not work except in Silence; neither will virtue work except in Secrecy. Let not thy left hand know what thy right hand doeth!" In *Walden,* Thoreau attacked the hypocrisy of reformers and philanthropists. "If you should ever be betrayed into any of these philanthropies, do not let your left hand know what your right hand does, for it is not worth knowing."

LETTER KILLETH

II Cor. 3:6

Paul wrote to the Corinthians saying that "the Spirit of the living God" is superior to the letter of the law. God "hath made us able ministers of the New Testament; not of the letter, but of the spirit: for the letter killeth, but the spirit giveth life." In

Chaucer's "The Summoner's Tale," the hypocritical friar tells Thomas that he has preached a sermon for Thomas's salvation. But since Thomas would find it hard to understand, ". . . therefore wol I teche you al the glose. / Glosynge is a glorious thynge, certeyn, / For lettre sleeth, so as we clerkes seyn." In *Studies in Classic American Literature,* D. H. Lawrence tells about Natty Bumppo, who, when an old hunter of seventy, was imprisoned for violating the new game laws. He was soon released, "but the thing was done. The letter killeth . . . . The old hunter disappears . . . severed away from his race. In the new epoch that is coming, there will be no Letter of the Law." In Butler's *The Way of All Flesh,* Ernest comes to see that "the spirit behind the Church is true, though her letter—true once —is now true no longer. The spirit behind the High Priests of Science is as lying as its letter."

LET THE DAY PERISH WHEREIN I WAS BORN   *see CURSE THE DAY I WAS BORN*

LET THE DEAD BURY THEIR DEAD

Matt. 8:21–22;
Luke 9:60

When Jesus was about to depart from a great multitude, one of His disciples said unto Him, "Lord, suffer me first to go and bury my father. But Jesus said unto him, Follow me; and let the dead bury their dead." In "A Psalm of Life," Longfellow wrote, "Trust no Future, howe'er pleasant! / Let the dead Past bury its dead!" In "A Plea for Captain John Brown," Thoreau said that Harper's Ferry made him aware of the fact of death. But there really was "no death in the case, because there had been no life; they merely rotted or sloughed off . . . . Let the dead bury their dead." And in Joyce's *A Portrait of the Artist as a Young Man,* Stephen reflects upon his revolt against his past. "*March 21, night.* Free. Soul free and fancy free. Let the dead bury the dead. Ay. And let the dead marry the dead."

LET THERE BE LIGHT

Gen. 1:3

When "In the beginning God created the heaven and earth . . . . God said, Let there be light: and there was light." The Vulgate said, "Dixitque Deus: Fiat lux. Et facta est lux." In Milton's *Paradise Lost,* Raphael tells Adam about the creation.

> Let ther be Light, said God, and forthwith Light
> Ethereal, first of things, quintessence pure
> Sprung from the Deep, and from her native East

To journie through the airie gloom began,
Sphear'd in a radiant Cloud, for yet the Sun
Was not; shee in a cloudie Tabernacle
Sojourn'd the while. God saw the Light was good;

Pope wrote this epitaph for Sir Isaac Newton:

Nature and Nature's laws lay hid in night:
God said, Let Newton be! and all was light.

In "Shakespeare," Carlyle asked, "Can the man say, Fiat lux,
Let there be light; and out of chaos make a world?"

LET THOU THY SERVANT DEPART IN PEACE   *see SIMEON THE JUST*

LET US REASON TOGETHER   *see SINS BE AS SCARLET*

LEVIATHAN

Job 41; Ps. 74:14; 104:26; Isa. 27:1

Leviathan in the Bible is a mythical sea monster, usually considered a whale in literature. The Lord spoke to Job out of the whirlwind saying, "Canst thou draw out leviathan with an hook? . . . Canst thou fill his skin with barbed irons . . . . The sword of him that layeth at him cannot hold: the spear, the dart, nor the habergeon. He esteemeth iron as straw . . . . The arrow cannot make him flee . . . . Darts are counted as stubble: he laugheth at the shaking of a spear." In *Moby Dick*, Melville asks of a whale struggling against the lines of three harpooners: "Is this the creature of whom it was once so triumphantly said—'Canst thou fill his skin with barbed irons? . . . The sword of him that layeth at him cannot hold, the spear, the dart, nor the habergeon; he esteemeth iron as straw; the arrow cannot make him flee; darts are counted as stubble; he laugheth at the shaking of a spear!' This the creature? this he? Oh! that unfulfilments should follow the prophets." In *Paradise Lost*, Milton compares Satan stretched out on the burning lake of hell to "that Sea-beast / Leviathan, which God of all his works / Created hugest that swim th' Ocean stream . . . ." And Raphael, in *Paradise Lost*, tells Adam of the creation of the fishes:

there Leviathan
Hugest of living Creatures, on the Deep
Stretched like a Promontorie sleeps or swimmes,
And seems a moving Land, and at his Gilles
Draws in, and at his Trunck spouts out a Sea.

LIGHT (CANDLE) UNDER A BUSHEL

Matt. 5:15; Mark
4:21; Luke 11:33

In the Sermon on the Mount, Jesus said, "Ye are the light of the world. A city that is set on an hill cannot be lid. Neither do men light a candle, and put it under a bushel, but on a candlestick; and it giveth light unto all that are in the house." In Shakespeare's *Measure for Measure*, the Duke ironically chides harsh Angelo for not showing his true virtue openly:

> Heaven doth with us as we with torches do.
> Not light them for themselves; for if our virtues
> Did not go forth of us, 'twere all alike
> As if we had them not.

In *Cape Cod*, Thoreau, at Provincetown, speaking of the lighthouse, said, "What avails it though a light be placed on the top of a hill, if you spend all your life directly under the hill? It might as well be under a bushel." In Hardy's *Far from the Madding Crowd*, when Joseph Poorgrass is praised, he admits he has his gifts. "But under your bushel, Joseph! under your bushel with 'ee! A strange desire, neighbors, this desire to hide, and no praise due."

LILIES OF THE FIELD

Matt. 6:28–34;
Luke 12:27–31

In the Sermon on the Mount, Jesus taught the superiority of spiritual to material values. "And why take ye thought for raiment? Consider the lilies of the field, how they grow; they toil not, neither do they spin: and yet I say unto you, That even Solomon in all his glory was not arrayed like one of these . . . . Take therefore no thought for the morrow: for the morrow shall take thought for the things of itself." Milton, in Sonnet XX, invites a friend to dinner, asking him to "help wast a sullen day," until the west wind shall "re-inspire / The frozen earth; and cloth in fresh attire / The Lilie and Rose, that neither sow'd nor spun." The motto for Keats's "Ode on Indolence" is "They toil not, neither do they spin." In "The Two Races of Men," Lamb says of borrowers, "What a careless, even deportment hath your borrower! . . . What a beautiful reliance on Providence doth he manifest,—taking no more thought than lilies!" In D. H. Lawrence's "Sun," Juliet, on her doctor's orders, took sun baths in the nude. "She would lie and turn to the sun, her tanned, pear-shaped breasts pointing up. She would take no thought for the morrow." In "Mrs. Battle's Opinions on Whist," Charles Lamb extols the beauty of the court cards: "the gay triumph-assuring scarlets—the contrasting deadly-killing sables—the 'hoary majesty of spades,' Pam in all his glory! . . ."

LILITH (lil'ith)

Lilith is the legendary first wife of Adam, nowhere named in the Bible. In Babylonian legend she was a demon of desolate places, and in later Jewish lore she deserted Adam and haunted the night. Isaiah (34:14) says, ". . . the screech owl also shall rest there, and find for herself a place of rest"; this, according to a marginal note in the Revised Version, refers to Lilith. In Browning's poem, "Adam, Lilith, and Eve," each wife, during a frightening storm, confessed to Adam truths about herself. As soon as the storm was over,

> Up started both in wonder,
> Looked round and saw that the sky was clear,
> Then laughed "Confess you believed us, Dear!"
> "I saw through the joke!" the man replied
> They re-seated themselves beside.

In *Sartor Resartus*, Carlyle said that Professor Teufelsdröckh's vast learning included writings about "Lilis, Adam's first wife, whom, according to the Talmudists, he had before Eve, and who bore him, in that wedlock, the whole progeny of aerial, aquatic, and terrestial Devils . . . ."

LILY AMONG THORNS   *see ROSE OF SHARON*

LILY OF THE VALLEYS   *see ROSE OF SHARON*

LINTEL OF THE DOOR   *see PASSOVER*

LION IN THE WAY . . . IN THE STREETS

Prov. 26:13

"The slothful man saith, There is a lion in the way; a lion is in the streets." Charles Lamb, in "The South-Sea House," says of John Tipp, an accountant with a kind of cowardice in his nature, ". . . it is mere temperament; the absence of the romantic and the enterprising; it sees a lion in the way . . . ." In "Poor Relations," Lamb says that a poor relation "is the most irrelevant thing in nature,—a lion in your path . . . ." In Butler's *The Way of All Flesh*, after Ernest was released from prison, he patrolled the streets for three or four nights. ". . . he had been scared, and now saw lions where there were none . . . ."

LION LIE DOWN WITH THE LAMB

Isa. 11:6 When the Messiah shall come forth, "a rod out of the stem of Jesse," "the wolf also shall dwell with the lamb, and the leopard shall lie down with the kid; and the calf and the young lion and the fatling together . . . ." In Shakespeare's *Henry VI, Part III*, King Henry, recounting his own virtues, asks Exeter why should the people

> love Edward more than me?
> No, Exeter, these graces challenge grace:
> And when the lion fawns upon the lamb,
> The lamb will never cease to follow him.

In Shelley's *Queen Mab*, the Queen pictures a future of peace and love among all creatures:

> The lion now forgets to thirst for blood:
> There might you see him sporting in the sun
> Beside the dreadless kid; his claws are sheathed,
> His teeth are harmless, custom's force has made
> His nature as the nature of a lamb.

In Henry James's "The Death of the Lion," the successful author, Neil Paraday, is lionized by Mrs. Weeks Wimbush, "proprietress of the universal menagerie . . . [at her house] the animals rub shoulders freely with the spectators and the lions sit down for whole evenings with the lambs."

LITTLE CLOUD NO BIGGER THAN A MAN'S HAND   *see* *CLOUD LIKE A MAN'S HAND*

LITTLE LOWER THAN THE ANGELS

Ps. 8:4–5 The Psalmist considers the excellence of the Lord's creation, nature and man. "What is man, that thou art mindful of him? and the son of man, that thou visitest him? For thou hast made him a little lower than the angels, and hast crowned him with glory and honour." In Shakespeare's *Hamlet*, Hamlet explains his recent melancholy to Rosencrantz and Guildenstern: "What a piece of work is man! How noble in reason! How infinite in faculty! In form and moving how express and admirable! In action how like an angel! . . . The paragon of animals! And yet, to me, what is this quintessence of dust?" Izaak Walton, in *The Life of Dr. John Donne*, said that Donne had doubts about his fitness for the clergy: ". . . he came to ask King David's thankful question, 'Lord, who am I that thou art so mindful of me?' " In "The Damned Human Race," Mark Twain wrote of man's "Moral Sense": "There is only one possible stage below the Moral Sense; that is the Immoral Sense. The Frenchman has it. Man is but little lower than the angels. This definitely locates him. He is between the angels and the French."

LIVE BY BREAD ALONE   see BY BREAD ALONE

LIVE, MOVE, AND HAVE OUR BEING

Acts 17:28

Paul, in Athens speaking on the Areopagus [ăr·ê·ŏp′a·gŭs], meaning the hill of Mars or Ares, declared that God dwells not in temples made with hands, but is near every one of us; "For in him we live, and move, and have our being; as certain also of your own poets have said, For we are also his offspring." The motto of Browning's poem "Cleon," about the first century Greek poet, is, "As certain also of your own poets have said—" In "Boswell's Life of Johnson," Carlyle asks if in modern times one can gather "any dimmest shadow of an answer to that great question: How men lived and had their being . . . ." Johnson, he said, was devoted to the highest truth: that man is "ever a Revelation of God to man; and lives, moves, and has his being in Truth only . . . ." In Butler's *The Way of All Flesh*, Ernest, writing "on the various marriage systems of the world," said that good breeding should be "the central faith in which [all] should live and move and have their being . . . ."

LIVING DOG IS BETTER THAN A DEAD LION

Eccles. 9:4

The Preacher argues that death brings all to the same end. So "to him that is joined to all the living there is hope: for a living dog is better than a dead lion." In the "Conclusion" of *Walden*, Thoreau said, "Some are dinning in our ears that we Americans, and moderns generally, are intellectual dwarfs compared with the ancients, or even the Elizabethan men. But what is that to the purpose? A living dog is better than a dead lion." In Galsworthy's *Over the River*, Dornford's comment on his family's loss of property and wealth when his father died was, "Live donkeys are better than dead lions." In Shaw's *Back to Methuselah*, the sculptor Martellus tells his fellow sculptor Arjillax that he will smash his busts of the ancients, as Martellus did, "because you cannot give them life. A live ancient is better than a dead statue."

LOAVES AND FISHES

Matt. 14:15–21;
John 6:5–14

A great multitude followed Jesus into a desert and when evening came there was no food for them except five loaves and two fishes. Jesus "took the five loaves, and the two fishes, and looking up to heaven, he blessed, and brake, and gave the loaves to his disciples, and the disciples to the multitude. And they did all eat, and were filled . . . about five thousand men, beside women and children." In "The Man of Law's Tale," Chaucer asked who fed Constance.while she was adrift at sea in a rudderless ship.

> no wight but Crist, sanz faille.
> Five thousand folk it was as greet mervaille
> With loves five and fisshes two to feede.
> God sente his foyson at hir grete neede.

Van Wyck Brooks, in *The Times of Melville and Whitman,* said that "Whitman grieved that so many young men were hungry for loaves and fishes and fat berths, that they seemed always ready to obey."

LOCUSTS AND WILD HONEY

Matt. 3:4; Mark
1:6

JOHN THE BAPTIST led an austere life in the wilderness, dressing in "raiment of camel's hair . . . and his meat was locusts and wild honey." In Shakespeare's *Othello,* Iago tells Roderigo, "These Moors are changeable in their wills . . . . The food that to him now is as luscious as locusts shall be to him shortly as bitter as coloquintida." Carlyle, in *Sartor Resartus,* says of Professor Teufelsdröckh, "In our wild Seer, shaggy, unkempt, like a Baptist living on locusts and wild honey, there is an untutored energy, a silent, as it were unconscious, strength . . . ." And in *Walden,* Thoreau, commenting on "modern improvements," said, "After all, the man whose horse trots a mile in a minute does not carry the most important messages; he is not an evangelist, nor does he come round eating locusts and wild honey."

LOCUSTS, PLAGUE OF   *see PLAGUE OF LOCUSTS*

LORD GAVE, AND THE LORD HATH TAKEN AWAY   *see NAKED CAME I OUT OF MY MOTHER'S WOMB*

LORD, HOW LONG?

Ps. 6:3; 89:46;
90:13; Isa. 6:11

The Psalmist, praying for help in time of trouble: "My soul is also sore vexed: but thou, O Lord, how long?" In "Clerical Oppressors," Whittier comments on a proslavery meeting of southern clergymen in 1835:

How long, O Lord! how long
Shall such a priesthood barter truth away,
And in Thy name, for robbery and wrong
At thy own altars pray?

At the end of Shaw's *Saint Joan,* Joan's last words after she has
been condemned to burning are: "O God that madest this beautiful earth, when will it be ready to receive Thy saints? How
long, O Lord, how long?"

LORD'S ANOINTED

I Sam. 16:6; 24:6,
10

One blessed or specially appointed or chosen by God: prophets,
priests, and particularly a king. When, after secretly cutting off
Saul's skirt in the night but sparing his life, David, feeling guilty,
spoke to Saul, saying that though men claimed that David
would kill Saul, "I will not put forth mine hand against my
lord; for he is the Lord's anointed." In Shakespeare's *Richard
II,* John of Gaunt refuses the plea of the Duchess of Gloucester
to avenge her husband's death, for it was caused by the king.

God's is the quarrel; for God's substitute,
His deputy anointed in His sight,
Hath caused his death: the which if wrongfully,
Let heaven revenge; for I may never lift
An angry arm against His minister.

And in *Macbeth,* Macduff cries out the murder of King Dun-
can, saying,

Confusion now hath made his masterpiece!
Most sacrilegious murder hath broke ope
The Lord's anointed temple, and stole thence
The life o' the building.

LORD'S PRAYER

Matt. 6:9–13

In the Sermon on the Mount, Jesus taught the Lord's Prayer,
which begins: "Our father, which art in heaven, Hallowed be
thy name. Thy kingdom come. Thy will be done in earth, as it
is in Heaven." The opening words in Latin are *pater noster.*
Longfellow's first "Divina Commedia" sonnet describes a devout laborer entering a cathedral:

Oft have I seen at some cathedral door
A laborer, pausing in the dust and heat,
Lay down his burden, and with reverent feet
Enter, and cross himself, and on the floor
Kneel to repeat his paternoster o'er . . . .

In *Cannery Row*, Steinbeck wrote a humanistic prayer: "Our father who art in nature, who has given the gift of survival to the coyote, the common brown rat, the English sparrow, the house fly and the moth, must have a great deal and overwhelming love for no-goods and blots-on-the-town and bums, and Mack and the boys." And in "A Clean, Well-Lighted Place," Hemingway wrote a naturalistic prayer, with existentialist tones. The old waiter, reflecting upon the despair which caused another old man to attempt suicide, thought, "It was a nothing that he knew too well . . . and man was a nothing too . . . . Our nada who art in nada, nada be thy name thy kingdom nada thy will be nada in nada as it is in nada . . . ."

LORD'S SUPPER   *see LAST SUPPER*

LOSE HIS LIFE   *see WHOSOEVER WILL SAVE HIS LIFE SHALL LOSE IT*

LOSE (LOST) ITS SAVOUR   *see SALT OF THE EARTH*

LOT AND HIS DAUGHTERS

Gen. 19:30–38

After Lot left Sodom, he dwelt in the mountain "in a cave, he and his two daughters." Because there was "not a man in the earth to come in unto [them] after the manner of all the earth," they made their father drink wine and then lay with him in order to "preserve seed of [their] father." The elder daughter bore Moab, the father of the Moabites, and the younger daughter bore Benammi, the father of the Ammonites. In Chaucer's "The Pardoner's Tale," the Pardoner cites the Bible to show how wine and drunkenness lead to lust and excess:

> The hooly writ take I to my witnesse
> That luxurie is in wyn and dronkenesse.
>   Lo, how that dronken Looth, unkyndely,
> Lay by his doghtres two, unwityngly;
> So dronke he was, he nyste what he wroghte.

In Mark Twain's *The Mysterious Stranger*, Satan presented the boys with a show portraying "the progress of the human race." After they saw Sodom and Gomorrah, "Next, Lot and his daughters in the cave."

LOT AND THE MEN OF SODOM

Gen. 19:1–14

While Lot was entertaining two angels, the men of Sodom surrounded his house and said, "Where are the men which came in to thee this night? bring them out unto us, that we may know them." Lot said, "I pray you, brethren, do not so wickedly," and he offered his two daughters instead. And the angels smote the men of Sodom with blindness "so that they wearied themselves to find the door." From this story we get the words "sodomite" and "sodomy." In his elegy "On His Mistress," John Donne urges his mistress not to accompany him on his journey disguised as "my feigned page":

> Th' indifferent Italian, as we pass
> His warm land, well content to think thee page,
> Will hunt thee with such lust and hideous rage
> As Lot's fair guests were vexed.

In "An Edict by the King of Prussia," Benjamin Franklin satirized the export by Britain of undesirables to America: they included "all the thieves, highway and street robbers . . . murderers, s-d-tes, and villains of every denomination . . . for the better peopling of that country." And in *White Jacket*, Melville told of homosexual tendencies among sailors held long in close confinement. "The sins for which the cities of the plain were overthrown still linger in some of these woodenwalled Gomorrahs of the deep."

LOT'S WIFE

Gen. 19:17–26

When Lot fled from Sodom (see SODOM AND GOMORRAH), the Lord said, "Escape for thy life; look not behind thee, neither stay thou in the plain . . . ." But Lot's wife "looked back from behind him, and she became a pillar of salt." Jesus said, "Remember Lot's wife" (Luke 17:32). In Bunyan's *Pilgrim's Progress*, Christian and his companion Hope came to an old monument that looked like "a Woman transformed into the shape of a Pillar." An inscription read, "Remember Lot's Wife," and they concluded that "that was the Pillar of Salt into which Lot's wife was turned, for her looking back with a covetous heart, when she was going from Sodom for safety." When Jane Eyre, in Charlotte Brontë's *Jane Eyre*, assumed a new position as schoolmistress with St. John Rivers, he warned her not "to yield to the vacillating fears of Lot's wife . . . . I counsel you to resist, firmly, every temptation which would incline you to look back." In *Don Juan*, Byron described one of the ladies of the Turkish harem who "as marble, statue-like and still, / Lay in a breathless, hush'd and stony sleep;" like "Lot's wife done in salt."

LOVE OF MONEY   *see ROOT OF ALL EVIL*

LOVE PASSING THE LOVE OF WOMEN

II Sam. 1:26

In his lament for the deaths of Saul and Jonathan, David wrote, "I am distressed for thee, my brother Jonathan: very pleasant hast thou been unto me: thy love to me was wonderful, passing the love of women. How are the mighty fallen!" Macaulay, in "Lord Clive," criticizes Sir John Malcolm's overpraise of Lord Clive: his "love passes the love of biographers, and [he] can see nothing but wisdom and justice in the actions of his idol." D. H. Lawrence, in *Studies in Classic American Literature*, summarizes the beginning of the plot of Hawthorne's *Blithedale Romance:* "I, Nathaniel, at once catch cold, and . . . am nursed with inordinate tenderness by the blacksmith, whose great hands are gentler than a woman's, etc. The two men love one another with a love surpassing the love of women, so long as the healing-and-salvation business lasts."

LOVE THY NEIGHBOR

Matt. 5:43; 19:19;
22:39; Lev. 19:18

The Lord taught through Moses and Jesus, "Thou shalt love thy neighbor as thyself." In Dryden's "Absalom and Achitophel," Shimei was a treasonous conspirator against David: "For Shimei, though not prodigal of pelf, / Yet loved his wicked neighbor as himself." In Sidney Lanier's "The Symphony," the flute sings of love:

> Later, a sweet Voice *Love thy neighbor* said;
> Then first the bounds of neighborhood outspread
> Beyond all confines of old ethnic dread . . .
> "All men are neighbors," so the sweet Voice said . . .
> Yea, man found neighbors in great hills and trees
> And streams and clouds and suns and birds and bees,
> And throbbed with neighbor-loves in loving these.

And in "The Damned Human Race," Mark Twain said, "Man is the only Religious Animal . . . . He is the only animal that loves his neighbor as himself, and cuts his throat if his theology isn't straight."

LOVE YOUR ENEMIES

Matt. 5:44

In the Sermon on the Mount, Jesus said, "Ye have heard that it hath been said, Thou shalt love thy neighbor, and hate thine enemy. But I say unto you, Love your enemies, bless them that curse you, do good to them that hate you, and pray for them which despitefully use you, and persecute you." In Shakespeare's *Macbeth*, when Macbeth hired Banquo's mur-

derers, he urged them to remember the wrongs Banquo had
done them:

> Are you so gospell'd
> To pray for this good man and for his issue,
> Whose heavy hand hath bow'd you to the grave
> And beggar'd yours for ever?

In *Walden*, Thoreau said of the stoical Indians being burned
at the stake by missionaries, ". . . the law to do as you would
be done by fell with less persuasiveness on the ears of those
. . . who loved their enemies after a new fashion, and came
very near freely forgiving them all they did." In *Innocents
Abroad*, Mark Twain wrote, "I know it is my duty to 'pray
for them that despitefully use me'; and therefore, hard as it is,
I shall still try to pray for these fumigating, macaroni-stuffing
organ grinders."

LUCIFER
(lū′sĭ·fẽr)

Isa. 14:12

"How art thou fallen from heaven, O Lucifer, son of the
morning." The name, meaning "light-bringer," refers to Venus
as the morning star. In Isaiah it refers to the fallen king of
Babylon. Jesus' saying "I beheld Satan as lightning fall from
heaven" (Luke 10:18) was later interpreted as a reference to
Isaiah. Lucifer thus became a literary term usually referring to
Satan expelled from heaven. Sometimes, however, it simply
means the fallen angel Lucifer himself. In Chaucer's "The
Monk's Tale," the Monk describes Lucifer as an example of
men fallen from high degree.

> At Lucifer, though he an angel were,
> And not a man, at hym wol I bigynne.
> For though Fortune may noon angel dere,
> From heigh degree yet fel he for his synne
> Doun into helle, where he yet is inne.
> O Lucifer, brightest of angels alle,
> Now artow Sathanas, that mayest nat twynne
> Out of miserie, in which that thou art falle.

Falstaff, in Shakespeare's *Henry IV, Part II*, ridicules Bardolph's
liquorous face with its inflamed nose: "The Fiend hath pricked
down Bardolph irrecoverable, and his face is Lucifer's privy
kitchen, where he doth nothing but roast malt worms." Milton,
in the *Areopagitica*, attacks licensing of books as "the imme-
diate image of a star-chamber decree . . . made in those very
times when that court did the rest of those her pious works,
for which she is now fallen from the stars with Lucifer." And
in *Paradise Lost*, Lucifer becomes Satan on his fall:

> Lucifer from Heav'n
> (So call him, brighter once amidst the Host
> Of Angels, then that Starr the Starrs among)
> Fell with his flaming Legions through the Deep.

When Aunt Polly, in Mark Twain's *Tom Sawyer,* said that Tom was "full of the Old Scratch," she referred to the devil as Lucifer—by way of the friction match, or the lucifer match.

MACCABEES

"I and II Maccabees" of the Apocrypha

The Maccabees, meaning perhaps "hammer," were the family who achieved independence and religious freedom for the Jews from 166 to 63 B.C. The rebellion against the Syrian tyrant Antiochus Epiphanes [ăn·tī′·ô·kŭs ê·pĭf′a·nēz] was led first by Judas Maccabaeus [măk·a·bē′ŭs]. When Antiochus tried to force heathen worship on the Jews, the priest Mattathias (măt·a·thī′ăs) of Modin, father of Judas and his four brothers, fled with his family to the hills, from where guerrilla attacks on Antiochus were made, until Judas Maccabaeus entered Jerusalem and restored the Temple, December 25, 165 B.C. After Judas died, his brothers continued the fight for political independence. In Chaucer's "The Tale of Melibee," Prudence advises her husband Melibeus not to start war against his enemies. She quotes "Judas Machabeus, which was Goddes knyght, whan he shold fighte agayn his adversarie that hadde a gretter nombre and a gretter multitude of folk and strenger than was this peple of Machabee." Judas told his people, says Prudence, that victory comes only by God's will; and no man, she argues, can be certain of that. In Shakespeare's *Love's Labour's Lost,* Holofernes, the schoolmaster, presents himself before the Princess as one of the Nine Worthies, Judas Maccabaeus: "Judas I am—" Dumain says, "A Judas!" Holofernes: "Not Iscariot, sir. Judas I am, ycliped Maccabaeus." Dumain: "Judas Maccabaeus clipt is plain Judas." And when Holofernes finally retires in confusion, the Princess says, "Alas, poor Maccabaeus, how he hath been baited!" In Milton's *Paradise Regained,* Satan tempts Christ with worldly kingdom. Often, he says, have tyrants violated

> The Temple, oft the Law with foul affronts,
> Abominations rather, as did once
> Antiochus: and think'st thou to regain
> Thy right by sitting still or thus retiring?
> So did not Machabeus: he indeed
> Retir'd unto the Desert, but with arms;
> And o'er a mighty King so oft prevail'd,
> That by strong hand his Family obtain'd,
> Though Priests, the Crown, and David's Throne usurp'd,
> With Modin and her suburbs once content.

MAGDALEN(E)

(măg'dȧ·lēn)

Matt. 27:56, 61; Mark 16:9; Luke 7:37–50

Mary, from the town of Magdala, was one of the women at the Crucifixion and was the one to whom Jesus appeared first after the Resurrection. She is usually remembered in literature as the repentant sinner who, when Jesus sat at meat in the Pharisee's house, "stood at his feet behind him weeping, and began to wash his feet with tears, and did wipe them with the hairs of her head . . . ." Jesus said, "Her sins, which are many, are forgiven; for she loved much . . ." The word "maudlin" derives from her name, and in paintings her eyes are usually swollen and red from weeping. In "Laus Veneris," Swinburne sang of love: " 'Sweeter,' I said, 'the little laugh of love / Than tears out of the eyes of Magdalen, / Or any fallen feather of the Dove.' " In "Burns," Whittier said of Burns's lawless loves and ribald lines, ". . . think, while falls the shade between / The erring one and Heaven, / That he who loved like Magdalen, / Like her may be forgiven." D. H. Lawrence, in *Studies in Classic American Literature,* said about Hester Prynne, "A man must be pure, just that you can seduce him to a fall. Because the greatest thrill in life is to bring down the Sacred Saint with a flop into the mud. Then when you've brought him down, humbly wipe off the mud with your hair, another Magdalen."

MAIMED, THE HALT, THE BLIND

Luke 14:13, 21

Jesus said to a group of "lawyers and Pharisees . . . when thou makest a feast, call the poor, the maimed, the lame, the blind . . . ." instead of friends and rich neighbors. And he told of a certain man who made a great supper and sent his servant to go out and "bring in hither the poor, and the maimed, and the halt, and the blind." In Goldsmith's *The Vicar of Wakefield,* cousins often came to visit the Wakefield family. "Some of them did us no great honour by these claims of kindred; as we had the blind, the maimed, and the halt amongst the number." In Vachel Lindsay's "General William Booth Enters Heaven," Jesus came out of the courthouse and "stretched his hands above the passing poor."

Then in an instant all that blear review
Marched on spotless, clad in raiment new.
The lame were straightened, withered limbs uncurled
And blind eyes opened on a new, sweet world.°

°Reprinted with permission of The Macmillan Company from *Collected Poems* by Vachel Lindsay. Copyright 1913 by The Macmillan Company.

MAINTAIN MINE OWN WAYS   *see THOUGH HE SLAY ME, YET WILL I TRUST IN HIM*

MAKING MANY BOOKS   *see OF MAKING MANY BOOKS*

MAMMON

Matt. 6:24; Luke 16:9, 11, 13

In the Sermon on the Mount, Jesus said, "No man can serve two masters: for either he will hate the one, and love the other; or else he will hold to the one, and despise the other. Ye cannot serve God and mammon." "Mammon" is from the Aramaic word *mamona*, meaning "riches." In the Middle Ages Mammon became the devil of avarice. In Spenser's *The Faerie Queene*, Sir Guyon meets Mammon:

> God of the world and worldlings I me call,
>   Great *Mammon*, greatest god below the skye,
>   That of my plenty poure out unto all,
>   And unto none my graces do enuye:
>   Riches, renowne, and principality,
>   Honour, estate, and all this worldes good,
>   For which men swinck and sweat incessantly,
>   Fro me do flow into an ample flood,
> And in the hollow earth have their eternal brood.

In Ben Jonson's *The Alchemist*, Sir Epicure Mammon is a worldly sensualist. In Milton's *Paradise Lost*, Mammon, one of the fallen angels, leads them in digging for gold for the devils' Palace of Pandemonium in hell.

> Mammon led them on,
> Mammon, the least erected Spirit that fell
> From heav'n, for ev'n in heav'n his looks & thoughts
> Were always downward bent, admiring more
> The riches of Heav'ns pavement, trod'n Gold,
> Then aught divine or holy else enjoy'd
> In vision beatific . . . .

MAN AFTER HIS OWN HEART   *see DAVID*

MAN BORN OF WOMAN

Job 14:1-2

In his debate with his friends about his sufferings, Job said, "Man that is born of a woman is of few days, and full of trouble. He cometh forth like a flower, and is cut down: he fleeth also as a shadow, and continueth not." In Carlyle's *Sartor Resartus*, Professor Teufelsdröckh tells of his childhood sufferings. "And yet, O Man born of Woman . . . wherein is my case peculiar?" In *The Way of All Flesh*, Butler said of Ernest, just come into his inheritance, ". . . when he fell—as who that is born of woman can help sometimes doing?—it was not till after a sharp tussle with temptation. . . ." And in Mark Twain's *Tom Sawyer*, Aunt Polly says of Tom, who has just tricked her, "Every time I let him off, my conscience does hurt me so, and every time I hit him my old heart most breaks. Well-a-well, man that is born of woman is of few days and full of trouble, as the Scripture says, and I reckon it's so."

MANNA

Exod. 16:13–35; Num. 11:6–9; Josh. 5:12; Ps. 78:24; John 6:31, 49, 58; Rev. 2:17

When the children of Israel became hungry in the wilderness, the Lord sent "quails [that] came up, and covered the camp," then "a small round thing, as small as the hoar frost on the ground." They called it manna, "for they wist not what it was." It was possibly a sweet secretion from the tamarisk tree. They gathered and divided it by the omer according to each man's need, every morning because "when the sun waxed hot, it melted." In Shakespeare's *The Merchant of Venice*, when Nerissa announces Shylock's "special deed of gift" to Lorenzo and Jessica, Lorenzo says, "Fair ladies, you drop Manna in the way / Of starved people." In *Areopagitica*, Milton, arguing for temperance in all things, said that when God "tabled the Jews from heaven, that omer, which was every man's daily portion of manna, is computed to have been more than might have well sufficed the heartiest feeder thrice as many meals." In *Walden*, Thoreau calls himself a reporter of nature, "waiting at evening on the hill-tops for the sky to fall, that I might catch something, though I never caught much, and that, manna-wise, would dissolve again in the sun." In Mark Twain's *Captain Stormfield's Visit to Heaven*, Captain Stormfield, newly arrived in heaven, sent a note to his old friend Sandy McWilliams "and asked him to come over and take his manna and quails with me next day."

MAN SHALL NOT LIVE BY BREAD ALONE   *see BY BREAD ALONE*

MANSIONS, HEAVENLY   *see MANY MANSIONS*

MANTLE OF ELIJAH   *see ELIJAH, THE TISHBITE*

MANY BE CALLED, BUT FEW CHOSEN

Matt. 20:16; 22:14

In the parable of the laborers, Jesus said, "So the last shall be first, and the first last: for many be called, but few chosen." (See FIRST SHALL BE LAST.) In *Discourses in America*, Matthew Arnold discussed the dangers of majority rule. "[Plato said] 'The majority are bad . . .' Much to the same effect, however, is the famous sentence of the New Testament: 'Many are called, few chosen.'" This may seem "a hard saying," said Arnold, but there is truth in it. In Aldous Huxley's *After Many a Summer*, Mr. Propter reflects upon salvation: more than good will and intelligence are needed; "there must also be the recollection which seeks to transform and transcend intelligence. Many are called, but few are chosen—because few even know in what salvation consists."

MANY MANSIONS

John 14:2

Jesus, in his farewell sermon, said to his disciples, "Let not your heart be troubled: ye believe in God, believe also in me. In my Father's house are many mansions: if it were not so, I would have told you. I go to prepare a place for you." Charles Lamb, in "The Old and the New Schoolmaster," wrote about his "lamentably desultory and unmethodical" reading. "Not that I affect ignorance—but my head has not many mansions, nor spacious; and I have been obliged to fill it with such cabinet curiosities as it can hold without aching." D. H. Lawrence, in *Studies in Classic American Literature*, said that Whitman's essential message was the free soul going down the open road. "'In my Father's house are many mansions.' 'No,' said Whitman. 'Keep out of mansions. A mansion may be heaven on earth, but you might as well be dead. Strictly avoid mansions. The soul is herself when she is going on foot down the open road.'"

MARAH
(mā′rȧ)

Exod. 15:23–25;
Ruth 1:20

Marah, which means "bitter," was the first oasis the Israelites reached after crossing the Sea of Reeds. "And when they came to Marah, they could not drink of the waters of Marah, for they were bitter . . . ." The people complained, and "the Lord shewed [Moses] a tree, which when he had cast into the waters, the waters were made sweet . . . ." When, in the book of Ruth, Naomi, whose name means "pleasant," returned a widow to Bethlehem, she said, "Call me not Naomi, call me Mara: for the Almighty hath dealt very bitterly with me." In Tennyson's *Becket*, Rosamund leaves her nunnery disguised as a monk to plead with Becket for mercy to the King. As she throws back her cowl, Becket says, "Breaking already from thy novitiate / To plunge into this bitter world again— / These wells of Marah!" In "The Jewish Cemetery at Newport," Longfellow expresses sympathy for the sufferings of the Jews:

All their lives long, with the unleavened bread
And bitter herbs of exile and its fears,
The wasting famine of the heart they fed,
And slaked its thirst with Marah of their tears.

MARANATHA   *see ANATHEMA MARANATHA*

MARK OF CAIN

Gen. 4:15   After Cain was banished as "a fugitive and vagabond," for killing Abel, he "cried unto the Lord . . . that everyone that
findeth me shall slay me." And in compassion the Lord said
unto him, "Therefore whosoever slayeth Cain, vengeance shall
be taken on him sevenfold. And the Lord set a mark upon
Cain, lest any finding him should kill him." Although the mark
of Cain, commonly called also the brand or curse of Cain, was
a mark of protection, and although its exact nature and location were not specified, in literature it is usually a mark of
punishment, of crimson color, branded on Cain's brow. In
Shakespeare's *Richard III*, Queen Elizabeth accuses Richard of
his murders:

Hidest thou that forehead with a golden crown,
Where should be graven, if that right were right,
The slaughter of the prince that owed that crown,
And the dire death of my two sons and brothers?

When Shelley in "Adonais" appears as a mourner and is asked
by Urania who he is,

He answered not, but with a sudden hand
Made bare his branded and ensanguined brow,
Which was like Cain's . . . .

And in "Adonais" also he invoked "the curse of Cain" on the
critics who he believed had killed Keats. Byron's Giaour, in
The Giaour, confesses that he had caused his mistress' death:

She died—I dare not tell thee how;
But look—'tis written on my brow!
There read of Cain the curse and crime,
In characters unworn by time.

Longfellow, in "The Arsenal at Springfield," says that if the
wealth spent on war were spent on education, "every nation,
that should lift again / Its hand against a brother, on its forehead / Would wear forevermore the curse of Cain!" And Hawthorne, in *The Scarlet Letter*, says that society "had set a mark

upon [Hester] more intolerable to a woman's heart than that
which branded the brow of Cain."

MARK OF THE BEAST

Rev. 13:16–17;
16:2

A beast from the earth gave power to the image of the beast
from the sea; "And he caused all, both small and great, rich
and poor, free and bond, to receive a mark in their right hand,
or in their foreheads: And that no man might buy or sell, save
he that had the mark, or the name of the beast . . . ." And an
angel poured out "the vials of the wrath of God . . . upon the
men which had the mark of the beast, and upon them which
worshipped his image." In Ben Jonson's *The Alchemist,* Ananias,
the deacon, says he has no faith in Subtle, the alchemist: "He
bears / The visible mark of the beast in his forehead." In Butler's *The Way of All Flesh,* Ernest, disgusted with editors'
treatment of his articles, says, "Editors are like the people who
bought and sold in the book of Revelation; there is not one
but has the mark of the beast upon him." In "Spiritual Laws,"
Emerson said that a man's character shows in every way. "His
vice glasses his eye, demeans his cheek, pinches the nose, sets
the mark of the beast on the back of his head, and writes, O fool!
fool! on the forehead of a king."

MARRIAGE IN CANA   *see CANA*

MARY MAGDALENA   *see MAGDALEN(E)*

MASSACRE OF THE INNOCENTS   *see HEROD THE GREAT*

MAUDLIN   *see MAGDALEN(E)*

MEASURE FOR MEASURE

Matt. 7:2; Mark
4:24

In the Sermon on the Mount, Jesus said, "Judge not, that ye
be not judged. For with that judgment ye judge, ye shall be
judged: and with that measure ye mete, it shall be measured
to you again." Shakespeare's title "Measure for Measure" is a
popular variant of this. In *Henry VI, Part III,* on the battlefield in Yorkshire, when Clifford is killed, Warwick says to
Richard,

> From off the gates of York fetch down the head,
> Your father's head, which Clifford placed there;
> Instead whereof let this supply the room:
> Measure for measure must be answered.

MEAT THAT YE KNOW NOT OF

John 4:32

When the disciples of Jesus "prayed him, saying, Master, eat . . . he said unto them, I have meat to eat that ye know not of." In Anne Bradstreet's "The Flesh and the Spirit," Spirit foretells her eventual conquest over her evil sister Flesh: "How I do live thou need'st not scoff, / For I have meat thou know'st not of." In E. A. Robinson's "Old King Cole," Old King Cole preferred to live rather than to weep over his misfortunes.

> There may be room for ruin yet,
> And ashes for a wasted love;
> Or, like One whom you may forget,
> I may have meat you know not of.°

MEDES AND THE PERSIANS see LAW OF THE MEDES AND PERSIANS

MELCHISEDEK
(mĕl·kĭz′ĕ·dĕk)

Gen. 14:18–20;
Ps. 110:4; Heb.
5:6, 10; 7:1–4,
10–17

Melchisedek, meaning "king of righteousness," was the "king of Salem, priest of the most high God, who met Abraham returning from the slaughter of the kings, and blessed him . . . . Without father, without mother, without descent, having neither beginning of days, nor end of life; but made like unto the Son of God; abiding a priest continually." Christ was "a priest forever after the order of Melchisedek." In *Sartor Resartus,* Carlyle said of Professor Teufelsdröckh, about whose parentage little was known, "Wits spoke of him secretly as if he were a kind of Melchizedek, without father or mother of any kind . . ." In Butler's *The Way of All Flesh,* Ernest in prison received a letter from his father but did not answer it. Longing for a total break with his parents, he "brooded over the bliss of Melchisedek who had been born an orphan, without father, without mother, and without descent." In Joyce's *A Portrait of the Artist as a Young Man,* the priest urging Stephen to join the priesthood seemed to be offering him secret knowledge and power: "He would hold his secret knowledge and secret power, being as sinless as the innocent; and he would be a priest forever according to the order of Melchisedec."

°Reprinted with permission of The Macmillan Company from *Collected Poems* by E. A. Robinson. Copyright 1916 by E. A. Robinson. Renewed 1944 by Ruth Nivison.

MENE, MENE, TEKEL, UPHARSIN

(mē′nê,
tĕk′êl,
u·fär′sĭn)

Dan. 5:25–31

These are the words which appeared in the handwriting on the wall at Belshazzar's feast in Babylon. They are Aramaic words meaning "numbered, numbered, weighed, and divisions." They were interpreted by Daniel for Belshazzar, whose thoughts were troubled, as meaning "God hath numbered thy kingdom, and finished it . . . . Thou art weighed in the balances, and art found wanting . . . . Thy kingdom is divided, and given to the Medes and the Persians." In Tennyson's "The Palace of Art" the Queen was plagued "with sore despair":

> When she would think, where'er she turn'd her sight,
> The airy hand confusion wrought,
> Wrote, "Mene, mene," and divided quite
> The kingdom of her thought.

When the fiery corposants appeared on the mast tops during a typhoon in Melville's *Moby Dick,* Stubb cursed, saying, "In all my voyagings, seldom have I heard a common oath when God's burning finger has been laid on the ship; when his 'Mene, Mene, Tekel, Upharsin' has been woven into the shrouds and the cordage." In *Don Juan,* Byron said of the words of Queen Catherine's general after his conquest of a Turkish city ("Glory to *God* and to the Empress!"): "Methinks these are the most tremendous words, / Since 'Mene, Mene, Tekel' and 'Upharsin,' / Which hands or pens have ever traced of swords. / Heaven help me! I'm but little of a parson:"

MERCY SEAT   *see ARK OF THE COVENANT*

MESS OF POTTAGE   *see SOLD HIS BIRTHRIGHT FOR A MESS OF POTTAGE*

METHUSELAH

Gen. 5:21–27

Methuselah, the son of Enoch, was the grandfather of Noah. "And all the days of Methuselah were nine hundred sixty and nine years: and he died." James Russell Lowell wrote about himself in *A Fable for Critics:*

> His lyre has some chords that would ring pretty well,
> But he'd rather by half make a drum of the shell,
> And rattle away till he's old as Methusalem,
> At the head of a march to the last new Jerusalem.

In *Walden,* Thoreau tells of an old man "who has come to his growth, and can hardly acquire more of natural love if he should live to the age of Methuselah . . . ." In Shaw's *Back to Methuselah,* Haslam, the rector, says to Franklyn, who was once in the Church, "Now I come to think of it, old Methuselah must have had to think twice before he took on anything for life. If I thought I was going to live nine hundred and sixty years, I don't think I should stay in the Church."

MICHAEL, ANGEL

Dan. 10:13, 21;
12:1; Jude 9;
Rev. 12:7

Michael, whose name means "Who is like God?" was a messenger of God who came to help Daniel against the Persians; an archangel, in Jude, who contended with the devil about the body of Moses; and, in Revelation, he fought with his angels against "that old serpent, called the Devil, and Satan" in the WAR IN HEAVEN. He is called the Prince of Angels. In Milton's *Paradise Lost,* Michael and GABRIEL lead the war in heaven against Satan. God commands him:

> Goe Michael of Celestial Armies Prince,
> And thou in military prowess next
> Gabriel, lead forth to Battel these my Sons
> Invincible, lead forth my armed Saints
> By Thousands and by Millions rang'd for fight;

In *The Vision of Judgment,* Byron said of Michael, receiving the soul of George III in heaven:

> 'Twas the archangel Michael; all men know
> The make of angels and archangels, since
> There's scarce a scribbler has not one to show,
> From the fiends' leader to the angels' prince;

And in Joyce's *A Portrait of the Artist as a Young Man,* "Michael, prince of the heavenly host, with a sword of flame in his hand, appeared before the guilty pair [Adam and Eve] and drove them forth" from the Garden of Eden.

MICHAL, WIFE OF DAVID   *see DAVID*

MIGHTY HUNTER   *see NIMROD*

MILK AND HONEY   *see LAND FLOWING WITH MILK AND HONEY*

MILLENIUM

Rev. 20:1-5

St. John the Divine envisioned a period of a thousand years when Christ would reign on earth and the Devil be chained in the bottomless pit, a period of great joy and peace. Macaulay, in "Milton," wrote of the pride of the Puritan: "he thought himself intrusted with the scepter of the millennial year." In Tennyson's *In Memoriam,* the Christmas bells

> Ring out old shapes of foul disease;
> Ring out the narrowing lust of gold;
> Ring out the thousand wars of old,
> Ring in the thousand years of peace.

In Butler's *The Way of All Flesh,* Christina was certain that a very great future was in store for her son Ernest: "there was to be a millenium shortly, certainly not later than 1866, when Ernest would be just about the right age for it, and a modern Elias would be wanted to herald its approach."

MILLSTONE ABOUT HIS NECK

Matt. 18:6; Mark 9:42; Luke 17:2

When Jesus' disciples asked him, "Who is the greatest in the kingdom of heaven?" he spoke of children, saying, "Whoso shall receive one such little child in my name receiveth me. But whoso shall offend one of these little ones which believe in me, it were better for him that a millstone were hanged about his neck, and that he were drowned in the depth of the sea." In Butler's *The Way of All Flesh,* Ernest thought he might get to Mr. Holt to try to convert him by ingratiating himself with the Holt children. "Ernest felt that it would indeed be almost better for him that a millstone should be hanged about his neck, and he cast into the sea, than that he should offend one of the little Holts." In Joyce's *A Portrait of the Artist as a Young Man,* at the Christmas dinner, Dante said that Parnell was a public sinner. "We are all sinners and black sinners, said Mr. Casey coldly." Mrs. Riordan said, " 'Woe be to the man by whom the scandal cometh! It would be better for him that a millstone were tied about his neck and that he were cast into the depth of the sea rather than that he should scandalise one of these, my least little ones.' That is the language of the Holy Ghost."

MISERABLE COMFORTERS   *see JOB'S COMFORTERS*

MITE   *see WIDOW'S MITE*

MOLOCH, MOLECH   *see TOPHET(H)*

MOLTEN CALF   *see GOLDEN CALF*

MONEY, ROOT OF ALL EVIL   *see ROOT OF ALL EVIL*

MONEYCHANGERS IN THE TEMPLE *see DEN OF THIEVES*

MORDECAI *see ESTHER*

MORNING STARS SANG TOGETHER

Job 38:7 The VOICE FROM THE WHIRLWIND reproved Job for his questioning of God's justice, asking, "Where wast thou when I laid the foundations of the earth? . . . When the morning stars sang together, and all the sons of God shouted for joy?" In Carlyle's *Sartor Resartus*, Professor Teufelsdröckh asks, "Is not God's universe a Symbol of the Godlike . . . is not Man's History . . . a perpetual Evangel? Listen, and for organ music thou wilt ever, as of old, hear the Morning Stars sing together." Whittier, in *The City of a Day*, praised two Swiss singers who carried him away "to that wonderful land where Nature seems still uttering from lake and valley . . . the echoes of that mighty hymn of a new-created world, when 'the morning stars sang together, and all the sons of God shouted for joy.'" Edwin A. Robinson, in "Ben Jonson Entertains a Man from Stratford," described Shakespeare in a pessimistic mood. Life is all nothing, Shakespeare said.

> It's all a world where bugs and emperors
> Go singularly back to the same dust,
> Each in his time, and the old, ordered stars
> That sang together, Ben, will sing the same
> Old stave to-morrow.°

MOSES AND ARK OF BULRUSHES

Exod. 2:1–6 When Moses was born, his mother, fearing Pharaoh's charge that "every [Hebrew] son that is born ye shall cast into the river, . . . took for him an ark of bulrushes . . . and put the child therein; and she laid it in the flags by the river's brink." Pharaoh's daughter came down to bathe, "and when she saw the ark among the flags, she sent her maid to fetch it." Taking compassion on the babe, she "drew him out of the water" and gave him to his mother to nurse. Mark Twain's *Huckleberry Finn* begins with the chapter headed "I Discover Moses and the Bulrushers." Huck says that after supper the Widow Douglas "got out her book and learned me about Moses and the Bulrushers, and I was in a sweat to find out all about him; but

°Reprinted with permission of The Macmillan Company from *Collected Poems* by E. A. Robinson. Copyright 1916 by E. A. Robinson. Renewed 1944 by Ruth Nivison.

by and by she let it out that Moses had been dead a considerable long time; so then I didn't care no more about him, because I don't take no stock in dead people." D. H. Lawrence, in the Foreword to *Studies in Classic American Literature,* said that the great American authors, such as Poe, Melville, Hawthorne, and Whitman, loved symbols, double meanings. "They prefer their truth safely swaddled in an ark of bulrushes, and deposited among the reeds until some friendly Egyptian princess comes to rescue the babe. Well it's high time now that someone came to lift out the swaddled infant of truth that America spawned some time back. The child must be getting pretty thin, from neglect."

MOSES' FACE SHONE

Exod. 34:29–30, 33–35

"When Moses came down from Mount Sinai with the two tables of testimony . . . [he] wist not that the skin of his face shone while he talked with him." Because "Aaron and all the children of Israel . . . were afraid to come nigh him . . . he put a veil on his face." The medieval representations of Moses with horns on his head, and statues such as Michaelangelo's great Moses are from the literal translation in the Vulgate of the Hebrew word for "shone," as *cornuta* meaning "horned." In "Absalom and Achitophel," Dryden said of Cora, rebel against David, "His long chin proved his wit; his saintlike grace / A church vermilion, and a Moses' face." In *Evangeline,* Longfellow describes the setting sun, as Evangeline waits at her father's door: "Down sank the great red sun, and in golden, glimmering vapors / Veiled the light of his face, like the Prophet descending from Sinai." In "Rabbi Ishmael," Whittier said that Rabbi Ishmael saw the face of the Lord in the HOLY OF HOLIES; then "Radiant as Moses from the Mount, he stood / And cried aloud unto the multitude: / 'O Israel, hear! The Lord our God is good!' "

MOSES, LEADER OF THE EXODUS

Exod. 3

The Lord said to Moses, "I have surely seen the affliction of my people which are in Egypt . . . . Come now therefore, and I will send thee unto Pharaoh, that thou mayest bring forth my people the children of Israel out of Egypt." Cotton Mather, in *Magnalia Christi Americana,* told of John Winthrop leading the American colonists: "Accordingly when the *Noble Design* of carrying a Colony of *Chosen People* into an *American* Wilderness, was by *some* Eminent Persons undertaken, This Eminent Person was, by Consent of all, *Chosen* for the *Moses*, who must be the Leader of so great an Undertaking . . . ." And James Russell Lowell, in *New England Two Centuries Ago,* writing on the wide influence of the Puritans, said, "Next to the fugitives whom Moses led out of Egypt, the little shipload of outcasts who landed at Plymouth two centuries and a half ago are destined to influence the future of the world."

MOSES' SEAT

Matt. 23:2

Jesus denounced the Pharisees to His disciples, saying, "The scribes and the Pharisees sit in Moses' seat: All therefore whatsoever they bid you observe, that observe . . . but do not ye after their works: for they say, and do not." In Milton's *Paradise Regained,* Satan tempts Jesus with wisdom, recalling His childhood when He was found in the Temple "Among the gravest Rabbies disputant / On points and questions fitting Moses Chair, / Teaching not taught . . . ." In "Swedenborg," Emerson said, "There is an air of infinite grief, and the sound of wailing, all over and through this lurid universe. A vampire sits in the seat of the prophet, and turns with gloomy appetite to the images of pain."

MOTE IN THY BROTHER'S EYE

Matt. 7:3–5

In the Sermon on the Mount, Jesus taught that you should "Judge not, that ye be not judged. And why beholdest thou the mote that is in thy brother's eye, but considerest not the beam that is in thine own eye?" The Reeve, in the Prologue to Chaucer's "The Reeve's Tale," attacks the Miller, who has just told a tale about a carpenter—read Reeve—beguiled.

> I pray to God his nekke mote to-breke;
> He kan wel in myn eye seen a stalke,
> But in his owene he kan nat seen a balke.

The Vulgate translates "mote" as "festucam," a "stalke." In Shakespeare's *Love's Labour's Lost,* Biron reproves his lovesick friends:

> But are you not ashamed? nay, are you not,
> All three of you, to be thus much o'ershot?
> You found his mote; the king your mote did see;
> But I a beam do find in each of three.

In *Hamlet,* when Bernardo interprets the appearance of the Ghost as an omen of "fierce events," Horatio comments, "A

mote it is to trouble the mind's eye." And Charles Lamb, in
"Poor Relations," defines a poor relation as, among other
things, "a mote in your eye . . . . ."

MOTH AND RUST CORRUPT   *see LAY NOT UP TREASURES UPON*
EARTH

MOUNTAINS SKIPPED LIKE RAMS

Ps. 114:4   The psalm called "A Hymn for Passover" begins "When Israel
went out of Egypt, the house of Jacob from a people of strange
language . . . . The mountains skipped like rams, and the little
hills like lambs." In his *Journals,* November 6, 1839, Emerson
said that people distrust you when you profess "unlimited alle-
giance" to the "Ideal life." If you "demand that these mountain circumstances should skip like rams and the little hills like
lambs before the presence of the Soul, then they distrust your
wisdom . . . ." In *Walden,* Thoreau hears a cattle train passing
by the pond. "When the old bell-weather [*sic*] at the head
rattles his bell, the mountains do indeed skip like rams and
the hills like lambs."

MOURNED AND WOULD NOT BE COMFORTED   *see RACHEL*
WEEPING FOR HER CHILDREN

MUCH STUDY IS A WEARINESS OF THE FLESH   *see OF MAKING*
MANY BOOKS

MUSTARD SEED   *see GRAIN OF MUSTARD SEED*

MY BROTHER'S KEEPER

Gen. 4:9   When the Lord asked, "Where is Abel thy brother?" Cain
replied, "I know not: Am I my brother's keeper?" In *Past and
Present,* Carlyle attacked mill owners who tried to justify paying starvation wages: "When Cain, for his own behoof, had
killed Abel, and was questioned, 'Where is thy brother?' he
too made answer, 'Am I my brother's keeper?' Did I not pay
my brother *his* wages, the thing he had merited from me?"
Somerset Maugham, in *The Summing Up,* wrote of his tol-
erance of the wickedness of his fellow men: "I am not my
brother's keeper. I cannot bring myself to judge my fellows;
I am content to observe them."

MY NAME IS LEGION   *see LEGION*

MY PUNISHMENT IS GREATER THAN I CAN BEAR

Gen. 4:13

When the Lord cursed Cain to be a fugitive and a vagabond in the earth, Cain, fearing that he would be slain, "said unto the Lord, My punishment is greater than I can bear." In Tennyson's *Harold*, Queen Aldwyth, viewing the body of her husband on the battlefield, cries, "My punishment is more than I can bear." As Henchard in Hardy's *The Mayor of Casterbridge*, rejected by Elizabeth-Jane, left Casterbridge alone, he said, "I—Cain—go alone as I deserve—an outcast and a vagabond. But my punishment is *not* greater than I can bear!"

MY SOUL CHOOSETH STRANGLING   *see SOUL CHOOSETH STRANGLING AND DEATH*

NAAMAN THE LEPER   *see ELISHA*

NABAL   *see ABIGAIL*

NABOTH'S VINEYARD   *see JEZEBEL*

NAKED, AND YE CLOTHED ME   *see STRANGER AND YE TOOK ME IN*

NAKED CAME I OUT OF MY MOTHER'S WOMB

Job 1:21

When Job heard of the destruction of his animals and of his sons, he said, "Naked came I out of my mother's womb, and naked shall I return thither: the Lord gave, and the Lord hath taken away; blessed be the name of the Lord." Chaucer's "The Clerk's Tale" tells of the testing of the wife, patient Griselda, much as God tested Job. When her husband sends her back to her father, she returns her rich clothing and wedding ring to him.

> "To you broght I noght elles, out of drede,
> But feith, and nakedness, and maydenhede . . .
> Naked out of my fadres hous," quod she,
> "I cam, and naked moot I turne agayn."

In *Abraham Lincoln: The Prairie Years*, Carl Sandburg wrote that Tom Lincoln arrived at Little Pigeon Creek with his wife, son and daughter, and little else. "Naked they had come into the world; almost naked they came to Little Pigeon Creek, Indiana." In Goldsmith's *The Vicar of Wakefield*, when the Vicar, enraged over the seduction of his daughter, is reproved by his son for cursing her unknown abductor, he becomes calmer and says, "Now, my son, I see it was more than human benevolence that first taught us to bless our enemies: Blessed be His holy name for all the good He hath given, and for all that He hath taken away."

NAME BLOTTED OUT   *see BOOK OF LIFE*

NAME IS LEGION   *see LEGION*

NAME TAKEN IN VAIN   *see TAKE THE NAME OF GOD IN VAIN*

NAOMI   *see RUTH*

NARROW PATH, WAY   *see STRAIT IS THE GATE, NARROW IS THE WAY*

NATHAN THE PROPHET   *see DAVID AND NATHAN*

NAZARITE, NAZIRITE

Num. 6:1–21;
Judg. 13:5,
7; 16:17

A Nazarite, meaning "separated" or "consecrated," was one devoted to God by special vows, sometimes made by the mother, as described in Numbers: "He shall separate himself from wine and strong drink . . . there shall no razor come upon his head . . . he shall come at no dead body," and he shall eat no unclean food. Samson was a practicing Nazarite, and others were consecrated to the order, such as Samuel and John the Baptist. It is sometimes confused with "Nazarene," one, like Jesus, who came from Nazareth. In Shakespeare's *The Merchant of Venice*, Shylock says to Bassanio, who has invited him to dinner, "Yes, to smell pork, to eat of the habitation which your prophet the Nazarite conjured the devil into." This is not an error of Shakespeare's, because no Bible before K.J. made the distinction. In Milton's *Samson Agonistes*, Samson assures the Chorus that he will go to the Philistine temple voluntarily: I will not "stain my vow of Nazarite."

> Shall I abuse this Consecrated gift
> Of strength, again returning with my hair
> After my great transgression . . .
> A Nazarite in place abominable
> Vaunting my strength in honour to thir Dagon?

In *Sartor Resartus*, Carlyle's Professor Teufelsdröckh says of the sect of "Dandies," "They affect great purity and separatism . . . and, on the whole, strive to maintain a true Nazarene [*sic*] deportment, and keep themselves unspotted from the world."

NEBO   *see PISGAH*

NEBUCHADNEZZAR, NEBUCHADREZZAR
(nĕb·û·kăd·nĕz'ẽr)

Dan. 1–4   He was the Babylonian ruler from 605 to 562 B.C. who destroyed Jerusalem and the Temple and carried the people into captivity (II Kings 24—25). He made a great "image of gold" which "he set up in the plain of Dura, in the province of Babylon," and commanded all to fall down and worship it on pain of being thrown into the FIERY FURNACE. Daniel's interpretation of Nebuchadnezzar's dream of the tree was fulfilled when Nebuchadnezzar "was driven from men, and did eat grass as oxen, and his body was wet with the dew of heaven, til his hairs were grown like eagles' feathers, and his nails like birds' claws." Chaucer, in "The Monk's Tale," tells the story of "Nabugodonosor," one who fell from "heigh degree." In Shakespeare's *All's Well That Ends Well*, when the Clown says that Helena "was the sweet-marjoram of the salad, or rather the herb of grace," Lafeu says, "They are not [salad] herbs, you knave; they are nose-herbs." The Clown replies, "I am no great Nebuchadnezzar, sir; I have not much skill in grass." When Jane Eyre, in Charlotte Brontë's *Jane Eyre*, sees Rochester after the fire in his home, she says, "You have a 'faux air' of Nebuchadnezzar in the fields about you, that is certain: your hair reminds me of eagles' feathers; whether your nails are grown like birds' claws or not, I have not yet noticed." In *Nature*, Emerson said that we "distrust and deny inwardly our sympathy with nature . . . . We are like Nebuchadnezzar, dethroned, bereft of reason, and eating grass like an ox." In *Unto This Last*, Ruskin, referring to modern material values, spoke of the "lying image of prosperity set up, on Dura plains dug into seven-times-heated furnaces" (Dan. 3:19).

NEW JERUSALEM

Rev. 21:2–22:5   John of Patmos wrote, "And I John saw the holy city, new Jerusalem, coming down from God out of heaven, prepared as a bride adorned for her husband." And, "I will write upon him . . . the name of the city of my God, which is new Jerusalem, which cometh down out of heaven from my God . . ." (Rev. 3:12). This is the vision of the Christian heavenly Para-

dise. Anne Bradstreet gives many of the details of the holy
city in "The Flesh and the Spirit."

> The City where I hope to dwell
> There's none on earth can parallel;
> The stately walls both high and strong
> Are made of precious jasper stone;
> The gates of pearl both rich and clear;
> And angels are for porters there;
> The streets thereof transparent gold,
> Such as no eye did e'er behold;
> A crystal river there doth run,
> Which doth proceed from the Lamb's throne;
> Of life there are the waters sure,
> Which shall remain forever pure;
> Nor sun nor moon they have no need,
> For glory doth from God proceed;
> No candle there, nor yet torchlight,
> For there shall be no darksome night.

In "The Pageant," Whittier describes the beauty of winter, a
"wild work of frost and light," a "glimpse of glory infinite."

> This foregleam of the Holy City
>   Like that to him of Patmos given,
>   The white bride coming down from heaven!

Matthew Arnold, in *Culture and Anarchy,* contrasting Hebraism with Hellenism, asks, is the "Greek notion of felicity . . .
when they walk about the New Jerusalem with palms in their
hands?" No. It is "when they think aright, when their thought
hits."

NEW WINE IN OLD BOTTLES

*Matt. 9:17; Mark
2:22; Luke 5:37*

When the disciples of John asked Jesus, "Why do we and the
Pharisees fast oft, but thy disciples fast not?" Jesus replied:
"No man putteth a piece of new cloth unto an old garment
. . . . Neither do men put new wine into old bottles: else the
bottles break, and the wine runneth out, and the bottles perish: but they put new wine into new bottles, and both are
preserved." In *Walden,* Thoreau said, ". . . beware of all
enterprises that require new clothes, and not rather a new
wearer of clothes . . . . Perhaps we should never procure a
new suit, however ragged or dirty the old, until we have . . .
so enterprised or sailed in some way, that we feel like new
men in the old, and that to retain it would be like keeping
new wine in old bottles."

NIMROD

Gen. 10:8-12

Nimrod, meaning "valiant," "strong," was a man of Babylon famed as a hunter, builder of cities, and founder of kingdoms. Nimrod "began to be a mighty one in the earth. He was a mighty hunter before the Lord . . . . And the beginning of his kingdom was Babel, and Erech, and Accad, and Calneh, in the land of Shinar." In medieval tradition he was the builder of the tower of Babel. In *Eikonoklastes*, Milton said that Charles I accused his parliament of being "vassals of certain nameless men, whom he charges to be such as 'hunt after faction with their hounds, the tumults.' And yet the bishops could have told them that Nimrod, the first that hunted after faction, is reputed by ancient tradition the first that founded monarchy; whence it appears, that to hunt after faction is more properly the king's game . . . ." And in *Paradise Lost*, Milton speaks of Nimrod, who "with a crew, whom like Ambition joyns," sought "Of Brick, and of that stuff they cast to build / A Citie & Towre, whose top may reach to Heav'n . . . ." In *Shooting Niagara: and After?* Carlyle said that the British aristocracy should quit flattering the common people with pretensions to democracy. Better the aristocrat should "shoot lions" in Africa—"or stay at home, and hunt rats. Why not? Is not, in strict truth, the Ratcatcher our one *real* British Nimrod now!"

NINTH PLAGUE   *see PLAGUE OF DARKNESS*

NOAH DRUNK   *see CANAAN, SON OF HAM*

NOAH'S ARK

Gen. 6:14-19

In preparation for the FLOOD, God commanded Noah, "Make thee an ark of gopher wood; rooms shalt thou make in the ark, and shalt pitch it within and without with pitch . . . . And of every thing of all flesh, two of every sort shalt thou bring into the ark . . . they shall be male and female." Genesis 7:2 says, "Of every clean beast thou shalt take to thee by sevens . . . and of beasts that are not clean by two . . . ." In Shakespeare's *As You Like It*, Jaques, remembering the unclean beasts, greeted Touchstone and Audrey with, "There is, sure, another flood toward, and these couples are coming to the ark. Here comes a pair of very strange beasts, which in all tongues are called fools." In "The South-Sea House," Charles Lamb said that the queer variety of clerks employed there "formed a sort of Noah's ark. Odd fishes." Mark Twain, in *Innocents Abroad*, said of the Americans touring Palestine that they were "a weird procession of pilgrims . . . astride of a

sorrier lot of horses, camels, and asses than those that came
out of Noah's ark, after eleven months of seasickness and
short rations."

NOD   *see LAND OF NOD*

NOISE OF MANY WATERS   *see VOICE (NOISE, SOUND) OF MANY WATERS*

NO JOT OR TITTLE   *see TITTLE*

NOLI ME TANGERE

(nō′·lĭ·mē
tăn′·jĕ·rē)

John 20:17

When Jesus appeared to Mary Magdalene (see MAGDALENE)
after the Resurrection, she said to Him, "Rabboni; which is to
say, Master. Jesus saith unto her, Touch me not; for I am not
yet ascended to my father . . ." The Vulgate version is: "Dicit
ei Jesus: Noli me tangere . . . ." In Tennyson's *Becket,* as Archbishop Becket fights off his murderers, he exclaims, "Touch me
not!" De Brito says, "How the good priest gods himself! / He
is not yet ascended to the Father." In *Studies in Classic American Literature,* D. H. Lawrence said that Melville found, in
Typee and *Omoo,* that civilized man cannot really go back to
the savage state. Primitive woman is attractive, ". . . but I
would never want to touch her . . . . She has soft warm flesh,
like warm mud. Nearer the reptile, the Saurian age. *Noli me
tangere.*"

NO MAN CAN SERVE TWO MASTERS

*Matt. 6:24; Luke
16:13*

In the Sermon on the Mount, Jesus said, "No man can serve
two masters: for either he will hate the one, and love the
other; or else he will hold to the one, and despise the other.
Ye cannot serve God and mammon." In "Life Without Principle," Thoreau says that "it is too much to read one newspaper a week." He tries it, and finds that he has "not dwelt
in my native region. The sun, the clouds, the snow, the trees
say not so much to me. You cannot serve two masters. It
requires more than a day's devotion to know and to possess
the wealth of a day." In Butler's *The Way of All Flesh,* Mr.
Hawke preaches to the young men at Cambridge: ". . . if
you value your eternal welfare, then give up the friendship of
this world; of a surety you must make your choice between
God and Mammon, for you cannot serve both." In Shaw's
Saint Joan, The English nobleman argues that neither the

French nor English factions can call themselves true French-
men nor true Englishmen. "Men cannot serve two masters. If
this cant of serving their country once takes hold of them,
goodbye to authority . . . ."

NO MORE SPIRIT IN HER   *see SHEBA (SABA) QUEEN OF*

NO NEW THING UNDER THE SUN

Eccles. 1:9

"The words of the Preacher," or Koheleth, "the son of David,
king in Jerusalem," traditionally Solomon, were that "all is
vanity . . . and there is no new thing under the sun." In *English Bards and Scotch Reviewers*, Byron attacked passing fads
of contemporary poetry: "Thus saith the Preacher: 'Nought
beneath the sun / Is new;' yet still from change to change we
run . . . ." In Melville's *Moby Dick*, Ishmael tells a story of a
whale in ancient days to show that "these marvels (like all
marvels) are mere repetitions of the ages; so that for the mil-
lionth time we say amen with Solomon—Verily there is nothing new under the sun." And in Shaw's *Man and Superman*,
the Devil says to Don Juan that history is but "the oscilations
of the world between the two extremes" of heaven and hell.
"You will discover the profound truth of the saying of my
friend Koheleth, that there is nothing new under the sun.
Vanitas vanitatum—"

NO OTHER GODS BEFORE ME

Exod. 20:3

The first of the TEN COMMANDMENTS is "Thou shalt have no
other gods before me." In Tennyson's *Becket*, King Henry,
angered at Thomas Becket's defiance, shouts, "No God but
one, and Mahound is his prophet. / But for your Christian,
look you, you shall have / None other God but me—me,
Thomas, son / Of Gilbert Becket, London Merchant. Out!"
Arthur H. Clough's "The Latest Decalogue" begins: "Thou
shalt have one God only; who / Would be at the expense of
two?"

NO RESPECTER OF PERSONS

Acts 10:34

Peter preached that the word of God was sent to all peoples.
"Of a truth I perceive that God is no respecter of persons
. . . ." Emerson, in "Spiritual Laws," said that every man has
a special talent because God incarnates himself in him. "The
pretense that he has another call . . . betrays obtuseness to
perceive that there is one mind in all individuals, and no re-

spect of persons therein . . . ." In *The Subjection of Women*, John Stuart Mill said that "there should be no restraint not required by the general good, and that the law should be no respecter of persons, but should treat all alike."

NOT PEACE BUT A SWORD

Matt. 10:34 When Jesus chose His disciples and sent them forth, He said, "Think not that I am come to send peace on earth: I came not to send peace, but a sword." In Shakespeare's *Henry VI, Part II*, when King Henry called for peace among his "furious peers," Cardinal Beaufort said, "Let me be blessed for the peace I make, / Against this proud protector, with my sword!" In his "Hymn of Man," Swinburne, pleading for the freedom of man from orthodox religion, addresses Jesus: "Ah, thou that darkenest heaven—ah, thou that bringest a sword— / By the crimes of thine hands unforgiven, they beseech thee to hear them, O Lord."

NOT WORTHY TO UNLOOSE   *see LATCHET OF WHOSE SHOES*

NOTHING NEW UNDER THE SUN   *see NO NEW THING UNDER THE SUN*

NO VARIABLENESS, NEITHER SHADOW OF TURNING

Jas. 1:17 James, the brother of Jesus, wrote "to the twelve tribes which are scattered abroad . . . . Every good gift and every perfect gift is from above, and cometh down from the Father of lights, with whom is no variableness, neither shadow of turning." In Carlyle's *Sartor Resartus*, Professor Teufelsdröckh agrees with those who say that the universe runs by "unalterable laws." "I, too, must believe that God, whom ancient inspired men assert to be 'without variableness or shadow of turning,' does indeed never change." Arthur Hugh Clough's poem "With Whom Is No Variableness, Neither Shadow of Turning" is as follows:

> It fortifies my soul to know
> That, though I perish, Truth is so:
> That, howse'er I stray and range,
> Whate'er I do, Thou dost not change.
> I steadier step when I recall
> That, if I slip, Thou dost not fall.

NUNC DIMITTIS   *see SIMEON THE JUST*

O DEATH, WHERE IS THY STING?   *see DEATH, WHERE IS THY*
        STING?

OF MAKING MANY BOOKS

Eccles. 12:12   In the conclusion, the Preacher admonishes "my son": "of
making many books there is no end; and much study is a
weariness of flesh." In Shakespeare's *Love's Labour's Lost,*
Biron asks, "What is the end of study?" Then he gives his own
answer:

> Why, all delights are vain; but that most vain,
> Which with pain purchased doth inherit pain:
> As, painfully to pour upon a book
>   To seek the light of truth; while truth the while
> Doth falsely blind the eyesight of his look . . . .

In *Areopagitica,* Milton says that God gave every man reason
to make his own choice of books. "Solomon informs us, that
much reading is a weariness to the flesh; but neither he, nor
other inspired author, tells us that such or such reading is
unlawful; yet, certainly had God thought good to limit us
herein, it had been much more expedient to have told us what
was unlawful, than what was wearisome." Thomas Fuller begins "Of Books," from *The Holy and the Profane State,* with:
"Solomon saith truly, 'Of making many books there is no end,'
so insatiable is the thirst of men therein: as also endless is the
desire of many in buying and reading them."

OF SUCH IS THE KINGDOM OF HEAVEN   *see SUFFER THE*
        LITTLE CHILDREN

OG, KING OF BASHAN   *see BASHAN*

OLD ADAM   *see ADAM*

OLD CLOOTIE   *see SATAN*

OLD MEN DREAM DREAMS   *see DREAM DREAMS, OLD MEN*

OLD SCRATCH   *see LUCIFER*

OLIVE BRANCH, BOUGH   *see DOVE OF NOAH*

ONAN
(ō'năn)

Gen. 38:4–10

Because Er, the husband of Tamar, was slain by the Lord for his wickedness, Judah, her father-in-law, said to his son Onan, "Go in unto thy brother's wife, and marry her, and raise up seed to thy brother. And Onan knew that the seed should not be his; and it came to pass, when he went in unto his brother's wife, that he spilled it on the ground, lest that he should give seed to his brother." Displeased, the Lord slew Onan. The word "onanism" is used today to mean masturbation, or, more accurately, a form of birth control. In *Letters from the Earth*, Mark Twain, speaking of Moses' killing of the Midianites, because "they had offended the Deity in some way," said, "It is more than likely that a Midianite had been duplicating the conduct of one Onan, who was commanded to 'go in unto his brother's wife'—which he did; but instead of finishing, 'he spilled it on the ground.' The Lord slew Onan for that, for the Lord could never abide indelicacy." In Aldous Huxley's *After Many a Summer*, the Fifth Earl of Hauberk theorized, in his diary, about the longevity of carp. "I have asked myself if the Fish's longer years might not be due to its peculiar mode of begetting its young. But again I am met by fatal Objections. The Males of Parrots and Ravens do not onanize, but copulate . . . ."

ON EARTH PEACE, GOOD WILL   *see PEACE, GOOD WILL TOWARD MEN*

ONE JOT OR TITTLE   *see TITTLE*

ONE LITTLE EWE LAMB   *see DAVID AND NATHAN*

OPHIR
(ō'fēr)

*I Kings 9:28;
10:11; 22:48*

Ophir was a region on the Red Sea in southwest Arabia, famed for its gold. Solomon traded in its gold, which he used in his Temple, throne, house, and furnishings. It took Solomon's ships three years to make the trip. In Milton's *Paradise Lost*, Michael shows Adam great earthly kingdoms of the future, among others "Sofala thought Ophir." In Ben Jonson's *The Alchemist*, Surly says to Sir Epicure Mammon, as they approach the alchemist's house to get the philosopher's stone which will bring fabulous riches:

> And there within, sir, are the golden mines,
> Great Solomon's Ophir! He was sailing to 't
> Three years, but we have reached it in ten months.

And in "Cargoes," Masefield writes of the "Quinquireme of Nineveh from distant Ophir, / Rowing home to haven in sunny Palestine . . . ."*

ORDER OF MELCHISEDEK   see MELCHISEDEK

OUR DAILY BREAD

Matt. 6:11

The Lord's Prayer: "Give us this day our daily bread." In "The Birds of Killingsworth," Longfellow wrote:

> And hungry crows, assembled in a crowd,
> Clamoured their piteous prayer incessantly,
> Knowing who hears the ravens cry, and said:
> "Give us, O Lord, this day, our daily bread!"

And in *Roughing It*, Mark Twain wrote of "a little, half-starved, wayside community that had no subsistence except what they could get by preying upon chance passengers who stopped over with them a day when travelling by the Overland stage, that in their Church service they had altered the Lord's Prayer to read: 'Give us this day our daily stranger!' "

OUTER DARKNESS   see WEEPING AND GNASHING OF TEETH

OUT-HEROD HEROD   see HEROD THE GREAT

OUT OF THE EATER CAME FORTH MEAT

Judg. 14:8–18

Samson killed a lion with his bare hands (Judg. 14:6), and later he saw "the carcase of the lion: and, behold, there was a swarm of bees and honey in the carcase of the lion." Then at his wedding feast given for his Philistine friends, he put forth a riddle unto them: "Out of the eater came forth meat, and out of the strong came forth sweetness." The Philistines got the answer only through the wiles of Samson's wife. In Carlyle's *Sartor Resartus*, Professor Teufelsdröckh, speaking of "growth and regenesis," said that the most "snow-and-rose-bloom maiden . . . has descended . . . from that same hair-mantled, flint-hurling Aboriginal Anthropophagus! Out of the eater cometh forth meat; out of the strong cometh forth sweetness." In *The Renaissance*, Walter Pater said that Michel-

---

*Reprinted with permission of The Macmillan Company from *Story of a Round House* by John Masefield. Copyright 1912 by The Macmillan Company. Renewed 1940 by John Masefield. Permission granted also by The Society of Authors and Dr. John Masefield O.M.

angelo, "because the gods loved him, lingered on to be of immense, patriarchal age, till the sweetness it had taken so long to secrete in him was found at last. Out of the strong came forth sweetness, *ex forti dulcedo*." Emerson, in the "Ode, Inscribed to W. H. Channing," said that the

> The over-god
> Who marries Right to Might,
> Who peoples, unpeoples,—
> He who exterminates
> Races by stronger races,
> Black by white faces,—
> Knows to bring honey
> Out of the lion;
> Grafts gentlest scion
> On pirate and Turk.

OUT OF THE MOUTH OF BABES AND SUCKLINGS

Ps. 8:2; Matt. 21:16

The psalm praising the Lord for the excellence of his creation: "Out of the mouth of babes and sucklings has thou ordained strength because of thine enemies, that thou mightest still the enemy and the avenger." When the chief priests and scribes were "sore displeased" because of the wonderful things Jesus did and because of the praise of the children, Jesus said, "Yea, have ye never read, Out of the mouth of babes and sucklings thou hast perfected praise?" In the Prologue to Chaucer's "The Prioress's Tale," about the murdered child, the Prioress paraphrases the first two verses of this psalm.

> "O Lord, oure Lord thy name how merveillous
> Is in this large world ysprad," quod she;
> "For noght oonly thy laude precious
> Parfourned is by men of dignitee,
> But by the mouth of children thy bountee
> Parfourned is, for on the brest soukynge
> Somtyme shewen they thyn heriynge."

In Tennyson's *Becket,* Archbishop Becket accepts the plaudits of the people, saying, "Out of the mouths of babes and sucklings, praise! / I thank you, sons . . . ."

OUT OF THE STRONG CAME FORTH SWEETNESS   *see OUT OF THE EATER CAME FORTH MEAT*

PAINTED JEZEBEL   *see JEZEBEL*

PALE HORSE

Rev. 6:8

St. John the Divine's vision on the opening of the fourth seal: "And I looked, and behold a pale horse: and his name that sat on him was Death, and Hell followed with him." Shelley, in *The Mask of Anarchy*, writes of visions he saw as he "lay asleep in Italy."

> Last came Anarchy; he rode
> On a white horse splashed with blood;
> He was pale even to the lips,
> Like Death in the Apocalypse.

Byron, in *Manfred*, describes the sun shining on the mountain torrent: its rays

> fling its lines of foaming light along,
> And to and fro, like the pale courser's tail,
> The giant steed, to be bestrode by Death,
> As told in the Apocalypse.

And Mark Twain, in *Tom Sawyer*, tells about Aunt Polly plying her patent medicines on Tom when he becomes depressed because Becky isn't at school: "She gathered together her quack periodicals and her quack medicines, and thus armed with death, went about on her pale horse . . . with 'hell following after.' "

PALM SUNDAY   *see JESUS, ENTRY INTO JERUSALEM*

PARABLE OF THE TALENTS

Matt. 25:14–30

Jesus compared the kingdom of heaven to the traveler who entrusted five talents to one servant, two to another, and one talent to a third. When he returned from his journey, he found that the first two servants had increased their talents by trade. The master praised each saying, "Well done, good and faithful servant . . . . Enter thou into the joy of thy lord." The third servant had been afraid and had hid his talent in the ground. The master reproved him saying he should have put the money to work so that "I should have received mine own with usury [interest]." Then, "Cast ye the unprofitable servant into outer darkness: there shall be weeping and gnashing of teeth." "Talent" then meant a large sum of money; now it means ability or gift. Milton's sonnet on his blindness is based on this parable. It begins:

> When I consider how my light is spent,
>   E're half my days, in this dark world and wide,
>   And that one Talent which is death to hide,
>   Lodg'd with me useless, though my Soul more bent

> To serve therewith my Maker, and present
> My true account, least he returning chide,
> Doth God exact day-labour, light deny'd,
> I fondly ask . . . .

In Robert Southey's *A Vision of Judgment,* King George III
appealed to God for pardon: "Bending forward he spake with
earnest humility. 'Well done, / Good and faithful servant!' then
said a voice from the Brightness; / 'Enter thou into the joy of
thy Lord.' " In *Sartor Resartus,* Carlyle said that we should not
call Professor Teufelsdröckh wicked when he suffered religious
doubts; "Unprofitable servants as we all are, perhaps at no era
of his life was he more decisively the Servant of God . . . ."
And in Hemingway's "The Snows of Kilimanjaro," the dying
writer, Harry, admitted that it was not his rich wife who had
destroyed his talent; "He had destroyed his talent by not using
it, by betrayals of himself and what he believed in . . . ."

PARABLE OF THE TARES AND WHEAT

Matt. 13:24–30

Jesus said that the kingdom of heaven was like the man who
sowed good seed in his field. Enemies came in the night and
sowed tares among the wheat. The man commanded his servants not to try to pull them out "lest while ye gather up the
tares, ye root up also the wheat with them." At harvest time the
reapers will separate them. In Shakespeare's *Henry IV, Part II,*
the Archbishop of York predicts that King Henry will forgive
the rebels and agree to peace,

> for full well he knows
> He cannot so precisely weed this land
> As his misdoubts present occasion.
> His foes are so enrooted with his friends
> That, plucking to unfix an enemy,
> He doth unfasten so and shake a friend.

The Genevan Bible used "plucke up." In *Areopagitica,* Milton
approved of some sectarian differences: "Not that I think well
of every light separation; . . . [but] it is not possible for man to
sever the wheat from the tares; . . . that must be the angel's
ministry at the end of mortal things."

PARABLE OF THE WISE AND FOOLISH VIRGINS

Matt. 25:1–13

Jesus compared the kingdom of heaven to "ten virgins, which
took their lamps, and went forth to meet the bridegroom."
Five were wise and "took oil in their vessels with their lamps";
five were foolish and "took no oil with them." While they all

waited sleeping, at midnight the bridegroom came, and "they that were ready went in with him to the marriage: and the door was shut." The foolish virgins cried, "Lord, Lord, open to us. But he answered and said, Verily, I say unto you, I know you not." Milton's "Sonnet IX" was addressed to a virtuous young girl:

> Thy care is fixt and zealously attends
>   To fill thy ordorous Lamp with deeds of light,
>   And Hope that reaps not shame. Therefore be sure
> Thou, when the Bridegroom with his feastfull friends
>   Passes to bliss at the mid hour of night,
>   Hast gain'd thy entrance, Virgin wise and pure.

In Tennyson's *Idylls of the King*, Queen Guinevere, fled to a convent to escape her enemies, hears a maid's song that reminds her of "her thought when first she came—" leaving Lancelot too late.

> Too late, too late! ye cannot enter now.
>   No light had we: for that we do repent;
> And learning this, the bridegroom will relent.
> Too late, too late! ye cannot enter now.

PARADISE   *see EDEN, GARDEN OF*

PASSOVER   Moses instructed the people to "strike the lintel and the two side posts" of their doors with "a bunch of hyssop" dipped in
Exod. 12:21–28   the blood of a lamb. "For the Lord will pass through to smite the Egyptians; and when he seeth the blood upon the lintel, and on the two side posts, the Lord will pass over the door, and will not suffer the destroyer to come in unto your houses to smite you. And ye shall observe this thing for an ordinance to thee and to thy sons for ever." The tenth plague was the smiting of the FIRSTBORN OF EGYPT. In Tennyson's *Becket*, King Henry describes the bloody reign of his predecessor, King Stephen. Murder, common

> As Nature's death, like Egypt's plague, had fill'd
>   All things with blood; when every doorway blush'd,
>   Dash'd red with that unhallow'd passover . . . .'

In "Self-Reliance," Emerson said that one should follow his own genius. "I would write on the lintels of the door-post, *Whim*." And in Longfellow's *Evangeline*, Evangeline finds her lover Gabriel dying.

> Hot and red on his lips still burned the flush of the fever,
> As if life, like the Hebrew, with blood had besprinkled its portals,
> That the Angel of Death might see the sign, and pass over.

PATERNOSTER   see LORD'S PRAYER

PATIENCE OF JOB   see JOB

PATMOS   see JOHN OF PATMOS

PAUL, CONVERSION OF

Acts 9:1–22;
22:1–22; 26:1–23

As Saul of Tarsus, (his Hebrew name; Paul is his Roman name) was on the road to Damascus to find followers of Jesus and bring them bound to Jerusalem, "suddenly there shined round about him a light from heaven: And he fell to the earth, and heard a voice saying unto him, Saul, Saul why persecutest thou me?" It was the Lord, and he said, "I am Jesus whom thou persecutest." Saul was converted, "and straightway he preached Christ in the synagogues, that he is the Son of God." In his *Life of Dr. John Donne*, Izaak Walton said that Donne was glad to return, by invitation of his old friends, to Lincoln's Inn, "where he had been a Saul, though not to persecute Christianity or deride it, yet in his irregular youth to neglect the visible practice of it, there to become a Paul and preach salvation to his beloved brethren." In Butler's *The Way of All Flesh*, Ernest at Cambridge wrote an essay exhorting the religious Simeonites "to a freer use of the tub . . . . He was something of a Saul and took pleasure in persecuting the elect . . . . It rose from an unconscious sympathy with them, which, as in St. Paul's case, in the end drew him into the ranks of those whom he had most despised and hated."

PAUL SHIPWRECKED

Acts 27:1–28:18

When Paul was being taken as prisoner to Rome by ship, "there rose against it a tempestuous wind, called Euroclydon" [û·rŏk'lĭ·dŏn] meaning in Greek "a stormy east wind." Paul gave the sailors guidance and good cheer, saying, ". . . there shall not an hair fall from the head of any of you." After several narrow escapes the ship finally ran aground on the island of Melita [mĕl'ĭ·tȧ], or Malta today, where they were hospitably welcomed. Shakespeare may have had this story in mind in the shipwreck scene in *The Tempest*: Ariel told Prospero that "not a hair perished," and Prospero told Miranda that the men came ashore "by divine Providence." William Bradford, in *Of Plymouth Plantation*, contrasted the Indians' cruelty to the Puritans with the Melitans' mercy to Paul: "It is recorded in Scripture as a mercy to the Apostle and his shipwrecked company, that the barbarians showed them no small kindness in refreshing them . . . ." Ishmael, in Melville's *Moby Dick,* found The Spouter Inn "a queer sort of place . . . which stood on a sharp bleak corner, where that tempestuous wind Euroclydon kept up a worse howling than ever it did about poor Paul's tossed craft. Euroclydon, nevertheless, is a mighty pleasant zeypher to any one in-doors, with his feet on the hob quietly toasting for bed."

PAY TITHE OF MINT AND ANISE *see TITHE OF MINT, ANISE, AND CUMMIN*

PEACE, GOOD WILL TOWARD MEN

Luke 2:14 When Jesus was born at Bethlehem, "suddenly there was with the angel a multitude of the heavenly host praising God, and saying, Glory to God in the highest, and on earth peace, good will toward men." In Tennyson's *In Memoriam,* the poet at Christmas time hears "four voices of four hamlets round."

> Each voice four changes on the wind,
>   That now dilate, and now decrease,
>   Peace and goodwill, goodwill and peace.
>   Peace and goodwill, to all mankind.

In "The Peace Convention at Brussels," Whittier said, about the peace effort, let us sing the old song of peace.

> Lend, once again, that holy song a tongue,
>   Which the glad angels of the Advent sung,
>   Their cradle-anthem for the Saviour's birth,
>   Glory to God, and peace unto earth.

PEACEMAKERS, BLESSED ARE *see BEATITUDES*

PEACE THAT PASSETH ALL UNDERSTANDING

Phil. 4:7 Paul wrote to the Philippians, "Be careful for nothing; but in every thing by prayer and supplication with thanksgiving let your requests be made known unto God. And the peace of God, which passeth all understanding, shall keep your hearts and minds through Christ Jesus." In *The American Crisis,* Thomas Paine urged his countrymen not to trust the mercies of the British by delivering up their arms. "The ministry recommended the same plan to Gage, and this is what the tories call making their peace, *a peace which passeth all understanding indeed!"* In *Black Boy,* Richard Wright told of religious quarrels in his grandmother's home. "Granny bore the standard for

God, but she was always fighting. The peace that passes understanding never dwelt with us."

PEARL OF GREAT PRICE

Matt. 13:45–46

Jesus said unto his disciples, "Again, the kingdom of heaven is
like unto a merchant man, seeking goodly pearls: Who, when
he had found one pearl of great price, went and sold all that
he had, and bought it." Othello's final words, in Shakespeare's
Othello, speaking of himself as "one whose hand, / Like the
base Indian [Iudean in the Folio], threw a pearl away / Richer
than all his tribe . . . ." may be an allusion to this passage. In
The Scarlet Letter, Hawthorne said that Hester "named the
infant 'Pearl,' as being of great price,—purchased with all she
had." And old Master Wilson admonished Pearl with great
solemnity, saying, "Pearl, thou must take heed to instruction,
that so, in due season, thou mayest wear in thy bosom the pearl
of great price."

PEARLS BEFORE SWINE *see CAST PEARLS BEFORE SWINE*

PENTECOST

Acts 2:1–4

Pentecost, meaning "fiftieth" day, was in Old Testament times
the time of the Feast of Pentecost, fifty days after the Feast of
the Passover; it celebrated the giving of the law on Mount
Sinai. In the New Testament it was the time when the Holy
Ghost descended upon the apostles and disciples gathered from
many nations together in Jerusalem. "And there appeared unto
them cloven tongues like as of fire, and it sat upon each of
them." And they "began to speak with other tongues, as the
Spirit gave them utterance." In Francis Bacon's *New Atlantis,*
the Governor tells how his people—drawn from many different
nationalities—were by a miracle enabled to read the writings
of St. Bartholomew. It was a miracle like that of the apostles
"in the original gift of tongues." In *The Scarlet Letter,* Hawthorne says of some of the saintly Puritan fathers, "All that
they lacked was the gift that descended upon the chosen disciples, at Pentecost, in tongues of flame . . . that of addressing
the whole human brotherhood in the heart's native language.
These fathers, otherwise so apostolic, lacked . . . the Tongue
of Flame." And in "The Problem," Emerson compared the
minister, poet, artist, and prophet as true "makers" bringing
God to men.

> Ever the fiery Pentecost
> Girds with one flame the countless host,
> Trances the heart through chanting choirs,
> And through the priest the mind inspires.

PENUEL   *see* JACOB WRESTLES WITH AN ANGEL

PETER'S VISION OF THE SHEET

Acts 10:9–18

Peter at his prayers, very hungry, fell into a trance, "and saw heaven opened, and a certain vessel descending unto him, as it had been a great sheet knit at the four corners . . . . Wherein were all manner of fourfooted beasts of the earth . . . and creeping things, and fowls of the air. And there came a voice to him, Rise, Peter; kill, and eat." But Peter refused, saying he never ate anything "common or unclean." Peter was puzzled, for he knew not "what this vision which he had seen should mean." In *Areopagitica,* Milton argued that the individual should be trusted to choose his own books. "For books are as meats and viands are; some of good, some of evil substance; and yet God in that unapocryphal vision said without exception, 'Rise, Peter, kill and eat;' leaving the choice to each man's discretion." In Carlyle's *Sartor Resartus,* Professor Teufelsdröckh expounds his philosophy of clothes: "Society is founded upon Cloth; Society sails through the Infinitude on cloth . . . like the Sheet of clean and unclean beasts in the Apostle's dream; and without such Sheet . . . should sink to endless depths . . . ." In Tennyson's *Becket,* Walter Map tells Herbert of Bosham about King Henry's crowning banquet: "And as for the flesh at table, a whole Peter's sheet, with all manner of game, and four-footed things, and fowls—" Herbert asks, "And all manner of creeping things too?" Walter replies, "Well, there are abbots—but they did not bring their women . . . ." Tennyson, in "To E. Fitzgerald," recalls his visit to the vegetarian Fitzgerald. He sat in his garden with his doves alighting on him, "As if they knew your diet spares / Whatever moved in that full sheet / Let down to Peter at his prayers."

PHARISEES

Matt. 3:7;
23:13–15; Luke
18:9–14

The Pharisees, meaning "separated," were a scholarly sect of Jews who believed in strict observance of the Law. Students and teachers, they did much to help preserve Judaism. They were accused by Jesus of stressing outward forms of religion at the expense of inward spirit; hence frequently in literature they stand for traditionalism, bigotry, hypocrisy, and self-righteousness, as in the word "pharisaical." Milton, for example, in *Animadversions,* said that the proposal to admit "papists to our churches . . . was pharisaical, and vain-glorious, a greedy desire to win proselytes by conforming to them unlawfully . . . ." In *Characteristics,* Carlyle said that "so soon as Prophecy among the Hebrews had ceased, then did the reign of Argumentation begin; and the ancient Theocracy, in its Sadduceeisms and Phariseeisms, and vain jangling of sects and doctors, give token that the *soul* of [religion] had fled." And in *Billy Budd,* Melville said of Claggart's hidden evil nature, "The Pharisee is the Guy Fawkes prowling in the hid chambers underlying some natures like Claggart's."

PHILISTINE

Gen. 21:32, 34; Judg. 16:5–30

The Philistines, meaning perhaps "immigrants," were invaders from Egypt or Crete who settled on the southern coastal plain of Palestine (the name derives from "Philistine"), and who became the enemies of the Israelites. The modern meaning— one who is crude and uncultured—derives from Matthew Arnold's application of the word to the materialistic middle class. Arnold adapted it from the term "Philister," applied to hostile townsmen by students of German universities. This meaning is said to have derived from a sermon text taken from Delilah's words, "Philister über dir, Simson!" The sermon was delivered in Jena in 1693 at the funeral of a student killed in a "town and gown" quarrel. Arnold's definition of "Philistinism" appears in *On the Study of Celtic Literature:* "We are imperilled by what I call the 'Philistinism' of our middle class. On the side of beauty and taste, vulgarity; on the side of morals and feeling, coarseness; on the side of mind and spirit, unintelligence,—this is Philistinism." And in *Culture and Anarchy,* Arnold said, "The people who believe most that our greatness and welfare are proved by our being very rich . . . are just the very people whom we call Philistines." And in "Puritanism as a Literary Force," Mencken said that Mark Twain was a great artist, but ". . . he could never throw off his native Philistinism . . . . In the presence of all beauty of man's creation—in brief, of what we roughly call art, whatever its form—the voice of Mark Twain was the voice of the Philistine."

PHILISTINES BE UPON THEE   *see SAMSON AND DELILAH*

PILATE, PONTIUS

Matt. 27; Mark 15; Luke 23; John 18–19

Pilate, the fifth Roman governor of Judea (A.D. 26–36), made mistakes during his rule which finally led to his banishment by Rome. Unable to find Jesus guilty, he sent Him to Herod, governor of Galilee; but Herod returned Him. PILATE WASHED HIS HANDS of the whole affair, and then "delivered Jesus . . . to be crucified." Matthew Arnold, in *Literature and Dogma,* compared Pilate to modern aristocrats, insensitive to true religion. "Even the Roman governor has his close parallel in our celebrated aristocracy, with its superficial good sense and good

nature, its complete inaptitude for ideas, its profound helpless-
ness in presence of all great spiritual movements." In "Clerical
Oppressors," Whittier wrote about a proslavery meeting in
Charleston, South Carolina, attended by the clergy:

> Pilate and Herod, friends!
> Chief priests and rulers, as of old, combine!
> Just God and holy! is that church, which lends
> Strength to the spoiler, thine!

PILATE WASHED HIS HANDS

Matt. 27:24
When Jesus was tried before him, Pilate could find nothing
evil that he had done. "When Pilate saw that he could prevail
nothing, but that rather a tumult was made, he took water,
and washed his hands before the multitude, saying, I am innocent of the blood of this just person: see ye to it." In the abdication scene of Shakespeare's *Richard II*, Richard says to his
accusers:

> Nay, all of you that stand and look upon me
> Whilst that my wretchedness doth bait myself,
> Though some of you with Pilate wash your hands
> Showing an outward pity; yet you Pilates
> Have here deliver'd me to my sour cross,
> And water cannot wash away your sin.

In *Richard III*, the Second Murderer of Clarence in the Tower
says,

> A bloody deed, and desperately dispatch'd!
> How fain, like Pilate, would I wash my hands
> Of this most grievous guilty murder done!

And in *Henry IV, Part I*, when Prince Hal, in the Boar's-Head
Tavern, tells Falstaff that he has paid back the money stolen at
Gadshill, Falstaff, thinking of Prince Hal become king, says,
"Rob me the exchequer the first thing doest, and do it with
unwash'd hands, too."

PILLAR OF CLOUD, OF FIRE

Exod. 13:20–22
When Moses led the children of Israel out of Egypt toward the
Red Sea, "the Lord went before them by day in a pillar of a
cloud, to lead them the way; and by night in a pillar of fire, to
give them light; to go by day and night: He took not away the
pillar of the cloud by day, nor the pillar of fire by night, from
before the people." "Rebecca's Hymn," in Scott's *Ivanhoe*,
begins:

> When Israel, of the Lord beloved,
>   Out from the land of bondage came,
> Her father's God before her moved,
>   An awful guide in smoke and flame
> By day, along the astonish'd lands
>   The cloudy pillar glided slow;
> By night, Arabia's crimson'd sands
>   Return'd the fiery column's glow.

In *Sartor Resartus,* Carlyle said, regarding modern materialism and unbelief, ". . . no Pillar of Cloud by day, and no Pillar of Fire by night, any longer guides the Pilgrim."

PILLAR OF SALT   *see LOT'S WIFE*

PISGAH
(pĭz′gȧ)

Deut. 34:1

"And Moses went up from the plains of Moab unto the mountain of Nebo, to the top of Pisgah, that is over against Jericho. And the Lord showed him all the land of Gilead, unto Dan." From this mountain top Moses looked over the PROMISED LAND, which the Lord forbade him to enter, and he died soon after. It is sometimes referred to as Nebo, a nearby hill. William Bradford, in the *History of Plymouth Plantation,* telling of the plight of the Pilgrims facing "a hideous and desolate wilderness," says that they could not "go up to the top of Pisgah, to view from this wilderness, a more goodly country to feed their hopes." In *The Return of the Native,* Thomas Hardy writes of Mrs. Yeobright, when she appears on Rainbarrow Hill after the Fifth-of-November festival fire, that "at moments she seemed to be regarding issues from a Nebo denied to others." Walt Whitman is compared to Moses by D. H. Lawrence in *Studies in Classic American Literature:* He stands high above the many little poets who imitate him. "Pisgah. Pisgah sights. And Death. Whitman like a strange, modern, American Moses. Fearfully mistaken. And yet the great leader."

PIT OF THE DRAGON   *see BOTTOMLESS PIT*

PITCH DEFILES   *see TOUCH PITCH AND BE DEFILED*

PLACE OF SKULLS   *see CALVARY*

PLAGUE OF DARKNESS

Exod. 10:21–23

The ninth plague that the Lord inflicted upon the Egyptians when Pharaoh "would not let the children of Israel go": the Lord told Moses, "Stretch out thine hand toward heaven, that there may be darkness over the land of Egypt, even darkness which may be felt . . . and there was a thick darkness in all the land of Egypt three days: They saw not one another, neither rose any from his place for three days." In Shakespeare's *Twelfth Night*, the clown baits Malvolio, who says that he is not mad, it's just that the closet in which he is shut is dark: "Madman, thou errest: I say, there is no darkness but ignorance: in which thou art more puzzled than the Egyptians in their fog." Hardy, in *The Hand of Ethelberta*, wrote, "On a moorland in wet weather, it is thirty perceptible minutes to any fireside . . . —minutes that can be felt, like the Egyptian plague of darkness." In *A Portrait of the Artist as a Young Man*, by Joyce, the preacher describes the never-ending darkness of hell: "Of all the plagues with which the land of the Pharoahs was smitten one plague alone, that of darkness, was called horrible. What name, then, shall we give to the darkness of hell which is to last not for three days alone but for all eternity?"

PLAGUE OF FROGS

Exod. 8:1–15

The second plague which Moses, at the Lord's command, inflicted on the Egyptians: "And the river shall bring forth frogs abundantly, which shall go up and come into thine house, and into thy bedchamber, and upon thy bed, and into the house of thy servants, and upon thy people, and into thine ovens, and into thy kneading troughs." In "Poor Relations," Charles Lamb said that a "poor relation—is the most irrelevant thing in nature . . . —a frog in your chamber . . . ." Gilbert White, in *The Natural History of Selborne*, said that crickets sometimes increase to such a degree that they overrun homes: "In families, at such times, they are, like Pharaoh's plague of frogs,— 'in their bedchambers, and upon their beds, and in their ovens, and in their kneading troughs.'"

PLAGUE OF LOCUSTS

Exod. 10:1–20

The eighth plague inflicted by Moses and Aaron on Pharaoh and the Egyptians: "And the locusts went up all over the land of Egypt, and rested in all the coasts of Egypt: very grievous were they; before them there were no such locusts as they, neither after them shall be such." In *Paradise Lost*, Milton described the gathering of the numberless "bad Angels" fallen on the dry plain of hell: they were

> As when the potent Rod
> Of Amram's Son in Egypts evill day
> Wav'd round the Coast, up call'd a pitchy cloud
> Of Locusts, warping on the Eastern Wind,
> That oer the Realm of impious Pharaoh hung
> Like Night, and darken'd all the land of Nile . . . .

In Browning's "Pippa Passes," the irreligious vagabond Bluphocks says he used a spelling book to study Syriac, "and what was the purport of this miraculous posy? Some cherished legend of the past, you'll say—'How Moses hocuspocussed Egypt's land with fly and locust . . . .' "

PLAGUES, TEN

Exod. 7–12   In order to free the Hebrews from their Egyptian bondage, for "Pharaoh's heart is hardened, he refuseth to let the people go," the Lord directed Moses and Aaron to afflict the Egyptians with plagues. The ten were successively: (1) the river turned to blood, (2) frogs, (3) lice, (4) flies, (5) murrain, (6) boils with blains, (7) hail, (8) locusts, (9) darkness, and (10) death of the Egyptian firstborn (see FIRSTBORN OF EGYPT). Then Pharoah "called for Moses and Aaron by night, and said, Rise up, and get you forth from among my people . . . and go serve the Lord, as ye have said." In Milton's *Paradise Lost*, the angel Michael pictures the future plagues to Adam. Pharaoh, "the lawless Tyrant"

> Must be compelled by Signes and Judgments dire;
> To blood unshed the Rivers must be turnd,
> Frogs, Lice and Flies must all his Palace fill
> With loath'd intrusion, and fill all the land;
> His Cattel must of Rot and Murren die,
> Botches and blaines must all his flesh imboss,
> And all his people; Thunder mixt with Haile,
> Haile mixt with fire must rend th' Egyptian Skie
> And wheel on th' Earth, devouring where it rouls;
> What it devours not, Herb, or Fruit, or Graine,
> A darksome Cloud of Locusts swarming down
> Must eat, and on the ground leave nothing green:
> Darkness must overshadow all his bounds,
> Palpable darkness, and blot out three dayes;
> Last with one midnight stroke all the first-born
> Of Egypt must lie dead. Thus with ten wounds
> This River-dragon tam'd at length submits
> To let his sojourners depart . . .

POOL OF BETHESDA   *see BETHESDA, POOL OF*

POOR ALWAYS YE HAVE WITH YOU

Matt. 26:11; John 12:8

Jesus, at the time that he was in the HOUSE IN BETHANY, was anointed by Martha with costly ointment. Judas, according to John, objected, saying the money could be better used for the poor. Jesus replied that Martha did well, "for the poor always ye have with you; but me ye have not always." In *Evangeline*, Longfellow said that the almshouse is now nearly lost, surrounded by the city,

> but still, with its gateway and wicket
> Meek, in the midst of splendour, its humble walls seem to echo
> Softly the words of the Lord:—"The poor ye always have
> with you."

In *Walden*, Thoreau writes of the burden of owning superfluous property: "What mean ye by saying that the poor ye have always with you . . . ?" Then he quotes Ezekiel (18:3) and , Jeremiah (31:29) that "ye shall not have occasion any more to use this proverb in Israel."

POTIPHAR'S WIFE   *see JOSEPH AND POTIPHAR'S WIFE*

POTTER'S FIELD   *see ACELDAMA*

POUR OUT THE VIALS OF WRATH   *see VIALS OF WRATH*

POWERS THAT BE

Rom. 13:1

Paul wrote to the Romans concerning submission to the state: "Let every soul be subject unto the higher powers. For there is no power but of God: the powers that be are ordained of God." James Russell Lowell, in "Democracy," said that some people fear that democracy endangers property rights. "But I believe that the real gravamen of the charges lies in the habit it has of making itself generally disagreeable by asking the Powers that Be at the most inconvenient moment whether they are the powers that ought to be. If the powers that be are in a condition to give a satisfactory answer to this inevitable question, they need feel in no way discomfort by it." In *The Flowering of New England*, Van Wyck Brooks said that Unitarianism abroad, in contrast to the Boston brand, "had always been accompanied by radical movements. Even in far-away Poland had been . . . pacifists . . . communists, trouble-makers for the powers that be."

THE PREACHER   *see ALL IS VANITY*

PRECURSOR   *see JOHN THE BAPTIST*

PREPARE THE WAY   *see* VOICE THAT CRIETH IN THE
                   WILDERNESS

PRIDE GOETH BEFORE . . . A FALL

Prov. 16:18   The proverb states, "Pride goeth before destruction, and a
haughty spirit before a fall." In Bunyan's *Pilgrim's Progress*,
Faithful tells Christian how he resisted Discontent who tried to
dissuade him from going through the Valley of Humility: "I
told him that as to this Valley, he had quite miss-represented
the thing: for . . . a haughty spirit [is] before a fall." Melville's
story "The Bell-Tower," about the man who built a great bell
tower with an automaton bell striker which finally killed him,
concludes, "So the creator was killed by the creature . . . .
And so pride went before the fall." In Shaw's *Saint Joan*, when
Joan defends her method of fighting to the Archbishop, he
says, "Pride will have a fall, Joan." She replies, "Oh, never
mind whether it is pride or not: is it true? is it commonsense?"

PRINCE OF DARKNESS   *see SATAN*

PRODIGAL SON

Luke 15:11–32   A parable of Jesus about the sinner that repents. The word
"prodigal"does not appear in the Bible except in the chapter
heading, "The Prodigal Son." A younger son of a certain man
took the portion of goods that belonged to him, journeyed
"into a far country, and there wasted his substance with riotous
living." During a mighty famine he was forced into the fields to
feed swine, and there "filled his belly with the husks that the
swine did eat . . . ." Then, repentant, he returned to his
father, who welcomed him with new clothes and the FATTED
CALF, saying, "For this my son was dead, and is alive again."
The elder son was angry, but his father urged him to be forgiving also. In Shakespeare's *As You Like It*, Orlando quarrels
with his elder brother Oliver for treating him as a rustic: "Shall
I keep your hogs, and eat husks with them? What prodigal
portion have I spent, that I should come to such penury?" In
Henry IV, Part I, Falstaff says of his ragged company of soldiers, ". . . you would think that I had a hundred and fifty
tattered prodigals lately come from swine-keeping, from eating
draff and husks." In Joyce's *A Portrait of the Artist as a Young
Man*, Stephen looked at the dean of his college, an English con-

vert to Catholicism, "with the same eyes as the elder brother
in the parable may have turned on the prodigal." In *Walden*,
Thoreau said of his pond in spring, "Walden was dead and is
alive again."

PROMISED LAND

Gen. 12:5–7;
26:3; Deut.
19:8; 34:4

"Abram took Sarai his wife and Lot" from Haran "into the
land of Canaan . . . and the Canaanite was then in the land.
And the Lord appeared unto Abram, and said, Unto thy seed
will I give this land:" Moses led his people to it through the
wilderness but was not permitted himself to enter it. The exact
phrase "promised land" is not to be found in the Bible; "land
of promise" appears in Hebrews 11:9. In the chapter "Natural
Supernaturalism" of *Sartor Resartus*, Carlyle says "the Philosophy of Clothes properly attains to Transcendentalism; this
last leap, can we but clear it, takes us safe into the promised
land." Matthew Arnold, in *Essays in Criticism*, wrote that a
great epoch of creative activity, like those of Aeschylus and
Shakespeare, "is the promised land, toward which criticism
can only beckon. That promised land it will not be ours to
enter, and we shall die in the wilderness: but to have desired
to enter it, to have saluted it from afar, is already, perhaps, the
best distinction among contemporaries." Lawrence Durrell's "A
Ballad of the Good Lord Nelson" begins

> The Good Lord Nelson had a swollen gland,
> Little of the scripture did he understand
> Till a woman led him to the promised land
> Aboard the Victory, Victory O.°

PROPHET IS NOT WITHOUT HONOR

Matt. 13:57;
John 4:44

When Jesus had finished teaching parables to his disciples and
to great multitudes, he returned to his own country and "taught
them in their synagogue." And they were astonished and offended that the local carpenter's son had "this wisdom and
these mighty works." "But Jesus said unto them, A prophet is
not without honour, save in his own country, and in his own
house." In Butler's *The Way of All Flesh*, Ernest, returning
home from Cambridge full of new religious enthusiasm, found
his father cold to his new ideas. "He said to himself that a
prophet was not without honour save in his own country, but
he had been lately . . . getting into an odious habit of turning

---

° From *Collected Poems* by Lawrence Durrell. Reprinted by permission
of E. P. Dutton & Co., Inc., and Faber and Faber, Ltd.

proverbs upside down, and it occurred to him that a country is sometimes not without honour save for its own prophet." In *The Big Money*, John Dos Passos wrote:

> Frank Lloyd Wright,
> patriarch of the new building
> not without honor except in his own country.°

PROPHET'S GOURD   *see JONAH'S GOURD*

PURE, UNTO THE   *see UNTO THE PURE ALL THINGS ARE PURE*

PUT NEW WINE INTO OLD BOTTLES   *see NEW WINE IN OLD BOTTLES*

PUT OFF THY SHOES

Exod. 3:5; Josh. 5:15; Acts 7:33

When God called to Moses from the BURNING BUSH, and Moses said, "Here I am," God said, "Draw not nigh hither: put off thy shoes from off thy feet, for the place whereon thou standest is holy ground." When Joshua was by Jericho, "the captain of the Lord's host" appeared before him and said, "Loose thy shoe from off thy foot; for the place whereon thou standest is holy ground." Emerson, in "Self-Reliance," said, ". . . let us sit at home with the cause. Let us stun and astonish the intruding rabble of men and books and institutions by a simple declaration of the divine fact. Bid them take their shoes from off their feet, for God is here within." In "The Miracle of Autumn," Whittier wrote of the flaming beauty of autumn, which

> Burned, unconsumed; a voice without a sound
> Spake to him from each kindled bush around,
> And made the strange new landscape holy ground.

And in "Laus Deo," hearing the bells pealing for the abolition of slavery in 1865, Whittier wrote:

> Let us kneel:
> God's own voice is in that peal,
> And this spot is holy ground.
> Lord, forgive us! What are we,
> That our eyes this glory see,
> That our ears have heard this sound!

QUAILS   *see MANNA*

°From *The Big Money* by John Dos Passos (Boston, Houghton Mifflin Company). Reprinted by permission of John Dos Passos.

QUEEN OF HEAVEN   see *ASHTORETH; ASHTAROTH*

QUEEN OF THE SOUTH   see *SHEBA (SABA) QUEEN OF*

QUICK AND THE DEAD

Acts 10:42; II Tim. 4:1; I Pet. 4:5

Peter taught that Jesus "was ordained of God to be the Judge of quick and dead." In *The English Mail-Coach*, De Quincey described a vision of a great cathedral: "Lo! as I looked back for seventy leagues through the mighty cathedral, I saw the quick and the dead that sang together to God . . . ." In Somerset Maugham's *Of Human Bondage*, Philip, after seeing his first cadaver in the dissecting room of the medical school, remembered Fanny Price. "She was the first dead person he had ever seen, and he remembered how strangely it had affected him. There was an immeasurable distance between the quick and the dead . . . ."

RACHEL   see *JACOB, LEAH, AND RACHEL*

RACHEL WEEPING FOR HER CHILDREN

Jer. 31:15; Matt. 2:18

Matthew said that after the slaughter of the innocents (see HEROD THE GREAT) in Bethlehem by King Herod, "Then was fulfilled that which was spoken by Jeremy the prophet, saying, In Rama [rā'mà] was there a voice heard, lamentation, and weeping, and great mourning, Rachel weeping for her children, and would not be comforted, because they are not." In *The Prioress's Tale*, Chaucer said that as the murdered child was carried in procession to the abbey,

> His mooder swownynge by his beer lay;
> Unnethe myghte the people that was theere
> This newe Rachel brynge fro his beere.

Charles Lamb, in "The Praise of Chimney Sweepers," said that some young chimney sweeps are victims of abductions from good families: "Many noble Rachels mourning for their children, even in our days, countenance the fact." In Melville's *Moby Dick*, Captain Ahab refused to stop to help the captain of the *Rachel*, who was hunting for his lost son. She continued searching. "But by her still halting course and winding, woful way, you plainly saw that this ship that so wept with spray, still remained without comfort. She was Rachel, weeping for her children, because they were not." In *Science and Poetry*,

I. A. Richards said that Thomas Hardy is "the poet who has
most steadfastly refused to be comforted. The comfort of for-
getfulness, the comfort of beliefs, he has put both these away."

RAVENS FED ELIJAH   *see ELIJAH FED BY RAVENS*

REAP THE WHIRLWIND   *see SOW THE WIND, AND REAP THE*
        WHIRLWIND

REAP WHAT ONE SOWS   *see WHATSOEVER A MAN SOWETH,*
        THAT SHALL HE ALSO REAP

RECHABITE   *see JONADAB THE RECHABITE*

RED SEA   The Hebrew words *yam suph,* translated "Red Sea," are now
understood to mean "reed—or weed—sea." The Hebrews, pur-
Exod. 10:19;   sued by Pharaoh in heavy chariots, probably crossed over the
14:1–31   swampy land above the Gulf of Suez, the northwestern arm of
the Red Sea. The Lord sent a strong east wind which divided
the waters, "and the children of Israel went into the midst of
the sea upon the dry ground: and the waters were a wall unto
them on their right hand, and on their left." Moses stretched
forth his hand "and the waters returned, and covered the chariots, and the horsemen, and all the host of Pharaoh . . . ." In
Paradise Lost, Milton described the fallen devils scattered on
the burning lake of hell: they lay like

> scattered sedge
> Afloat, when with fierce winds Orion arm'd
> Hath vext the Red-Sea coast, whose waves orethrew
> Busiris and his Memphian chivalrie,
> While with perfidious hatred they pursu'd
> The Sojourners of Goshen, who beheld
> From the safe shore their floating carkases
> And broken chariot wheels . . . .

Philip Freneau, in "On a Honey Bee—Drinking from a Glass
of Wine and Drowned Therein," warns the bee not to take too
deep a drink: "Here bigger bees than you might sink, / Even
bees full six feet high. / Like Pharaoh, then, you would be said
/ To perish in a sea of red."

REFUSED TO BE COMFORTED   *see RACHEL WEEPING FOR HER*
        CHILDREN

REMNANT   *see SAVING REMNANT*

RENDER UNTO CAESAR

Matt. 22:21;
Luke 20:25

Trying to entangle Jesus, the Pharisees send their disciples with the Herodians to ask Him, "Is it lawful to give tribute unto Caesar, or not?" Jesus asks for the tribute money, and when they bring Him a penny, He asks whose "image and super-scription" are upon it. "They say unto him, Caesar's. Then saith he unto them, Render therefore unto Caesar the things which are Caesar's; and unto God the things which are God's." In *Table Talk,* John Selden said, regarding kings: "The text, 'Render unto Caesar the things that are Caesar's,' makes as much against Kings as for them; for it says plainly that some things are not Caesar's. But divines make choice of it, first in flattery, and then because of the other part adjoined to it, 'Render unto God the things that are God's,' where they bring in the Church." In *Walden,* Thoreau wrote of the burdens of rich men.

The best thing a man can do for his culture when he is rich is to en-deavor to carry out those schemes which he entertained when he was poor. Christ answered the Herodians according to their condition. "Show me the tribute-money," said he;—and took one penny out of his pocket;—if you use money which has the image of Caesar on it . . . that is, *if you are men of the State,* and gladly enjoy the advantages of Caesar's government, then pay him back some of his own when he demands it. "Render therefore to Caesar that which is Caesar's, and to God those things which are God's,"—leaving them no wiser than before as to which was which; for they did not wish to know.

RESURRECTION   *see JESUS, RESURRECTION*

REVELATION, BOOK OF   *see APOCALYPSE*

REVOLT OF THE ANGELS   *see WAR IN HEAVEN*

RICH MAN ENTER HEAVEN   *see CAMEL GO THROUGH AN EYE OF A NEEDLE*

RICH YOUNG RULER

Matt. 19:16–22;
Mark 10:17–22;
Luke 18:18–23

A certain rich young man, called a ruler by Luke, asked Jesus what he should do to have eternal life. When Jesus bade him keep the TEN COMMANDMENTS, and he said that he had done so all his life, "Jesus said unto him, If thou wilt be perfect, go and sell that thou hast, and give to the poor, and thou shalt have treasure in heaven: and come and follow me. But

when the young man heard that saying, he went away sorrowful: for he had great possessions." The expression "counsel of
perfection" derives from this passage. In *The Summing Up*,
Somerset Maugham said, "Every production of an artist should
be the expression of an adventure of his soul. This is a counsel
of perfection . . . but this surely is the aim he should keep
before him." In Chaucer's Prologue to "The Wife of Bath's
Tale," the good wife of Bath discourses on virginity:

> Virginitee is greet perfeccion,
> And continance eek, with devocion;
> But Crist, that of perfeccion is welle,
> Bad not every wight sholde go selle
> All that he hadde and gyve it to the poore,
> And in swich wise folwe hym and his foore.
> He spak to hem that wolde live parfitly;
> And, lordynges, by youre leve, that am nat I.

In Shaw's *Saint Joan*, the Inquisitor says of Joan, "A gentle
and pious girl, or a young man who has obeyed the command
of our Lord by giving all his riches to the poor, and putting
on the garb of poverty . . . may be the founder of a heresy
that will wreck both Church and Empire if not ruthlessly
stamped out in time."

RIGHT HAND KNOW WHAT LEFT HAND DOETH   *see LET NOT*
THY LEFT HAND KNOW

RIMMON

II Kings 5:8-18

Rimmon was a Syrian god worshiped at Damascus. Naaman
worshiped with his master in the house of Rimmon before he
was cured of leprosy by ELISHA. He asked the Lord's pardon
for going "into the house of Rimmon to worship" with his
master. King Ahaz saw an altar at Damascus, presumably
Rimmon's, according to Milton, and had one made like it on
which he made burnt offerings (II Kings 16:10-16). In Milton's *Paradise Lost*, Rimmon is one of the fallen angels on the
Plain of Hell. After Dagon

> follow'd Rimmon, whose delightful Seat
> Was fair Damascus, on the fertil Banks
> Of Abbana and Pharphar, lucid streams.
> He also against the house of God was bold:
> A Leper once he lost and gain'd a King,
> Ahaz his sottish Conqueror, whom he drew
> Gods Altar to disparage and displace
> For one of Syrian mode, whereon to burn
> His odious offrings, and adore the Gods
> Whom he had vanquisht.

RINGSTRAKED AND SPOTTED   *see JACOB AND LABAN*

RISE, TAKE UP THY BED, AND WALK   *see BETHESDA, POOL OF*

RIVER OF WATER OF LIFE

Rev. 22:1, 17

John's vision of the New Jerusalem: "And he shewed me a pure river of water of life, clear as a crystal, proceeding out of the throne of God and of the Lamb . . . . And whosoever will, let him take of the water of life freely." William Hazlitt, in "On Going on a Journey," said, "O sylvan Dee . . . thou shalt always be to me the river of Paradise, where I will drink of the waters of life freely." Hardy, in *Tess of the D'Urbervilles*, said that the waters of the river Froom, in the Valley of the Great Dairies where Tess worked, "were clear as the pure River of Life shown to the Evangelist." And Poe, in "Landor's Cottage," said of the lakelet in the lower vale, "No crystal could be clearer than its waters."

RIVERS OF BABYLON   *see BY THE RIVERS OF BABYLON*

ROCK IN HOREB   *see SMITE THE ROCK*

ROOT OF ALL EVIL

I Tim. 6:10

Paul wrote to Timothy concerning the "temptation and snare of riches." "For the love of money is the root of all evil: which while some coveted after, they have erred from the faith, and pierced themselves through with many sorrows." In the Prologue to Chaucer's "The Pardoner's Tale," the avaricious Pardoner, in the tavern, announces the theme of his tale:

> I preche of no thyng but for coveityse.
> Therefore my theme is yet, and evere was,
> *Radix malorum est Cupiditas.*
> Thus kan I preche agayne that same vice
> Which that I use, and that is avarice.

In Melville's *Moby Dick*, Ishmael reflects upon the money motive for going to sea: "The urbane activity with which a man receives money is really marvelous, considering that we so earnestly believe money to be the root of all earthly ills . . . . Ah! how cheerfully we consign ourselves to perdition!" And in *Typee*, Melville says that the Typees were free from many of the ills of civilization—mortgages, notes, bills and "debts of honour . . . . The root of evil was not to be found in the valley."

ROSE OF SHARON

Song of Sol.
2:1–2

"The Bride," or the maiden, sings of her love: "I am the rose of Sharon, and the lily of the valleys. As the lily among thorns, so is my love among the daughters." In *Personal Narrative*, Jonathan Edwards says that, in his meditations and reading on Christ, "Those words, Cant. ii:1, used to be abundantly with me, *I am the Rose of Sharon, and the Lily of the valleys.* The words seemed to me, sweetly to represent the loveliness and beauty of Jesus Christ . . . ." Matthew Arnold, in *Essays in Criticism*, called Dr. Chalmers "the Scotch thistle valiantly doing duty as the rose of Sharon, but keeping something very Scotch about it all the time." Somerset Maugham said, in *Of Human Bondage*, "The greatest portrait painters have painted both, man and the intention of his soul; Rembrandt and El Greco; it's only the second-raters who've only painted man. A lily of the valley would be lovely even if it didn't smell, but it's more lovely because it has perfume."

RUTH

Book of Ruth

Ruth, a Moabitess widow, against the advice of Naomi, her widowed mother-in-law, loyally accompanied Naomi on her return to Judah, saying, "Intreat me not to leave thee, or to return from following after thee: for whither thou goest, I will go . . . ." She gleaned wheat in the fields of a kinsman Boaz and slept at his feet one night. Then, because of her devotion to Naomi and to preserve the family line, Boaz married her. Her first son Obed became the grandfather of David. When Charles Strickland, the painter in Somerset Maugham's *The Moon and Sixpence*, suggests that his native wife return to Papeete, she replies, "Thou art my man and I am thy woman. Whither thou goest I will go, too." Whittier, in "Among the Hills," describes the beauty of a mountain lake under the moon: it "Sleeps dreaming of the mountains, fair as Ruth / In the old Hebrew pastoral, at the feet / Of Boaz." O. W. Holmes, in *The Autocrat of the Breakfast Table*, says of reading books that a sensitive woman "reading after a man, follows him as Ruth followed the reapers of Boaz, and her gleanings are often the finest of wheat." And Keats, in "Ode to a Nightingale," hearing the song of the bird, writes:

> Perhaps the self-same song that found a path
> Through the sad heart of Ruth, when, sick for home,
> She stood in tears amid the alien corn.

SABA, QUEEN OF   *see SHEBA (SABA) QUEEN OF*

SACKCLOTH AND ASHES

Jonah 3:6; Esther 4:1, 3; Matt. 11:21

When Jonah preached to the Ninevites, the King of Nineveh "arose from his throne, and he laid his robe from him, and covered him with sackcloth, and sat in ashes." The expression is widely used in the Bible for abject repentance and lamentation. In Shakespeare's *Henry IV, Part II,* Falstaff tells the Lord Chief Justice about Prince Hal giving him a box on the ear: "I have check'd him for it, and the young lion repents; marry, not in ashes and sackcloth, but in new silk and old sack." In "The Gentle Boy," Hawthorne tells of the Quaker Catherine denouncing the Puritans in their own meeting house. When she took off her cloak and hood, she "appeared in a most singular array. A shapeless robe of sackcloth was girded about her waist with a knotted cord; her raven hair fell down upon her shoulders, and its blackness was defiled by pale streaks of ashes which she had strown upon her head." In *The Adventures of Mark Twain,* Albert Bigelow Paine said that Mark Twain one summer in New Hampshire "rented" three kittens so they would have a home until fall. He named them Sackcloth and Ashes, "Sackcloth being a black-and-white kit, and Ashes a joint name owned by the two others, who were grey and exactly alike."

SADDUCEE   *see PHARISEE*

SAINT PETER   *see KEYS OF THE KINGDOM*

SALOME   *see HEROD ANTIPAS*

SALT OF THE EARTH

Matt. 5:13

In the Sermon on the Mount, Jesus said, "Ye are the salt of the earth: but if the salt have lost his savour, wherewith shall it be salted? it is thenceforth good for nothing, but to be cast out, and to be trodden under the foot of men." In Chaucer's "The Summoner's Tale," when the friar, excited and wrathful, rushes to tell his friend about the unsavory hoax just played on him, the friend replied, "Distempre yow noght, ye be my confessour; / Ye been the salt of the erthe and the savour. / For Goddes love, your pacience ye holde!" Thoreau, in "A Plea for Captain John Brown," attacks the hypocrisy of churches regarding slavery: "Away with your broad and flat churches! Take a step forward, and invent a new style of out-houses. Invent a salt that will save you, and defend our nostrils."

And in Melville's "I and My Chimney," the narrator, a lover of old things, says of his wife, who loves new things, that she keeps him from stagnating. "My wife, good soul, is the salt of the earth, and none the less the salt of my sea, which otherwise were unwholesome."

SAMARITAN WOMAN

John 4:6–29   When Jesus stopped at Jacob's well in Samaria, He asked a woman of Samaria to give Him drink. She was surprised because "Jews have no dealings with the Samaritans." Jesus gave her "that living water" that whosoever should drink of it should never thirst, but have everlasting life. And He told her that it was not necessary for her to go to Jerusalem to worship God, for "the true worshippers shall worship the Father in spirit and in truth." And Jesus revealed Himself unto her as Christ the Messiah come. In Tennyson's "Sir John Oldcastle," Sir John, a Wycliffite, fled to Wales, contemplates a fountain and a cross:

> To thee, dead wood, I bow not head nor knees . . .
> Rather to thee, thou living water, drawn
> By this good Wiclif mountain down from heaven,
> And speaking clearly in thy native tongue—
> No Latin—He that thirsteth, come and drink.

In Whittier's "Mogg Megone," Ruth Boniton recalls the tales her mother used to tell her:

> Of her, Samaria's humble daughter,
>   Who paused to hear, beside her well,
>   Lessons of love and truth, which fell
> Softly as Shiloh's flowing water;
>   And saw, beneath his pilgrim guise,
> The Promised One, so long foretold
> By holy seer and bard of old,
>   Revealed before her wondering eyes!

In "Two Rivers," Emerson sees the actual river as a symbol of the ideal river:

> So forth and brighter fares my stream,—
> Who drinks it shall not thirst again;
> No darkness stains its equal gleam
> And ages drop in it like rain.

And Cecil Day-Lewis satirizes science in "The Magnetic Mountain":

God is an electrician,
And they that worship him must worship him
In ampere and volt.°

SAMSON A NAZARITE

*Judg. 13:4–5;
16:17*

Samson's mother consecrated him to become a NAZARITE, as the angel of the Lord commanded: "Now therefore beware, I pray thee, and drink not wine nor strong drink, and eat not any unclean thing: for, lo, thou shalt conceive, and bear a son; and no razor shall come on his head: for the child shall be a Nazarite unto God from the womb . . . ." And when Samson told Delilah the secret of his strength, he said, "There hath not come a razor upon mine head; for I have been a Nazarite unto God from my mother's womb . . . ." In Chaucer's "The Monk's Tale," Samson fell because he told "his lemman Dalida . . . that in his heeris al his strength lay . . . ."

This Sampson nevere ciser drank ne wyn,
Ne on his heed cam rasour noon ne sheere,
By precept of the messager divyn,
For alle his strength in his heeres weere.

Milton admired Samson for his sobriety and temperance. In *The Reason of Church Government Urged against Prelaty*, Milton said, "I cannot better liken the state and person of a king than to that mighty Nazarite Samson; who being disciplined from his birth in the precepts and the practice of temperance and sobriety, without the strong drink of injurious and excessive desires, grows up to a noble strength and perfection with those his illustrious and sunny locks, the laws, waving and curling about his godlike shoulders." And in *The Citizen of the World*, Goldsmith said of the English gentleman, "To make a fine gentleman several trades are required, but chiefly a barber. You have undoubtedly heard of the Jewish Champion whose strength lay in his hair. One would think that the English were for placing all wisdom there."

SAMSON AND DELILAH

Judg. 16:1–21

Samson fell in love with Delilah, meaning "coquette," a Philistine woman. She betrayed him to the lords of the Philistines, binding him, at his suggestion, first with "seven green withs" then with "new ropes." Then she wove "the seven locks of

°Copyright 1933 and 1961 by C. Day-Lewis. Reprinted by permission of the Harold Matson Co., Inc.

[his] head with the web," and finally "she called for a man . . . to shave off the seven locks of his head." Each time, as the waiting Philistines approached, Delilah woke him, calling out, "The Philistines be upon thee, Samson." Three times he escaped, but the fourth time he was caught, blinded, and taken captive to Gaza to "grind in the prison house." In Thomas Hardy's *Far from the Madding Crowd*," Liddy, discovering an ominous file of men and women approaching the house, called out to Bathsheba, her mistress, "The Philistines be upon us!" In "The Lost Occasion," Whittier regretted that Daniel Webster did not live long enough to see his flag trampled under the feet of slavery; it would have broken "the spell about [him] wound / Like the green withes that Samson bound." Chaucer's Wife of Bath in her Prologue told how her jolly husband Jankin read to her about unfaithful wives: "Tho redde he me how Sampson lost his heres: / Slepynge, his lemman kitte it with hir sheres; / Thurgh which treson loste he bothe hise eyes." In Shakespeare's *Love's Labour's Lost*, Moth tells his master Don Armado, in love with "a base wench," that Delilah surely "had a green wit."

SAMSON AND PILLARS OF THE TEMPLE

Judg. 16:25–30   The Philistines took blind Samson from prison and set him between the pillars of their temple of DAGON to make sport of him. Guided by a boy, he took hold of the two middle pillars and said, "Let me die with the Philistines. And he bowed himself with all his might; and the house fell upon the lords, and upon all the people that were therein. So the dead which he slew at his death were more than they which he slew in his life." Chaucer described the event in "The Monk's Tale":

> The ende of this caytyf was as I shal seye.
> His foomen made a feeste upon a day,
> And made hym as hire fool biforn hem pleye;
> And this was in a temple of greet array.
> But atte laste he made a foul affray;
> For he two pilers shook and made hem falle,
> And doun fil temple and al, and ther it lay;
> And slow hymself, and eek his foomen alle.

Francis Thompson, in "The Hound of Heaven," recalls his dissipated youth:

> In the rash lustihead of my young powers,
> I shook the pillaring hours

And pulled my life upon me; grimed with smears,
I stand amid the dust o' the mounded years—
My mangled youth lies dead beneath the heap.

SAMSON, BLIND, GRINDS IN PRISON

Judg. 16:21

After Delilah betrayed Samson, "the Philistines took him, and put out his eyes, and brought him down to Gaza, and bound him with fetters of brass; and he did grind in the prison house." In the Prologue of Milton's *Samson Agonistes*, Samson, alone in prison, asks why, if destined for great exploits,

> I must dye
> Betray'd, Captiv'd, and both my Eyes put out,
> Made of my Enemies the scorn and gaze;
> To grind in Brazen Fetters under task
> With this Heav'n-gifted strength? . . .
> O loss of sight, of thee I most complain!
> Blind among enemies, O worse then chains,
> Dungeon, or beggery, or decrepit age!

In "Boswell's Life of Johnson," Carlyle said that Johnson suffered so much as usher at Market Bosworth that he resigned: "Young Samson will grind no more in the Philistine mill of Bosworth."

SAMSON'S FIREBRANDED FOXES

Judg. 15:3–6

Samson's Philistine father-in-law refused to let Samson in to see his wife, saying he had given her to Samson's companion and offering him instead her younger sister. In revenge Samson "caught three hundred foxes, and took firebrands, and turned tail to tail, and put a firebrand in the midst between two tails." Then "he let them go into the standing corn of the Philistines, and burnt up both the shocks, and also the standing corn, with the vineyards and olives." So the Philistines burnt Samson's wife and her father with fire. Keats, in *Endymion*, attacked lords and kings who preyed upon the poor:

> There are who lord it o'er their fellow-men
> With most prevailing tinsel . . .
> Who, through an idiot blink, will see unpacked
> Fire-branded foxes to sear up and singe
> Our gold and ripe-ear'd hopes.

In Mark Twain's *The Mysterious Stranger*, Satan "told some very cunning things . . . about the time that Samson tied the torches to the foxes' tails and set them loose in the Philistines' corn, and Samson sitting on the fence slapping his thighs and laughing, with the tears running down his cheeks, and lost his balance and fell off the fence, the memory of that picture got him to laughing too, and we did have a most lovely and jolly time."

SAMSON SLEEPING, WAKING, AND SHAKING HIMSELF

Judg. 16:20 After Delilah had "a man . . . shave off the seven locks of his head" while Samson slept, she said, "The Philistines be upon thee, Samson. And he awoke out of his sleep, and said, I will go out as at other times before, and shake myself. And he wist not that the Lord was departed from him." In *Moby Dick*, Melville described the calm sea just before the final chase: ". . . the robust and man-like sea heaved with long, strong, lingering swells, as Samson's chest in his sleep." In *Areopagitica*, Milton said that England must arise and cast off the corruption of conformity. "Methinks I see in my mind a noble and puissant nation rousing herself like a strong man after sleep and shaking her invincible locks." In Hardy's *Tess of the D'Urbervilles*, Angel Clare, the morning after his sleepwalking with Tess in his arms, awakened "from a sleep deep as annihilation; and during those first few moments in which the brain, like a Samson shaking himself, is trying its strength, he had some dim notion of an unusual nocturnal proceeding."

SANCTUM SANCTORUM   *see HOLY OF HOLIES*

SAPPHIRA   *see ANANIAS*

SATAN   Satan, meaning "hater" or "accuser," is known variously as the Devil, the Dragon, Old Serpent, Prince of Darkness, Prince of Hell, Old Clootie, Old Nick, Old Scratch, Lucifer, Beelzebub, and Mephistopheles. In the Old Testament he is a son of God, mainly "an adversary"; whereas in the New Testament he also becomes the tempter and the devil. Although in literature he is generally the personification of evil, some writers view Satan with considerable sympathy, if not admiration. Milton's Satan, in *Paradise Lost*, is the capable and courageous commander of the devils. As he reviewed his fallen hosts,

I Chron. 21:1;
Job 1-2; Matt.
4:1-11; Rev.
20:1-10

> he above the rest
> In shape and gesture proudly eminent
> Stood like a Tower; his form had not yet lost
> All her Original brightness, nor appear'd
> Less than Arch Angel ruind, and th' excess
> Of Glory obscur'd . . . .

Robert Burns's "Address to the Deil" begins:

> O thou! whatever title suit thee—
> Auld Hornie, Satan, Nick, or Clootie
> Wha in cavern grim an sootie,
>   Clos'd under hatches,
> Spairges[1] about the brunstane cootie,[2]
>   To scaud[3] poor wretches!
>
> Hear me, Auld Hangie, for a wee,
> An' let poor damned bodies be;
> I'm sure sma' pleasure it can gie,
>   Ev'n to a deil,
> To skelp[4] an' scaud poor dogs like me,
>   An' hear us squeel.

And Emily Dickinson wrote:

> The Devil, had he fidelity,
> Would be the finest friend—
> Because he has ability,
> But Devils cannot mend.
> Perfidy is the virtue
> That would he but resign,—
> The Devil, so amended,
> Were durably divine.[*]

SAUL, KING

I Sam. 9–31

Saul, the son of Kish, was anointed the first King of Israel by Samuel. He helped to unite the people by his successful wars against the Philistines and other neighbors, but his jealous and moody temperament led to clashes with Samuel, David, and his son Jonathan. Finally, defeated by the Philistines at Mount Gilboa, he killed himself with his own sword. (The Amalekite messenger told David that he had killed Saul at Saul's request.) In *Eikonoklastes*, Milton refers to Saul's disobedience in sparing the "best of the sheep and of the oxen" of the Amalekites, as the people wished, for "sacrifice unto the Lord." Samuel reproved him for this, because God had commanded the destruction of everything, and he repented. Milton attacks Charles I for catering to unworthy courtiers and clergymen, although Charles I claimed that he feared God more than man. "Thus boasted Saul to have 'performed the commandment of God,' and stood it in against Samuel; but it was found at length, that he had feared the people more than God, in saving those fat

[1]Splashes.
[2]Brimstone tub.
[3]Scald.
[4]Slap.
[*]From *Poems by Emily Dickinson* by Emily Dickinson, by permission of Little, Brown and Co. Copyright 1914, 1942 by Martha Dickinson Bianchi.

oxen for the worship of God, which were appointed for destruction." So had Charles "for fear to displease his court and mon-
grel clergy . . . upheld . . . those beasts of Amalec, the prel-
ates . . . ; in this more unexcusable than Saul . . . Saul was at
last convinced." In *Billy Budd*, Melville said that Claggart's
envy of Billy did not "partake of that streak of apprehensive
jealousy which marred Saul's visage perturbedly brooding on
the comely young David." And in "Saul," Browning portrays
David playing for the moody King Saul. As he sang of the rich-
ness of life, "in the darkness Saul groaned."

And I paused, held my breath in such silence, and listened apart;
And the tent shook, for mighty Saul shuddered: and sparkles 'gan
    dart
From the jewels, that woke in his turban, at once with a start,
All its lordly male-sapphires, and rubies courageous at heart.
So the head: but the body still moved not, still hung there erect.
And I bent once again to my playing, pursued it unchecked,
As I sang,—

SAUL OF TARSUS   *see PAUL, CONVERSION OF*

SAVE HIS LIFE   *see WHOSOEVER WILL SAVE HIS LIFE SHALL LOSE IT*

SAVING REMNANT

Isa. 10:20–23   Isaiah said that, after the Lord sends Assyria to punish the sinful people, "The remnant shall return, even the remnant of
Jacob, unto the mighty God. For though thy people Israel be
as the sand of the sea, yet a remnant of them shall return: the
consumption decreed shall overflow with righteousness." Matthew Arnold, in *Discourses in America*, used this term for the
intelligent minority who would save the state—especially the
United States—from "the unsound majority." Athens fell, he
said, because "the majority were bad, and the remnant were
impotent." Plato spoke of "the very small remnant which hon-
estly sought wisdom." "The remnant!—it is the word of the
Hebrew prophets also, and especially it is the word of the greatest of them all, Isaiah . . . 'Though thy people Israel be as the
sand of the sea, only a remnant of them shall return.'"

SCALES FELL FROM HIS EYES

Acts 9:18   After Saul (Paul), on his way to Damascus to persecute the
Christians, was struck blind by "a light from heaven," Jesus
sent Ananias to him. Ananias put his hands on Saul, and told

him, Jesus "hath sent me, that thou mightest receive thy sight, and be filled with the Holy Ghost. And immediately there fell from his eyes as it had been scales: and he received sight forthwith, and arose, and was baptized." Converted, he "straightway preached Christ in the synagogues . . . ." In *Ways of Nature*, John Burroughs wrote, "There are not only scales upon our eyes so that we do not see, there are scales upon our ears so that we do not hear." In Butler's *The Way of All Flesh*, when Ernest discovered that his wife, Ellen, had been misusing their money, and she "reproached him downright with having married her— on that moment the scales fell from Ernest's eyes as they had fallen when" he had become disillusioned about his old friend Townley. "A touch had again come which had revealed him to himself."

SCAPEGOAT

Lev. 16:8, 10, 26

Aaron cast lots for two goats, "one lot for the Lord, and the other lot for the scapegoat." The first was offered for a sin offering, the second was "presented alive before the Lord, to make an atonement with him, and to let him go for a scapegoat into the wilderness." Thus it means someone who bears the blame or burden of others. The word is William Tyndale's translation of the Hebrew word "azazel." The scapegoat is sometimes called Azazel [à·zā'zĕl], who is also an evil demon of the desert. In *Paradise Lost*, Milton makes Azazel the proud standard-bearer of Satan's devils in hell. In Tennyson's *Maud*, Maud's lover

> heap'd the whole inherited sin
> On that huge scapegoat of the race,
> All, all upon the brother.

When Jane was serving as governess for Mrs. Reed, in Charlotte Brontë's *Jane Eyre*, the servants made her "the scapegoat of the nursery."

SCARLET WOMAN *see BABYLON AS SCARLET WOMAN, WHORE*

SCRIBES AND PHARISEES *see PHARISEE*

SEA OF REEDS *see RED SEA*

SEAT OF CHRIST, OF GOD *see JUDGMENT DAY*

SECOND COMING *see MILLENIUM*

SECOND DEATH *see LAKE OF FIRE AND BRIMSTONE*

SEEK, AND YE SHALL FIND

Matt. 7:7–8;
Luke 11:9–10

In the Sermon on the Mount, Jesus said, "Ask, and it shall be given you; seek, and ye shall find; knock, and it shall be opened unto you: For every one that asketh receiveth; and he that seeketh findeth; and to him that knocketh it shall be opened." When Christian, in Bunyan's *Pilgrim's Progress*, got up to the strait Gate, he found "over the Gate there was written, Knock and it shall be opened unto you." In "Compensation," Emerson said, "All things are double, one against the other.—Tit for tat; . . . blood for blood; . . . love for love.—Give, and it shall be given you." In *Cape Cod*, Thoreau, describing a "Charity-house" built on the shore for shipwrecked sailors, tells about peeking through a knothole in the door hoping to see perhaps some dead men's bones: we were "looking with the eye of faith, knowing that, though to him that knocketh it may not always be opened, yet to him that looketh long enough through a knot-hole the inside shall be visible . . . ."

SEE THROUGH A GLASS DARKLY   *see THROUGH A GLASS DARKLY*

SEE VISIONS, YOUNG MEN   *see DREAM DREAMS, OLD MEN*

SELL ALL THAT THOU HAST   *see RICH YOUNG RULER*

SELL DOVES   *see DEN OF THIEVES*

SEPARATE SHEEP FROM GOATS

Matt. 25:32–33

Jesus said that when JUDGMENT DAY shall come, the Son of man shall "sit upon the throne of his glory . . . and before him shall be gathered all nations; and he shall separate them one from another, as a shepherd divideth his sheep from the goats: And he shall set the sheep on his right hand, but the goats on the left." In Shakespeare's *As You Like It*, Touchstone jests Corin about being a shepherd, getting "a living by the copulation of cattle . . . If thou beest not damned for this, the Devil himself will have no shepherds. I cannot see else how thou shouldst 'scape." In "The Reading of Books," Carlyle said, "I conceive that books are like men's souls—divided into sheep and goats." And Arnold, in *Culture and Anarchy*, said that some English people took pride in large families, as if "the British Philistine would have only to present himself before the Great Judge with his twelve children, in order to be received among the sheep as a matter of right!"

SERMON ON THE MOUNT   *see BEATITUDES*

SERPENT AS THE DEVIL

Gen. 3:1; Rev.
12:9; 20:2

It was the serpent, who "was more subtil than any beast of the field which the Lord God had made," that tempted Eve in the Garden of Eden. Although not so identified in Genesis, the serpent was later thought of as the devil. In Revelation, for example, he is "the dragon, that old serpent, which is the Devil, and Satan." In Milton's *Paradise Lost*, Satan chose the serpent as his disguise for tempting Eve. He roamed "the Orb"

> With narrow search; and with inspection deep
> Consider'd every Creature, which of all
> Most opportune might serve his Wiles, and found
> The Serpent suttlest Beast of all the Field.

Melville's Billy Budd was intelligent, but "with little or no sharpness of faculty or any trace of the wisdom of the serpent." In Joyce's *A Portrait of the Artist as a Young Man*, the preacher tells the boys about the fall of Adam and Eve: how "the devil, once a shining angel . . . now a foul fiend came in the shape of a serpent, the subtlest of all the beasts of the field."

SERVANT OF SERVANTS   *see CANAAN, SON OF HAM*

SERVE GOD AND MAMMON   *see MAMMON*

SERVE TWO MASTERS   *see NO MAN CAN SERVE TWO MASTERS*

SET TEETH ON EDGE   *see FATHERS HAVE EATEN A SOUR GRAPE*

SEVEN PILLARS OF WISDOM

Prov. 9:1

"Wisdom hath builded her house, she hath hewn out her seven pillars." In *In Memoriam*, Tennyson said that Wisdom is loved by all:

> Who loves not Knowledge? Who shall rail
> Against her beauty? May she mix
> With men and prosper! Who shall fix
> Her pillars? Let her work prevail.

In *Unto This Last*, Ruskin said that profit seeking is unstable, "business being . . . essentially restless—and probably contentious . . . whereas the olive feeding and bearing birds look for rest for their feet: thus it is said of Wisdom that she 'hath builded her house, and hewn out her seven pillars.' "

SEVENTY TIMES SEVEN

Matt. 18:22   Peter asked Jesus, "Lord, how oft shall my brother sin against me, and I forgive him? till seven times? Jesus saith unto him, I say not unto thee, Until seven times: but, Until seventy times seven." In "Marcus Aurelius," Matthew Arnold quotes this saying in comparing it with a similar one by Epictetus. Although Jesus, says Arnold, did not give a reason, as Epictetus did, his morality is the better, because "the warmth, the emotion, of Jesus's answer fires his hearer to the practice of forgiveness of injuries, while the thought in Epictetus's leaves him cold." In Emily Brontë's *Wuthering Heights*, Ellen Dean dreams of hearing a tedious sermon on the text, "Seventy Times Seven." It was divided into 490 parts. Suddenly Ellen arose to denounce the preacher "as the sinner of the sin that no Christian need pardon. 'Sir,' I exclaimed, 'sitting here, within these four walls, at one stretch, I have endured and forgiven the four hundred and ninety heads of your discourse. Seventy times seven times have I plucked up my hat and been about to depart—Seventy times seven times have you preposterously forced me to resume my seat. The four hundred and ninety-first is too much. Fellow martyrs, have at him! Drag him down, and crush him to atoms, that the place which knows him may know him no more!'"

SEVEN YEARS OF PLENTY   *see JOSEPH, JACOB'S SON*

SHADOW OF DEATH   *see VALLEY OF THE SHADOW OF DEATH*

SHADRACH, MESHACH, AND ABEDNEGO   *see FIERY FURNACE*

SHAKE OFF THE DUST OF YOUR FEET

Matt. 10:14;
Mark 6:11; Acts
13:51

When Jesus chose his disciples and sent them forth to preach, he said, "And whosoever shall not receive you, nor hear your words, when ye depart out of that house or city, shake off the dust of your feet." In Whittier's "Letter from a Missionary of the Methodist Episcopal Church South," a missionary, who is having trouble promoting Christianity and slavery in Kansas, looks for a job elsewhere. A voice tells him: "Shake off the dust of Kansas. Turn to Cuba— / . . . Keep pace with Providence, or, as we say, / Manifest Destiny." In "Milton," Macaulay said that, upon graduation, "It was probably with relief that Milton shook the dust of his University from his feet, free at last to study in his own way."

SHARON, ROSE OF   *see ROSE OF SHARON*

SHEBA (SABA) QUEEN OF

I Kings 10:1–13;
II Chron. 9:1–12;
Matt. 12:42;
Luke 11:31

Sheba, or Saba [sā′bå], referred to in the New Testament as "the queen of the south," was queen of the kingdom of Saba in southwest Arabia, the present Yemen. She visited King SOLOMON, bringing a great train of camels, spices, gold and precious stones. "She came to prove him with hard questions," and was so impressed with his wisdom and wealth that "there was no more spirit in her." In Shakespeare's *Henry VIII*, Archbishop Cranmer prophesied the brilliant future of Elizabeth the child.

> She shall be . . .
> A pattern to all princes living with her,
> And all that shall succeed. Saba was never
> More covetous of wisdom and fair virtue
> Than this pure soul shall be.

In his *Second Defence*, Milton praised Queen Christina of Sweden, who had detected the imposture of Salmasius, the controversialist. "Henceforth, the queen of the south will not be alone renowned in history; for there is a queen of the north, who would not only be worthy to appear in the court of the wise king of the Jews, or any king of equal wisdom . . . ." In Hardy's *Tess of the D'Urbervilles*, when Angel Clare asks Tess why she looks so sad, she replies, "When I see what you know, what you have read, and seen, and thought, I feel what a nothing I am! I'm like the poor Queen of Sheba who lived in the Bible. There is no more spirit in me."

SHEEP FROM GOATS   *see SEPARATE SHEEP FROM GOATS*

SHEET OF BEASTS   *see PETER'S VISION OF THE SHEET*

SHEM

Gen. 5:32;
9:23–27

Shem, meaning "renown," was Noah's eldest son. When he and his brother Japheth respected their father Noah when he was drunk, (see CANAAN, SON OF HAM) Noah blessed them saying, God "shall dwell in the tents of Shem." By tradition Shem is the ancestor of the Arabs, Aramaeans, Assyrians, and Hebrews —hence the words, "Semite" and "Semitic." In Knickerbocker's *A History of New York*, Washington Irving says that Noah divided the earth among his three sons, Asia going to Shem. If Noah had had another son, "he would doubtless have inherited America." In *Suspiria de Profundis*, De Quincey said that Our Lady of Sighs "walks among the outcasts of mankind . . . . For her kingdom is chiefly amongst the tents of Shem, and the houseless vagrant of every clime." In "The Long Trail," Kipling interprets the "tents of Shem" as comfortable homes:

> Ha' done with the Tents of Shem, dear lass,
> We've seen the seasons through,
> And it's time to turn on the old trail . . . .

SHIBBOLETH
(shĭb′ō·lĕth)

Judg. 12:4–6

Shibboleth was the word, meaning "stream in flood," which Jephtha and the Gileadites used to test the enemy, the Ephraimites trying to escape across the Jordan. "Then said they unto him, Say now Shibboleth: and he said Sibboleth: for he could not frame to pronounce it right. Then they took him and slew him at the passages of Jordan . . . ." The meaning today is test word, password, or slogan. Samson, in Milton's *Samson Agonistes*, likens his betrayal by Judah to Jephtha's betrayal by the Ephraimites and his subsequent revenge. Jephtha's

> prowess quell'd their pride
> In that sore battel when so many dy'd
> Without Reprieve adjudged to death,
> For want of well pronouncing Shibboleth.

Whittier's poem "Letter from a Missionary of the Methodist Episcopal Church South" tells how a vigilance committee was organized in Kansas to catch Yankees:

> A score in all—to watch the river ferry,
> (As they of old did watch the fords of Jordan,)
> And cut off all whose Yankee tongues refuse
> The Shibboleth of the Nebraska bill.

H. L. Mencken attacked American "supernaturalism of politics" in "Puritanism as a Literary Force": "The most successful American politicians . . . have been those most adept at twisting the ancient gauds and shibboleths of Puritanism to partisan uses." In *Don Juan*, Byron said that Juan "did not understand a word / Of English, save their shibboleth, 'God damn!' "

SHIMEI, SON OF GERA
(shĭm′ē·ī)

*II Sam. 16:5–13;
19:16–23;
I Kings 2:8–9,
36–46*

When ABSALOM rebelled against his father, and King David fled, ". . . behold, thence came out a man of the family of the house of Saul, whose name was Shimei, the son of Gera [gē′rȧ]: he came forth, and cursed still as he came . . . and threw stones at him, and cast dust." David did not retaliate, and later forgave him; but his dying words to Solomon were: "hold him not guiltless . . . but his hoar head bring thou down to the grave

with blood." So Solomon did. In Shakespeare's *Richard III*, as
Richard sets out to meet the rebels on Bosworth Field, Queen
Margaret and the Duchess of York intercept him, crying out
against his foul murders. King Richard says:

> A flourish, trumpets! strike alarum, drums!
> Let not the heavens hear these tell-tale women
> Rail on the Lord's anointed . . .

In Dryden's "Absalom and Achitophel," Shimei is one of the
plotters against David (Charles II):

> The wretch who heaven's anointed dared to curse . . . .
> Shimei was always in the midst of them;
> And if they cursed the king when he was by,
> Would rather curse than break good company.

In Butler's *The Way of All Flesh*, when Ernest returned home
during his mother's last illness, his unforgiving father read to
the family "about David's dying injunction to Solomon in the
matter of Shimei, but he did not mind it."

SHINAR: LAND, PLAIN, TOWER   *see BABEL*

SHINING LIGHT

Prov. 4:18; John 5:35

The way of the wicked is as darkness, "But the path of the just
is as the shining light, that shineth more and more unto the perfect day." And Jesus said of John, "He was a burning and a
shining light: and ye were willing for a season to rejoice in his
light." In his *Life of Dr. John Donne*, Izaak Walton said that
after Donne was converted, "his life was as a shining light among
his old friends" of Lincoln's Inn. In *The Way of All Flesh*, Butler
said that Theobald had known Dr. Skinner of Cambridge as "a
burning and a shining light in every position he had filled from
his boyhood upwards."

SIGNS OF THE TIMES

Matt. 16:3

When the Sadducees and the PHARISEES asked Jesus to show
them a sign from heaven, he replied that they could well
prophesy weather by watching the sky. "O ye hypocrites, ye
can discern the face of the sky; but can ye not discern the signs
of the times?" In Joyce's *A Portrait of the Artist as a Young
Man*, the politically minded McCann spoke to the students "of
the Tsar's rescript, of Stead, of general disarmament, arbitra-
tion in cases of international disputes, of the signs of the times
. . . ." And in *Essays, Critical and Historical*, Macaulay wrote:

"The more we read the history of past ages, the more we observe the signs of our times," the more we have hope for the future of the human race.

SILOA(M), SHILOAH, WATERS OF

Isa. 8:6; Neh. 3:15

Isaiah, predicting the coming of the Assyrians as a punishment of the people, said, "The Lord spake also unto me again, saying, Forasmuch as this people refuseth the waters of Shiloah that go softly . . . . Now therefore, behold, the Lord bringeth up upon them the waters of the river, strong and many, even the king of Assyria and all his glory . . . ."—perhaps referring by contrast to the turbulent Euphrates. The softly flowing waters of Shiloah probably are the stream which flowed by way of an old canal built from the Spring of Gihon outside Jerusalem to the Pool of Siloam inside the walls. Milton's invocation in *Paradise Lost* is to the Heavenly Muse, that inspired Moses on Mount Sinai:

> or if Sion Hill
> Delight thee more, and Siloa's Brook that flowed
> Fast by the Oracle of God; I thence
> Invoke thy aid to my adventrous Song . . . .

In *Sartor Resartus,* Carlyle said that Professor Teufelsdröckh, when a child, would muse on how the little brook Kuhbach flowed in time before history: "assiduous as Siloa [it] was murmuring on across the wilderness, as yet unnamed, unseen . . . ." And in "To the Memory of Thomas Shipley," abolitionist and philanthropist, Whittier wrote:

> Gone to thy Heavenly Father's rest!
> The flowers of Eden round thee blowing,
> And on thine ear the murmers blest
> Of Siloa's waters softly flowing.

SILOAM TOWER   *see TOWER IN SILOAM*

SILVER CORD   *see GOLDEN BOWL BE BROKEN*

SIMEON THE JUST

Luke 2:22–34

When Jesus' parents "brought him to Jerusalem, to present him to the Lord" in the temple, Simeon who "was just and devout" recognized Jesus as the Messiah. He took him up in his arms and said, "Lord, now lettest thou thy servant depart in peace, according to thy word: For mine eyes have seen thy salvation, Which thou hast prepared before the face of all the people; A light to lighten the Gentiles, and the glory of thy people Israel." This is the "Nunc Dimittis," meaning "farewell" or "departure," from the Vulgate: "Nunc dimittis, servum tuum, Domine . . . ." In Milton's *Paradise Regained*, Christ in the wilderness recalls his mother telling him about his discovery in the temple:

> Just Simeon and Prophetic Anna, warn'd
> By Vision, found thee in the Temple, and spake
> Before the Altar and the vested Priest,
> Like things of thee to all that present stood.

In *Reflections on the Revolution in France*, Edmund Burke quoted disapprovingly the glowing peroration of a pro-French sermon by Dr. Richard Price: "What an eventful period is this! I am thankful that I have lived to it; I could almost say, Lord now lettest thou thy servant depart in peace, for mine eyes have seen thy salvation."

SIMON MAGUS

Acts 8:9-24

Simon "used sorcery, and bewitched the people of Samaria, giving out that himself was some great one"—hence the term "Magus" later added to his name. "And when Simon saw that through laying on of the apostles' hands the Holy Ghost was given, he offered them money, saying, Give me also this power . . . ." Peter rebuked him so severely that he asked Peter to pray to the Lord for his forgiveness. From Simon Magus we get the word "simony." Milton, in *The Tenure of Kings and Magistrates*, attacked those divines who opposed the deposing of tyrants on religious grounds. They are "a pack of hungry churchwolves, who in the steps of Simon Magus their father, follow the hot scent of double livings, and pluralities, advowsons, donatives, inductions, and augmentations . . . by the mere suggestion of their bellies . . . ." In Bunyan's *Pilgrim's Progress*, Christian attacked the religion of Mr. Moneylove and Mr. Hold-the-world, saying, "Simon the Witch was of this Religion too; for he would have had the Holy Ghost, that he might have got Money therewith, and his sentence from Peter's mouth was according . . . ." There were male witches in those days. In Joyce's "The Sisters," the young boy would say strange words at night like "paralysis," and "like the word simony in the Catechism." And when Father Flynn died, he felt, after hearing the old men criticizing his dead friend, "that I too was smiling feebly as if to absolve the simoniac of his sin."

SIMON THE LEPER   *see HOUSE IN BETHANY*

SINAI   Mount Sinai, or Horeb, was the sacred mountain, on the present Sinai Peninsula, where Moses received the TEN COMMAND-
Exod. 19:10–20   MENTS. ". . . there were thunders and lightnings, and a thick
cloud upon the mount, and the voice of the trumpet exceeding
loud; so that all the people that was in the camp trembled . . . .
And mount Sinai was altogether on a smoke, because the Lord
descended upon it in a fire: and the smoke thereof ascended as
the smoke of a furnace, and the whole mount quaked greatly."
In Milton's *Paradise Lost*, Michael tells Adam of the future
giving of the Law:

> God from the Mount of Sinai, whose gray top
> Shall tremble, he descending, will himself
> In Thunder Lightning and loud Trumpets sound
> Ordaine them Lawes . . . .

Cotton Mather, in *Magnalia Christi Americana*, said of John
Eliot's preaching: "He would sound the *Trumpets* of God
against all *Vice* with a most penetrating Liveliness, and make
his Pulpit another Mount *Sinai*, for the Flashes of Lightning
therein display'd against the Breaches of the *Law* given upon
that *Burning Mountain*."

SINS BE AS SCARLET, THEY SHALL BE WHITE AS SNOW

Isa. 1:18   The prophet pleaded with the sinful people: "Wash you, make
you clean . . . . Come now, and let us reason together, saith
the Lord: though your sins be as scarlet, they shall be as white
as snow; though they be red like crimson, they shall be as wool."
In Shakespeare's *Hamlet*, Claudius soliloquizes about his guilt
after seeing the play:

> What if this cursed hand
> Were thicker than itself with brother's blood,
> Is there not rain enough in the sweet heavens
> To wash it white as snow?

In *A Defense of Poetry*, Shelley said that great poets are great
men; their errors are minor: ". . . if their sins were as scarlet,
they are now white as snow . . . ." In Butler's *The Way of All
Flesh*, Theobald tries to comfort the cottager's fearful dying
wife, Mrs. Thompson, with thoughts of the lake of everlasting
fire at Judgment Day. " 'Mrs. Thompson, compose yourself, be
calm . . . though [your sins] be as scarlet, yet shall they be as
white as wool,' and he makes off as fast as he can from the fetid
atmosphere of the cottage to the pure air outside."

SINS OF THE FATHERS

Exod. 20:5

The second of the TEN COMMANDMENTS prohibits man from bowing down or serving idols, "for I the Lord thy God am a jealous God, visiting the iniquity of the fathers upon the children unto the third and four generation of them that hate me." In Shakespeare's *King John,* Lady Constance tells Queen Elinor that her son John has usurped the "royalties and rights" of Arthur, Lady Constance's son.

> Thy sins are visited in this poor child;
> The canon of the law is laid on him,
> Being but the second generation
> Removed from thy sin-conceiving womb.

The clown Launcelot Gobbo, in Shakespeare's *The Merchant of Venice,* teases Jessica about Shylock, her father: ". . . look you, the sins of the father are to be laid upon the children . . . . Therefore be o' good cheer, for truly I think you are damn'd. There is but one hope . . . that your father got you not . . . ." To which Jessica replies, "That were a kind of bastard hope, indeed. So the sins of my mother should be visited upon me." In Butler's *The Way of All Flesh,* Ernest, in rebellion against his schoolmasters and his father, communes with his inner self. It says to him, "Obey me, your true self, and things will go tolerably well with you, but only listen to that outward and visible old husk of yours which is called your father, and I will rend you in pieces even unto the third and fourth generation as one who has hated God; for I, Ernest, am the God who made you."

SINS WASHED WHITE   *see SINS BE AS SCARLET, THEY SHALL BE WHITE AS SNOW*

SIN WILL FIND YOU OUT

Num. 32:23

When the children of Gad and of Reuben were discouraged about crossing over the Jordan, Moses told them that if they would go over armed until the enemies were driven out and then return, they would be guiltless before the Lord. "But if ye will not do so, behold, ye have sinned against the Lord: and be sure your sin will find you out." In Chaucer's "The Nun's Priest's Tale," Chauntecleer argues with his wife Dame Pertelote that dreams must be believed; his dreams of his friend murdered came true:

> Mordre wol out, that se we day by de.
> Mordre is so wlatsom and abhomynable

> To God, that is so just and reasonable,
> That he ne wol nat suffre it heled be,
> Though it abyde a yeer, or two, or thre.
> Mordre wol out, this my conclusion.

D. H. Lawrence, in *Studies in' Classic American Literature,*
said of the theme of *The Scarlet Letter:* "*Be good! Be good!* war-
bles Nathaniel. *Be good, and never sin! Be sure your sins will
find you out.*"

SION   *see ZION*

SISERA   *see JAEL*

SIT AT THE FEET OF

Acts 22:3   When Paul, taken for an Egyptian seditionist, was arrested in
the Temple in Jerusalem, he defended himself, saying, "I am
verily a man which am a Jew, born in Tarsus, a city in Cilicia,
yet brought up in this city at the feet of Gamaliel, and taught
according to the perfect manner of the law of the fathers . . . ."
Gamaliel was a noted Pharisee teacher of the liberal school of
Hillel. In Trollope's *Barchester Towers,* the new Rev. Mr. Slope
stirred up such controversy that parties formed. Chiefly the
upper-class ladies were on his side. "No man—that is no gentleman—could possibly be attracted by Mr. Slope, or consent to
sit at the feet of so abhorrent a Gamaliel." In "Boswell's Life
of Johnson," Carlyle said that Boswell was a Tory "of quite
peculiarly feudal, genealogical, pragmatical temper; had been
nurtured in an atmosphere of Heraldry, at the feet of a very
Gamaliel in that kind . . . ." And in "The American Scholar,"
Emerson said, "I ask not for the great, the remote, the romantic . . . . I embrace the common, I explore and sit at the feet of
the familiar, the low."

SIT IN MOSES' SEAT   *see MOSES' SEAT*

SLAUGHTER OF THE INNOCENTS   *see HEROD THE GREAT*

SMITE THEM HIP AND THIGH

Judg. 15:8   In revenge for the Philistines' burning of his wife and her father,
Samson "smote them hip and thigh with a great slaughter." In
The Biglow Papers, James Russell Lowell wrote of the difficulty
of dealing with the South on the slavery question. Grandfather
lacked patience: " 'Smite 'em hip an' thigh!' / Sez gran'ther,

'an let every man-child die!' " Van Wyck Brooks, in *New England: Indian Summer,* said that Dr. Holmes had been a leader in making Boston a center of culture. "It was he who had smitten the Philistines hip and thigh . . . ."

SMITE THE ROCK

Exod. 17:6; Num.
20:11

When the children of Israel, journeying in the wilderness of Sin, murmured against Moses because there was no water, Moses cried unto the Lord for help. And the Lord said unto Moses, "Behold, I will stand before thee there upon the rock in Horeb; and thou shalt smite the rock, and there shall come forth water out of it, that the people may drink. And Moses did so in the sight of the elders of Israel." In "One Word More," Browning writes of the critical and ungrateful attitudes of people toward the acts of a prophet, an artist, or a leader.

> Wherefore? Heaven's gift takes earth's abatement!
> He who smites the rock and spreads the water,
> Bidding drink and live a crowd beneath him,
> Even he, the minute makes immortal,
> Proves, perchance, but mortal in the minute . . . .

Matthew Arnold, in "The Progress of Poesy," wrote:

> Youth rambles on life's arid mount,
> And strikes the rock, and finds the vein,
> And brings the water from the fount,
> The fount which shall not flow again.

And in Melville's *Moby Dick,* Ishmael describes sharks attacking a wounded whale. They "rushed to the fresh blood that was spilled, thirstily drinking at every new gash, as the eager Israelites did at the new bursting fountains that poured from the smitten rock."

SODOM AND GOMORRAH

Gen. 18:20;
19:23–25

The Lord, because of their sinfulness, rained brimstone and fire upon these two cities of the plain on the Dead Sea. "And he overthrew those cities, and all the plain, and all the inhabitants of the cities, and all that which grew upon the ground." In "The Burden of Nineveh," Matthew Arnold wrote of the great fallen cities of the past:

> The day [Nineveh's] builders made their halt,
> Those cities of the lake of salt
> Stood firmly 'stablished without fault,
> Made proud with pillars of basalt,
>   With sardonyx and porphyry.

In Melville's *Moby Dick*, Ishmael one dark night stumbled over an ash-box on the porch of a Negro church in New Bedford. "Ha! thought I, ha, as the flying particles almost choked me, are these ashes from that destroyed city, Gomorrah?" The idealistic Melvilles, in D. H. Lawrence's "The Lovely Lady," lived a free and beautiful life in Europe: "America for twelve years had been their anathema, the Sodom and Gomorrah of industrial materialism."

SODOMITE   *see LOT AND THE MEN OF SODOM*

SOLD HIS BIRTHRIGHT FOR A MESS OF POTTAGE

Gen. 25:29–34

ESAU came in from the field one day faint with hunger, and JACOB, his younger brother, was cooking red pottage. Esau asked for some, and Jacob said, "Sell me this day thy birthright." "And he sold his birthright unto Jacob . . . and he did eat and drink, and rose up, and went his way: thus Esau despised his birthright." The expression "mess of pottage" appears only in the chapter heading of some earlier translations of the Bible. In Bunyan's *Pilgrim's Progress*, Christian makes a detailed comparison between Esau and Little-faith, who was robbed of all but his jewels: "Esau's Birth-right was typical, but Little-faith's Jewels were not so: Esau's belly was his god, but Little-faith's belly was not so: Esau's want lay in his fleshly appetite, Little-faith's did not so . . . ." In Byron's *Don Juan*, Don Juan's companion says, when Don Juan suggests knocking their captor over the head, no, we might be worse off later;·"Besides, I'm hungry, and just now would take, / Like Esau, for my birthright a beef-steak." And in "Life without Principle," Thoreau writes of the importance of his freedom and leisure: "If I should sell both my forenoons and afternoons to society, as most appear to do, I am sure that for me there would be nothing left worth living for. I trust that I shall never thus sell my birthright for a mess of pottage."

SOLOMON

I Kings 1–11

Solomon, meaning "peaceable," the son of David and Bathsheba, was King of Israel from c. 960 to 922 B. C. He was famous for his wisdom, his wealth, and his many wives. He built the great Temple and magnificent palaces for himself and his wives. "And he spake three thousand proverbs; and his songs were a thousand and five." It has been believed that he wrote such books as Proverbs, Ecclesiastes, and the Song of Songs. Much about Solomon is related by Queen Proserpina, in Chau-

cer's "The Merchant's Tale." Pluto, her husband, argues that
Solomon found no woman faithful.

What rekketh me of youre auctoritees?
I woot wel that this Jew, this Salomon,
Foond of us wommen fooles many oon . . . .
What make ye so much of Salomon?
What though he made a temple, Goddes hous?
What though he were riche and glorious?
So made he eek a temple of false goddis.
How myghte he do a thyng that moore forbode is?
Pardee, as faire as ye his name emplastre,
He was a lecchour and an ydolastre,
And in his elde he verray God forsook;
And if that God ne hadde, as seith the book,
Yspared him for his fadres sake, he sholde
Have lost his regne rather than he wolde.

SOLOMON IN ALL HIS GLORY   *see LILIES OF THE FIELD*

SOLOMON'S JUDGMENT OF THE CHILD

I Kings 3:16–28

Two harlots came before King Solomon, each claiming the living child was hers. The child of one was dead. Solomon called
for a sword and said, "Divide the living child in two, and give
half to the one, and half to the other." Then spoke the woman
whose child it was, saying, "O my lord, give her the living
child, and in no wise slay it." The other woman said, "Divide
it." Then Solomon gave the child to the first woman, and all
Israel "saw that the wisdom of God was in him, to do judgment."
In *The Newcomes*, Thackeray said that a critic is "a Solomon
that sits in judgment over us authors and chops up our children." In Mark Twain's *Huckleberry Finn*, Jim cannot believe
that Solomon was wise " 'bout dat chile dat he 'uz gwyne to
chop in two . . . . Warn' dat de beatenes' notion in de worl? . . .
Now I want to ast you: . . . what use is a half chile? I wouldn'
give a dern for a million un um."

SOLOMON'S WISDOM

I Kings 3:9, 12;
4:29–34

God said unto Solomon, "Behold, I have done according to
thy words: lo, I have given thee a wise and understanding
heart; so that there was none like thee before thee, neither after
thee shall any arise like unto thee." Solomon had knowledge
of nature: "And he spake of trees, from the cedar tree that is in
Lebanon even unto the hyssop that springeth out of the wall:
he spake also of beasts, and of fowl, and of creeping things,

and of fishes." In Francis Bacon's *The New Atlantis*, Solomon's House was the center of learning "dedicated to the study of the works and creatures of God." It was so named, the Governor said, "for we have some parts of [Solomon's] works which with you are lost; namely that Natural History which he wrote of all plants, from the cedar of Libanus to the moss that groweth out of the wall; and of all things that have life and motion." In *Barchester Towers*, Trollope said that had Dr. Grantly suggested the marriage of Eleanor and Mr. Arabin "when he first brought Mr. Arabin into the country, his character for judgment and wisdom would have received an addition which would have classed him at any rate next to Solomon." In "Literature of Knowledge and Literature of Power," Thomas De Quincey said that the Scriptures stressed the literature of power which appeals to man's higher faculties: "when speaking of man in his intellectual capacity, the Scriptures speak, not of the understanding, but of 'the understanding heart' . . . ." In Mark Twain's *Huckleberry Finn*, Jim doesn't think "Sollermun de wises' man dat ever liv' "—with all those wives: ". . . would a wise man want to live in de mids er sich a blim-blammin' all de time? No—'deed he wouldn't. A wise man 'ud take en buil' a biler-factry; en den he could shet down de biler-factry when he want to res'."

SOLOMON'S WIVES

1 Kings 11:1–8

"But king Solomon loved many strange women, together with the daughter of Pharaoh, women of the Moabites, Ammonites, Edomites, Zidonians, and Hittites . . . . And he had seven hundred wives, princesses, and three hundred concubines: and his wives turned away his heart." Chaucer's good Wife of Bath, in the Prologue to her tale, sees no wrong in having had five husbands and in seeking a sixth:

> Lo, heere the wise kyng, daun Salomon;
> I trowe he hadde wyves mo than oon.
> As wolde God it were leveful unto me
> To be refresshed half so ofte as he!
> Which yifte of God hadde he for alle his wyvys!
> No man hath swich that in this world alyve is.
> God woot, this noble kyng, as to my wit,
> The firste nyght had many a myrie fit
> With ech of hem, so wel was hym on lyve.
> Yblessed be God that I have wedded fyve!
> Welcome the sixte, whan that evere be shal.

In Ben Jonson's *The Alchemist*, Sir Epicure Mammon contem-

plates the luxuries he will enjoy when he gets the philosopher's
stone from the alchemist:

> For I do mean
> To have a list of wives and concubines
> Equal with Solomon, who had the stone
> Alike with me; and I will make me a back
> With the elixer that shall be as tough
> As Hercules, to encounter fifty a night.

In Mark Twain's *Huckleberry Finn*, Huck tells Jim about Solomon's harem, where "he had about a million wives." Jim replies,
"Why, yes, dat's so; I—I'd done forgot it. A harem's a bo'd'n-
house, I reck'n. Mos' likely dey has rackety times in de nussery.
En I reck'n de wives quarrels considable; en dat 'crease de
racket." And in Mark Twain's *Letters from the Earth*, Satan
writes to God about sexual relations on earth. Women, he
argues, should have harems. "Solomon, who was one of the
Deity's favorites, had a copulation cabinet composed of seven
hundred wives and three hundred concubines. To save his life
he could not have kept two of those young creatures satisfac-
torily refreshed, even if he had had fifteen experts to help him.
Necessarily almost the entire thousand had to go hungry years
and years on a stretch. Conceive of a man hardhearted enough
to look daily upon all that suffering and not be moved to miti-
gate it. He even wantonly added a sharp pang to that pathetic
misery; for he kept within those women's sight, always, stal-
wart watchmen whose splendid masculine forms made the poor
lassies' mouths water but who hadn't anything to solace a candlestick with, these gentry being eunuchs. A eunuch is a person
whose candle has been put out. By art."[1]

SONG OF DEBORAH   *see DEBORAH*

SON(S) OF BELIAL   *see BELIAL*

SON OF HAM   *see CANAAN, SON OF HAM*

SONS OF THUNDER   *see BOANERGES*

SOUL CHOOSETH STRANGLING AND DEATH

Job 7:15   In his sufferings Job cries to God that he loathes his life: "So
that my soul chooseth strangling, and death rather than my

[1]"I purpose publishing these Letters here in the world before I return
to you. Two editions. One, unedited for Bible readers and their children; the
other, expurgated, for persons of refinement. [M. T.]"

life. I loathe it; I would not live alway . . . ." In Bunyan's
Pilgrim's Progress, Christian, lying in the dungeon of Doubting
Castle, and beaten by Giant Despair, says to his fellow prisoner
Hopeful, "What shall we do? . . . I know not whether is best,
to live thus, or to die out of hand. *My soul chuseth strangling
rather than life,* and the Grave is more easy for me than this
Dungeon." In Hardy's *Tess of the D'Urbervilles,* when Tess,
after her downfall, met Angel Clare in a melancholy mood,
she thought, "How could this admirable and poetic man ever
. . . have felt with the man of Uz . . . 'My soul chooseth strangling and death rather than my life. I loathe it; I would not live
alway.' "

SOUNDING BRASS, OR A TINKLING CYMBAL

I Cor. 13:1 Paul wrote to the Corinthians about love: "Though I speak
with the tongues of men and of angels, and have not charity, I
am become as sounding brass, or a tinkling cymbal." In Bunyan's *Pilgrim's Progress,* Christian says of Talkative's fine discourse, "Paul calleth some men, yea and those great Talkers
too, *sounding Brass and tinckling Cymbals* . . . ." In *Vanity
Fair,* after Becky Sharp appeared at Lord Steyne's "private
and select parties," Thackeray said, "Ah, ladies!—ask the Reverend Mr. Thurifer if Belgravia is not a sounding brass, and
Tyburnia a tinkling cymbal." Hazlitt, in "On Familiar Style,"
said about the florid style, much admired by the vulgar, "Keep
to your sounding generalities, your tinkling phrases, and all will
be well."

SOUND OF MANY WATERS   *see VOICE (NOISE, SOUND) OF MANY WATERS*

SOW THE WIND, AND REAP THE WHIRLWIND

Hos. 8:7 Hosea reproves Israel for her sins: ". . . the calf of Samaria
shall be broken in pieces. For they have sown the wind, and
they shall reap the whirlwind . . . ." In *The Scarlet Letter,*
Hawthorne says that Hester can see her own "wild, desperate,
defiant mood" in Pearl. The "very colored-shapes of gloom . . .
were now illuminated by the morning radiance of a young
child's disposition, but later in the day of earthly existence
might be prolific of the storm and the whirlwind." In *New England: Indian Summer,* Van Wyck Brooks, speaking of "the Boston authors," said, "Thus the vitality of Boston turned against

Boston. Its culture-philistinism sowed the wind; the creators of
its culture reaped the whirlwind."

SOWN IN CORRUPTION   see *CORRUPTIBLE AND INCORRUPTIBLE; CORRUPTION AND INCORRUPTION*

SPARE THE ROD

Prov. 13:24

"He that spareth his rod hateth his son: but he that loveth
him chasteneth him betimes." The expression "Spare the rod
and spoil the child," which is based on this, is found in Butler's
Hudibras, II, Canto 1, l. 843. In "The Legend of Sleepy Hollow," Washington Irving said that Ichabod Crane "ever bore
in mind the golden maxim, 'Spare the rod and spoil the child.'
—Ichabod Crane's scholars certainly were not spoiled." Aunt
Polly, in Mark Twain's *Tom Sawyer*, said, after one of Tom's
escapades, "I ain't doing my duty by that boy, and that's the
Lord's truth, goodness. Spare the rod and spile the child, as
the Good Book says." Lawrence, in *Studies in Classic American Literature*, said that when the captain, in Dana's *Two
Years before the Mast*, flogged Sam, it was good for both of
them, because they were "in a very unsteady equilibrium of
command and obedience . . . . Spare the rod and spoil the
physical child. Use the rod and spoil the *ideal* child."

SPARROW'S FALL

Matt. 10:29

When Jesus chose the apostles, he said to them, "Are not two
sparrows sold for a farthing? and one of them shall not fall
on the ground without your Father . . . . Fear ye not therefore, ye are of more value than many sparrows." In Shakespeare's *Hamlet*, when Horatio suggests postponing the duel
with Laertes because of evil omens, Hamlet replies: "Not a
whit, we defy augury: there's a special providence in the fall
of a sparrow . . . ." In Mark Twain's *The Mysterious Stranger*,
when poverty-stricken old Ursula tells Satan that God will
help her care for the stray kitten she wants to keep, and
Satan asks, "What makes you think so?" Ursula says angrily,
"Because I know it. Not a sparrow falls to the ground without
His seeing it." Emily Dickinson sent this poem to her cousins
Louise and Frances when their mother died:

> Mama never forgets her birds,
> Though in another tree,
> She looks down just as often

> And just as tenderly
> As when her little mortal nest
> With cunning care she wove—
> If either of her "sparrows fall,"
> She "notices" above.°

SPEARS INTO PRUNINGHOOKS   *see SWORDS INTO PLOWSHARES*

SPECKLED AND SPOTTED   *see JACOB AND LABAN*

SPIRIT GIVETH LIFE   *see LETTER KILLETH*

SPIRIT IS WILLING   *see FLESH IS WEAK*

STIFFNECKED PEOPLE   *see GOLDEN CALF*

STILL SMALL VOICE

I Kings 19:11–12   Elijah fled for his life and hid in a cave on Mount Horeb. There the word of the Lord came to him and told him to "stand upon the mount before the Lord. And, behold, the Lord passed by, and a great and strong wind rent the mountains, and brake in pieces the rocks before the Lord; but the Lord was not in the wind: and after the wind an earthquake; but the Lord was not in the earthquake: And after the earthquake a fire; but the Lord was not in the fire: and after the fire a still small voice." In "Lines Composed a Few Miles above Tintern Abbey," Wordsworth tells of his growth into manhood:

> For I have learned
> To look on nature, not as in the hour
> Of thoughtless youth; but hearing oftentimes
> The still, sad music of humanity.

In "The Brewing of Soma," Whittier tells of ancient man using drink, dance, and drugs to stimulate religious feelings. Let us, he says, avoid this "strain and stress": "Let us be dumb, let flesh retire; / Speak through the earthquake, wind, and fire, / A still, small voice of calm." And in "First-Day Thoughts," Whittier pictures the Quaker silent meeting: "There, syllabled by silence, let me hear / The still small voice which reached the prophet's ear;"

°Reprinted by the permission of the publishers and the Trustees of Amherst College. Thomas H. Johnson, Editor *The Poems of Emily Dickinson* (Cambridge, Mass., The Belknap Press of Harvard University Press), Copyright 1951, 1955, by The President and Fellows of Harvard College.

STRAIGHT AND NARROW PATH   *see STRAIT IS THE GATE, NARROW IS THE WAY*

STRAIN AT A GNAT, AND SWALLOW A CAMEL

Matt. 23:24

Jesus attacked the PHARISEES for their excessive formalism, calling them hypocrites and "blind guides, which strain at a gnat, and swallow a camel." It should be "strain out" a gnat, as from drinking water. "Strain at" is probably an error in the King James translation. In *Eikonoklastes,* Milton satirized King Charles's repentance for executing the Earl of Strafford. "To the Scribes and Pharisees wo was denounced by our Saviour, for straining at a gnat and swallowing a camel, though a gnat were to be strained at: but to a conscience with whom one good deed is so hard to pass down as to endanger almost a choking, and bad deeds without number . . . go down currently without straining, certainly a far greater wo appertains." In his Preface to "Adonais," Shelley attacked the critics who he thought had killed Keats: "Are these the men who in their venal good nature presumed to draw a parallel between the Rev. Mr. Milman and Lord Byron? What gnat did they strain at here, after having swallowed all those camels?"

STRAIT IS THE GATE, NARROW IS THE WAY

Matt. 7:13–14; Luke 13:24

In the Sermon on the Mount, Jesus taught, "Enter ye in at the strait gate: for wide is the gate, and broad in the way, that leadeth to destruction, and many there be which go in thereat: Because strait is the gate, and narrow is the way, which leadeth unto life, and few there be that find it." In Shakespeare's *All's Well That Ends Well,* Lavache the clown jests about serving "the darkness." "I am for the house with the narrow gate, which I take to be too little for pomp to enter. Some that humble themselves may; but the many will be . . . for the flowery way that leads to the broad gate and the great fire." In *Macbeth,* the drunken porter plays porter at the gate of hell: "I'll devil-porter it no further: I had thought to have let in some of all professions that go the primrose way to the everlasting bonfire." In Butler's *The Way of all Flesh,* the Rev. Gideon Hawke preaches to the Simeonites at Cambridge: "My dear young friends, strait is the gate, and narrow is the way which leadeth to Eternal Life, and few there be that find it. Few, few, few, for he who will not give up ALL for Christ's sake, has given up nothing." In *The Ordeal of Mark Twain,* Van Wyck Brooks said that it is very humiliating to

see "great American writers behind the scenes, given 'rats'
by their wives whenever they stray for an instant from the
strait and narrow path that leads to success."

STRANGER, AND YE TOOK ME IN

Matt. 25:35

When judgment comes, said Jesus, "Then shall the King say
unto them on his right hand, Come, ye blessed of my Father,
inherit the kingdom prepared for you from the foundation of
the world: For I was an hungred, and ye gave me meat:
I was thirsty, and ye gave me drink: I was a stranger, and
ye took me in: Naked, and ye clothed me . . . ." In *Sesame
and Lilies*, Ruskin says that the ancient art of building has
decayed: "The ant and the moth have cells for each of their
young, but our little ones lie in festering heaps . . . and night
by night, from the corners of our streets, rises up the cry of
the homeless—'I was a stranger, and ye took me not in.'" In
the same book, Ruskin says that nature clothes her children
better than man does his: ". . . every winter's wind bears up
to heaven its wasted souls, to witness against your hereafter,
by the voice of their Christ,—'I was naked, and ye clothed
me not.'" In Byron's *Don Juan*, the beautiful Haidee rescued
Don Juan, starved and naked, from the sea. She found

> Don Juan, almost famished, and half drown'd;
> But being naked, she was shock'd, you know,
>   Yet deem'd herself in common pity bound,
>   As far as in her lay 'to take him in,
>   A stranger,' dying, with so white a skin.

STREETS OF GOLD

Rev. 21:21

St. John the Divine's vision of the NEW JERUSALEM: "And the
twelve gates were twelve pearls; every several gate was of
one pearl: and the street of the city was pure gold, as it were
transparent glass." In Bunyan's *Pilgrim's Progress,* as Christian
drew near "the heavenly City," he could see "It was builded
of Pearls and Precious Stones, also the Street thereof was
paved with Gold . . . ." Anne Bradstreet pictures the New
Jerusalem in "The Flesh and the Spirit":

> The gates of pearl both rich and clear;
> And angels are for porters there;
> The streets thereof transparent gold
> Such as no eye did e're behold.

In Hawthorne's *The Scarlet Letter,* Dr. Chillingworth says,
when the Reverend Dimmesdale declares that he would be

content to die rather than resort to medical aid: "Youthful men . . . give up their hold on life so easily! And saintly men, who walk with God on earth, would fain be away, to walk with him on the golden pavements of the New Jerusalem."

STUMBLING BLOCK

Lev. 19:14; Isa. 57:14; Rom. 14:13; I Cor. 1:23

This is a common expression throughout the Bible. Paul, for example, wrote to the Corinthians: "For the Jews require a sign, and the Greeks seek after wisdom: But we preach Christ crucified, unto the Jews a stumbling block, and unto the Greek foolishness." In *The Crown of Wild Olive*, Ruskin said that great architecture grows out of a great national religion. "The Greeks essentially worshipped the God of Wisdom; so that whatever contended against their religion,—to the Jews a stumbling block, was, to the Greeks—Foolishness." Henry Adams, in *The Education of Henry Adams*, said, "The Legal Tender decision, which had been the first stumbling block to Adams at Washington, grew in interest till it threatened to become something more serious than a block; it fell on one's head like a plaster ceiling, and could not be escaped."

SUFFER THE LITTLE CHILDREN

Matt. 19:14; Mark 10:14; Luke 18:16

When the people brought little children to Jesus "that he should put his hands on them, and pray: and the disciples rebuked them," Jesus said, "Suffer little children, and forbid them not, to come unto me: for of such is the kingdom of heaven." In Shakespeare's *Richard II*, Richard, imprisoned in Pomfret Castle, soliloquizes on his loneliness. With his thoughts he will "people this little world":

> The better sort,
> As thoughts of things divine, are intermix'd
> With scruples and do set the word itself
> Against the word:
> As thus, "Come little ones, ..."

In "Jonathan Edwards," Oliver Wendell Holmes said that Edwards called children who are "out of Christ" "young vipers." "Is it possible," Holmes asked, "that Edwards read the text mothers love so well, 'Suffer little *vipers* to come unto me, and forbid them not, for such is the Kingdom of God'?" And in Joyce's *A Portrait of the Artist as a Young Man*, when the students argue about religion, Glynn, a teacher of youngsters, says, "I suffer little children to come unto me." Temple replies, "That phrase you said now . . . is from the

new testament about suffer the children to come to me . . .
if Jesus suffered the children to come why does the church
send them all to hell if they die unbaptized? " Swinburne's
"Of Such Is the Kingdom of Heaven" concludes:

> Earth's creeds may be seventy times seven
> And blood have defiled each creed:
> If such be the kingdom of heaven,
> It must be heaven indeed.

SUFFICIENT UNTO THE DAY

Matt. 6:34

In the Sermon on the Mount, Jesus taught: "Seek ye first the
kingdom of God, and his righteousness; and all these things
shall be added unto you. Take therefore no thought for the
morrow: for the morrow shall take thought for the things of
itself. Sufficient unto the day is the evil thereof." In Trollope's
Barchester Towers, Charlotte Stanhope says to her brother
Bertie, " 'I look forward to the time when the governor must
go. Mother, and Madeline, and I,—we shall be poor enough,
but you will have absolutely nothing.' 'Sufficient for the day
is the evil thereof,' said Bertie." In Galsworthy's *Indian Summer of a Forsyte*, Old Jolyon Forsyte wondered if there was
"any cupboard love" in Irene's affection for him. "No, she
was not that sort . . . . Besides he had not breathed a word
about that codicil, nor should he—sufficient unto the day was
the good thereof."

SUN STAND STILL   *see JOSHUA, SUN AND MOON STAND STILL*

SUSANNA

*"The History of
Susanna" of the
Apocrypha*

Susanna, the beautiful and virtuous wife of Joakim in Babylon,
was spied upon lustfully by two elders while she was in her
garden bath. She refused to submit to them, so they accused
her in court of having lain with a young man. Convicted, she
prayed, and "the Lord raised up the holy spirit of a young
youth, whose name was Daniel." By cross-examination Daniel
exposed the false elders, and they were put to death. Parallel
is the story of Constance in Chaucer's "The Man of Law's
Tale." Accused of murder by a false knight, Constance prays
for help as her husband puts the knight to a test.

> She sette hire down on knees, and thus she sayde,
> "Immortal God, that savedest Susanne
> Fro false blame, and thou, merciful mayde,
> Marie I meene, doghter to Seint Anne . . . .
> If I be giltlees of this felonye,
> My socour be, for ellis shal I dye!"

As the false accuser swore on a Bible that she was guilty,

> An hand hym smoot upon the nekke-boon,
> That doun he fil atones as a stoon,
> And bothe his eyen broste out of his face
> In sighte of every body in that place.

In Shakespeare's *All's Well That Ends Well,* the King is reluctant to try Helena's remedy for his affliction. She says:

> He that of greatest works is finisher
> Oft does them by the weakest minister:
> So holy writ in babes hath judgement shown
> When judges have been babes . . . .

The Genevan Bible said: "For when she was led foorth to death, the Lorde raised up the spirit of a young childe, whose name was Daniel." Wallace Stevens's "Peter Quince at the Clavier" reflects the story of Susanna. Thinking of you

> is like the strain
> Waked in the elders by Susanna:

> Of a green evening, clear and warm,
> She bathed in her still garden, while
> The red-eyed elders, watching felt
> The basses of their beings throb
> In witching chords, and their thin blood
> Pulse pizzicati of Hosanna.°

SWEAT OF THY FACE (BROW)

Gen. 3:19

Because Adam disobeyed God by eating the FORBIDDEN FRUIT, God punished Adam, saying, ". . . cursed is the ground for thy sake. . . . In the sweat of they face shalt thou eat bread, till thou return unto the ground . . . ." "Sweat of thy brow," which is not in the Bible, is the usual form of the expression. In *Sesame and Lilies,* Ruskin writes of the joys of both creation of art and common labor. "No true workmen will ever tell you, that they have found the law of heaven an unkind one—that in the sweat of their face they should eat their bread, till they return to the ground . . . ." In *Walden,* Thoreau said that if man lives simply and wisely it is no "hardship but a pastime . . . to maintain one's self on this earth . . . . It is not necessary that a man should earn his living by the sweat of his brow, unless he sweats easier than I do." And in the Preface to *Saint Joan,* Shaw said, "To a professional

°From *The Collected Poems of Wallace Stevens.* Reprinted by permission of Alfred A. Knopf, Inc.

critic . . . theatre-going is the curse of Adam. The play is the
evil he is paid to endure in the sweat of his brow; and the
sooner it is over, the better."

SWORDS INTO PLOWSHARES

Isa. 2:4; Mic. 4:3;
and Joel 3:10

Both Isaiah and Micah prophesy universal world peace in
these words: "And he shall judge among the nations, and shall
rebuke many people: and they shall beat their plowshares, and
their spears into pruninghooks: nation shall not lift up sword
against nation, neither shall they learn war any more." In
"The Witch of Atlas," Shelley tells of soldiers dreaming they
were blacksmiths: "Round the red anvils you might see them
stand / Like Cyclopses in Vulcan's sooty abysm, / Beating
their swords to ploughshares . . . ." In "The Peace Convention at Brussels," Whittier wrote of a cynic sneering at the
peace meeting:

> And round the green earth, to the church bells' chime,
> The mourning drum-roll of the camp keeps time.
> To dream of peace amidst a world in arms,
> Of swords to plowshares changed by Scriptural charms.

James Russell Lowell, in "A Fable for Critics," spoke of
Whittier and the Quakers who opposed war and worked for
social reform:

> They were harsh, but shall *you* be so shocked at hard words
> Who have beaten your pruning hooks up into swords,
> Whose rewards and hurrahs men are surer to gain
> By the reaping of men and of women than grain?

TABLES (TABLETS) OF THE LAW   *see TEN COMMANDMENTS*

TAKE A LITTLE WINE

I Tim. 5:23

Paul advised Timothy: "Drink no longer water, but use a little
wine for thy stomach's sake and thine often infirmities." Oliver
Wendell Holmes, in "On Lending a Punch-Bowl," traced its
history from its beginning with the Spanish galleon:

> But, changing hands, it reached at length a Puritan divine,
> Who used to follow Timothy, and take a little wine,
> But hated punch and prelacy; and so it was, perhaps,
> He went to Leyden, where he found conventicles and schnapps.

In Hemingway's *Farewell to Arms*, Frederick Henry renews
his friendship with Rinaldi, who says, "We'll drink once more
for your liver's sake." "Like Saint Paul." "You are inaccurate.

That was wine and the stomach. Take a little wine for your stomach's sake." "Whatever you have in the bottle. For any sake you mention."

TAKE, EAT, THIS IS MY BODY   see LAST SUPPER

TAKE IN VAIN   see TAKE THE NAME OF GOD IN VAIN

TAKE NO THOUGHT FOR THE MORROW   see LILIES OF THE FIELD

TAKE THE NAME OF GOD IN VAIN

Exod. 20:7

The Third Commandment is "Thou shalt not take the name of the Lord thy God in vain; for the Lord will not hold him guiltless that taketh his name in vain." In Chaucer's "The Pardoner's Tale," the Pardoner preaches against "fals sweryng":

> Bihold and se that in the firste table
> Of heigh Goddes heestes honurable,
> Hou that the seconde heeste of hym is this:
> "Take nat my name in ydel or amys."

In "Sea Dreams," Tennyson said of a pious but crooked businessman that he was one "Who never [named] God except for gain, / So never took that useful name in vain . . . ." In *Elmer Gantry,* Sinclair Lewis describing Elmer's preaching said that "all his profounder philosophy" could be heard except "his mother's stream of opinions on hanging up his overcoat, wiping his feet . . . and taking the name of the Lord in vain." And Van Wyck Brooks, in *The World of Washington Irving,* said that Irving's *History of New York* was a "masterpiece of learned spoofing that offended some of the old New Yorkers who felt that the names of their ancestors were taken in vain."

TAKE THE WINGS OF MORNING

Ps. 139:9–10

The Psalmist sings joy and praise to the Lord: "If I take the wings of morning, and dwell in the uttermost parts of the sea; Even there shall thy hand lead me, and thy right hand shall hold me." The goddess of the dawn arose in the east and flew, for the Hebrews, over into the Mediterranean Sea. In Carlyle's *Sartor Resartus,* Professor Teufelsdröckh's thoughts rise to ever higher and dizzier heights—for example, about "Nature being not an Aggregate but a Whole: 'Well sang the Hebrew Psalmist: "If I take the wings of the morning and dwell in the uttermost parts of the universe, God is there." ' " Washington Irving, in "The Broken Heart," says that man disappointed in love, in contrast to woman, "can shift his abode at will, and taking as it were the wings of the morning, can 'fly to the uttermost parts of the earth, and be at rest.'" And in Butler's *The Way of All Flesh,* when Ernest was sentenced to prison, he felt that he should sever himself from his parents completely, "and go to some place in the uttermost parts of the earth . . . ."

TAKE UP THY BED AND WALK   *see BETHESDA, POOL OF*

TALE THAT IS TOLD

Ps. 90:9 The Psalmist sings of God as the refuge of man in his troubles: "Thou hast set our iniquities before thee, our secret sins in the light of thy countenance. For all thy days are passed away in thy wrath: we spend our years as a tale that is told." This is a favorite idea of Shakespeare's. At the end of Shakespeare's *Romeo and Juliet,* Friar Laurence begins his account of the tragedy:

> I will be brief, for my short date of breath
> Is not so long as is a tedious tale.
> Romeo, there dead, was husband to that Juliet . . . .

In *King John,* Lewis, Dauphin of France, ordered by the Pope to make war with his father, King Philip, against the English, says:

> There's nothing in this world can make me joy:
> Life is as tedious as a twice-told tale
> Vexing the dull ear of a drowsy man . . . .

And when Macbeth hears that his wife is dead, he says:

> Life's but a walking shadow . . . .
>   It is a tale
> Told by an idiot, full of sound and fury,
> Signifying nothing.

And Washington Irving, in "Westminster Abbey," contemplating the tombs of the great, says, "Thus man passes away; his name perishes from record and recollection; his history is as a tale that is told, and his very monument becomes a ruin."

TALENTS   *see PARABLE OF THE TALENTS*

TARES AND WHEAT   *see PARABLE OF THE TARES AND WHEAT*

TARSHISH   *see JONAH*

TEETH SET ON EDGE   *see FATHERS HAVE EATEN A SOUR GRAPE*

TEKOAH   *see AMOS*

TELL IT NOT IN GATH

II Sam. 1:20

David's lament for the deaths of Saul and Jonathan begins: "The beauty of Israel is slain upon thy high places: how are the mighty fallen! Tell it not in Gath, publish it not in the streets of Askelon; lest the daughters of the Philistines rejoice, lest the daughters of the uncircumcised triumph." Thoreau, in *Cape Cod*, watching a little boy stealing swallows' eggs from nests in the bank near the Highland Light, said, "Tell it not to the Humane Society!" And in Sinclair Lewis' *It Can't Happen Here*, "Doremus announced to his family and told it loudly in Gath that he was still looking for an option on an apple orchard to which they might retire."

TEMPTATION IN THE WILDERNESS   *see JESUS, TEMPTATION*

TEN COMMANDMENTS

Exod. 20:3–17; Deut. 5:7–21

The Ten Commandments, known also as the Decalogue, from the Greek *deka logos*, "the ten words," were given to Moses on Mount SINAI by the Lord, and were inscribed on two tablets, or tables, of stone. Hence they are known also as the Tables of the Law and the Tables of Testimony. All the commandments, except two, begin with "Thou shalt not." The first group of commandments deal with man's duties to God, the second group with man's duties to his fellow man. Milton's *Paradise Lost* begins with an invocation to Urania, the Heavenly Muse who on Mount Sinai inspired Moses, the author of the Pentateuch:

> Sing Heav'nly Muse, that on the secret top
> Of *Oreb*, or of *Sinai*, didst inspire
> That Shepherd, who first taught the chosen Seed,
> In the Beginning how the Heav'ns and the Earth
> Rose out of Chaos . . .

In Shakespeare's *King Lear*, Edgar, feigning madness in the hut with Lear and Kent, says, "Take heed o' the foul fiend. Obey thy parents, keep thy word justly, swear not, commit not with man's sworn spouse, set not thy sweet heart on proud array. Tom's a-cold." In "First-Day Thoughts," Whittier, speaking of the Quaker inner light, said, "Read in my heart a still diviner law / Than Israel's leader on his tables saw!" In "Characteristics," Carlyle, arguing that morality really begins in society, wrote, "The Duties of Man . . . to what is Highest in himself make but the First Table of the Law: to the First Table is now superadded a Second, with the Duties of Man to his Neighbour; whereby also the significance of the First now assumes its importance." John Stuart Mill, in "On Liberty," argued that Christian morality is negative and passive, rather than positive: "in its precepts . . . 'thou shalt not' predominates unduly over 'thou shalt.'" And D. H. Lawrence, in *Studies in Classic American Literature*, said that American liberty is "a liberty of THOU SHALT NOT . . . . The land of THOU SHALT NOT. Only the first commandment is: THOU SHALT NOT PRESUME TO BE A MASTER. Hence democracy."

TENDER MERCIES

Prov. 12:10   "A righteous man regardeth the life of his beast: but the tender mercies of the wicked are cruel." In his *Journal*, John Woolman tells of killing a bird with a stone, and then killing all its young to spare their suffering. He believed he had fulfilled the proverb about "the tender mercies." "Thus He whose tender mercies are on all his works, hath placed a principle in the human mind, which incites to exercise goodness towards every living creature . . . ." In Galsworthy's "The Juryman," Mr. Bosengate heard the other jurymen agree that the deserter had tried to commit suicide, but he abstained. "Guilty! Well—yes! There was no way out of admitting that, but his feelings revolted against handing 'that poor little beggar' over to the tender mercy of his country's law."

TEN THOUSANDS   *see THOUSANDS AND TENS OF THOUSANDS*

TENTH PLAGUE   *see FIRSTBORN OF EGYPT*

TENTS OF SHEM   *see SHEM*

TENTS OF WICKEDNESS   *see DOORKEEPER IN THE HOUSE OF MY GOD*

THERE IS A TIME AND A PLACE   *see TIME FOR ALL THINGS*

THERE IS NO END   *see OF MAKING MANY BOOKS*

THERE'S NOTHING NEW UNDER THE SUN   *see NO NEW THING UNDER THE SUN*

THERE WAS NO MORE SPIRIT IN HER   *see SHEBA (SABA)*
              QUEEN OF

THEY KNOW NOT WHAT THEY DO   *see FATHER, FORGIVE THEM*

THEY TOIL NOT   *see LILIES OF THE FIELD*

THIEF IN THE NIGHT

I Thess. 5:2   Paul wrote to the Thessalonians that they knew not when the Lord would come. "But of the times and the seasons, brethren, ye have no need that I write to you. For yourselves know perfectly that the day of the Lord so cometh as a thief in the night." In "Peter Bell the Third," Shelley said that the devil is "A thief, who cometh in the night, / With whole boots and net pantaloons / . . . ." In the concluding paragraph of "The Masque of Red Death," Poe wrote: "And now was acknowledged the presence of the Red Death. He had come like a thief in the night." And in Butler's *The Way of All Flesh*, Mr. Hawke, preaching to the boys at Cambridge, urged them to turn quickly: "For the Son of Man cometh as a thief in the night, and there is not one of us can tell but what this day his soul may be required of him."

THIEVES BREAK THROUGH AND STEAL   *see LAY NOT UP*
              TREASURES UPON EARTH

THIN EARS AND FULL EARS   *see JOSEPH, JACOB'S SON*

THINGS SEEN ARE TEMPORAL

II Cor. 4:18   Paul wrote: ". . . we look not at the things which are seen, but at the things which are not seen: for the things which are seen are temporal; but the things which are not seen are eternal." In Bunyan's *Pilgrim's Progress*, the Interpreter explains to Christian that "things that are last are lasting." Christian says, "Then I perceive 't is not best to covet things that are now, but to wait for things to come." And the Interpreter replies, "You say the truth: For the things that are not seen are Eternal." In the chapter "Idealism" in *Nature*, Emerson says that both religion and ethics "put nature under foot. The first and last lesson of religion is, The things that are seen, are temporal; the things that are unseen, are eternal."

THIRD AND FOURTH GENERATION   *see SINS OF THE FATHERS*

THIRTY PIECES OF SILVER

Matt. 26:15;
27:3–5

Judas "went unto the chief priests, And said unto them, What will ye give me, and I will deliver him unto you? And they covenanted with him for thirty pieces of silver." After Judas betrayed Jesus, he repented and "cast down the pieces of silver in the temple, and departed, and went and hanged himself." Robert Browning probably referred to this story in "The Lost Leader," attacking Wordsworth for his supposed desertion of the liberal cause. It begins: "Just for a handful of silver he left us . . . ." In *The Crown of Wild Olive*, Ruskin suggested a sculpture for the British exchange: "a statue of Britannia of the Market . . . her corslet, of leather, folded over her heart in the shape of a purse, with thirty slits in it, for a piece of money to go in it, on each day of the month." Judas was the expert, among the disciples, in financial management. In "The Present Crisis," about the annexation of Texas and the slavery issue, James Russell Lowell wrote: "For humanity sweeps onward: where to-day the martyr stands, / On the morrow crouches Judas with the silver in his hands."

THORN IN THE FLESH

II Cor. 12:7

Paul wrote that he would not glory in himself. "And lest I should be exalted above measure through the abundance of the revelations, there was given to me a thorn in the flesh, the messenger of Satan to buffet me, lest I should be exalted above measure." Various suggestions as to the nature of Paul's affliction have been made: epilepsy, blindness, stammering, and malaria. Jung believed that his blindness was psychogenetic. In *Don Juan*, Byron said that Juan was a bachelor, a matter "of import both to virgin and to bride / . . . A rib's a thorn in a wed gallant's side, / Requires decorum, and is apt to double / The horrid sin—and what's still worse, the trouble." In *Studies in Classic American Literature*, D. H. Lawrence said of Franklin's *Poor Richard's Almanac*, "And probably I haven't got over those Poor Richard tags yet. I rankle still with them. They are thorns in young flesh."

THORNS, FELL AMONG

Matt. 13:7

In the parable of the sower, Jesus told of a sower who sowed seeds, some of which "fell among thorns; and the thorns sprung up, and choked them." In Shakespeare's *King John*, after Arthur has leaped from the castle wall, Philip the Bastard says, "Go, bear him in thine arms. / I am amazed, methinks, and lose my way / Among the thorns and dangers of this world." Washington Irving, in *The Sketch Book*, "Roscoe," said that nature "scatters the seeds of genius to the winds, and though . . . some be choked by the thorns and brambles of early adversity, yet others will now and then strike root even in the clefts of the rocks." And in Hardy's *The Mayor of Casterbridge*, Farfrae admires the new corn drill: "No more sowers flinging their seed about broadcast, so that some falls by the wayside and some among thorns . . . ."

THOU SHALT NOT STEAL

Exod. 20:15

The eighth of the TEN COMMANDMENTS. In Shakespeare's *Measure for Measure*, Lucio jests with his companions: "Thou conclud'st like the sanctimonious pirate, that went to sea with the Ten Commandments, but scrap'd one out of the table." The Second Gentleman replies, " 'Thou shalt not steal' ?" Lucio: "Ay, that he raz'd." First Gentleman: "Why, 't was a commandment to command the captain and all the rest from their functions; they put forth to steal." Arthur Hugh Clough, in "The Latest Decalogue," writes, "Thou shalt not steal, an empty feat, / When it's so lucrative to cheat." Mark Twain's fox, in the essay "In the Animal's Court," broke the law, "Thou shalt not steal"; he pleaded that he had obeyed the divine law, "The Fox shall steal," but he was imprisoned for life. Byron's "poetical commandments," in Don Juan, included:

> Thou shalt not steal from Samuel Rogers, nor
> Commit—flirtation with the muse of Moore.

THOU ART THE MAN   *see DAVID AND NATHAN*

THOUGH HE SLAY ME, YET WILL I TRUST IN HIM

Job 13:15

Job, defying his friends' accusations, desires "to reason with God." "Though he slay me, yet will I trust in him: but I will maintain mine own ways before him." (This is an example of a passage that is lost in modern translations.) In *Past and Present*, Carlyle said that modern men are the victims of the atheistic "Quack" (the opposite of the "Hero"). Let the Quack "come swiftly, that I may at least have done with him; for in his Quack-world I can have no wish to linger. Though he slay me, yet will I not trust in him." In the Preface to *Saint Joan*, Shaw, questioning the certainty of a priest's knowledge of God's intentions, said, "And Joan's answer is also the answer of old: 'Though He slay me, yet will I trust in Him; *but I will maintain my own ways before Him.*' "

THOUSANDS AND TENS OF THOUSANDS

I Sam. 18:5–8

When David returned with the head of Goliath, the "women came out of all cities of Israel, singing and dancing, to meet king Saul . . . . And the women answered one another as they played, and said, Saul hath slain his thousands, and David his ten thousands. And Saul was very wroth . . . ." Thomas Paine, in *The American Crisis,* called for a stand against the British despite Tory desertions: "Say not that thousands are gone, turn out your tens of thousands." Archibald Henderson, in *Bernard Shaw,* addresses Shaw: "A master of invective, with the dour ferocity of a Carlyle and the esthetic perceptiveness of a Ruskin, you have slain your thousands and your tens of thousands."

THOU SHALT, THOU SHALT NOT   *see TEN COMMANDMENTS*

THREESCORE YEARS AND TEN

Ps. 90:10

The Psalmist speaks of the fleetingness of time: "we spend our years as a tale that is told. The days of our years are threescore years and ten; and if by reason of strength they be fourscore years, yet is their strength labour and sorrow; for it is soon cut off, and we fly away." In "The Custom House" introduction to *The Scarlet Letter,* Hawthorne tells about the gallant old general who "had already numbered, nearly or quite, his threescore years and ten, and was pursuing the remainder of his earthly march, burdened with infirmities . . . ." Ruskin, in *Unto This Last,* said that we pursue death "frantically all our days, he flying or hiding from us. Our crowning success at threescore and ten is utterly and perfectly to seize, and hold him in his eternal integrity—robes, ashes, and sting." And Housman's beautiful lines from "Loveliest of Trees":

> Now, of my threescore years and ten,
> Twenty will not come again,
> And take from seventy springs a score,
> It only leaves me fifty more.°

° From "A Shropshire Lad"—Authorized Edition—from *The Collected Poems of A. E. Housman.* Copyright 1940 by Holt, Rinehart and Winston, Inc. Reprinted by permission of Holt, Rinehart and Winston, Inc., The Society of Authors, and Jonathan Cape, Ltd.

THROUGH A GLASS DARKLY

I Cor. 13:12

Paul wrote to the Corinthians, "For now we see through a glass, darkly; but then face to face: now I know in part; but then shall I know even as also I am known." The modern sense would be: "see in a mirror imperfectly." In *Areopagitica*, Milton argued against the censoring of books. We are thankful, he said, for the "great measure of truth" which exists "between us and the Pope . . . but he who thinks . . . we have attained the utmost prospect of reformation, that the mortal glass wherein we contemplate can show us . . . is yet far short of the Truth." William Hazlitt, in "On the Feeling of Immortality in Youth," said, "It is only as present objects begin to pall upon sense . . . that we by degrees become weaned from the world, and allow ourselves to contemplate 'as in a glass darkly,' the possibility of parting with it for good." Poe, in "Dream-Land," said that travelers through dreamland "dare not openly view it"; "thus the sad Soul that here passes / Beholds it but through darkened glasses."

THROW THE FIRST STONE   *see WOMAN TAKEN IN ADULTERY*

THY WILL BE DONE

Matt. 6:10

The Lord's Prayer begins: "Our father which art in heaven, Hallowed be thy name. Thy kingdom come. Thy will be done in earth, as it is in heaven." Pope's "The Universal Prayer" contains these lines:

> This day be bread and peace my lot:
> All else beneath the sun
> Thou know'st if best bestowed or not,
> And let thy will be done.

Emily Dickinson, in "I Have a King Who Does Not Speak," says that when she has unpleasant dreams,

> the little Bird
> Within the Orchard is not heard,
> And I omit to pray,
> "Father, thy will be done" to-day
> For my will goes the other way,
> And it were perjury!°

°From *Poems of Emily Dickinson* by Emily Dickinson (Boston, Little, Brown and Co.).

TIDINGS OF GREAT JOY   *see GOOD TIDINGS OF GREAT JOY*

TIME FOR ALL THINGS

Eccles. 3:1–8   The poem on time and seasons begins: "To every thing there is a season, and a time to every purpose under the heaven: A time to be born, and a time to die; a time to plant, and a time to pluck up that which is planted." Chaucer referred to this passage several times. For example, in the Prologue to "The Clerk's Tale," the Host calls for a story from "Sire Clerk of Oxenford," who has been quiet as "a mayde newe spoused."

> I trowe ye studie about som sophyme;
> But Salomon seith "every thyng hath tyme."
> For Goddes sake, as beth of bettre cheere!
> It is no tyme for to studien heere.

In Shakespeare's *Comedy of Errors,* Antipholus and Dromio of Syracuse jest about time. It is dinner time, and Dromio tells his master not to eat meat lest it makes him "choleric and purchase me another dry basting." Antonio says, "Well, sir, learn to jest in good time. There's a time for all things." In Hardy's *Tess of the D'Urbervilles,* when Angel Clare carried Tess and her dairymaid friends across the flooded road, Izz said, "There is a time for everything, a time to embrace, and a time to refrain from embracing; the first is now going to be mine." "Fie—it is Scripture, Izz!" said Tess. "Yes," said Izz, "I've always a 'ear at church for pretty verses."

TINKLING CYMBAL   *see SOUNDING BRASS, OR A TINKLING*
                    CYMBAL

TISHBITE   *see ELIJAH, THE TISHBITE*

TITHE   The tithe, meaning "tenth," is the tenth part of one's income devoted to political or religious uses. In his *Autobiography,* Franklin said that whereas his elder brothers were apprenticed to different trades, "I was put to the grammar school at eight years of age, my father intending to devote me as the tithe of his sons to the service of the church." And Lamb, in "The Two Races of Men," said that his old friend Ralph Bigod, Esq., was a great borrower. In his triumphant tour of "this island, it has been calculated that he laid a tythe part of the inhabitants under contribution."

Gen. 14:20; Lev. 27:30, 32; Deut. 26:2–4, 10, 12

TITHE OF MINT, ANISE, AND CUMMIN

Matt. 23:23

Jesus attacked the PHARISEES, saying, ". . . hypocrites! for ye pay tithe of mint and anise and cummin, and have omitted the weightier matters of the law, judgment, mercy, and faith: these ought ye to have done, and not to leave the other undone." In *Characteristics*, Carlyle said that when virtue becomes self-conscious it begins to decline: ". . . humane Courtesy and Nobleness of mind dwindle into punctilious Politeness . . . 'paying tithe of mint and anise, neglecting the weightier matters of the law.' " In "The Pennsylvania Pilgrim," Whittier told of an early Quaker meeting that rejected Daniel Pastorious' plea against slaveholding:

> So it all passed; and the old tithe went on
> Of anise, mint, and cummin, till the sun
> Set, leaving still the weightier work undone.

In *The Atlantic Monthly* (April, 1953), Van Wyck Brooks accused the new critics of neglecting "the psychological problem of the writer's life." "This is one of the weightier matters that critics have ignored in their recent preoccupation with the mint and cummin, the grammatical and rhetorical minutiae of literary texts . . . ."

TITTLE

Matt. 5:18; Luke 16:17

In the Sermon on the Mount, Jesus said that he came not to destroy, but to fulfill, the law and the prophets. "For verily I say unto you, Till heaven and earth pass, one jot or one tittle shall in no wise pass from the law, till all be fulfilled." The jot, the smallest letter in the Hebrew alphabet, was the *yodh* or "y," the Greek *iota* or "i." The tittle was a small mark or stroke that distinguished one letter from another. In Bunyan's *Pilgrim's Progress*, Faithful gave Hope "a Book of Jesus . . . and he said concerning that Book, that every jot and tittle thereof stood firmer than Heaven and Earth." In *Of Prelatical Episcopacy*, Milton argued that, according to the Gospel, there were only two ecclesiastical orders. Let him be accursed who claims three, "for Christ has pronounced that no tittle of his word shall fall to the ground: and if one jot be alterable, it is as possible that all should perish . . . ."

TO EVERY THING THERE IS A SEASON   *see TIME FOR ALL THINGS*

TO HIM THAT HATH   *see WHOSOEVER HATH, TO HIM SHALL BE GIVEN*

TOIL NOT, NEITHER DO THEY SPIN   *see LILIES OF THE FIELD*

TONGUES OF FIRE (FLAME)   *see PENTECOST*

TOOTH FOR A TOOTH   *see EYE FOR AN EYE*

TOPHET(H)

II Kings 23:10;
Isa. 30:33; Jer.
7:31–32;
19:1–15; 32:35

King Josiah "defiled Topheth [tō′fĕth], which is in the valley of the children of Hinnom, that no man might make his son or daughter to pass through the fire to Molech" [mō′lĕch]. Tophet, or Topheth, was a "high place" in the Valley of Hinnom near Jerusalem, where parents sacrificed their children in the fires of the god Molech, or Moloch. Josiah abolished the practice, and Jeremiah and Ezekiel denounced it. *Gehenna* (Greek), meaning "hell," derives from the Hebrew *Hinnom.* In Milton's *Paradise Lost,* Moloch was one of the fallen angels on the plain of hell.

> First Moloch, horrid King besmear'd with blood
> Of human sacrifice, and parents tears,
> Though for the noyse of Drums and Timbrels loud
> Their childrens cries unheard, that past through fire
> To his grim idol.

Solomon built him a temple, said Milton,

> and made his Grove
> The pleasant Vally of Hinnom, Tophet thence
> And black Gehenna call'd, the Type of Hell.

In Hardy's *Tess of the D'Urbervilles,* Tess watched the engineer firing a threshing machine on the farm, Flintcomb-Ash: "The isolation of his manner and colour lent him the appearance of a creature from Tophet. . . . He served fire and smoke." Ben Jonson, in Edwin Arlington Robinson's "Ben Jonson Entertains a Man from Stratford," met Shakespeare one afternoon down Lambeth way, "and on my life I was afear'd of him: / He gloomed and mumbled like a soul from Tophet . . . ."*

TO THE PURE ALL THINGS ARE PURE   *see UNTO THE PURE ALL THINGS ARE PURE*

TOUCH ME NOT   *see NOLI ME TANGERE*

*Reprinted with permission of The Macmillan Company from *Collected Poems* by E. A. Robinson. Copyright 1916 by E. A. Robinson. Renewed 1944 by Ruth Nivison.

TOUCH PITCH AND BE DEFILED

Ecclus. 13:1

Jesus, the son of Sirach, wrote: "He that toucheth pitch, shall be defiled therewith, and he that hath fellowship with a proud man, shall be like unto him." This passage was a favorite with Shakespeare. For example, in *Othello*, Iago resolves to turn Desdemona's kindness to Cassio against her:

> So will I turn her virtue into pitch,
> And out of her own goodness make the net
> That shall enmesh them all.

In *Henry IV, Part I*, Falstaff, playing the part of Prince Hal's father, chides him for his low companions: "There is a thing, Harry, which thou hast often heard of and it is known to many in our land by the name of pitch: this pitch, as ancient writers do report, doth defile; so doth the company thou keepest . . . ." In Stevenson's *Treasure Island*, Cap'n Flint, Long John Silver's parrot, swore "blue fire." " 'There,' John would add, 'you can't touch pitch and not be mucked, lad.' "

TOUCH THE HEM OF HIS GARMENT   *see HEM OF HIS GARMENT*

TOWER IN SILOAM

Luke 13:4

When certain people told Jesus that Pilate had caused the Galileans great suffering, Jesus said they did not suffer because they were sinners. "Or those eighteen, upon whom the tower in Siloam [sĭ·lō'ăm] fell, and slew them, think ye that they were sinners above all men that dwelt in Jerusalem? I tell you, Nay: but, except ye repent, ye shall all likewise perish." In Butler's *The Way of All Flesh*, when Ernest was sentenced to prison, his friend speculates about Theobald and Christina's responsibility. "Why then should it have been upon them, of all people in the world, that this tower of Siloam had fallen? Surely it was the tower of Siloam that was naught rather than those who stood under it; it was the system rather than the people that was at fault." Thomas H. Huxley, in "The Struggle for Existence in Human Society," said that the governing principle of nature, in human terms, "is intellectual and not moral . . . . That the rain falls upon the just and the unjust [Matt. 5:45] and that those upon whom the Tower of Siloam fell were no worse than their neighbours, seem to be Oriental modes of expressing the same conclusion."

TOWER OF IVORY

Song of Sol. 7:4   From a passage in praise of the woman's beauty: "Thy neck is as a tower of ivory . . . ." (This is not "ivory tower" in the sense of seclusion or retreat.) Swinburne's poem "Dolores," is written to "Our Lady of Pain":

> O garment not golden but gilded,
>   O garden where all men may dwell,
>   O tower not of ivory, but builded
>   By hands that reach heaven from hell.

In Oscar Wilde's *Salome,* Salome addresses John the Baptist in the dungeon: "Thy hair is horrible. It is covered with mire and dust . . . . I love not thy hair . . . . It is thy mouth that I desire, Jokanaan. Thy mouth is like a band of scarlet on a tower of ivory. It is like a pomegranate cut with a knife of ivory." In Joyce's *A Portrait of the Artist as a Young Man,* at the Christmas dinner table Dante tells young Stephen not to play with Protestants. They made "fun of the litany of the Blessed Virgin. *Tower of Ivory,* they used to say, *House of Gold!* How could a woman be a tower of ivory, or a house of gold?" Then Stephen remembered Protestant Eileen; she "had long white hands. One evening when playing tig she had put her hands over his eyes: long and white and thin and cold and soft. That was ivory: a cold white thing. That was the meaning of *Tower of Ivory.*"

TREASURES UPON EARTH   *see LAY NOT UP TREASURES UPON EARTH*

TREE IS KNOWN BY HIS FRUIT

Matt. 12:33;   Jesus taught: "Either make the tree good, and his fruit good; or
Luke 6:44   else make the tree corrupt, and his fruit corrupt: for the tree is known by his fruit." In Shakespeare's *Richard III*, when the citizens of London offer him the crown, he hypocritically says:

> God be thanked, there's no need of me,
> And much I need to help you, if need were;
> The royal tree hath left us royal fruit,
> Which, mellow'd by the stealing hours of time,
> Will well become the seat of majesty . . . .

In *Henry IV, Part I,* Falstaff, playing the part of Prince Hal's father, advises Hal to avoid all evil companions—except Falstaff. "If that man should be lewdly given, he deceiveth me, for, Harry, I see virtue in his looks. If then the tree may be known by the fruit, as the fruit by the tree, then, peremptorily I speak

it, there is virtue in that Falstaff. Him keep with, the rest ban-
ish." In *Lady Chatterley's Lover*, Lawrence wrote, "No, there's
something wrong with the mental life, radically. It's rooted in
spite and envy, envy and spite. Ye shall know the tree by its
fruits."

TREE OF KNOWLEDGE

Gen. 2:9, 17;
3:2–6

The Lord God commanded Adam, saying, "Of every tree of
the garden thou mayest freely eat: but of the tree of the knowledge of good and evil, thou shalt not eat of it: for in the day that
thou eatest thereof thou shalt surely die." Tempted by the serpent, "when the woman saw that the tree was good for food,
and that it was pleasant to the eyes, and a tree to be desired to
make one wise, she took of the fruit thereof, and did eat, and
gave also unto her husband with her; and he did eat." In Milton's
Paradise Lost, Adam tells the angel Raphael of God's prohibi-
tion. God said to Adam,

> Of every Tree that in the Garden growes
> Eate freely with glad heart; fear here no dearth:
> But of the Tree whose operation brings
> Knowledge of good and ill, which I have set
> The Pledge of thy Obedience and thy Faith,
> Amid the Garden by the Tree of Life,
> Remember what I warne thee, shun to taste,
> And shun the bitter consequence: for know,
> The day thou eat'st thereof, my sole command
> Transgrest, inevitably thou shalt dye . . . .

In *Sartor Resartus*, Carlyle writes, "In every well-conditioned
stripling . . . there already blooms a certain prospective Paradise, cheered by some fairest Eve: nor, in the stately vistas, and
flowerage and foliage of that Garden, is a Tree of Knowledge,
beautiful and awful in the midst thereof, wanting." In Christopher Fry's *The Lady's Not for Burning*, Thomas says to Humphrey, who has been propositioning Jennet, "And as for you /
I'll knock your apple-blossom back into the roots / Of the Tree
of Knowledge where you got it from!"*

TREE OF LIFE *see EDEN, GARDEN OF*

TRIBUTE MONEY *see RENDER UNTO CAESAR*

---

*From *The Lady's Not for Burning* by Christopher Fry. Reprinted by
permission of Oxford University Press.

TRIED AND FOUND WANTING   *see WEIGHED IN THE BALANCES AND FOUND WANTING*

TRUMPET OF LAST JUDGMENT

I Cor. 15:52

Paul wrote that at the Resurrection "In a moment, in the twinkling of an eye, at the last trump; for the trumpet shall sound, the dead shall be raised incorruptible, and we shall be changed." In Shakespeare's *Romeo and Juliet,* when the Nurse tells Juliet that both Romeo and Tybalt are dead, she cries:

> Is Romeo slaughtered, and is Tybalt dead?
> My dear-loved cousin, and my dearer lord?
> Then, dreadful trumpet, sound the general doom!
> For who is living if these two are gone?

In "Self-Reliance," Emerson wrote, "Speak your latent conviction, and it shall be the universal sense . . . our first thought is rendered back to us by the trumpets of the Last Judgment." As Abraham Davenport, in Whittier's "Abraham Davenport," continued reading "an act to amend an act to regulate the shad and alewive fisheries," the sky darkened with a great cloud of smoke; ". . . all ears grew sharp / To hear the doom-blast of the trumpet shatter / The black sky, that the dreadful face of Christ / Might look from the rent clouds . . . ."

TRUTH SHALL MAKE YOU FREE

John 8:32

Jesus said "to those Jews which believed on him, If ye continue in my word, then are ye my disciples indeed; And ye shall know the truth, and the truth shall make you free." Chaucer's "Truth," advising contentment and self-control, has this expression for its refrain:

> Savour no more than thee bihove shal;
> Reule wel thyself, that other folk canst rede;
> And trouthe thee shal delivere, it is no drede.

In Sonnet XII, Milton replied to the hostile reactions to his liberal ideas on divorce expressed in the *Tetrachordon.* These barbarous cries are like "Hoggs"

> That bawl for freedom in their senceless mood,
> And still revolt when truth would set them free.

TUBAL-CAIN
(tū′băl-kān)

Gen. 4:22

Tubal-cain, one of three sons of LAMECH and Zillah, was "an instructor of every artificer in brass and iron," in legend a traveling metalworker. Jabal [jā′băl] was the father of such as dwell in tents, and of such as have cattle," and JUBAL was "the father of all such as handle the harp and organ." In *The History of the World*, Sir Walter Raleigh, with questionable accuracy, said, "Jubal, Tubal, and Tubal Cain [were] inventors of pastorage, smiths'-craft, and music, the same which were called by the ancient profane writers, Mercurius, Vulcan, and Apollo." In Sir Thomas Overbury's *Characters*, "A Tinker is a movable: for he hath no abiding place . . . . His house is as ancient as Tubalcain's, and so is a runagate by antiquity."

TURN THE OTHER CHEEK

Matt. 5:39; Luke 6:29

In the Sermon on the Mount, Jesus said, "Ye have heard that it hath been said, An eye for an eye, and a tooth for a tooth: But I say unto you, That ye resist not evil: but whosoever shall smite thee on thy right cheek, turn to him the other also." In *Walden*, Thoreau said, "When the frost had smitten me on one cheek, heathen as I was, I turned to it the other also." In Galsworthy's *Flowering Wilderness*, Dinny's uncle says that when Wilfred's poems are published, trouble will begin about Wilfred and Dinny's marriage: "There beginneth a real dog-fight. 'Turn the other cheek' and 'too proud to fight' would have been better left unsaid . . . it's asking for trouble . . . ." And in "Gothic Architecture," William Morris wrote of "the warlike pilgrimages of the Crusades amongst races by no means prepared to turn their cheeks to the smiter."

TWINKLING OF AN EYE

I Cor. 15:52

Paul wrote of Judgment Day: "Behold, I will shew you a mystery; We shall not all sleep, but we shall all be changed, In a moment, in the twinkling of an eye, at the last trump . . . ." In *Confessions of an English Opium Eater*, De Quincey tells of dreaming of meeting his young friend Ann in an Oriental setting. He gazed at her beauty, but "in a moment, all had vanished . . . and, in the twinkling of an eye, I was . . . by lamplight in Oxford Street, walking with Ann—just as we walked seventeen years before . . . ." Robert Louis Stevenson, in "A Plea for Gas Lamps," wrote: "Fiat Lux, says the sedate electrician. What a spectacle, on some clear, dark nightfall, from the edge of Hampstead Hill, when in a moment, in the twinkling of an eye, the design of the monstrous city flashes into vision!"

TWO ARE BETTER THAN ONE

Eccles. 4:9–10

The Preacher wrote: "Two are better than one; because they have a good reward for their labour. For if they fall, the one will lift up his fellow: but woe to him that is alone when he

falleth; for he hath not another to help him up." In Chaucer's
Troilus and Criseyde, Pandarus tries to persuade the lovesick
Troilus to confide in him:

> The wise seith, "Wo hym that is allone,
> For, and he falle, he hath non helpe to ryse";
> And sith thow hast a felawe, tel thi mone . . . .

In Bunyan's *Pilgrim's Progress,* when Christian and his friend
Hope reach The Inchanted Ground, Hope wants to sleep, but
Christian warns against it. Hope acknowledges the danger, and
says, "I see it is true that the Wise Man saith, Two are better
than one. Hitherto hath thy company been my mercy, and thou
shalt have a good reward for thy labour."

TWO OR THREE GATHERED TOGETHER   *see WHERE TWO OR THREE ARE GATHERED TOGETHER*

TWO THIEVES

*Matt. 27:38;
Mark 15:27;
Luke 23:33,
39–43; John
19:18*

When Jesus was crucified, "there were two thieves crucified
with him, one on the right hand, and another on the left." Luke
said that Jesus forgave one "malefactor" who had rebuked the
other for railing on Jesus. In *Time and Tide,* Ruskin said that
theft by unjust profits is the worst of sins. " 'And with Him they
crucified two thieves' . . . the sin of theft is again and again
indicated as the chiefly antagonistic one to the law of Christ."
In *Moby Dick,* Melville described a flogging. In "The Town-
Ho's Story," the captain, "seizing a rope, applied it with all his
might to the backs of the two traitors, till they yelled no more,
but lifelessly hung their heads sideways, as the two crucified
thieves are drawn."

UNDER A BUSHEL, CANDLE, LIGHT   *see LIGHT (CANDLE) UNDER A BUSHEL*

UNDERSTANDING HEART   *see SOLOMON'S WISDOM*

UNDER THE PALM TREE   *see DEBORAH*

UNDER THE SUN   *see NO NEW THING UNDER THE SUN*

UNJUST STEWARD   *see CHILDREN OF LIGHT*

UNKNOWN GOD

Acts 17:23

When Paul visited Athens, certain Epicurean and Stoic philosophers took him to the Areopagus [ăr·ê·ŏp'à·gŭs] to hear his new doctrine. He said to them: "Ye men of Athens, I perceive that in all things ye are too superstitious. For as I passed by, and beheld your devotions, I found an altar with this inscription, TO THE UNKNOWN GOD. Whom therefore ye ignorantly worship, him declare I unto you." In *Hellas*, Shelley wrote:

> In sacred Athens, near the fane
> Of Wisdom, Pity's altar stood:
> Serve not the unknown God in vain.

Ruskin, in *Sesame and Lilies*, said: "You cannot lead your children faithfully to those narrow axe-hewn church altars of yours, while the dark azure altars in heaven—the mountains that sustain your island throne . . . remain for you without inscription; altars built, not to, but by an Unknown God."

UNPROFITABLE SERVANT   *see PARABLE OF THE TALENTS*

UNTO DUST SHALT THOU RETURN   *see DUST, CLAY*

UNTO THE PURE ALL THINGS ARE PURE

Titus 1:15

Paul wrote to Titus [tī'tŭs]: "Unto the pure all things are pure: but unto them that are defiled and unbelieving is nothing pure; but even their mind and conscience is defiled." In *Areopagitica*, Milton cites Paul in support of his argument against censorship of books. The individual should have freedom to choose what he should read. Paul said, "Prove all things, hold fast that which is good" (I Thess. 5:21). And one should add "another remarkable saying of the same author: 'To the pure, all things are pure.'" D. H. Lawrence, in *Studies in Classic American Literature*, says, of *The Scarlet Letter*, that Dimmesdale's "spiritual love was a lie . . . . We are so pure in spirit. Hi-tiddly-i-ty! Till she tickled him in the right place, and he fell. Flop. Flop goes spiritual love. But keep up the game. Keep up appearances. Pure are the pure. To the pure all things, etc."

UNTO (UPON) THE THIRD AND FOURTH GENERATION   *see SINS OF THE FATHERS*

URIAH THE HITTITE   *see DAVID AND BATHSHEBA*

URIEL
(ū′·rĭ·ĕl)

"II Esdras 1–11,"
of the Apocrypha

Uriel, meaning "God is light," was an angel sent by God to instruct the prophet Esdras, and one of the seven archangels, in later lore. In Milton's *Paradise Lost*, Uriel is the Regent of the Sun, "the sharpest sighted Spirit of all in Heav'n." Satan meets him on his way to the Garden of Eden, and deceives him with "hypocrisie, the only evil" which "neither Man nor Angel can discern." In Longfellow's "The Golden Legend," Uriel is one of the Angels of the Seven Planets bearing the star of Bethlehem: "I am the Minister of Mars, / The strongest star among the stars!"

URIM AND THUMMIN

(ū′rĭm,
thŭm′ĭm)

Exod. 28:30;
Levit. 8:8; Deut.
33:8

When AARON became priest, the Lord instructed Moses: "And thou shalt put in the breastplate of judgment the Urim and the Thummim; and they shall be upon Aaron's heart, when he goeth in before the Lord. . . ." The words mean "lights" and "perfection." They were possibly small stones or jewels used by the priest for oracular purposes. In Milton's *Paradise Regained*, Satan praises Christ for rejecting the temptation of wealth.

> Should Kings and Nations from thy mouth consult,
> Thy Counsel would be as the Oracle
> *Urim* and *Thummim*, those oraculous gems
> On *Aaron's* breast . . . .

In Tennyson's "The Coming of Arthur," in *The Idylls of the King*, Bellicent describes King Arthur's sword Excalibur

> That rose from out the bosom of the lake,
> And Arthur row'd across and took it—rich
> With jewels, elfin Urim, on the hilt,
> Bewildering heart and eye . . . .

UR OF THE CHALDEES   *see ABRAHAM*

USE A LITTLE WINE   *see TAKE A LITTLE WINE*

USURY   *see PARABLE OF THE TALENTS*

UTTERMOST PARTS OF THE SEA (EARTH)   *see TAKE THE WINGS OF MORNING*

UZ   *see JOB*

VALE OF TEARS   *see BACA, VALE OF*

VALLEY OF DECISION   *see VALLEY OF JEHOSHAPHAT*

VALLEY OF DRY BONES

Ezek. 37:1–14

The Lord set Ezekiel "down in the midst of the valley which was full of bones . . . and they were very dry. And he said unto [Ezekiel], Son of man, can these bones live?" On the Lord's command, Ezekiel prophesied upon the bones and upon the wind, and with a shaking the bones came together and lived—an allegory of the restoration of all Israel. According to Izaak Walton, in his *Life of Dr. John Donne,* when Donne preached his own funeral sermon, he was so ill that "many did secretly ask that question in Ezekiel: 'Do these bones live?' " In *Benito Cereno,* Melville, describing a neglected whaleboat, said, "Her keel seemed laid, her ribs put together, and she launched, from Ezekiel's Valley of Dry Bones." And Whittier, in "Howard at Atlanta," describes a group of slaves reading the Bible together:

> Behold!—the dumb lips speaking,
> The blind eyes seeing!
> Bones of the Prophet's vision
> Warmed into being!

VALLEY OF HINNOM   *see TOPHET(H)*

VALLEY OF JEHOSHAPHAT

Joel 3:2

Joel wrote that all nations shall be finally judged here: "I will also gather all nations, and will bring them down into the valley of Jehoshaphat [jē·hŏsh'a·făt], and will plead with them for my people and for my heritage Israel, whom they have scattered among the nations, and parted my land." The word means "God is judge," and the valley is later called by Joel "the valley of decision" (v. 14). Many Jews and Moslems are buried in the Kidron Valley outside Jerusalem, which has been believed to be the site of the coming Judgment Day. In *Culture and Anarchy,* Arnold advised young Liberals not to oppose the Philistine Parliament too strenuously: "For our part, we rejoice to see our dear old friends, the Hebraizing Philistines, gathered in force in the Valley of Jehoshaphat previous to their final conversion, which will certainly come." In Joyce's *A Portrait of the Artist as a Young Man,* Stephen, after hearing a powerful sermon on sin and judgment, contemplates the fate of all sinners: "Time is, time was, but time shall be no more. At the last blast the souls of universal humanity throng towards the valley of Jehoshaphat, rich and poor, gentle and simple, wise and foolish, good and wicked." And in "What of the Day?" Whittier says of the battle for freedom led by Frémont, a "sound of tumult" grows.

> Behold the burden of the prophet's vision;
> The gathering hosts,—the Valley of Decision,
> Dusk with the wings of eagles wheeling o'er.
> Day of the Lord, of darkness and not light!
> It breaks in thunder and the whirlwind's roar!

VALLEY OF THE SHADOW OF DEATH

Ps. 23:4 "Yea, though I walk through the valley of the shadow of death, I will fear no evil: for thou art with me; thy rod and thy staff they comfort me." The phrase "shadow of death" here probably means "deep gloom." But elsewhere in the Bible and in literature since then "shadow of death" means approaching death, as in Job 3:5 and Jeremiah 2:6. In Bunyan's *Pilgrim's Progress*, Christian was forced to go through the Valley of the Shadow of Death on his way to the Celestial City. "Now this Valley is a very solitary place. The Prophet Jeremiah thus describes it: A Wilderness, a land of Desarts and of Pits, a land of drought, and of the Shadow of Death, a land that no man (but a Christian) passeth through, and where no man dwelt." And as Christian neared The Mouth of Hell where Satan spoke blasphemies into his mind, he heard "a voice of a man, as going before him, saying, Though I walk through the Valley of the Shadow of Death, I will fear none ill, for thou art with me." In Poe's "Eldorado," the "pilgrim shadow" tells the "gallant knight" that he will find the land of Eldorado "Over the Mountains / Of the Moon, / Down the Valley of the Shadow." And Van Wyck Brooks, in *New England: Indian Summer,* said that New England in the new twentieth century was facing the Epigoni —Robert Frost especially. "But, first of all, it had to dree its weird. It had to pass through the valley of the shadow. Only then was it ripe for these new revelations."

VANITAS VANITATUM   *see ALL IS VANITY*

VANITY OF VANITIES   *see ALL IS VANITY*

VARIABLENESS, NOR SHADOW OF TURNING   *see NO VARIABLENESS, NEITHER SHADOW OF TURNING*

VASHTI   *see ESTHER*

VEIL OF THE TEMPLE RENT

Matt. 27:51;
Mark 15:38;
Luke 23:45

When Jesus, on the cross, "cried again with a loud voice [and] yielded up the ghost . . . behold, the veil of the temple was rent in twain from the top to the bottom; and the earth did quake, and the rocks rent;" Whittier, in "The Crucifixion," wrote:

> The Temple of the Cherubim,
> The House of God is cold and dim;
> A curse is on its trembling walls,
> Its mighty veil asunder falls!

In "A Plea for Captain John Brown," Thoreau said, of the events at Harpers Ferry, "There was no death in the case, because there had been no life; they merely rotted or sloughed off. . . . No temple's veil was rent, only a hole dug somewhere." In O'Neill's *The Hairy Ape,* Yank and Long walk down Fifth Avenue hearing the voices of passing churchgoers:

> Dear Doctor Caiphas! He is so sincere!
> What was his sermon? I dozed off . . .
> We can devote the proceeds to rehabilitating the veil of the
>   temple.
> But that has been done so many times.

VENGEANCE IS MINE

Rom. 12:19

Paul wrote to the Romans that they should not recompense evil for evil. "Dearly beloved, avenge not yourselves, but rather give place unto wrath: for it is written, Vengeance is mine; I will repay, saith the Lord." In Byron's *Manfred,* the Abbot urges Manfred to repent for his sins. He speaks of pardon, not punishment. The latter, he says,

> I leave to heaven,—"Vengeance is mine alone!"
> So saith the Lord, and with all humbleness
> His servant echoes back the awful word.

In Tennyson's "The Voyage of Maeldune," Maeldune, wearied of his quest for vengeance for his father's murder, meets a saint who says, "O Maeldune, let be the purpose of thine! / Remember the words of the Lord when he told us, 'Vengeance is mine!' "

VIALS OF WRATH

Rev. 16:1–17

John of Patmos envisioned seven punishments to be visited upon the earth. "And I heard a great voice out of the temple saying to the seven angels, Go your ways, and pour out the

vials of wrath of God upon the earth." (Modern translations
say "bowls of wrath.") In *The English Mail-Coach*, De Quincey
said that the mail-coach had "terrific beauty" because of its
"awful *political* mission" when it "distributed over the face of
the land, like the opening of apocalyptic vials, the heart-shak-
ing news of Trafalgar, of Salamanca, of Vittoria, of Waterloo."
In *Typhoon*, Conrad described the coming of a storm as "something formidable and swift, like the sudden smashing of a vial
of wrath."

VISIT THE INIQUITY (SINS) OF THE FATHERS   *see SINS OF THE FATHERS*

VOICE FROM THE WHIRLWIND

Job 38:1

The chapter telling of the Lord reproving Job for his questioning is headed "The Voice from the Whirlwind" in the King
James Version, and it begins, "Then the Lord answered Job
out of the whirlwind . . . ." In *Modern Painters*, Ruskin argued
that faithlessness can be cured by the love of nature. Just because "we have been led, according to those words of the Greek
poet . . . 'to dethrone the gods, and crown the whirlwind,' it is
no reason that we should forget there was once a time when
'the Lord answered Job out of the whirlwind.' " In "Laus Deo,"
celebrating the abolition of slavery, Whittier said that "God's
own voice is in that peal" of bells. "For the Lord / On the
whirlwind is abroad . . . ."

VOICE IS JACOB'S VOICE

Gen. 27:22

Jacob schemed to obtain his father's blessing, which belonged
to Esau, his older brother. With his mother's help, he cooked
savory meat and covered his hands and neck with hairy
skins of kids and goats. Jacob told his blind old father Isaac that
he was Esau and had come for his blessing. Isaac then "felt
him, and said, The voice is Jacob's voice, but the hands are
the hands of Esau." But Jacob got the blessing. In Dryden's
"Absalom and Achitophel," David (Charles II) speaks of the
rebels supporting Absalom (the Duke of Monmouth) who make
a show of loyalty: "True, they petition me t'approve their
choice; / But Esau's hands suit ill with Jacob's voice." In his
biography *Mark Twain*, Stephen Leacock wrote, "The voice is
Yankee but the hand is from Missouri." And in Shaw's *Saint
Joan*, Ladvenu cross-examined Joan about her voices which she
felt came from God: "Joan, Joan: does not that prove to you
that the voices are the voices of evil spirits?"

VOICE (NOISE, SOUND) OF MANY WATERS

Ps. 93:4; Ezek. 1:24; 43:2; Rev. 1:15

The Psalmist sings: "The Lord on high is mightier than the noise of many waters, yea, than the mighty waves of the sea." John of Patmos was charged to write his revelation by a great voice, "as the sound of many waters." Whittier, in "Massachusetts to Virginia," protesting the fugitive-slave laws, wrote:

> The voice of Massachusetts! Of her free sons and daughters,
> Deep calling unto deep aloud, the sound of many waters!"

Poe concludes "The Fall of the House of Usher" with the collapse of the house of Usher: "I saw the mighty walls rushing asunder—there was a long tumultuous shouting sound like the voice of a thousand waters—and the deep and dank tarn at my feet closed suddenly and silently over the fragments of the HOUSE OF USHER." In *A Portrait of the Artist as a Young Man,* Joyce describes Stephen's feelings as he watches the swallows from the library steps—"ever leaving the homes they had built to wander": "A soft liquid joy like the noise of many waters flowed over his memory and he felt in his heart the soft peace of silent spaces of fading tenuous sky above the waters, of oceanic silence, of swallows flying through the seadusk over the flowing waters."

VOICE OF THE TURTLE

Song of Sol. 2:12

In the spring song the lover calls to his beloved: "The flowers appear on the earth; the time of the singing of birds is come, and the voice of the turtle is heard in our land . . . ." It is the turtledove, the mourning dove. In Chaucer's "The Merchant's Tale," Old January calls to his young wife, May, to come out into the garden one spring morning:

> Rys up, my wyf, my love, my lady free!
> The turtles voyse is herd, my dowve sweete;
> The wynter is goon with alle his reynes weete.

In Bunyan's *Pilgrim's Progress,* Christian and Hope "solaced themselves for a season" in the Country of Beulah. "Yea, here they heard continually the singing of Birds, and saw every day the Flowers appear in the earth, and heard the voice of the Turtle in the Land." D. H. Lawrence, in *Studies in Classic American Literature,* said, about De Crevecœur's statement that "unfortunately our king-birds are the destroyers of those industrious insects (the bees)": "This is a sad blow to the sweet-and-pureness of Nature. But it is the voice of the artist in contrast to the voice of the ideal turtle."

VOICE THAT CRIETH IN THE WILDERNESS

Isa. 40:3; Matt. 3:3; Mark 1:3; Luke 3:4; John 1:23

Isaiah's vision of the redemption of Jerusalem: "The voice of him that crieth in the wilderness, Prepare ye the way of the Lord, make straight in the desert a highway for our God," was quoted by all four of the New Testament Evangelists as "the voice of one crying in the wilderness." In literature it usually means an unheeded voice. In his Preface to *Pygmalion*, Shaw said that we need "an energetic phonetic enthusiast" to improve our language. "There have been heroes of that kind crying in the wilderness for many years past." In *Studies in Classic American Literature*, D. H. Lawrence said of De Crevecœur's idealized wife on the American frontier, "Poor haggard drudge, [she was] like a ghost wailing in the wilderness, nine times out of ten." And R. D. Skinner said of Eugene O'Neill, "Among modern writers he was almost a voice in the wilderness crying for moral values when the world about him was smugly preaching economic determinism and the fatalism of matter."

WAGES OF SIN IS DEATH

Rom. 6:23

Paul wrote to the Romans about freedom from, and slavery to, sin: "For the wages of sin is death: but the gift of God is eternal life, through Jesus Christ our Lord." In Bunyan's *Pilgrim's Progress*, when Christian meets Apollyon (see ABADDON) in the Valley of Humiliation, Apollyon claims that Christian is one of his subjects. Christian replies: "I was born indeed in your dominions, but your service was hard, and your wages such as a man could not live on, for the Wages of Sin is death . . . ." In "Wages," Tennyson wrote: "The wages of sin is death: if the wages of Virtue be dust, / Would she have the heart to endure for the life of the worm and the fly? / . . . Give her the wages of going on, and not to die." In *Black Boy*, Richard Wright said that when he returned home from a trip with a salesman-evangelist, his religious Granny thought that some of his sins must have evaporated, "for she felt that success spelled the reward of righteousness and that failure was the wages of sin."

WALK (WENT) BACKWARD   *see CANAAN, SON OF HAM*

WALK WITH GOD   *see ENOCH*

WALL OF JERICHO   *see JERICHO*

WAR IN HEAVEN

Rev. 12:7–9

"And there was war in heaven: Michael and his angels fought against the dragon; and the dragon fought and his angels, And prevailed not; neither was their place found any more in heaven. And the great dragon was cast out, that old serpent, called the Devil, and Satan, which deceiveth the whole world; he was cast out." In Milton's *Paradise Lost*, Raphael describes to Adam the revolt of Satan and his angels against God. Satan fraught

> With envie against the Son of God, that day
> Honourd by his great Father, and proclaimd
> Messiah King anointed, could not beare
> Through pride that sight, and thought himself impaird
> Deep malice thence conceiving & disdain,
> Soon as midnight brought on the duskie houre
> Friendliest to sleep and silence, he resolv'd
> With all his Legions to dislodge, and leave
> Unworshipt unobey'd the Throne supream
> Contemptuous . . . .

The three-day war in heaven, led by Michael and Gabriel, and involving cannons and the tossing about of mountains, was won when Christ the champion threw out the rebels single-handed:

> Nine dayes they fell; confounded Chaos roard,
> And felt tenfold confusion in thir fall
> Through his wilde Anarchie, so huge a rout
> Incumberd him with ruin: Hell at last
> Yawning receavd them whole, and on them clos'd,
> Hell thir fit habitation fraught with fire
> Unquenchable, the house of woe and paine.

And in Melville's *Moby Dick*, when the *Pequod* finally sank, a sky-hawk caught on the mast by Tashtego's hammer,

> . . . with archangelic shrieks . . . and his whole captive form folded in the flag of Ahab, went down with his ship, which, like Satan, would not sink to hell till she had dragged a living part of heaven along with her, and helmeted herself with it.

WASHED HIS HANDS   *see PILATE WASHED HIS HANDS*

WASHED IN THE BLOOD OF THE LAMB   *see BLOOD OF THE LAMB, WASHED IN*

WATER INTO WINE   *see CANA*

WATERS OF BABYLON   *see BY THE RIVERS OF BABYLON*

WATER(S) OF LIFE   *see RIVER OF WATER OF LIFE*

WAY OF TRANSGRESSORS

Prov. 13:15   Among the proverbs on virtues and vices is this: "Good understanding giveth favour: but the way of transgressors is hard." In "Life without Principle," Thoreau spoke of the similarity between gold diggers and gamblers: "It is not enough to tell me that you worked hard to get your gold. So does the Devil work hard. The way of the transgressors may be hard in many respects." In Somerset Maugham's *Of Human Bondage*, Chitton came to the art studio late, saying it was a good day to "lie in bed and think how beautiful it was out." When Miss Price remarked seriously that it would have been better to get up and enjoy it, Chitton said gravely, "The way of the humorist is very hard."

WEAKER VESSEL

I Pet. 3:7   Peter advised wives to be in subjection to their husbands; and "ye husbands, dwell with them according to knowledge, giving honour unto the wife, as unto the weaker vessel, and as being heirs together of the grace of life; that your prayers be not hindered." This was a favorite passage with Shakespeare. In *Love's Labour's Lost*, Don Adriano de Armado reports to the King that one Costard, "a shallow vassal," unlawfully "sorted and consorted" with "Jaquenetta, so is the weaker vessel called which I apprehended with the aforesaid swain,—I keep her as a vessel of the law's fury." In *Romeo and Juliet*, Samson and Gregory, Capulet servants, jest about "taking the wall"—the inside of the sidewalk. Samson: "I will take the wall of any man or maid of Montague's." Gregory: "That shows thee a weak slave, for the weakest goes to the wall." Samson: " 'T is true, and therefore women, being the weaker vessels, are ever thrust to the wall. Therefore I will push Montague's men from the wall and thrust his maids to the wall." In *Euphues*, Lyly said, "Men are always laying baytes for women, which are the weaker vessels." When Othello accuses Desdemona of being a strumpet, she says:

> No, as I am a Christian,
> If to preserve this vessel for my lord
> From any other foul unlawful touch
> Be not to be a strumpet, I am none.

WEARINESS OF FLESH   *see OF MAKING MANY BOOKS*

WEAVER'S BEAM   *see DAVID AND GOLIATH*

WEAVER'S SHUTTLE

Job 7:6

In his sufferings, Job contemplates death: "My flesh is clothed with worms and clods of dust; my skin is broken, and become loathsome. My days are swifter than a weaver's shuttle, and are spent without hope." In Shakespeare's *The Merry Wives of Windsor*, Falstaff tells Ford, disguised as Master Brook, that Mistress Ford's husband beat him grievously when he was "in the shape of a woman." But "in the shape of a man, Master Brook, I fear not Goliath with a weaver's beam; because I know also life is a shuttle." In "New Year's Eve," Lamb said that "as the years both lessen and shorten, I set more count upon their periods . . . I am not content to pass away 'like a weaver's shuttle.' Those metaphors solace me not . . . ."

WEDDING IN CANA   *see CANA*

WEEPING AND GNASHING OF TEETH

Matt. 8:12; 22:13;
24:51; 25:30;
Luke 13:28

Jesus used this expression several times; for example, when He cured the centurion's servant, He said, "But the children of the kingdom shall be cast out into outer darkness; there shall be weeping and gnashing of teeth." In the parable of the tares, Jesus said, "There shall be wailing and gnashing of teeth" (Matt. 13:42). In Melville's *Moby Dick*, Ishmael enters a Negro church in New Bedford where the preacher "was beating a book" in his pulpit; his text was about "the blackness of darkness, and the weeping and wailing and teeth-gnashing there." In *Life on the Mississippi*, Mark Twain said that when the steamboat captains, under pressure from the Pilots' Benevolent Association, fired the nonmembers, "There was weeping and wailing and gnashing of teeth in the camp of the outsiders now." In Christopher Fry's *The Lady's Not for Burning*, Skipps, drunk, when asked by the justice if he is Matthew Skipps, replies, "Who give me that name? . . . Baptized I blaming was . . . and baptized I will be, win holy weeping and washing of teeth. And immersion upon us miserable offenders."*

*From *The Lady's Not for Burning* by Christopher Fry. Reprinted by permission of Oxford University Press.

WEIGHED IN THE BALANCES AND FOUND WANTING

Dan. 5:27

At Belshazzar's feast Daniel explained to the king the meaning of the HANDWRITING ON THE WALL. The words written were MENE, MENE, TEKEL, UPHARSIN. "Tekel" was interpreted to mean "Thou art weighed in the balances, and art found wanting." That night Belshazzar was slain. Shelley, in *A Defense of Poetry*, argues that great poets are great men whose faults are trivial: "Their errors have been weighed and found to have been dust in the balance." Robert Southey's "Ode on Negotiations with Buonaparte" opposes negotiations with the wicked tyrant: "Have ye not seen him in the balance weighed, / And there found wanting?" In *Past and Present*, Carlyle attacks the "Idle Aristocracy" who "are 'sliding' even faster, towards a . . . balance-scale whereon is written *Thou art found wanting . . . .*"

WEIGHTIER MATTERS   *see TITHE OF MINT, ANISE, AND CUMMIN*

WELL DONE, GOOD AND FAITHFUL SERVANT   *see PARABLE OF THE TALENTS*

WHAT IS A MAN PROFITED, IF HE SHALL GAIN THE WHOLE WORLD?

Matt. 16:26;
Mark 8:36

Jesus said to his disciples that any man who would follow him must deny himself. "For what is a man profited, if he shall gain the whole world, and lose his own soul? or what shall a man give in exchange for his soul?" In "Boswell's Life of Johnson," Carlyle said that Johnson saw that "wrong is not only different from Right, but that it is in strict scientific terms infinitely different; even as gaining of the whole world set against the losing of one's own soul." In Galsworthy's *The Forsyte Saga*, Aunt Juley, at Swithin's dinner, said to Soames, "Only last Sunday dear Mr. Scoles had been so witty in his sermon, so sarcastic: 'For what,' he had said, 'shall it profit a man if he gain his own soul, but lose all his property?' That, he had said, was the motto of the middle-class; now, what *had* he meant by that?"

WHAT IS MAN, THAT THOU ART MINDFUL OF HIM?   *see LITTLE LOWER THAN THE ANGELS*

WHAT IS TRUTH?

John 18:37–38

When Jesus was tried before Pilate, saying, "I came into the world, that I should bear witness unto the truth . . . . Pilate saith unto him, What is truth? And when he had said this, he went out again unto the Jews, and saith unto them, I find in him no fault at all." Francis Bacon, in "Of Truth," wrote, " 'What is truth,' said jesting Pilate; and would not stay for an answer." In "Boswell's Life of Johnson," Carlyle, recalling Bacon's allusion, said that Johnson's "England was all confused," regarding truth; and that Johnson's own life also made the search for the truth difficult. " 'What is Truth?' said jesting Pilate. What is Truth? might earnest Johnson much more emphatically say." In "The Irresponsibles," Archibald MacLeish accused the modern scholar of being "as indifferent to values, as careless of significance, as bored with meanings as the chemist . . . . He has taught himself to say with the physicist—and with some others whom history remembers— 'What is truth?' "

WHATSOEVER A MAN SOWETH, THAT SHALL HE ALSO REAP

Gal. 6:7; II Cor. 9:6

Paul wrote to the Galatians that "every man shall bear his own burden . . . . Be not deceived; God is not mocked: for whatsoever a man soweth, that shall he also reap." In "Lines Written among the Euganean Hills," Shelley said, of Padua's sufferings under tyranny, that poisonous weeds overgrow

> Sheaves of whom are ripe to come
> To destruction's harvest-home:
> Men must reap the things they sow,
> Force from force must ever flow . . . .

In "Sister Songs," Francis Thompson said that a poet is not master of poetic inspiration; it comes unexpectedly: "Where he sows he doth not reap, / He reapeth where he did not sow." And Ruskin, in *Unto This Last,* said, "You may grow for your neighbour . . . grapes or grapeshot; he will also . . . grow grapes or grapeshot for you, and you will each reap what you have sown."

WHATSOEVER THINGS ARE TRUE, WHATSOEVER THINGS ARE HONEST . . . .

Phil. 4:8

Paul wrote to the Philippians: "Finally, brethren, whatsoever things are true, whatsoever things are honest, whatsoever things are just, whatsoever things are pure, whatsoever things are lovely, whatsoever things are of good report; if there be any virtue, and if there be any praise, think on these things." In *Modern Painters,* Ruskin said, "Modern art . . . consists neither in altering, nor in improving nature; but in seeking throughout nature for 'whatsoever things are lovely, and whatsoever things are pure.' " In *God and the Bible*, Matthew Arnold said that the early Christians were justly accused of a lack of intellectual seriousness by Celsus, in spite of Paul's motto of Christianity which should be translated "whatever things are nobly serious." In Hardy's *Tess of the D'Urbervilles*, Angel Clare courts Tess. When she says she is not worthy of him, he replies, "Distinction does not consist in the facile use of a contemptible set of conventions, but in being numbered among those who are true, and honest, and just, and pure, and lovely, and of good report—as you are, my Tess."

WHATSOEVER THY HAND FINDETH TO DO

Eccles. 9:10 The Preacher advised: "Whatsoever thy hand findeth to do, do it with thy might; for there is no work, nor device, nor knowledge, nor wisdom, in the grave, whither thou goest." Carlyle, in *Sartor Resartus*, concluded "The Everlasting Yea," saying, work for the Ideal. "Produce! Produce! Were it but the pitifullest, infinitesimal fraction of a Product, produce it, in God's name! . . . Up, Up! Whatsoever thy hand findeth to do, do it with thy whole might." In *Sesame and Lilies*, Ruskin said that labor brings happiness if truly creative, not if in response to "an unrewarded obedience, if, indeed, it was rendered faithfully to the command—'Whatsoever thy hand findeth to do—do it with thy might.' " And in Clarence Day's *Life with Father*, young Clarence was advised by his father: "King Solomon had the right idea about these things. Whatsoever thy hand findeth to do,' Solomon said, 'Do thy damnedest.' "

WHEELS WITHIN WHEELS

Ezek. 1:15–28 In Babylon by the river of Chebar [kē′bär] Ezekiel had a vision of the glory of the Lord. Amid whirlwind, fire, and lightning "as I beheld the living creatures, behold one wheel upon the earth by the living creatures, with his four faces. The appearance of the wheels and their work was like unto the color of a beryl . . . and their appearance and their work was as it were a wheel in the middle of a wheel . . . and their rings were full of eyes . . . the spirit of the living creature was in the wheels." "The likeness of the firmament . . . was as the colour of the terrible crystal . . . . And above the firmament was the likeness of a throne, as the appearance of a sapphire stone . . . . And I saw the colour of amber . . . and the appearance of the bow that is in the cloud in the day of

rain . . . ." In Milton's *Paradise Lost,* Christ rushed forth in
his chariot to do battle with the rebellious angels:

> forth rush'd with whirlwind sound
> The Chariot of Paternal Deitie,
> Flashing thick flames, Wheele within Wheele undrawn,
> It self instinct with Spirit, but convoyd
> By four Cherubic shapes, four Faces each
> Had wondrous, as with Starrs thir bodies all
> And Wings were set with Eyes, with Eyes the Wheel
> Of Beril, and careering Fires between;
> Over thir heads a chrystal Firmament,
> Whereon a Saphir Throne, inlaid with pure
> Amber, and colours of the showrie Arch.

In "Lucy Hooper," Whittier said that Lucy Hooper had a
firm faith based on old rites and liturgy:

> A life in every rite and form,
> As when on Chebar's banks of old,
> The Hebrew's gorgeous vision rolled.
> A spirit filled the vast machine,
> A life "within the wheels" was seen.

WHERE NEITHER MOTH NOR RUST DOTH CORRUPT   see *LAY NOT TREASURES UPON EARTH*

WHERE TWO OR THREE ARE GATHERED TOGETHER

Matt. 18:20   Jesus said, "For where two or three are gathered together in
my name, there am I in the midst of them." In Dryden's
"Absalom and Achitophel," SHIMEI was a conspirator against
David (Charles II). "When two or three were gathered to
declaim / Against the monarch of Jerusalem, / Shimei was
always in the midst of them." In "Characteristics," Carlyle
said that the individual becomes truly moral in sharing life in
society with "his brother men. 'Where two or three are gathered together' in the name of the Highest, then first does the
Highest, as it is written, 'appear among them to bless them
. . . .' " In "The Meeting," Whittier describes his Quaker faith:

> God should be most where man is least:
> So, where is neither church nor priest
> And never rag or form or creed . . .
> I turn my bell-unsummoned feet . . .
> "Where, in my name, meet two or three,"
> Our Lord hath said, "I there will be!"

WHITE AS SNOW   see *SINS BE AS SCARLET . . .*

WHITED SEPULCHRES

Matt. 23:27 Jesus denounced the scribes and PHARISEES, saying, "Woe unto you, scribes and Pharisees, hypocrites! for ye are like unto whited sepulchres, which indeed appear beautiful outward, but are within full of dead men's bones, and of all uncleanness." It was a Jewish custom to whitewash their tombs to avoid accidental touching, which would mean defilement. In Chaucer's "The Squire's Tale," the falcon tells of her false lover:

> As in a toumbe is al the faire above,
> And under is the corps, swich as ye woot,
> Swich was this ypocrite, bothe coold and hoot.

In Joyce's *A Portrait of the Artist as a Young Man*, Stephen reflects upon the words of the Preacher on Judgment Day: "O you hypocrites, O you whited sepulchres, O you who present a smooth smiling face to the world while your soul within is a foul swamp of sin, how will it fare with you in that terrible day?" In Eugene O'Neill's *Mourning Becomes Electra*, Christine, bringing flowers from the greenhouse, says to Lavinia, about their house, "I felt our tomb needed a little brightening. Each time I come back after being away it appears more like a sepulchre! The 'whited' one of the Bible—pagan temple front stuck like a mask on Puritan gray ugliness!"

WHITHER THOU GOEST, I WILL GO   *see RUTH*

WHOLE DUTY OF MAN

Eccles. 12:13 The Preacher concludes his book with: "Let us hear the conclusion of the whole matter: Fear God, and keep his commandments: for this is the whole duty of man." In "The South-Sea House," Charles Lamb said that John Tipp, accountant, had his diversions, but at his desk he was strictly business. "The whole duty of man consisted in writing off dividend warrants." In Carlyle's *Sartor Resartus*, Professor Teufelsdröckh says that "The Everlasting Yea" philosophy is "Applied Christianity." "We have here not a Whole Duty of Man, yet a Half Duty, namely the Passive half: could we but do it, as we can demonstrate it!"

WHOM GOD HATH JOINED TOGETHER, LET NOT MAN PUT ASUNDER

Matt. 19:6; Mark 10:9 When the Pharisees tested Jesus about divorce, he said, "What therefore God hath joined together, let not man put asunder."

The Prayer Book version is: "Those whom God hath joined together let no man put asunder." In Shakespeare's *Henry VI, Part III*, Gloucester says, in reply to King Edward's question whether he is offended by Edward's marriage to Lady Grey:

> Not I:
> No, God forbid that I should wish them sever'd
> Whom God hath join'd together; ay, and 't were pity
> To sunder them that yoke so well together.

In *Cape Cod*, Thoreau told of a Truro man who found the bodies of a man and a woman washed up on the shore together. "Perhaps," said Thoreau, "they were man and wife, and whom God had joined the ocean currents had not put asunder." Huxley, in *Brave New World*, told of "Neo-Pavlovian Conditioning" of the "Delta" infants to hate books and flowers. These and loud noises with electric shocks were in the infant minds "couples compromising linked." After two hundred repetitions they "would be wedded indissolubly. What man has joined, nature is powerless to put asunder."

WHORE OF BABYLON   *see BABYLON AS SCARLET WOMAN, WHORE*

WHOSOEVER HATH, TO HIM SHALL BE GIVEN

Matt. 13:12; 25:29; Mark 4:25; Luke 8:18; 19:26

This statement of Jesus appears several times, the first in connection with the parable of the sower, when his disciples asked why he spoke in parables. He explained, "Because it is given unto you to know the mysteries of the kingdom of heaven, but to them it is not given. For whosoever hath, to him shall be given, and he shall have more abundance: but whosoever hath not, from him shall be taken away even that he hath." Robert Herrick, in a poem beginning "Once poore, still penurious," wrote:

> Goes the world now, it will with thee goe hard.
> The fattest Hogs we grease the more with Lard.
> To him that has, there shall be added more;
> Who is penurious, he shall still be poore.

John Stuart Mill, in "Three Essays on Religion," said that "good and evil naturally tend to fructify, each in its own kind, good producing good, and evil, evil. It is one of Nature's general rules . . . that 'to him that hath shall be given, but from him that hath not, shall be taken even that which he hath.'"

WHOSOEVER WILL SAVE HIS LIFE SHALL LOSE IT

Matt. 16:25;
Mark 8:35; Luke
9:24; 17:33

Jesus said to his disciples, "If any man will come after me, let him deny himself, and take up his cross and follow me. For whosoever will save his life shall lose it: and whosoever will lose his life for my sake shall find it." In *Unto This Last,* Ruskin said of the worker, "Treat him kindly without any economical purpose, and all economical purposes will be answered; in this, as in all other matters, whosoever will save his life shall lose it, and whoso loses it shall find it." In *Civil Disobedience,* Thoreau argued against Paley's "Duty of Submission to Civil Government": "If I have unjustly wrested a plank from a drowning man, I must restore it to him though I drown myself. This, according to Paley, would be inconvenient. But he that would save his life, in such a case, shall lose it. America must cease to hold slaves, and to make war on Mexico, though it cost them their existence as a people."

WIDOW'S MITE

Mark 12:42–44;
Luke 21:2–4

As Jesus watched the rich cast much money into the treasury, "there came a certain poor widow, and she threw in two mites, which make a farthing." A mite was the smallest Jewish coin, about a tenth of our penny. And Jesus said to His disciples, ". . . this poor widow hath cast more in, than all they which have cast into the treasury: For all they did cast in of their abundance; but she of her want did cast in all that she had, even all her living." In *Don Juan,* Byron speaks of Antony, who gave all for love, and of himself who, when younger, and "had no great plenty," gave all he had—a heart. " 'T was the boy's 'mite,' and, like the 'widow's,' may / Perhaps be weigh'd hereafter, if not now . . . ." In Thackeray's *Vanity Fair,* Amelia, now a poor widow, watched her son George from a distance being taken to church by his well-to-do aunt. George stopped and gave a little chimney sweep money. "Emmy ran around the square, and coming up to the sweep, gave him her mite too."

WIND BLOWETH WHERE IT LISTETH

John 3:8

Jesus told Nicodemus the Pharisee that he must be born again, but Nicodemus could not understand how he could enter his mother's womb a second time and be born. Jesus explained: ". . . that which is born of the Spirit is spirit . . . . The wind bloweth where it listeth, and thou hearest the sound thereof, but canst not tell whence it cometh, and whither it goeth:

so is every one that is born of the Spirit." In *Childe Harold,*
Byron wrote of Voltaire's "fire and fickleness." His chief talent

> Breathed most in ridicule—which, as the wind
> Blew where it listed, laying all things prone,—
> Now to o'erthrow a fool, and now to shake a throne.

In "On the Tragedies of Shakespeare," Charles Lamb said that
King Lear cannot be acted. Only when we read it do we discover "a mighty irregular power of reasoning . . . exerting its
powers, as the wind blows where it listeth, at will upon the
corruptions and abuses of mankind."

WIND (THUNDER), EARTHQUAKE, AND FIRE   *see STILL SMALL VOICE*

WINGS LIKE (OF) A DOVE

Pss. 55:6; 68:13

The Psalmist, weary "of the oppression of the wicked," cries,
"Oh that I had wings like a dove! for then would I fly away,
and be at rest." In *Don Juan,* Byron said that Don Juan, at
Queen Catherine's court, was flush with youth, vigor, and
beauty, "and those things / Which for an instant clip enjoy-
ment's wings." / "But soon they grow again and leave their
nest. / 'Oh!' saith the Psalmist, 'that I had a dove's Pinions
to flee away, and be at rest!'" In *Confessions of an English
Opium Eater,* De Quincey said that during his "first mournful
abode in London," he would think of the road north to Gras-
mere, and "if I had the wings of a dove, *that* way I would
fly for comfort." Charles Lamb said, in "A Chapter on Ears,"
that in spite of his own musical limitations, he enjoyed hearing
his good Catholic friend play solemn anthems such as that one
"in which the psalmist, weary of the persecutions of bad men,
wisheth to himself dove's wings . . . ."

WINGS OF THE MORNING   *see TAKE THE WINGS OF MORNING*

WISDOM CRIETH IN THE STREETS

Prov. 1:20, 24

"Wisdom crieth without; she uttereth her voice in the streets
. . . . Because I have called, and ye refused; I have stretched
out my hand, and no man regarded . . . . I also will laugh at
your calamity; I will mock when your fear cometh." In Shakespeare's *Henry IV, Part I,* Falstaff cast aspersion on Prince
Hal's reputation. "An old lord of the Council rated me the
other day in the street about you, sir, but I marked him not;
and yet he talked very wisely, but I regarded him not; and yet

he talked wisely, and in the street too." Hal replied, "Thou didst well, for wisdom cries out in the streets, and no man regards it." In *Main Currents in American Thought*, Vernon L. Parrington said of Thoreau: "'Wisdom crieth in the streets and no man regardeth her' . . . . Thoreau proved his right to be called a philosopher by seeking wisdom as a daily counselor and friend, and following such paths only as wisdom suggested."

WISDOM HATH HEWN OUT HER SEVEN PILLARS   *see SEVEN PILLARS OF WISDOM*

WISE AND FOOLISH VIRGINS   *see PARABLE OF THE WISE AND FOOLISH VIRGINS*

WISE AS SERPENTS, AND HARMLESS AS DOVES

Matt. 10:16   Jesus chose his apostles and said, "Behold, I send you forth as sheep in the midst of wolves: be ye therefore wise as serpents, and harmless as doves." In *Modern Painters*, Ruskin, speaking of the gentleman, said that there is a "difference between honorable and base lying . . . . 'Be ye wise as serpents, harmless as doves,' is the ultimate expression of this principle." Melville, in *Billy Budd*, said of Billy that "with little or no sharpness of faculty or any trace of the wisdom of the serpent, nor yet quite a dove, he possessed that kind . . . of intelligence which goes along with the unconventional rectitude of a sound human creature." And in Butler's *The Way of All Flesh*, Aunt Althea Pontifex said of Dr. Skinner, Ernest's teacher, that "he had the harmlessness of the serpent and the wisdom of the dove."

WISE AND UNDERSTANDING HEART   *see SOLOMON'S WISDOM*

WISE AS SOLOMON   *see SOLOMON'S WISDOM*

WISE KING   *see SOLOMON*

WISER IN THEIR GENERATION   *see CHILDREN OF LIGHT*

WITCH OF ENDOR

I Sam. 28:3-25   Sore distressed at the approach of the Philistine army, and defying his own edict against consulting "those that have familiar spirits, and the wizards," Saul asked the "woman that hath a familiar spirit at Endor" to bring up Samuel. When Samuel appeared, Saul "stooped with his face to the ground, and bowed himself." Samuel told him not what to do, but prophesied accurately his defeat and death at the hands of the Philistines. The expression "Witch of Endor" appears only in the chapter heading. In Chaucer's "The Friar's Tale," the Summoner asked Satan if he always made new bodies from the elements. The fiend answered, Nay,

> Somtyme we feyne, and somtyme we aryse
> With dede bodyes, in ful sondry wyse,
> And speke as renably and faire and well
> As to the Phitonissa dide Samuel.

"Phitonissa" is the Vulgate form commonly used in the Middle Ages. In Hardy's *The Mayor of Casterbridge*, Henchard consulted "a man of curious repute as a forecaster or weather-prophet." As he entered the isolated cottage, "Henchard felt like Saul at his reception by Samuel; he remained in silence for a few moments." In *The Return of the Native*, when Wildeve came at the call of Eustacia Vye's festival fire, she said, "I merely lit that fire because I was dull, and thought I would get a little excitement by calling you up and triumphing over you as the Witch of Endor called up Samuel. I determined you should come; and you have come! I have shown my power."

WOE IS ME

Jer. 4:31; 15:10; 45:3; Isa. 6:5; Ps. 120:5

This is a common Biblical expression, but frequently associated with Jeremiah's laments. "Woe is me, my mother, that thou hast borne me a man of strife and a man of contention to the whole earth!" Milton, for example, in *The Reason of Church Government*, spoke of the burden of knowledge and truth-speaking. God's prophets "are made the greatest variance and offence, a very sword and fire, both in home and city over the whole earth. This is that which the sad prophet Jeremiah laments: 'Woe is me, my mother, that thou hast borne me, a man of strife and contention.'" In Whittier's "The Farewell," a slave mother laments her daughters sold into slavery:

> Gone, gone,—sold and gone,
> To the rice-swamp dank and lone,
> From Virginia's hills and waters;
> Woe is me, my stolen daughters.

At the end of Shaw's *Saint Joan*, Joan, condemned to the stake, cries, "Woe is me when all men praise me!"

WOE TO THEM THAT ARE AT EASE IN ZION   *see AT EASE IN ZION*

WOLVES IN SHEEP'S CLOTHING

Matt. 7:15

In the Sermon on the Mount, Jesus said, "Beware of false prophets, which come to you in sheep's clothing, but inwardly they are ravening wolves." In Shakespeare's *Henry VI, Part I*, Gloucester, facing the Bishop of Winchester before the Tower of London, says,

> Winchester goose, I cry, a rope! a rope!
> Now beat them hence; why do you let them stay?
> Thee I'll chase hence, thou wolf in sheep's array.

In *Romeo and Juliet*, when the Nurse brings news of Tybalt's death and Romeo's banishment, Juliet cries, "Beautiful tyrant! fiend angelical! / Dove-feather'd raven! wolfish-ravening lamb!" In *The Way of All Flesh*, Butler says of Ernest's attitude, in later years, toward the clergy of the Church of England: "Also, now thaᵗ he has seen them more closely, he knows better the nature of those wolves in sheep's clothing, who are thirsting for the blood of their victim . . . ." In "A Plea for Captain John Brown," Thoreau said, in regard to the clergy and the slavery issue, "some pastors are wolves in sheep's clothing."

WOMAN TAKEN IN ADULTERY

John 8:3–11

The scribes and Pharisees brought unto Jesus a woman taken in adultery, saying that according to the law of Moses she should be stoned. Jesus said unto them, "He that is without sin among you, let him first cast a stone at her." Then "he stooped down, and wrote on the ground," and the men "being convicted by their own conscience, went out one by one . . . ." When Jesus looked up and saw none but the woman, He said unto her, ". . . hath no man condemned thee? She said, No man, Lord. And Jesus said unto her, Neither do I condemn thee: go, and sin no more." In his Preface to "Adonais," Shelley said of the critics who he believed had caused Keats's death, "Against what woman taken in adultery dares the foremost of these literary prostitutes to cast his opprobrious stone? Miserable man! you, one of the meanest, have wantonly defaced one of the noblest specimens of the workmanship of God." In Tennyson's *Queen Mary*, Sir Thomas White said of the citizens who left hastily as Queen Mary entered the Guildhall, "Let them go. / They go like those old Pharisees in John

/ Convicted by their conscience, arrant cowards." William Morris, in *News from Nowhere*, said that in Utopia legal penalties are mild. "Paying a severe legal penalty, the wrong-doer "can 'go and sin again' with comfort . . . . Remember Jesus had got the legal penalty remitted before he said, 'Go and sin no more.'"

WORD, THE

John 1:1, 14

Saint John wrote: "In the beginning was the Word, and the Word was with God, and the Word was God." "And the Word was made flesh, and dwelt among us, (and we beheld his glory, the glory as of the only begotten of the Father,) full of grace and truth." King Richard, in Shakespeare's *Richard II,* imprisoned in Pomfret Castle, peoples his world with his own "still breeding thoughts." "No thought is contented":

> The better sort,
> As thoughts of things divine, are intermixed
> With scruples, and do set the word itself
> Against the word.

In "The Poet," Emerson said that the poet is impelled by his own inner compulsion to beauty: "Hence the necessity of speech and song; hence these throbs and heart-beatings in the orator, at the door of the assembly, to the end, namely, that thought may be ejaculated as Logos, or Word." Edwin Arlington Robinson satirized American materialism in "Cassandra":

> I heard one who said: "Verily,
> What word have I for children here?
> Your Dollar is your only Word,
> The wrath of it your only fear."°

WORD MADE FLESH

John 1:14

This is the Incarnation: "And the Word was made flesh, and dwelt among us, (and we beheld his glory, the glory as of the only begotten of the Father,) full of grace and truth." In *In Memoriam,* Tennyson said that spiritual truths, latent in all men's intuitions, were made living in Christ.

> And the Word had breath, and wrought
> With human hands the creed of creeds
> In loveliness of perfect deeds,
> More strong than all poetic thought . . . .

Emerson, in "Self-Reliance," said, "Let a Stoic open the resources of man and tell him . . . that a man is the word made flesh, born to shed healing to the nations . . ." (Rev. 22:2). And Shaw, in his Preface to *Saint Joan,* said: "When Joan maintained her own ways she claimed, like Job, that there was not only God and the Church to be considered, but the Word made Flesh: that is, the unaveraged individual . . . ."

WORM THAT DIETH NOT

Mark 9:44, 46, 48; Isa. 66:24

Jesus said that if thy hand, or foot, or eye offend thee, cut it off: "it is better for thee to enter into life maimed, than having two hands [or feet, or eyes] to go into hell, into the fire that never shall be quenched: Where their worm dieth not, and the fire is not quenched." In *Much Ado about Nothing,* Shakespeare may have had this idea in mind when Benedict justifies blowing his own trumpet while still alive. He says to Beatrice, ". . . therefore it is most expedient for the wise, if Don Worm, his conscience, find no impediment to the contrary, to be the trumpet of his own virtues, as I am to myself." Conscience was the gnawing of the worm, as in the old morality plays. De Quincey, in "The Affliction of Childhood," suffered endless sorrow after his sister's death: "The worm was at my heart; and, may I say, the worm that could not die." In Poe's "Morella," the husband, hearing expressions of his dead wife on the lips of his daughter, "found food for consuming thought and horror—for a worm that would not die." And in Poe's "Ulalume," Astarte's crescent moon "has seen that the tears are not dry on / These cheeks, where the worm never dies."

WORSHIP IN SPIRIT AND IN TRUTH   *see SAMARITAN WOMAN*

WOULD NOT BE COMFORTED   *see RACHEL WEEPING FOR HER CHILDREN*

WRATH TO COME   *see GENERATION OF VIPERS*

WRESTLES WITH AN ANGEL   *see JACOB WRESTLES WITH AN ANGEL*

WRITING ON THE WALL   *see HANDWRITING ON THE WALL*

YE SHALL KNOW THE TRUTH   *see TRUTH SHALL MAKE YOU FREE*

YOUNG MEN SEE VISIONS   *see DREAM DREAMS, OLD MEN*

ZABA, QUEEN OF   *see SHEBA (SABA) QUEEN OF*

ZION

II Sam. 5:6–9;
Pss. 2:6; 126:1;
137:1, 3; Amos
6:1; Rev. 14:1

Zion, meaning "fortress," sometimes spelled Sion, was at first the southeast stronghold hill captured by David from the Jebusites that became the City of David, then the city of Jerusalem. It is referred to variously as "the holy hill," the "habitation of the Lord," and as Mount Zion. Bunyan, in *Pilgrim's Progress*, calls the climax of Christian's pilgrimage "Mount Sion, the heavenly Jerusalem [where] the innumerable company of Angels, and the Spirits of Just Men are made perfect." In *Literature and Dogma*, Matthew Arnold said that Christianity has taught the "world's chief nations . . . to reckon and profess themselves born in Zion,—born that is, in the religion of Zion, the city of righteousness." In Butler's *The Way of All Flesh*, Ernest's friend tells of seeing some of the very old members of Theobald's church come out of a dissenting chapel with "a look of contentment on their faces that made [him] feel certain that they had been singing . . . the songs of Sion and no new fangled papistry."